Dancing the Black Question

Dancing the
Black Question

The Phoenix Dance Company Phenomenon

Christy Adair

DANCE BOOKS

First published in 2007 by Dance Books Ltd
The Old Bakery
4 Lenten Street
Alton
Hampshire GU34 1HG

Arts & Humanities
Research Council
Research for this book was supported by the AHRC

ISBN: 978 185273 116 8

A CIP catalogue record for this book is available from the British Library

Produced by Jeremy Mills Publishing Ltd.
www.jeremymillspublishing.co.uk

To Bonnie and Tansy

Contents

Illustrations

Acknowledgements

This research was initially undertaken because I became aware that the achievements of Phoenix Dance Company were not formally acknowledged in the dance canon. I am grateful to the members of the Company who generously shared their experiences with me and without whom this study would not exist. I would particularly like to mention the founding members – Donald Edwards, David Hamilton, Villmore James, Merville Jones and Edward Lynch – and the Phoenix Plus dancers: Sharon Donaldson (now Watson), Dawn Donaldson (now Holgate), Pamela Johnson and Seline Thomas (now Derrick). I also appreciate the many discussions with Thea Barnes and her generosity in allowing me access to the Archive Project.

I would like to thank Griselda Pollock, who both challenged and encouraged me. Ramsay Burt, Andrée Grau, Mary Luckhurst and Claudia Sternberg also offered insightful comments on my work, which I very much appreciate. In addition, l received valuable feedback from Jane Scott Barratt, Beth Cassani, Doran George, Keyna Paul, Jo Stanley and Myna Trustram. My students at the Northern School of Contemporary Dance, Hull University and York St John University offered stimulating questions, and I would like to thank the librarians from these institutions, who have been extremely helpful. My colleagues at York St John University have been exceptionally supportive and I was fortunate to be granted study leave from Hull University and York St John University and to be funded by the Arts and Humanities Research Council.

Finally, I am grateful to my daughters Bonnie and Tansy and my parents Joan and Jack Baker for their continuing support and encouragement; and I would like to thank Ben Arnup, Tom Cantrell, Kathryn Gallon, Jack Johnson, Ruth Steinberg, Teresa Stenson and Christine Wilde for their assistance during this project.

Introduction

Phoenix Dance Company 1981–2001

This book considers dance in relation to gender and ethnicity through a case study of Phoenix Dance Company.[1] The historical narrative of this Company and the critical responses to it not only provides insights into the significance of its achievements, but also underscores general themes of British dance history specifically and raises issues for dance history generally. This introduction sets out the context of my research of the Company, including the methodology used and the issues arising from it. It also explains my relationship to the Company during the research process.

Dancing the Black Question: The Phoenix Dance Company Phenomenon is the development of research that emerged both from my earlier book, *Women and Dance: sylphs and sirens* published in 1992 by Macmillan Press, and from my teaching of dance studies. My research agendas and questions are apparent in my previous book and are extended in this study. From the outset, the work located 'dance firmly within the domain of a broader critical discourse' (Carter, 1992-93: 49),[2] engaging with issues of both ethnicity and gender.

There have been significant shifts in theoretical concerns since the publication of *Women and Dance*, with clear recognition that 'feminism signifies a set of positions' (Pollock, 1996: 5). As research has progressed, it has become clear that, as Ann Cooper Albright argues, 'bodies are both producing and being produced by cultural discourses of gender, race, ability, sexuality and age' (1997: xxiii). This is a perspective that I held in 1992 and am extending in this study.

Chapter 8 in *Women and Dance*, entitled *Black power – black dance*, both documented the achievements of African American and Black British female artists and raised some controversial issues about the use of language and terms. When I wrote that chapter, I was aware that there was further research that would be useful but was beyond the boundaries of that project. This case study of Phoenix Dance is a result of some of those investigations.

---

[1] Throughout the study, Phoenix Dance Company may be referred to as 'Phoenix' or 'the Company'.

[2] For further responses to this work, see Bramley (1993), Burt (1993), Brown (1994), Fowler (1994), Morley (1994), Aalten (1995), Sayers (1995), Phoca and Wright (1999) and Claid (2006).

Preliminary research of Phoenix Dance Company

In 1995 I was asked to contribute to a 'Women and Dance' panel' with
Pamela Johnson, a dancer and choreographer with Phoenix Dance
Company, as part of a conference entitled *Women and Performance:
Rethinking the Politics of Representation* (1995). It was at this conference
that I met Thea Barnes, who became the fourth director of Phoenix
Dance Company and who later facilitated some of my research by giving me access to Company rehearsals, education projects and archival
materials. This book is a result of close dialogues with personnel of the
Company and investigations of the archives. As I was involved with
Phoenix in a variety of ways, I was writing with insider knowledge similar to that of the participant/observer of ethnography.[3] This book is
not, however, an ethnographic study. It is a cultural history charting an
important historical moment of a particular group at the interface
between cultural creativity and arts policy and arts institutions. This is
a complex narrative, which is paradoxically about loss at the same time
as the Company was developing into an internationally acclaimed
organisation. The narrative is played out through gender, ethnicity and
class evident in the body, representation, politics and cultural discourses, economics and critical rhetoric.

My first memory of the Company is of discussions of a performance
in 1983 at the International Dance Festival at Dartington College in
Devon. I was intrigued. I had missed a performance of a very popular
company. The dancers had presented work that drew on street jazz and
contemporary dance: a significant contrast to the festival's culture of
release techniques and experimental choreography. Ramsay Burt, writing in *New Dance*, portrayed some of the Company's characteristics as
'tense, hyper muscular [...] the tightest contemporary technique'
(1983: 21). He also suggested that some of their choreography was
'naïve'[4] but that 'Phoenix put themselves so completely into it that I had
to respect it' (1983: 21). Burt's article offers a snapshot of the Company
in the spring of 1983 when they were becoming established, but before
they became clients of the Arts Council. The dancers were informed by
mainstream dance rather than by an experimental context, but the fact
that they had engaged such an unlikely audience caught my attention.

During the 1980s, however, my priorities were investigating feminism in relation to dance and going to many of the cutting-edge workshops and performances at alternative dance spaces and festivals in

---

[3] Theresa Buckland outlines this approach in *Dance in the Field: Theory, Method and Issues in
Dance Ethnography* (1999).

[4] The members of Phoenix at this point had, of course, less than two years' experience of
choreographing for the Company.

London. The context of a political division between men and women and the ways in which this was theoretically framed, meant that an all-male dance group was not part of my research remit. An interesting overlap, however, was my study of Irie!, a dance company of African Caribbean performers led by their artistic director, Beverley Glean.[5] I attended one of their performances at their home base near the Albany Empire in Deptford, south-east London, an area with a culturally diverse population. This was also a venue for one of the early Phoenix performances. The Empire was a community centre and performance venue that offered opportunities for educational, community and artistic events. When Irie! performed, the atmosphere was warm, vibrant and inclusive. The audience did not hesitate to show their appreciation by clapping, stamping and calling out. When later I watched Phoenix Dance Company perform at the Riley Theatre at the Northern School of Contemporary Dance (NSCD), I reflected on the similarities between the enthusiastic audience responses to the two companies.

My interest in Phoenix Dance Company developed further in 1993 when I began teaching at the NSCD and discovered the close connections between the people involved with the Company and the School. Until that point, my information about the Company had been through reviews and opinions from dance colleagues who knew their work. During the early years of my teaching at NSCD, several students had dual heritages from the Caribbean and Britain. They were curious about dancers and choreographers who drew on such heritages in their work, and were frustrated by the dance canon, which appeared to be one-dimensional and dominated by European and American[6] aesthetics. Their questions prompted my reflection on issues of inclusion and exclusion in relation to the dance canon and led to further investigations of less well-recognised artists, particularly those with African American or Caribbean-British backgrounds.

The School introduced a one-year course that offered professional dancers an opportunity to gain a degree. Villmore James, one of the founders of Phoenix Dance Company, was in an early cohort of students and I supervised his dissertation. During our many discussions, I realised that the achievements of this Company were barely documented.

In this book I want to catch something of the historical moment of the formation of the Company and its subsequent development over a twenty-year period, through accounts given by the participants. In

---

[5] See Chapter 8 in *Women and Dance: sylphs and sirens*.
[6] The terms 'America' and 'American' throughout the book refer to North America and North American.

doing this I both touch on analytical issues and challenge an analytical approach to this material. There is a tension between the source of the material and theorising about it. The model I am using moves between self-accounting oral histories and a research-based framework. I confront elements of that history in which Phoenix are Black British citizens with a relationship to other cultural possibilities or with access to them through parental memory. I am writing from a position that tries not to take on the role of colonial superior and to place dancers as 'other'. As a dance historian, I have a responsibility to write about a company that I knew well from several different perspectives and connections. The challenge is not to reduce them or their work.

I have endeavoured to write from a position of cultural equity[7] rather than cultural diversity. The latter term condemns the diverse to *be* diverse rather than to have equal rights to the same resources for cultural development. The discussion is conducted from a position that considers cultures and practices. The history is of a society coming to terms with changes through cultural diversity, multiculturalism and now cultural equity, rather than through expressionist models of identity. This study engages with these theoretical shifts. In addition, I acknowledge and write from a position which considers that 'Writing itself is a political issue and a political practice for many contemporary feminists' (Gatens, 1992: 133).

I do not find it possible to explore this history without being sensitive to my own. One of the key aspects of this is a sense of my own changing identity and my understanding of the country in which I grew up. Reading about the experiences of African Caribbean people in Britain in the 1950s and the developments through the following decades, I am aware of my background and the reasons for my beliefs and prejudices. Working closely with the members of Phoenix has enabled me to expand my understanding of issues of gender and ethnicity and to reconsider dance history.

Methodology

This book examines the formation and development of Phoenix Dance Company from 1981 to 2001. The approach used draws upon the disciplines and methodologies of cultural studies, postcolonial theories and dance studies. The investigation of this company offers an opportunity

---

[7] 'Cultural equity' was a term referred to by Victor Leo Walker in an oral presentation at the International Association for Politics and Literature (IAPL) at the University of Leeds, 21 May 2004. The term was also used in the National Arts Strategy and Cultural Equity Discussion Paper (1991).

to raise questions about dance history, dance structures, critical response and cultural equity.

Until this book, the significance of Phoenix Dance Company's contribution to British dance history had largely been overlooked. This study takes an approach that differs from the one found in British dance history books, such as *London Contemporary Dance Theatre* (Clarke and Crisp, 1989) and *Dance Umbrella* (Rowell, 2000). These books give a chronological history of a specific topic within the context of British dance history, which is more typical of the approach to Western Theatre Dance. There have been cultural histories written on contemporary dance topics, for example *Ecstasy and the Demon: Feminism and Nationalism in the Dances of Mary Wigman* (Manning, 1993), but they have typically engaged with a re-writing of history from a specific perspective. More recently, there has been a reconsideration of approaches to dance history, as evidenced in *Re-Thinking History* (Carter, 2004) and *moving history/dancing cultures* (Albright and Dils, 2001).[8]

The present book, however, is concerned with establishing the significance of Phoenix Dance Company and ensuring that its history is recorded. Although this work is to some extent chronological, my approach locates Phoenix's history in the cultural and political contexts of the Company's existence, recognising that

> dance can be a central, indeed a crucial, discourse for our time [...] contemporary dance foregrounds a responsive dancing body, one that engages with and challenges static representations of gender, race, sexuality and physical ability, all the while acknowledging how deeply these ideologies influence our daily experience. (Cooper Albright, 1997: xiii)

As well as establishing the contribution of Phoenix Dance Company to British dance history, I also consider the institution of dance criticism. As Cooper Albright (1997) has noted, cultural studies provide a tool for locating specificity which counters the abstracted philosophy and universalising approach of dance critics such as Edwin Denby and John Martin and philosophers such as Susanne Langer and Maxine Sheets Johnson.

---

[8] *Europe Dancing: Perspectives on Theatre, Dance and Cultural Identity* is another example of a text that engages with an emerging paradigm shift (Grau and Jordan, 2000). Bonnie Rowell's chapter in that book, 'United Kingdom: An expanding map', although attempting to discuss identity and multiculturalism, separates this issue from the remainder of the chapter, which discusses contemporary dance and names several artists. The only artist mentioned who is not of European heritage is Shobana Jeyasingh. Phoenix is not mentioned, but the foundation of the Company is noted in a table of developments in contemporary dance in the UK.

My role as a researcher has been influenced by my relationships with members of the Company, including being a teacher of some of the members. My research was carried out at a key moment in the Company's history when many of the dancers still had connections with the community in which they grew up and the cultural contexts that made the Company unique. The research methods employed were varied. I conducted interviews with the founders, members of the Company in 1997 and 1998 (many of whom had been with the Company for eight or nine years), the artistic directors, some rehearsal directors, some administrators and some choreographers who had worked with the Company. These taped, transcribed and edited interviews created an archive of Company memories of those who had been, or still were, closely involved with Phoenix, to add to earlier recorded interviews held at the Yorkshire Dance Centre in 1988. During my close connection with the Company throughout the period of Thea Barnes' artistic directorship (1997–2001), I had frequent conversations with her about the running of the Company, the choice of repertoire and the response of the critics. I observed Company rehearsals and spoke to the dancers, rehearsal directors and administrative staff. I also observed and was involved in education and training initiatives of the Company, including the Education and Research Development Initiative (1997) and Ballroom Blitz (1999). I participated in a number of dance workshops with Company members. I analysed a selection of formal documents concerning the Company: for example, mission statements, Board minutes and Arts Council documents. I analysed a sample of reviews from the twenty-year period studied, selected to illustrate specific themes of critical response to the Company. In addition, I observed and analysed a wide range of the Company's repertoire available as live performance and recorded on video.

The process of my research led me to reflect that what I was writing was both a cultural history of a dance company and an analysis of a case study that draws on several pertinent elements. The traces of the Company's history are the narratives of Phoenix from people's memories; the documents related to the Company, the records of Company performances and education from video recordings and critical responses. These factors contribute to the history of the Company, but they are traces open to interpretation. This study is one approach to this material, but many other approaches could have been taken. This book, which is a reading of aspects mentioned above, reveals the multi-layered complexity and contradictions in the many strands that create a history of Phoenix Dance Company.

So what is revealed from these traces? Evidence of a remarkable group of dancers emerges from their testimonies and records through reviews and official documents. Aspects of the relationship of the Company to the funding bodies are revealed through readings of official documents, which provide insights into issues of ethnicity, class and gender. All these elements, however, are only traces of the primary concern of the Company – that is, performance. As Peggy Phelan articulates, 'Performance's only life is in the present. Performance cannot be saved, recorded, documented or otherwise participate in the circulation of representations: once it does so, it becomes something other than performance' (1993: 146). Clearly, Phelan's insights confirm that there are no 'original' 'authentic' performances to study or interpret. My research necessarily relies on the traces and contexts of performances.

The importance of attempting the task of narrating the complexities of Phoenix's history is confirmed by Catherine Ugwu's comments about the lack of recognition of black artists and the preconceptions of what their work should be. She states:

> The invisibility of black artists and their work, coupled with the general expectation that the work of black artists, when visible, may in one way or another be characteristic of a universal black experience, or only communicate with the marginalised community from which it comes, has been detrimental. (1995: 56)

She also makes clear that there is no 'homogenous essentialised black culture [....but there is a need] to embrace the diversity of black experience' (1995: 56).

Terminology

Several terms used throughout the book are necessarily dealt with differently at specific points in the writing. For example, I draw on terms related to identity and specificity, such as black, whiteness, ethnicity, gender, masculinity and class. In addition, at particular points in the study, discussions focus on approaches to the body, and on dance repertoire and institutions such as the Arts Council.

Janet Wolff identified a liberal notion that influenced dance practice and some dance writing, and that is relevant to perceptions of Phoenix. She suggested that dance is often viewed as articulating authentic expression of the body and, therefore, the assumption is that liberation may be discovered through the body in dance; but she argues that there is no pre-linguistic or pre-social experience of the body (1995). This argument counters any notion that people of the African Diaspora will have inherent rhythm and a disposition towards dance. In this book I argue that the social context informed the outstanding achievements of Phoenix Dance Company.

Another issue that has been problematic for Phoenix concerns the terms used to describe Company members and their work. At the time of writing, I do not think there is a clear solution. I have chosen to use 'people of the African Diaspora', 'people with African heritage', African Caribbean' and for the early history 'Black British' or 'black' artists. The latter terms are those used by the founders and are in various documents from the Arts Council and from the Company itself. Caroline Muraldo argued in *Dance Theatre Journal* (2003) that precise terms needed to be used for dance informed by the African Diaspora. She pointed out that there is no generic term for people of African descent except 'Black British', whereas in America people of such heritage are referred to as African American. Her argument in relation both to dances from African and African Caribbean traditions and to the terms that are used for them is for specificity. This does not, however, clarify the situation in relation to a contemporary company such as Phoenix who want their specificity recognised but who do not want their access to contemporary dance to be restricted because of that recognition.

Initially, one aspect of the Company's specificity was gender. Phoenix was unusual because it comprised solely male dancers in a context in which dance was identified with women (Adair, 1992). Gender, however, is acknowledged to be more fluid, following Butler's insights that gender is a category that is constructed through performance, rather than an innate social or cultural attribute (1990).

Another element of the Company's composition that was significant, but also not fixed, was that of ethnicity. The term 'ethnicity' offers more fluid interpretation than that of 'race' with its associations of fixed biological categories and heritage. Indeed, 'ethnicity and its components are relative to time and place [...] they are dynamic and prone to change [...an ethnic group may be defined as one] that is socially distinguished or set apart, by others and/or by itself, primarily on the basis of cultural or national characteristics' (Ashcroft, Griffiths and Tiffin, 1998: 81).

This definition accommodates the complex status of groups such as [...] black British, whose identity may be putatively constructed along racial as well as ethnic lines [...] black ethnicity in America and Britain becomes more intricately dependent upon politics in the process of ethnic legitimation than is evident with white ethnic groups [...]. Ethnic identities thus persist beyond cultural assimilation

into the wider society and the persistence of ethnic identity is not necessarily related to the perpetuation of traditional cultures. (Ashcroft,
Griffiths and Tiffin, 1998: 84)

It is clear, then, that the term 'ethnicity' is far from unproblematic, but
it encompasses some of the complexities of the members of Phoenix
Dance Company. Evidently, the problems with such terminology are a
legacy of nineteenth-century colonialism and the historical categorisation in which certain societies and cultures were perceived as intrinsi-
cally inferior (Ashcroft, Griffiths and Tiffin, 1998).

There is also an interesting parallel in relation to the use of language
in dance and in colonial contexts. For example, it is still common in
dance classes and dance companies for dancers to be called boys and
girls. This undermines their professional training or professional status.
Adults are infantilised by being referred to as girls and boys rather than
women and men. In colonial countries, such as South Africa, it was for
many years accepted practice for white people to address black men as
boys. Language is an important critical referent, and these examples, as
also the discussion of the use of the word 'black', illustrate how the use
of such terms can reinforce the status quo and undermine a specific person's position (Hall, 1997: 263).

Black and Blackness

Rasheed Araeen, in a 1982 talk at the First National Black Art
Convention in Wolverhampton, argued that the term 'black' emerged
from a specific set of historical and cultural circumstances and was not
a fixed term. In order for it to be more than a categorisation in a racist
society, he suggested that the term needed to be situated in its historical
context of 'struggles against colonial and neo-colonial domination'
(1988: 37). As Gabrielle Griffin pointed out in relation to women and
identity politics:

The 'blackification' of women from diverse communities in Britain
facilitated the adoption of the term 'black' as the signifier of political
allegiance of people who suffer/ed racialized oppression in Britain
[...]. However, it also became clear that the strategic utility of the term
had its limits in the very different needs and issues diverse communities faced. (2003: 10)

Clearly, then, terms of discussion are important, and in a consideration of these the Arts Council's *Cultural Grounding Report* quotes from an article by Guillermo Gomez-Pena in 1989 in which he stated that:

> The colonized cultures are sliding into the space of the colonizer, and in doing so, they are redefining its borders and its culture (A similar phenomenon is occurring in Europe and African immigration) [...]. We need to find a new terminology, a new iconography and a new set of categories and definitions. We need to rebaptize the world in our own terms. The language of postmodernism is ethnocentric and insufficient. And so is the existing language of cultural institutions and funding agencies. Terms like 'Hispanic', 'Latino', 'ethnic', 'minority', 'marginal', 'alternative' and 'Third World' among others, are inaccurate and loaded with ideological implications. (In ACGB, 1990: 12)

As well as considering language, the *Cultural Grounding Report* called for arts-funding institutions to take account of diverse cultural practices, aesthetics, critical discourses and participants contributing to an integral development of contemporary art and national culture within an international context. These findings had direct impact on companies such as Phoenix. So what was the historical context, in relation to terminology, from which this report emerged?

By the 1960s a cultural shift was evident, with a move away from the term 'negro', which was associated with acquiescence, to the term 'black'. The latter was considered more assertive, and symbolic of a significant perspective shift by an oppressed group who were challenging their oppression.

In relation to this study, the use of the terms 'black' and 'blackness' are pertinent to considerations of when the terms might be used strategically as opposed to being an imposed category. The term 'black' was used by the Black Power Movement in the US in the 1960s as a process of reclaiming African heritage for African Americans who had not had access to it because of racism (Brah, 1992). The context in which the word is used and who is using it affect the precision and relevance of this controversial term (Badejo, 1993). It does not have to be interpreted in essentialist terms, as it can have different political and cultural meanings in different contexts. Within Britain the term has been used to seek political accord against racism, and in this sense has included South Asian people, although clearly their political struggles and issues are different from those for people of African Caribbean heritage.

When asked about the role of a black consciousness in his work, Jack Whitten (a non-figurative painter in the 1970s) replied:

> I can't define what is black in my work. I think it's not necessary that I have to define it as much as I should know that it's there [...]. I'm black, and my sensibility derives from my being black. But I'm also dealing with art [...] on the highest universal level. And that's what I want to be known for. I want to maintain that search for what it means to be black, whatever it is [...]. But at the same time, I must deal with this within the issues that have grown out of the history of art. (In Powell, 1997: 137)

Many of the dancers, choreographers and artistic directors of Phoenix have echoed Whitten's comments over the twenty-year period of this study. For example, Sharon Donaldson[9] states:

> *My work [is] not as a black dancer but as a dancer, someone who has put time into my art and delivered it. Part of me says that Phoenix should not have to make that statement [about identity]. You look at the Company and people see it as a black dance company but whether you utilise those words and start using it as a political thing is where conflicts happen. I questioned the Board on many occasions about the Arts Council. [I asked] Do they see us as a black dance company? Do they fund us as a black dance company? (1998)[10]*

Donaldson's questions underline the tensions concerning the categorisation of the Company. Although the Arts Council did not specifically fund Phoenix as a black dance company, excerpts from the *Glory of the Garden* report (1984) indicate that the fact that the Company was comprised of black dancers was one reason for the allocation of funding.
But as Gilroy points out:

> Blackness is a diverse, complex, sometimes contradictory category which forms itself in opposition to a multiplicity of oppressions, and in response to different creativities [...]. What is being resisted and by what means? slavery? capitalism? coerced industrialisation? racial terror? Or ethnocentrism and European solipsism? How are the discontinuous histories of Diaspora to be thought, to be theorised by

---

[9] Sharon Donaldson's equity name is Chantal Donaldson.
[10] Throughout the book, the Company members' quotations from my interviews with them are italicised in order to highlight their perspectives of their history.

those who have experienced the consequences of racial domination?
(Gilroy, 1990–91: 4)

The questions that Gilroy posed continue to be asked. Furthermore, the
issues concerning blackness as a category and the use of the term
'black' have not been resolved. Kadiatu Kanneh made the point that
there has been a conflation of 'immigrant' with 'black' in Britain in the
twentieth century, which has created a separation 'between citizen and
ethnicity, between British and foreign, so that home and unbelonging
take on confusing and harrowing dimensions' (1998: 147).

During the 1980s, the emphasis on common experience (of racial
oppression in particular) as the rationale for black unity led to a further
change in the meaning of the term 'black'. It came to mean 'people
affected by racism' (Braham, Rattansi and Skellington, 1992: 80).

Class

Although it is clear from any investigation of Phoenix Dance Company
that ethnicity and gender are key categories to be considered, class is
more problematic. 'Class' is an uneasy term at the beginning of the
twenty-first century. The clear categorisations of Marxism, which provided a means to understand the social divisions apparent when there
was a significant manufacturing foundation, are no longer relevant for
global capitalism. Nonetheless, there remain inequalities and divisions
to which Phoenix allude when they describe themselves as working
class. This is an identity that I share, and Valerie Walkerdine's research
and writing echoes several of my concerns and experiences. A film that
she screened and discussed in her paper *Rethinking classed subjectivity* at
the *Translating Class/Altering Hospitality Conference* held at CentreCATH,
University of Leeds, in 2002 was entitled, *Didn't she do well*. In this film,
Walkerdine:

> explored narratives of upward mobility presented by a group of pro-
> fessional women who had grown up working class in Britain at differ-
> ent historical moments and who had all made a transition to the
> middle class by virtue of education and professional work. (2002: 11)

Walkerdine identified a common theme for these women, which she
termed 'survival guilt'. This she interpreted as the tension between
doing comparatively well materially themselves and knowing that their
families had suffered from limited material resources. Walkerdine's film
holds particular interest for me, as it documents a group run by Pamela

Trevithick that drew on the theory and practice of co-counselling. In the 1980s Trevithick ran several of these groups at the Women's Therapy Centre in London, and I attended as her assistant. The ideas on which the groups were based were outlined in an unpublished paper written by Trevithick in 1985.

It is clear from interviews with the Phoenix dancers that the founders identified themselves as working class. My identification with this class position allowed me an insight into some of their perspectives, while at the same time I was aware of our different experiences in relation to ethnicity and gender. The founders' perceptions of themselves as working class affected their views of themselves, their work and their audiences. It is interesting in this context to pose the question of whether there were tensions for the early Company between success and keeping a connection with their community. This study and the questions it raises are timely, not least because there have been, in the last few years, several initiatives in the arts and the media in the form of festivals, conferences and reports that indicate a growing awareness of the issues this book investigates. For example, the report *The Issue of Multi-Ethnic Britain in 2000* was commissioned by the Runnymede Trust, and the aim of *decibel*, the Arts Council's initiative, was 'to put cultural diversity central to [their] work' (Evans, 2004: 1). As there have been shifts in perspectives about ethnicity, gender and class, so too has history been re-considered.

Historical perspectives

History as it has traditionally been approached has been about telling and ordering the facts so that the 'true' story of past events may be told. This has entailed researchers' and writers' viewpoints being hidden, as though there were facts that were constant, regardless of viewpoints. More recently, investigation into the nature of history has called such approaches into question. In his book *Re-thinking History*, Keith Jenkins argues that accuracy of accounts are checked by comparing historians' accounts and that there will be variations between these rather than one 'correct text' (1991: 11). History is, therefore, an interpretation of the past, and the selection of materials for, and the slant of, any account is determined by the concerns and choices of the particular historian. As dance historian Brenda Dixon Gottschild suggests, 'Deconstruction theory has taught us that to formulate a history means to interpret selected events' (1998: 167). It is not possible to step outside one's ideas and beliefs, because history is a discourse that changes depending on whose perspective is recorded and in what ways. Jenkins argues that history is frequently presented by dominant groups as non-ideological. History that is constructed from a viewpoint of a marginal group, however, is usually considered to be ideological. But there is no 'true' history separate from those who are interpreting the past from their own perspectives. History is, as Jenkins clearly states, 'an ideological construct' (1991: 17). It also has different meanings for different groups, and contributes to people's understanding and sense of their own identities. This is powerful territory, and if people feel that history is integral to their identities, it is not surprising that history is a discourse that is contested.

Both White and Jenkins discuss Roland Barthes' *The Discourse of History* (1987) and his argument that some histories drew attention to the manner in which they were produced and, therefore, illuminated their constructed aspects and were less mythological than those that referred to sources as though they were proof of the 'truth' or facts. As Anita Loomba points out:

The historian and the critic [...] are also part of a discursive order rather than outsiders – what they say, indeed what they *can* say is also determined and shaped by their circumstances. Thus the concept of discourse extends the notion of an historically and ideologically inflected linguistic field – no utterance is innocent and every utterance tells us something about the world we live in. But equally, the world we live in is only comprehensible to us via its discursive representations. (1998: 39–40)

It is evident from this comment that, as Jacques Derrida (1981) points out (following Althusser), there is not a single, general history but histories. This is particularly evident in Gayatri Spivak's account of the Rani of Sirmur (1985). She discusses the records constructed by the colonial administrators and soldiers of the East India Company and suggests that these were a fiction, which was then 'misread'. Dominick LaCapra (1983: 344, cited in Spivak, 1985: 249) argues as follows:

The archive as fetish is a literal substitute for the 'reality' of the past which is 'always already' lost for the historian. When it is fetishized, the archive is more than the repository of traces of the past which may be used in its inferential reconstruction. It is a stand-in for the past that brings the mystified experience of the thing itself – an experience that is always open to question when one deals with writing or other inscriptions.

The archive holds a particular significance for dance because of the art form's transitory nature. Unlike visual art and literature, a dance work exists only in the moment. The study of dance relies on records of specific dance works, which take the form of film recordings, critics' reviews and articles, photographs, company records, set and costume designs and written or verbal accounts of the artists involved. However, as Alexandra Carter points out in *Re-thinking Dance History* (2004), 'all the past is ephemeral' (14); so whatever the art form, people attribute meaning from a range of specific viewpoints and interpretations to the documents or the art objects that exist.

In this book my own experiences and perspectives will inevitably inform my readings of the research material that I have selected. I am writing at a time when it is increasingly acknowledged that many artists who identify as Black British have made a significant input to the British Dance infrastructure, and it is important that their contributions are both acknowledged and documented.[11] My location as a dance historian with close connections to Phoenix is a significant aspect of both my access to resources and my interpretation of them for this account. Hayden White (1987) describes the narrative historian's method as one in which documents are scrutinised so that the most likely account of events can be related from this source. Clearly, the ways in which dance historians approach their work will affect the outcomes.

Issues arising from the research

A key element of my research has been the taped interviews I have made, which contribute to an oral history of Phoenix and which I have interpreted for this study. The recorded tapes offer individual accounts of the Company members' experiences and understanding of the Company. The relationship I had as the interviewer with each interviewee shaped the tone and content of the interview. The interview's setting also affected its outcome. Most interviews were conducted in workplaces but some were in social settings, as these were the only locations available within the time frame that the interviewer and interviewee had available.

In *History and the myth of realism* (1990), Elizabeth Tonkin discusses the problematics surrounding access to authoritative voices, and suggests that some people are disadvantaged in relaying their understandings of the past because they do not have status or are not conversant

---

[11] An important example of such documentation is the Photographic Exhibition, *Moments: Black dance in Britain from the 1930s to the 1990s* organised by ADAD (The Association of Dance of the African Diaspora) in 2006.

with specific genres. This is a consideration in relation to Phoenix because the people interviewed held a variety of positions in the Company, including as artistic directors, rehearsal directors and dancers. The early dancers' accounts differ from others because what, in effect, they are telling is an important aspect of their own life stories. The stories of the other Company members, however, are more like reflections of their particular experiences in a specific employment. In a discussion of what she terms *Myths in life stories* (1990), Jean Peneff suggests that what is mythical in life stories is the construct that is used to arrange memories and events. I was aware of this tendency when interviewing the founders. While keen that their stories were told, they understandably emphasised their successes rather than their difficulties. Peneff suggests that when collecting life stories one must try to distinguish between observation and imagination – that is, to understand when the subject is attempting to show himself or herself in a good light. It is also important to be aware of sensitive areas and favoured fantasies. I have taken these considerations into account in my readings of the interviews, which I shall refer to throughout the study.

This research has necessarily been drawn from incomplete archives. In the contemporary dance world, dance archives have not been a priority for organisations that are frequently underfunded and have difficulty meeting their performance and education targets with the resources at their disposal. In such a climate, it is not surprising that archives are such a low priority. Anna Furse of Blood Group Women's Experimental Theatre of the 1980s now laments the fact that she and her colleagues were so focused on their live performances that archives seemed remote and unnecessary (2000 and 2002). Now performance and dance artists are attempting to archive what is available from the past and are preparing to record the future.[12] An important example of this is the archive project that Thea Barnes set up in 1999 to 'strongly reflect the diversity of Phoenix choreographic history' (1999). Important as this work has been, however, many of the early records were already lost, and since her departure the archives have been boxed up and stored in places without public access. In addition, the focus for both dance companies and dance training is on performance practice in the studio and on the stage, rather than on the historical and theoretical aspects of the art form. Cynthia Novack articulates the divide between academic education and creative, physical education and also the fact that the subject cultural studies rarely includes dance (1995).[13]

---

[12] Anna Furse was also involved with X6 Dance Space, the experimental dance venue in London.
[13] Jane Desmond makes a similar point in *Embodying Difference: Issues in Dance and Cultural Studies* (1997).

As well as the complexities of research using substantial but incomplete and poorly organised archives, there is also an issue about my role within this work. In writing about what she termed the New Epic dance by African Americans, Ann Cooper Albright voiced her concern about how she, as a white feminist dancer and writer, could 'negotiate the position of witness and critic' (2001: 441). This is my concern too in writing about Phoenix. As with Cooper Albright's writing, this work gives insight into a specific cultural situation and an emerging critical tradition. It is also 'compelled by the conviction that this work is too important not to deal with, even if that means taking a risk by putting myself in a less comfortable critical position' (Cooper Albright, 2001: 441). Another context relevant to this study is Richard Schechner's observation that students of performance studies and the humanities in the academy are predominantly women, while their lecturers tend to be men. He suggests that, as with the history of modern dance, the gender balance is likely to shift as some of the graduates begin to teach (2003). So although in this context my gender and ethnicity place me in a majority category, that place is not fixed and shifts in relation to my interactions with the Company at specific times and places.

Although I was to some extent reassured by Cooper Albright's position, which reflected my own, I also carefully considered the points bell hooks raised in a discussion with Cornell West. She questioned whether, when white intellectuals made 'Black culture and Black experience the subject of their intellectual and discursive practices' (1991: 36), black people were being appropriated. My intention, of course, is not to do this but rather to locate Phoenix Dance Company as a significant artistic force in contemporary British dance, because this history is important. I hope that this initial cultural history will provide resources for future scholars with other agendas and positions.

Further developments

The reflections in this book acknowledge the Company's contributions to dance culture and dance history. Phoenix closed for some months in 2001 after the difficulties discussed in Chapter 5, but the Arts Council decided that the loss of a northern repertory company should be avoided. Darshan Singh Bhuller was appointed artistic director in 2002. He was a contemporary of the founders of Phoenix and studied at both Harehills Middle School and Intake High School. He became an acclaimed dancer with London Contemporary Dance Theatre (LCDT) and an internationally renowned choreographer. His connections to the founders and the Company's past provided a significant continuity for Phoenix. Moreover, his experience as a dancer and choreographer and his connections with Robert Cohan, a key figure in the development of contemporary dance in this country, ensured his authority as artistic director.

Bhuller had close contact with the Company throughout its development, creating five works for Phoenix as a freelance choreographer. As artistic director he created new works: *Class* (2002), *Requiem* (2003), *Eng-er-land* (2005) and *Laal* (2006); restaged *Planted Seeds* (2003 and 2005); and re-worked a duet, *Source 2* (2004). Like artistic directors Campbell and Barnes, he wanted a more flexible image for the Company that was not fixed to ethnicity. In an interview with Debra Craine (2006) he stated that he had modelled the Company on LCDT. He had achieved what was required of him: that is, to direct a company that attracted top British and international choreographers to make work which was then performed in middle-scale theatres (including Sadler's Wells Theatre in London) and toured internationally. His own ambitions, which he satisfied, were for the Company to perform good work made by artists whose work he found interesting, ranging from young British choreographers to more established international dance makers (Bhuller, 2006). When he left in 2006, Phoenix was acknowledged to be a challenge to the other key British repertory company, Rambert. At the time he said, 'The company is strong, it's a good time to leave. The new director will be blessed with great dancers and a great organisation' (Craine, 2006).

Javier De Frutos has taken over from Bhuller at the time of writing and offers influences from his Venezuelan background and his experiences as a solo artist and choreographer for a range of companies. De Frutos claims that he aims to make Phoenix 'the hottest [company]' in Britain (Berry, 2006: 27). He will, however, have to negotiate restrictive funding, issues of how artistic excellence is judged and stakeholders' expectations of the Company. In addition, its funding was at the outset connected to the contribution the Company made to contemporary dance in relation to the 'black dancing body'. More recently, this requirement has been questioned by artistic directors but continues to be a complex factor of the Company's heritage. Expectations of representing 'blackness' have contained and constrained these artists, who were expected to represent an imagined ethnicity. Their 'dancing body' became an ambiguous, political tool both satisfying and dissatisfying their own and everyone else's vision. The future of Phoenix will inevitably be informed by its history. This book focuses on the Company's history to 2001 and thus on the period before Bhuller's and De Frutos's directorships.

In writing this history I was aware of conflicting demands to discharge my responsibility to the Company to document the unwritten narrative from detailed archival work and at the same time to investigate the theoretical issues that play across this account in relation to ethnicity and cultural equity. The decisions I have taken about interweaving specific events entail a transformation. There is a play between, on the one hand, archival material and events, and on the other hand theoretical issues, which are themselves subject to translation. This process, moreover, problematises class, ethnicity and gender.

The structure of this book is a narrative. Chapters 1, 3, 4 and 5 form a chronological account of the Company's development in the context of social and historical events, artistic issues and arts policies. I have considered specific issues in particular chapters. Thus Chapter 1 discusses the founders of the Company in relation to the their achievements in the cultural contexts of the 1980s and dance developments in Britain. Chapter 2 sets out historical and cultural contexts, including debates about the Black Arts Movement and 'black dance', that have implications for the Company and raise theoretical concerns. Chapter 3 investigates Neville Campbell's directorship, the growth of Phoenix and the introduction of female dancers. It also considers the effects of the more formal organisation required of the Company at that time. Chapter 4 considers the implications for Phoenix of its establishment as a middle-scale company together with growing international success during the time Margaret Morris was artistic director. Company documents reveal numerous debates concerned with Phoenix as a 'black dance company' at this point. Chapter 5 discusses the issues confronting the Company in the creation and touring of its retrospective. In her role as artistic director, Thea Barnes was concerned both to acknowledge Phoenix's past and to promote its future as a Company performing with artistic excellence.

These chapters complete the readings of the archives in relation to history. The last chapter then examines critical responses to the repertoire, investigating the representation of Phoenix and specific critical writings from local and national newspapers and dance journals. Formal critical analyses of the Company do not exist, and so I have studied what is available, which offers insight into reception of their work at specific times. The critical response to the Company, despite the critics' support and enthusiasm for Phoenix, frequently exposes the writers' prejudices rather than offering readers informative accounts of its artistic achievements. Such responses raise serious questions about the limited understanding and effective support for companies from the African Diaspora. Both the critical responses and historical contexts frame the Company within contemporary dance in Britain in the last twenty years of the twentieth century.

Chapter 1: Beginnings: Phoenix Rising

This chapter introduces Phoenix Dance Company, as it was during the first six years of its existence, in a historical and cultural framework of contemporary dance in Britain in the 1970s and 1980s. I argue that the Company was unique in several ways both within contemporary dance and within wider artistic and cultural contexts in Britain. Its members were in their teens when they formed the Company in 1981, and gained recognition very early in their careers through an established television arts programme, *The South Bank Show*, in 1984. They were skilful performers but had not received the usual formal three-year dance training.[1] They were based in the north of England at a time when most dance activity was in London. In addition, they were Black British men, who had known each other from childhood and came from a tight-knit community, working in an art form that was associated with femininity (Adair, 1992). All these features were unusual for a dance company, and contributed to a story of success that became legendary. This chapter describes the Company members' backgrounds, and influences on their work and sense of identity. I show the complexity of the factors that affected the Company's work, and indicate both the reasons for and the problems involved in their success.

Early developments

The founders

Phoenix Dance Company has been described as 'the group of five young black men who changed the face of British contemporary dance when they founded Phoenix in 1982' (Senior, in Judd 1997–8: 32). Did they in fact do this? Unravelling possible answers to this question will raise a number of other questions in the process. From the interviews I have conducted, it is evident that there are as many perceptions of Phoenix as there are people who remember their early performances and/or who were connected with the Company in some way. The history and legacy of the Company is a complex one over which a number of people have a sense of ownership. Although my research has been rigorous because of

---

[1] Merville Jones stated in an article in *Animated*, 'I decided to work with Phoenix for a year whilst I was at school [...] I decided that if I wanted to continue with dance, the best way was to stay with Phoenix and not go into vocational training' (in Taylor, 1997: 13). This comment indicates the confidence the young dancers had in their ability to gain the physical skills they needed for performance without undergoing the typical three-year training. Such training was offered at London Contemporary Dance School and included daily technique classes in Graham technique and choreography classes.

the investment that people have in the Company, I am aware that my interpretations are just that and are unlikely to satisfy the need of those who want, as David Hamilton suggested, the 'correct' story (2003). One of the aspects of my research that I wanted to document was how the founders and later Company members perceived themselves; but is it possible to recover such information? This material has not previously been investigated in depth, nor have such questions been asked,[2] but this is one of the aims of this project. According to the founders, the group had certainly formed by November 1981 (Jones, 1997)[3] and this is the formation date accepted in this study. The starting date of the Company, however, is sometimes cited as 1982.

Phoenix Dance Company was founded by David Hamilton[4] (b. 1963), Villmore James (b. 1964) and Donald Edwards (b. 1963); Merville Jones (b. 1964) and Edward Lynch (b. 1965) joined them in 1982. Their local area was Harehills and Chapeltown, Leeds, which was home for most of the African Caribbean community. They were born in Britain, but their parents[5] had travelled to the 'mother country' (Phillips and Phillips, 1999). People from the first generation to arrive were encouraged to migrate to Britain; 'There were adverts everywhere: "Come to the mother country! The mother country needs you!" [...] I felt stronger loyalty towards England' (quoted in Webster, 1998: 42). The accounts in Webster's book, as in many others written about this migration, make evident the shock experienced by people who were received with hostility rather than welcomed to the country in which they expected to have a sense of belonging. (Fryer, 1984; Gilroy, 1987). These narratives are part of the heritage with which Hamilton, James, Edwards, Jones and Lynch were brought up and which informed their creativity.

The group began when David Hamilton mentioned the idea of forming a company to Villmore James, who was working at the Civic Theatre, Leeds, as part of a Youth Opportunities Scheme organised by the Manpower Services Commission.[6] James suggested that Donald Edwards join them. At this point the dancers were seventeen and eighteen years old (Edwards, 1997), influenced by their dance teachers from

---

[2] In 1997, Company member Dawn Holgate wrote an in-house resource/study pack that briefly charted the history of the Company.

[3] 1981 is the date given in one of the publicity leaflets for Phoenix (1987).

[4] David Hamilton's equity name was Leo Hamilton and he is frequently referred to as Leo.

[5] Their parents came from a range of islands: Hamilton – St Kitts and Nevis; James and Edwards – Jamaica; Jones – Barbados; and Lynch – Antigua.

[6] The theatre manager stated on the Certificate of Experience that Villmore had gained useful experience in preparing and building props, and in general stage management. He found him to be a very reliable and willing worker, and regretted that Villmore could not continue working in the theatre once the scheme finished. The scheme was basically a government initiative to deal with unemployment (Goddard, 1982).

1.   Studio Photograph, 1984. Villmore James, Edward Lynch, Merville Jones, David Hamilton, Donald Edwards. photographer Terry Cryer

Harehills Middle School and Intake High School who had introduced them to Laban's work (see below), and '*subconsciously using resources from social surroundings, from parents, reggae dance and using music that* [we] *liked* [and we] *choreographed from those resources*' (Edwards, 1997). As Paul Gilroy points out, 'The musics of the black Atlantic world were the primary expressions of cultural distinctiveness which this population [working-class black settlers] seized upon and adapted to its new circumstances' (1993: 81–2). An important example of such music was reggae, which the founders valued and which will be discussed later.

A contemporary at the school, Neville Campbell, reported that the group formed when they were unemployed. They therefore had the luxury of time when making work, without external pressures, because there were no expectations about what they would produce. They formed a close and unique bond with each other, and had a good deal of fun working together. Many of the works were narrative-based, familiar territory for them from their schooldays (Edwards, 1997; Jones, 1997; Campbell, 2000). The founders were past pupils of Harehills Middle School, and only Lynch did not attend Intake High School. James, Jones and Lynch were in the same year at school, Edwards was in the year above them and Hamilton was two years above them (Auty, 2006).

Backgrounds

The context of dance for young people in Chapeltown was wider than just their families and schools. Pamela Johnson, who joined the Company as a dancer in 1989, talked about events in Chapeltown in the 1970s as being 'really special' (1998). She told of a woman called Grandma who taught the songs and dances of Jamaica to local children, who then travelled and performed around the community. For the parents it became the norm to watch their children dancing and performing. '*Our greatest performance was performing for the Queen at Elland Road*'[7] (Johnson, 1998). Johnson described her experience in a production as part of her everyday life, as it was for the other children. Johnson's description offers insight into the role of dance and music in the lives of many of the children who studied dance at Harehills Middle School. It is also likely that the children's experience of dance predisposed them to be fully involved with the dance that the school provided.

---

[7] This reference is to the Elland Road of Leeds United Football Club, which the Queen visited. Caryl Phillips later discusses this club in relation to his experience of going to matches as a young boy. It is also the venue of a football dance project in which Pamela Johnson, when a member of Phoenix Dance Company, taught dance to some members of the Leeds United team (Wang, 1998).

When discussing his background and some of the influences upon his creativity, Edward Lynch described his family:

They would have parties and dance and we'd sit and watch, or we'd come downstairs and look through and see how they were dancing and imitate them. We kept something from that. I think that's where the rhythm and style came from. My parents would show us off; we'd dance and my parents would watch us, and when they got their friends round they would say, 'Look at Edward – do ska step' or whatever. All that home culture, I would express that in what I did in the youth group. (1997)

The home culture that Lynch describes evolved partly because of the hostility that first-generation Caribbean migrants experienced in Britain in the 1950s and 1960s. There was little access to entertainment because of 'the no-coloured policy [...] there was nothing for black people so you had to create your own social environment' (in Phillips and Phillips, 1999: 111). A dance environment similar to the one that Edwards described was also part of the lives of many African Americans who also 'learned to dance at home' (M.A. McQuirter, in DeFrantz, 2002: 95). As one interviewee described in a study by John W. Roberts of Philadelphians who danced in the 1940s, 'My parents used to literally roll back the carpet for us [...] All my brothers learned how to dance initially from my father, who was a magnificent dancer, and my mother, who was a wonderful dancer' (M.A. McQuirter, in DeFrantz, 95).

While Edward Lynch learnt from his family, he also developed his dance skills at school and as a member of the Youth Group. He said:

From an early age I was good at dance. I could watch things on TV and pick up the steps, so we had technique from this. We learnt a lot from London Contemporary Dance Theatre, and people coming in opened doors to other companies. We'd watch videos of Twyla Tharp, Netherlands Dance Company, Dance Theatre of Harlem and the Alvin Ailey Company. (1997)

Lynch's comment highlights the exposure to dance that the students received from a key contemporary dance company in Britain in the 1970s and 1980s (Senior, 1998). Lynch also indicates that the students gained a sense of a wider dance culture by watching videos of American and European companies. These elements formed an important part of the founders' dance education.

Education – Harehills Middle School

The secondary school system in Britain in the 1970s when David Hamilton, Villmore James, Merville Jones, Donald Edwards and Edward Lynch were at school was organised by local education authorities. Leeds Education Authority had a three-tier system from 1972 to 1986 (Senior, 1998). Pupils left primary school at the age of nine years and transferred to a middle school until the age of thirteen years, after which they went to a high school until the age of sixteen or eighteen years.

Three aspects of the education of the founders of Phoenix Dance Company are significant for this study. The first is that they all studied at Harehills Middle School; many dancers who joined the Company, once it was established, also studied at this institution. The second is that several dancers associated with Phoenix were also members of the Harehills Youth Theatre.[8] The third important aspect is that some of the pupils continued their studies at Intake High School.

Harehills Middle School had 450 pupils aged between nine and thirteen years old, of whom seventy-five per cent were from African Caribbean or Asian backgrounds, and many did not have English as their first language (Judd, 1997–8). It was situated in a densely populated, culturally mixed and economically deprived area. The school became well known within the education system and the contemporary dance networks for the quality of its dance education. So why was this particular school so successful in its dance education?

Several key elements appear crucial to the achievements of the staff and pupils at Harehills Middle School. Jack Bramwell[9] was appreciated by his staff as an enlightened and supportive head (Senior, 1998). He believed that engagement with the arts could encourage pupils from a variety of backgrounds to participate fully in their education, and he provided a structure within which teachers could work creatively with pupils. He thought dance had the potential to offer pupils at Harehills ways to communicate and contribute equally. He viewed working together towards a production as a social training and a means for pupils to appreciate one another's efforts, regardless of verbal skills or racial background (BBC Radio Leeds, 1988). He also valued dance sufficiently to make it an important part of the curriculum and to provide a structure that was developmental, so that by the end of the fourth year the students had experienced dance study based on Laban's principles. It is arguable that without Bramwell's unusual perceptiveness about the

---

[8] Harehills Youth Theatre is sometimes also referred to as Harehills Youth Dance Theatre.
[9] Jack Bramwell was White British.

value of the arts in education Phoenix Dance Company might never have come to fruition.

The approach to dance in schools in Britain in the 1960s and early 1970s was based on Rudolf von Laban's methods. Laban was motivated to create his movement principles by his concern over the limitations and artificiality of ballet at the beginning of the twentieth century, as was Isadora Duncan, another contemporary dance innovator. He wrote books and essays, developed a notation system, and taught and choreographed for professional dancers and for movement choirs of lay dancers. He was appointed director of Allied State Theatres in 1930 but left Nazi Germany in 1938. He moved to England to work with his colleague Kurt Jooss and where he already had followers – which is why his work made such an impact. In 1946 he founded the Art of Movement Studio, initially based at Manchester and then at Addlestone in Surrey (Rowell, 2000). He continued his investigations into movement, and his work in England was developed in education rather than in the theatre (Bruce, 1965).[10] Education Authorities accepted his theories of modern educational dance as an aspect of creative development for children and students, and his ideas were particularly popular in Yorkshire. He also developed a method of dance-and-movement analysis that gained acceptance within the contemporary dance field (Winearls, 1958: 1973). There was, however, 'no universally accepted canon of ideas or biography' (McCaw, 2001: 20). Each person who had been taught by Laban developed their own sense of both the man and his movement principles. The approach allowed teachers to develop their students' expressivity and creativity by teaching them physical and spatial awareness and providing a structure within which students could create their own work.

Hamilton said that the '*Laban approach encouraged you to create – that's its main strength*' (1997). This educational approach to dance enabled the founders of Phoenix, and other students who were taught at Harehills Middle School and Intake High School, to gain confidence in their abilities. It fed their desire to continue making work and to pass on their positive dance experiences to others. This commitment to education was noted in their publicity and programme notes. In the programme for Harrogate International Festival held at Royal Hall on

---

[10] There is controversy about the reasons Laban left Nazi Germany, and about his relationship with the regime. Marion Kant (2004) suggests that Laban benefited from the Nazi regime, whereas Violet Bruce (1965) and Valerie Preston-Dunlop (1988) suggest that he co-operated with the Nazis in order to survive artistically and politically, until eventually he refused to join the party in 1936. This left him without work or finances, and he left for Paris and then went on to England.

7 August 1985, it was noted that:

> Although Phoenix is primarily a performing company, they have a
> great interest in working with community, school and youth groups.
> They have a special interest in linking performances and workshops –
> especially as a way of encouraging others to dance. They have been
> enormously successful in stimulating and encouraging dance activi-
> ties during residencies in theatres, arts centres and summer schools.
> (49)

In 1972 Nadine Senior[11] was the senior mistress of physical education
at Harehills Middle School. In an interview, she spoke of her role as a
dance educator:

> I think it is easy for people to look back and assume that I had some
> complex theory about dance in education which I rigorously pursued.
> At the time I was simply trying to be a good physical education
> teacher, offering the children something that would interest and
> motivate them, artistically and physically. I had studied Laban's theo-
> ries of movement and this was very important in terms of the wide
> range of abilities and commitment we had to deal with, as it could be
> applied fairly flexibly. (In Judd, 1997–98: 32)

Every pupil took one dance lesson a week as part of the physical education curriculum.[12] In the fourth year, a devised performance was the
culmination of three years' work. There was a philosophy of self-disci-
pline and working for success, which evidently benefited the pupils, and
Senior was clear that she was developing the children's physical and
artistic intentions. She said, 'I can look at the youngsters who have got
so much from dance and that for me makes it all worthwhile because I
see their lives opening up' (in Hitchens, 1985:4). She valued the technique that the teachers from London Contemporary Dance Theatre
(LCDT) could bring to the occasional after-school classes they gave

---

[11] Nadine Senior is White British.

[12] An article in *The Times Educational Supplement*, 30 May 2003, reports that a school in
Dagenham, Essex, is successfully involving boys in the weekly dance lessons. From the
photographs, most appear to be African Caribbean. A teacher at the school, Caroline
Watkins, suggests, 'For quite a few of the boys who are low achievers academically, it has
given them a sense of belonging, doing something worthwhile and gaining praise for their
achievement in a new aspect of school curriculum [...]. It must have an impact on their
academic performance' (in McGavin, 2003: 11). It is interesting that this article was written
as though this work was innovative, yet such work was developed at Harehills Middle School
and Intake High School in the 1970s.

when they were in Yorkshire. She was, however, concerned to ensure that this remained an occasional experience, because she thought that there was a danger that pupils would limit themselves to reproducing technique rather then exploring their own intentions (1997). Modern dance as a professional performance form, in England before the foundation of LCDT and in Wales before Moving Being, scarcely existed. Laban-based work was modern dance in education without the example of trained professional dancers to aspire towards.

Nadine Senior considered Laban's movement principles a means of encouraging children to work at their own capacity and to achieve a sense of satisfaction (Bayliss, 1985). This approach she contrasted with traditional technique classes in which an exercise or a phrase of movement is copied from the teacher. She distinguished between dance for education, in which self-expression and personal development are the focus, and dance for theatrical performance, being a profession in which technique is required to enable the dancer to dance safely without injury and to extend the performer's range of movement possibilities (1988). The views that Senior communicates about teaching dance to young people are from Laban's educational discourse, which:

> claims that every child has the right to express his or her inner human emotions through a process of self-autonomy, experience, imagination and individuality. Laban supports the idea that any human being can move, therefore dance, and explore his or her human 'spontaneous and inborn' abilities. During his lifetime Laban tried to formulate a central theory that could encompass this universality of movement forms in order to master the contemporary aspects of dance and human experience (Marques, 1998: 175)

A Laban-based approach was one of my own experiences of dance movement, and on reflection I realise that I, as did the founders, internalised many of the beliefs noted above.

The particular view that Senior offered the pupils at Harehills is clear. She considered the work to be:

> [...] child-centred. It is non-stylistic, non-cultural, it deals with movement concepts and it works for any level of ability, because the concepts are the same for all the children but the response to the tasks depends on the individual, so there is no right or wrong answer. Nobody is failing, everyone is succeeding, because every answer is correct and that gives children enormous confidence to challenge themselves. (1998)

This comment indicates Senior's values of treating children equally, but also her assumptions. Her use of the term 'non-cultural' is an attempt to state that the work was accessible to children whatever their background. As Gilroy points out, in the 1980s the premises of racism did not so much connect 'race' with biology as exist as a cultural issue (1987). Cultural analysis in more recent times has offered the potential for understanding that 'identities are [...] constituted within, not outside representation' (Hall and du Gay, 1996: 4). It follows from this viewpoint that the idea of an approach being non-cultural is untenable.

Isabel Marques (1998), in an analysis of her application of Laban's theories in her work with young Brazilian dancers, highlights some issues relevant to the comments above and to the impact of Laban's work on the founders of Phoenix. From her research she challenges Laban's notion of the 'free, natural and spontaneous' body, arguing, as I have in an earlier publication, that the body is socially and culturally constructed (Adair, 1992). In addition, she counters Laban's notion of universal movement:

> Laban, a white European man born at the end of the 19th century, imprinted into his movement analysis his own views of the body, movement and dance that were inseparable from his personal, cultural, historical and social condition. Understanding his work as a claim for universal movement, as Laban himself pledged at that time, meant to me resisting and opposing in many ways diversity, multiplicity, and a polyphonic educational process in which I believed. Above all, I concluded that Laban's belief for universal movement patterns did not meet or complete the needs of the multicultural Brazilian contemporary society. (1998: 176)

Marques's observations are an example of the reconsideration of Laban's approach to movement. There is an assumption evident in Laban's work that Eurocentric values are superior and should, therefore, be adopted as universal. Despite this assumption, David Hamilton finds Laban's work useful in his current projects that fuse different dance styles and approaches. He suggests that the issue is about how Laban's concepts are applied, and that the process of experimentation is an important factor when working from such a method (2006).

Nadine Senior's quotation about her approach to teaching these young students is also an example of approaches to education that evolved from progressive educational policies advocated in the teacher training colleges in Britain in the 1960s and 1970s and that were practised in some progressive schools, particularly primary and middle schools. There were many successes as a result of these policies, not least a clear commitment to and development of children's creativity. Phoenix came about partly because of opportunities for creativity within schools offered by educational policies in the 1960s and 1970s. Such a success would be much less likely now after the educational policies of the 1990s. The recent focus on educational achievement in literacy and numeracy and on frequent assessment has resulted in schools' management and staff no longer being in a position to focus on creativity as they were in previous decades. The National Campaign for the Arts, in *Evidence to the National Advisory Committee on Creative and Cultural Education* (1997), made clear that, despite the Labour Party's encouraging manifesto, *Create the Future* (1997), it was still necessary to argue the case for arts in education. Indeed, they stressed that many children were likely to receive inadequate arts education because of government policies. Moreover, dance was not even mentioned in the 1994–5 report, *Subjects and standards: Issues for school development arising from OFSTED inspection findings.*

Senior suggested that the children she worked with had not been told what was 'good' or 'bad' art by their parents and did not have preconceptions about 'art' or 'dance'. '[...] as soon as we were able to establish dance as a regular event for the children, it became simply, "what people did" and lost all of its gender or class baggage' (in Judd, 1997–98: 32). This statement is at odds with the dancers' recollections of their experiences. Although dance was studied by all pupils, including the boys, in a social context in which dance activity was equated with femininity, that did not mean that gender was not an issue. Indeed, Senior herself suggests that when the boys studied dance 'they understood that you had to be fit and strong to dance [and] became more committed than the girls – dance became a macho thing to do' (in Judd, 1997–8: 34).

In the interviews that I undertook, the young men were very aware of the gendered aspects of dance. For example, Merville Jones recounts how the male dancers attracted female attention and that wearing tights was viewed as acceptable because of this appeal. They gained status through their role as dancers in the productions (1997). In addition, some had a family background of dance, so that the idea of participating in dance was not new to them and they were not first introduced to such participation at school (Lynch, 1997).

Newspaper cuttings from the national and local press paid tribute to the success of the school's dance work, including that from the youth group. One writer described it as '[...] that legend in the field, Harehills Youth Dance Theatre, a lesson if there ever was of what can be accomplished' (*The Sunday Times*, quoted in Holgate, 1997: 5). From reviews and from descriptions given by the Harehills performers, it is apparent that the school productions were devised projects with a dramatic focus. Pauline Fitzmaurice,[13] the drama teacher at Harehills (and later administrator for Phoenix), worked with Senior on the productions. Examples included *Jesus Christ Superstar, Tommy, Lord of the Rings* and *The Wizard of Oz*. All but the last of those had strong male leads, and Fitzmaurice said that there was positive discrimination towards the boys (1996). The founders acknowledged the importance of the drama work with Fitzmaurice, which complemented their dance work (Lynch, 1988).

The significance of Harehills Middle School is twofold. Firstly, in 1973 dance was introduced as a subject for every pupil in the school. This was unusual, as dance was often either not on the timetable or only taught to girls. There was enthusiasm for a subject in which pupils could express themselves and excel even though they might struggle in other aspects of the curriculum. Secondly, Harehills Youth Theatre, based at the school, provided a chance for pupils to have technique classes from visiting teachers and to have opportunities to make and rehearse their dances. The Youth Theatre was invited to perform at all the National Youth Festivals, held in venues in England, Scotland, and Wales (Holgate, 1997).

Pauline Fitzmaurice and Nadine Senior established the Harehills Youth Dance Theatre in 1976 because many of the children had nowhere to develop their dance work (Senior, 1988). They met regularly in the evenings and worked towards public performances. Dance technique was offered as well as choreographic workshops. Some students went into the school every day in the holidays to rehearse with David Hamilton, who had returned to Leeds after studying at the London Contemporary Dance School in London for a year (1988). Edwards, Jones and Lynch also attended the week-long course at the Yorkshire Ballet seminars, where they received tuition from highly acclaimed teachers (*Sports News*, 1982: PA). As these young dancers developed their own technique, they began to teach the younger students (Evans, 1984).

The aims of Harehills Youth Dance Theatre (1976–86) were to:

encourage and foster the growth of creativity in young people from the Harehills and Chapeltown areas of Leeds;

break down the artificial barriers between arts and society for both participants and audience;

---

[13] Pauline Fitzmaurice is White British.

break down pre-conceptions regarding race, sex and artistic involvement and achievement;
provide possible alternative career structures from those traditionally
available. (Holgate, 1997: 7)

The Youth Dance Theatre closed in 1986 when Harehills Middle School
closed and Leeds City Council changed to a two-tier system of education
(Senior, 1998). Senior left the school in 1985 to set up the Northern
School of Contemporary Dance in Leeds. At this point, the infrastructure for dance in the region, both in school and beyond, had diminished.[14] Previously, a number of boys as well as girls were interested in
dance because of their weekly dance lessons and the opportunity to pursue their interest in the Youth Dance Theatre group. Some of the students then went on to audition successfully for further training at the
London Contemporary Dance School. The other significant institution
in relation to dance experience for some of the founders was Intake High
School.

Education – Intake High School
This high school offered a specialist Theatre Arts course and was one of
several high schools specialising in a particular subject as part of Leeds
Education Authority's education policy. This was the route available to
students leaving Harehills who wanted to continue their dance studies,
and who included the founders of Phoenix. The school was in the west
of Leeds, which entailed a long bus journey to a post-war, predominantly working-class housing estate contrasting with the high-density,
nineteenth-century housing of Harehills. The headmaster of the
school, Charles Gardner,[15] had studied at the Laban Centre in London,
taught movement and dance himself, and actively encouraged dance
within the school. It was Gardner who suggested that the founders call
themselves 'Phoenix' from the myth of the visionary, immortal bird
(Hamilton, 1997; Auty, 2006).

The experience gained at Intake High School was significant for the
founders' dance development (Hamilton, 1997; Holgate, 1997). Nadine
Senior had taught at the school. John Auty,[16] however, became the
Head of Dance, which allowed him to pursue his approach to dance;
and he suggested that his gender had contributed to his career success
in a predominantly female profession.

---

[14] The Yorkshire Dance Centre, Leeds, offered some dance provision.
[15] Charles Gardner was White British.
[16] John Auty is White British.

Merville Jones remembers the school as strongly disciplinarian. The pupils were predominantly white in a white area. Some of the black pupils, who were mostly from Harehills, had a difficult time there. *'If you went to do the performing arts course you weren't really pushed, because they didn't see you in an academic light – they saw you in a theatrical way'* (Jones, 1997). Nevertheless, some of the Phoenix dancers gained valuable experience at Intake, including performing in theatres and on local television. Also, as Auty noted, they had the opportunity to give 'a great deal to each other when they were young' (in Keech, 1991).

Neville Campbell, the second artistic director of Phoenix, remembers John Auty teaching both practical and theory lessons based on Laban's principles. Auty's approach to teaching is illustrated in his book *Dance Ideas* (1991), written with Kate Harrison. He believed in the necessity of technique, and Campbell acknowledges Auty's influence as being as significant as Senior's for the Phoenix dancers.

John Auty was an expert in karate as well as dance, and was training part-time at London Contemporary Dance School when he was offered the position at Intake High School. He accepted the position because he was concerned that dancers were emerging mainly from private dance classes and that few pupils in state schools were being offered the chance to dance. He had an enthusiastic approach to his work, which he viewed as facilitating his students' abilities. The Phoenix founders experienced him as demanding and strict but as a good teacher from whom they learnt a good deal. David Hamilton remembered John Auty telling him that the basis of Laban's work was the effort actions – that is, the impulse behind movements (1988). This approach to movement influenced Hamilton's work and differed from the technical training of ballet or Graham technique, although the latter was an important part of the Company's work. In the excerpts from classes in videos of the Company's work throughout the 1980s and into the early 1990s, it is Graham technique that the Company are either participating in or teaching (Evans, 1984; Keech, 1991). The founders Edwards, James, Jones and Hamilton all studied at Intake and are clear about the significance for their future careers of what they learned at that institution. They were concerned that there should be recognition for the part that John Auty played in their dance development; the focus on Harehills sometimes meant that only some of their influences were readily acknowledged. The students went to Intake in the day and to Harehills Youth Dance Theatre in the evenings and sometimes at weekends and during holidays. This regime meant that they had to negotiate the different approaches to dance teaching offered by Auty and by Senior, together with clashes of rehearsal schedules (Auty, 2006). Nevertheless, these experiences were formative influences.

Youth dance movement

The youth dance movement evolved from work in schools and was a significant aspect of the supportive context within which Phoenix worked. It was an important part of the dance infrastructure in Britain that was eroded by the loss of the local education authorities in the restructuring under the Thatcher government. With that loss, many young people who did not have money for classes at private dance schools lost access to participation in dance.

The Education Reform Act of 1988 set up a National Curriculum, which introduced a single course of study in ten subjects for all primary and secondary schools. The curriculum was organised into core (English, maths and science) and foundation subjects. Dance was included under the umbrella of physical education but had only limited provision in the timetable. At the same time, there were fewer opportunities for dance clubs out of school hours because of teachers' rising workloads, and the youth dance movement significantly diminished.

In addition, as Hewison argues:

> The decision to establish a 'national curriculum' in schools is an attempt to reassert a particular view of national identity through a prescribed history and literature. The manipulation of the idea of a 'national heritage' performs a similar function in reuniting contemporary Britain with a particular version of its past and reconciling it to that past. (1995: 16-17)

However, as Paul Gilroy points out, the concept of nation is problematic for Britain's black settlers and their descendants, as they have been viewed as 'an illegitimate intrusion into a vision of authentic British national life' (1993: 3). Although the founders of Phoenix made clear in my interviews with them that they identify as British, they also indicated their experience of racism, which, as Gilroy articulates, has been fuelled by a notion that authenticity was disrupted by the settlers. Moreover, as Naz Rassool points out, 'analyses of different "black" experiences and the shaping of "black identities" in Britain cannot lose sight of the reality that racism is materially grounded' (1997: 189).

Nevertheless, when Phoenix was emerging as a new dance company, such concerns were not paramount for the young dancers. On Wednesday 15 September 1982 at 7.30 pm, Harehills Youth Dance

Theatre[17] performed as part of the Youth Dance National Festival organised by West Glamorgan Education Authority and held at the West Glamorgan Institute of Higher Education, Swansea. The Company members, many of whom went on to dance professionally, are listed as follows:

> David Hamilton, Donald Edwards, Vilmore James,[18] Merville Jones, David Hughes, Douglas Thorpe, Edward Lynch, Junior Willocks, Dwight Powell, Robert Edwards, Hugh Davis, Paul Liburd, Tony Louis, Sharon Donaldson, Pamela Johnson, Seline Thomas, Donna Gentiles.

Of those, only three did not dance with Phoenix at some time. The names include the founders of Phoenix and three of the women who were to join the Company in 1989. The fourth-year dance group, the youth group and Phoenix Dance Company were included in The Dance Umbrella of Harehills Middle School, Leeds, and each performed at the Youth Dance Festival. The Umbrella received some funding from the Gulbenkian Foundation (Fitzmaurice, April 2003). The programme note stated:

> The members of all three companies are either past or present pupils of the school, where dance is a part of the curriculum for every boy and girl in the school. The Harehills Youth Dance Umbrella will present a selection of short pieces from all three companies including four pieces especially choreographed for a recent residency at Ripon Cathedral. (1982: 7)

This programme note, together with a photograph illustrating some of the company, is evidence of the kind of performance experience Phoenix had in their early career. In addition, the eight-day programme for the Youth Dance National Festival included daily class in a choice of contemporary, ballet or t'ai chi, and daily workshops with a choice of mime, jazz, contact improvisation, music and partnering. The teachers were from the London-based training schools, including Ballet Rambert, Arts Educational, Royal Ballet and London Contemporary

---

[17] The programme for the National Youth Dance Theatre held in West Glamorgan on 12–19 September 1982 lists the Harehills company as 'Harehills Youth Dance Theatre'. Holgate (1997), in her overview of the company, writes of 'Harehills Youth Theatre'.

[18] Villmore James's name is spelt both as 'Vilmore' and as 'Villmore' in Company documents and reviews of the Company. He endorses the second spelling, and that is the one used for this study.

Dance School. There was also a sharing event coordinated by Geoff Moore and Moving Being,[19] and evening performances by the participating groups followed by performances by professional dancers. This festival provided good opportunities for the young people to experience their own work in a national context and to gain valuable dance experience with professional performers.

As well as offering a valuable learning opportunity through its classes, the Festival also provided an extremely useful networking opportunity. Several people listed in the programme made contributions later to the new company, Phoenix. For example, John Travis from London Festival Ballet became a member of their Board when it was formed. The dancers also performed *Blood Wedding* (1986), choreographed by David Glass, who had an international reputation in mime and performance and who also had contemporary dance training. This work was for four dancers. Merville Jones did not dance in it because of his injury. He described it as:

Amazing dance theatre, very different to what Phoenix were doing, and everyone knocked it [...]. People were saying, "You shouldn't be doing it"; we were energetic, fast, lively that's what people wanted to see. So it was shelved after about two performances; that was sad. It called on the guys to push all the skills they had and develop others. The costume and lighting worked well. (1997)

Jones's observations are an indication of the difficulties the Company experienced when attempting to diversify their repertoire.

One of the factors that contribute to the mythology about Phoenix is that they were not trained. There is an assumption linked with this that fits into racist ideology, which is that people of African and African Caribbean descent have inherent rhythm and physicality and that the dancers 'danced naturally'. In a 1938 interview with Frederick L. Orme, Katherine Dunham, a key early modern dancer, explains that 'dancing ability is not based on biology, but on rigorous training, even if this training occurs informally within the context of the activities of daily life' (in Fischer-Hornung, 2001: 92).

---

[19] Geoff Moore's Moving Being was formed in 1968. The dance critic John Percival suggested that 'almost single-handed, Geoff Moore had provided British ballet with its avant-garde' (1969: 43). The company included dancers, actors and technicians, who produced complex multi-media productions (Percival, 1971). They were housed at The Place, where the London Contemporary Dance School and London Contemporary Dance Theatre were based (Murray, 1979). They moved to a base in Cardiff in 1972 (Jordan, 1992).

The founders, however, not only received dance classes at school but also had classes and workshops from dancers from London Contemporary Dance Theatre and Ross McKim of English Dance Theatre who, unlike LCDT, were based in the north of England. McKim also made an early work for the Company, *Reach* (1982). Their physicality was developed through a range of other experiences, including sports, martial arts and boxing. They played on the streets doing dares and taking risks, and as they got older they went dancing in clubs and brought all of those influences to the stage. Undoubtedly, a dance training that provides rigorous technique classes on a daily basis and regular access to the expertise of teachers who have danced in contemporary companies is something that the founders, with the exception of Hamilton, did not have. That is not, however, the same as asserting that they had no training. They had high-quality physical and dance training, but not the usual three-year training at a dance school.

First appearances and early choreographies

At first, Phoenix Dance Company's performances were to audiences in the communities in Leeds to which the school group performed. Performances were in school halls and church halls and not necessarily attended by the black community. They danced at the Civic Theatre, but James reported that '*we always felt we were looked down upon by the Leeds community and by the Arts Council and Leeds City Council*' (1997). This is an interesting comment and one that has resonance today because, despite the recognition that the Company has received, the founders have not fully benefited from their early success. They have a sense of being exploited and they have not received the mentoring and facilitation that would have been appropriate for the development of young artists (Edwards, 1997; Hamilton, 1997).

They performed in small-scale venues such as Bradford's Theatre in the Mill. Edwards said that it was not until they were invited to perform at Battersea Arts Centre, London, in 1983 that they really attracted black audiences[20]. Several factors made the existence and development of the Company possible. They had access to free rehearsal space at Harehills Middle School. They also had many contacts within the Leeds area and gradually widened them to other areas, so that there was a network within which they could develop both their performance and their education work.

---

[20] Some of the documentation related to these performances, schedules and so on no longer exists. Lynch said that he had thrown away some of the material, but subsequently regretted it (1997).

David Hamilton cites the Company's first appearance as a show that was put together for the University and the Studio Theatre in Leeds (1997). An article from the Northern School of Contemporary Dance archives, however, states that their first appearance was in February 1982 at St Chad's Hall, Headingley, Leeds. They also appeared in their first television recording for the BBC morning programme *Get Set for Summer*. The reporter noted that the Company:

> [...] still had not worked out the complete choreography for the television performance, but their confidence under pressure, and their ability to laugh it off ("Where the hell do I put my leg now" said Donald Edwards, having vaulted gracefully on to David's shoulder) showed the confidence of seasoned performers. (NSCD AF, 1982)

This comment illustrates the youth of the dancers, the fact that they were working out how to operate as performers as they went along, and the opportunities they had for local and national coverage in the media early in their careers.

A review by Helen Scott in the *Yorkshire Evening Post* (7 January 1982) stated that the first performance was a charity concert held at Leeds Civic Theatre on 16 February 1982. This was where Villmore James was on a work experience scheme. The opportunity to perform was offered to the Company by Brian Goddard, the theatre's manager, and they were to perform there on various other occasions, notably 25 September 1983 for a Gala Charity Show and 20–23 May 1987 (Simpson, 2003). The 1983 programme notes indicate that they had also performed for BBC2's programme *Riverside* and represented Great Britain in an International Dance Festival (programme, 1983). This was less than two years after the Company first formed.

In an interview, Donald Edwards said:

> *For our first performance as Phoenix, myself, Villmore and David, we got £10 from the Albany Empire* [London]. *It was very difficult because we weren't trained dancers. A lot of people hated us for that, envied us, I think because* [they wondered] *how it was possible for five guys coming out of the education system, one of them had one year's training at the Place* [David], *all of a sudden to become a success. A lot of people said there is no way you are going to survive. For one, you haven't got the technical capability, you are dancing on your talent, you are going to burn yourselves out; and there were times when it came close to us saying, 'Well, let's just call it a day'.* (Edwards, 1997)

Edward Lynch sites the Company's first appearance as Battersea Arts Centre, London. He also says that, because they were so focused on the work, they did not really consider their audiences but thought that an audience would enjoy what the Company presented (Lynch, 1997). When he saw them perform before he joined, he thought they were unique and he felt inspired by what he saw (Lynch, 1997). Merville Jones identifies the first performance as at a conference in Loughborough, 1981, which Pauline Fitzmaurice also mentioned (2003).[21]

The discrepancies in the Company's recall of the first performance have several causes. As we have seen, the Company performed together while they were defining themselves as a Company. Each performer may have mentioned the performance that seemed most significant to him. Another factor that the varied recollections raises is the lack of clearly dated, catalogued and accessible archive material from the early years.

The first recording of Phoenix that I have located is a video directed by Bronwyn Williams at Leeds University. Gary Lyons provided the commentary, which accompanied a class directed by Nadine Senior with second-year pupils and a rehearsal of the Youth Dance Theatre in which Sharon Donaldson, Pamela Johnson and Seline Thomas[22] were dancing; they joined the company in 1989. The commentary continued:

> In Leeds at the moment is a group called Phoenix establishing themselves as a small touring company set up by David Hamilton in 1981. Phoenix dance with a heartfelt power and energy which is compelling to watch. They use their varied and imaginative talents in choreographing their own dances, developing a distinctive and dynamic style. (Lyons, in Williams, 1982)

David Hamilton is shown leading Donald Edwards, Villmore James and Merville Jones through a series of contemporary dance warm-up exercises, including standing bounces, leg extensions and changing directions with leg extensions and arm circles. There is a precision to the movement and all the dancers are focused. They then perform *Running Shadows* choreographed by Donald Edwards (1982). This work was one of eight that Edwards made for the Company between 1982 and 1988

---

[21] The dance context in which Phoenix emerged included several small companies in the early 1980s who explored a range of dance styles and reached wide audiences. Such companies included Corps de Jazz, Inner Visions Dance Co. and Union Dance Company (Charlemagne, 1984).

[22] These dancers were of African Caribbean heritage but born in Britain.

and was part of their current programme at the time the video was made.

The movement style of the choreography is from contemporary dance, with some moves familiar from martial arts and boxing. The piece opens with a figure (Merville Jones) lying on the floor with a bare torso crossed with black braid and with loose, slashed white trousers. He moves into leg and arm extensions reaching away from the floor into a back arch. The three figures who join him (Donald Edwards, David Hamilton and Villmore James) are dressed in similar trousers but in black, with white braid in a zigzag pattern binding the legs and bare torsos. The piece is reminiscent of contemporary dance work, particularly Robert North's *Troy Games* of the late 1970s and early 1980s. The movement vocabulary includes lunges, extensions, small side steps with weight over the toes (a movement often seen in boxing) and more acrobatic moves, including cartwheels. The structure is very simple, with some unison movement while at other times the three figures surround the figure dressed in white, providing a solo and group structure. This piece is an example of the Company's propensity to work with a range of movements, not only those defined as contemporary dance.

In an interview with Ramsay Burt in 1987, Hamilton talked about an early piece he had made, *Triad within the Tao* (1982), based on Chinese Taoism and the idea that:

> within the Tao there are always three; The Mystic, The Prophet, and The Genius. You always see them as individuals, but together as a group they are inseparable, they're one [...]. I gave Donald and Villmore poems which I felt represented the parts they were dancing. Donald was the Prophet, Villmore The Genius and I was The Mystic. The Mystic being the character who represents the heart and devotion, The Prophet representing imagination, vision and the importance of change, The Genius representing study and concentration. Behind the characters we assumed in that dance and the way we danced the parts, you can trace the way each of us choreographs. (Hamilton, in Holgate, 1997: 13)

It is evident from this statement that each founder was deeply committed to and involved with the practice of dance within the Company and to each other and their mission to express aspects of themselves. Here we see the potential conflict between the arts management, once the Company had become established, and the creative self and identity of the dancer as artist.

2. *Triad within the Tao*, 1982. Choreographer David Hamilton; dancers
David Hamilton, Villmore James, Donald Edwards; photographer Terry Cryer

'Phoenix Dance' for *The South Bank Show* was filmed in Leeds during 1–6 July 1984. Several choreographic excerpts were included that illustrated the diversity of the Company's work. The crew travelled to Leeds on Monday and based themselves at the Civic Theatre ready to film the dancers on Tuesday in four choreographies: *Traffic Variations* (1983) by Veronica Lewis, *Nightlife at the Flamingo* (1983) by Edward Lynch, *Speak Like a Child* (1983) by Darshan Singh Bhuller and *Forming of the Phoenix* (1982) by David Hamilton. On Wednesday the crew filmed Harehills Middle School and interviewed the dancers and Pauline Fitzmaurice (administrator). They filmed at Martine's Night Club at the Corn Exchange that evening. Thursday was a full day at Harehills Middle School, with Nadine Senior and footage of children working from different eras. The last day was spent with the dancers and in filming some footage of the Chapeltown Road (PA). This television programme was important for the dancers, as it offered insight into the relationship between their background and their dance work and presented a range of their early repertoire. It also gave Phoenix national publicity and became an important historic record of the Company.

Photographs by Pete Huggins, in an early publicity leaflet, also give insight into the Company. They were taken in a school hall (apparent from the background) and two of them illustrate the dancers' emphasis on physicality and risk-taking. One photograph has three dancers balancing on the shoulders of three other dancers, and in another photograph one dancer is astride a rope suspended from the ceiling while the others are engaged with each other and with the rope below. A posed photograph shows six dancers but lists the names of only five (Edwards, James, Jones, Hamilton and Lynch; the other dancer was identified by Pauline Fitzmaurice as Neville Campbell).

Although one person was named as the choreographer for the pieces in the Company repertoire, the members '*all had a hand in developing the pieces. There would be five brains thinking about this thing and where it was actually travelling*' (Jones, 1997). This statement is another example of the early co-operative approach with which the Company operated. It is also significant because at that time a named choreographer received a good deal of prestige within the mainstream modern dance tradition.

Hamilton identified the Company's strengths as the emphasis on creating their own work, developed from their experiences of Laban principles from school, and their use of jazz, soul and reggae music. '*Our first involvement in performance was like a process we were continually burning, always learning*' (1997). He also felt that there were expectations and standards within contemporary dance often set by one or two companies, against which other companies were judged, seldom appropriately.

(LCDT tended to be the standard by which contemporary dance was judged in the late 1970s and early 1980s; see discussions in *New Dance*.) '*We did it, lived it*' (Hamilton, 1997).

The work and the Company's concerns were from:

a British experience because we never did African pieces, Caribbean pieces; in the early days we did reggae, but that was more to do with what was happening here in England. The steppers, the skanking, the lovers' rock that was happening here in the 1970s time [when] we were growing up. We would go to dance halls and see what was going on. It was British even though we knew reggae music was from Jamaica; we didn't say all this dancing is from Jamaica. We had our own interpretations. Personal expression is very important because we had that opportunity to tell people about our lives and culture through dance. (Lynch, 1997)

As well as showing group pieces, the Company also occasionally performed solos, which Merville Jones said were sometimes useful as programme fillers so that there was time for costume changes and to allow some of the dancers to have a break. He made one solo based on Eleo Pomare's solo *Junkie* from *Blues for the Jungle* (1966):

I thought I could do that with my eyes closed. I've seen enough films, I don't need music. In the end I went on stage, had a costume, stumbled around and I pretended I was feeling high and that's what I called a solo. I remember it because I think it was taking the mickey, but in terms of the development of the group we needed things like that. (1997)

Merville Jones's comment indicates a paradox in relation to the Company's training and professionalism. On the one hand they worked extremely hard and developed their technical and choreographic abilities. On the other hand they were young men who wanted to have fun and were willing to take risks with improvisation and their stage performances, and were sometimes not fully prepared (Jones, 1997). I think Jones's statement also reflects a lack of understanding of other artists' work, in particular that of African American artists. Thomas DeFrantz discusses Eleo Pomare's solo *Junkie* in the context of the Black Arts Movement. He explained that:

Pomare's work reached off the stage and into the audience, forcing the issue of social change on his dancers and their audience. [In *Junkie*...] the dancer careers across the stage in search of a fix, finally tumbling off the stage and directly entreating the audience to satisfy his needs. The dance assumes the involvement of its audience in its construction [...]. The dance itself was conceived as an act of protest, and the inclusion and subsequent rejection of the audience here is an expression of that protest. (1999: 86)

This analysis identifies elements of the work that Jones had clearly over-looked. Moreover, the Company tended to look for inspiration to British artists, who either were dancing with London Contemporary Dance Theatre or had trained at the school. They were aware of some of the significant dance artists in America, but it was clear from my interviews that the founders had only limited information about such artists and did not regard them as role models. Another important point from Merville Jones was that there was competition within the group, particularly over choreography. Each choreographer wanted his work to be the best, and Jones suggested that there was often insufficient respect for each other's work (1997).

An early work that Donald Edwards choreographed for the Company was *Ritual for Death* (1982). Villmore James remembered, '*I saw Pina Bausch's* Rite of Spring. *Donald's* Ritual for Death *could have been influenced by Bausch because of the ritual of the whole game and the violence of the structure of the piece*'[23] (James, 1997). The work, accompanied by classical music, had the theme of sacrifice, which is also the basis of *Rite of Spring*. Jones described the work as '*a male bonding piece*' (1997). He went on to say:

Once in Scotland we were doing a tour and we got so much stick for being black, and racial abuse was flying around in the auditorium. I remember saying ok, let's go and get them. We just went on stage and made them crap themselves and then the respect the school had for us because the piece was so physical [...] we thought, we'll show you what we're made of [...] the experience for me was one of the most positive that we'd ever done. (1997)

Here Merville Jones is offering an example of the racism that the group sometimes encountered. It is interesting to reflect on the group's response in this situation; they took the opportunity to use their physical skills and artistry to empower themselves and to challenge the pre-conceptions and prejudices of their audience.

---

[23] There was a video of *Rite of Spring* (BBC, late 1970s, introduced by Nureyev), which may have been the recording that James remembered viewing.

Merville Jones is the only member from the early group who did not have a choreography in the repertoire. Between 1982 and 1988 Villmore James choreographed five works for the Company. His first piece was *Tribal Vibes* (1982). The movement vocabulary included turns, lunges, bounces, stretched arms and clenched fists, and stillness into wide second-position jumps. The structure was very simple, consisting of a solo (Edwards) joined by another dancer (Hamilton) for a duo, and then the remaining dancer (Hamilton) continuing with a solo. Jones said of it, '*I remember being kicked out of that because I wasn't giving it enough, and I ended up drumming for it in the end*' (1997). The movements in this work were those the Company were familiar with from the mainstream contemporary dance work available in Britain in the late 1970s and early 1980s. Merville Jones's comment demonstrates the difficulties the Company sometimes had in working with each other to a high professional standard during rehearsals.

It is interesting at this point to reflect on how they might have perceived working with choreographers from outside the Company. During the period 1982–88, forty works are listed in the Company repertoire; of these, only twelve are not choreographed by the founders. Of those twelve, seven are choreographed by Neville Campbell, four of them in 1987 when he had become the Company's artistic director. The other choreographers, who all choreographed one work for the Company, are Ross McKim, Darshan Singh Bhuller, Veronica Lewis, Jane Dudley and David Glass; of these, the only choreographer who was not white European or American was Bhuller. As we have seen, the Company had worked with both McKim and Bhuller either through workshops or at school.

Veronica Lewis[24] was filmed working with Phoenix Dance Company for television's *The South Bank Show* (Evans, 1984). In the programme, she talks enthusiastically about sharing the lyrical approach to movement which she enjoyed and which she felt would broaden the male dancers' movement style and allow their work to become more sensitive. The work she made for the dancers and which she is seen rehearsing is *Traffic Variations*, to Loillet's Flute Suite (1983). Although undoubtedly Lewis would have introduced the dancers to other ways of working, it is questionable whether this was an appropriate work for the Company at that time. From the comments the dancers made in interviews, it seems that they were committed to making their own work, and there were

---

[24] Veronica Lewis choreographed for the Company because she had met the dancers and Pauline Fitzmaurice at the National Youth Dance Summer Schools. Lewis was the founder of the Cheshire Dance Project, one of the most successful early youth dance projects. She is now joint principal of the Conservatoire of Dance and Drama, and Director of the London Contemporary Dance School (LCDS).

3.   *The Story of the Phoenix*, 1985. Choreographer David Hamilton; dancers
     Edward Lynch, Villmore James, Donald Edwards, David Hamilton; photographer
     Terry Cryer

sometimes difficulties making work with choreographers who had perhaps not taken sufficient account of who the dancers were. For example, Villmore James said:

> *She* [Lewis] *kept making jokes about 'accident black spots'. The piece was in*
> *four sections and the last one was called 'accident black spot'. The whole*
> *thing was playing on car accidents and so forth. Everything like that we*
> *took a step back, we never played into anyone's hands, if any racial abuse*
> *came out unconsciously.* (James, 1997)

It is clear from the television programme that Lewis's intentions were to
offer another approach to movement; but, unfortunately, from James's
statement it appears that her lack of awareness of cultural differences
meant that the dancers had to deal with inappropriate remarks. At that
time, I would suggest (and to some extent this is still the case), in most
dance companies there was a widely held belief that art transcends cultural specificities. However, even though this may be the case, it is also
necessary for cultural specificity to be taken into account so that artists
receive the cultural recognition that they require.

Another of the choreographers who made a work with the dancers
but did not have connections with the Company was Jane Dudley, a former dancer of the Martha Graham Dance Company, who also choreographed her own work and was Director of Graham Studies at LCDS in
1972. She created *Running* in 1985. As Merville Jones observes, this
was:

> [...] *one of those pieces that was imposed upon the company. We learnt a lot*
> *from Jane – her passion for dance and life. The piece itself was a challenge*
> *to do because it was physically demanding, but it was* [also] *boring.*
> (1997)

Jones's depiction of the work as 'imposed' and 'boring' is interesting
because it highlights a tension for the Company. In order to extend their
skills they needed to work with other teachers and choreographers, but
for that to be successful it was important that they worked with people
who were perceptive about their shared background and their understanding of dance. Dudley valued the Company's work. She was particularly impressed by their ability to make connections with audiences
who were not usually interested in contemporary dance. Nonetheless,
her comments in *The South Bank Show* make her preconceptions clear.
She says that she thinks it would be a pity if Phoenix became 'too arty,

4.   *Running*, 1985. Choreographer Jane Dudley; dancers Edward Lynch, Villmore James, Donald Edwards; photographer Terry Cryer

intellectual or formalist' (Evans, 1984). There is a subtext in this phrase
that alludes not only to ethnicity but also to class. There is a tendency to
associate art with the middle class, which clearly was not the background of the Company members. In addition, Dudley seems to be sug-
gesting that their strengths were better suited to content-based pieces
rather than to more abstract work. Her remark about not wanting them
to be 'too intellectual' is potentially racist, founded in the stereotype of
people of African heritage being associated with physicality rather than
intellect. Undoubtedly, her comments would have been unconscious
and her desire, apparent from her appreciation of the Company, was to
see it succeed. It was, however, this very unconsciousness evident in the
infrastructure of dance, from the Arts Council to the critics, that
unhelpfully categorised Phoenix.[25]

Before they received Arts Council funding, the Company operated on
a very tight budget. Moira Benoit (née Smith), costume designer from
1982 until 1988, designed and made the Company's costumes with
'great ingenuity', as an early programme stated. She costumed all the
works with the exceptions of *Traffic Variations* (1983) choreographed by
Veronica Lewis, *Running* (1985) choreographed by Jane Dudley and
Blood Wedding (1986) choreographed by David Glass. These works were
by the three choreographers who were not part of the Company or who
did not have close connections to it (Benoit did, however, provide the
costumes for Bhuller's and McKim's works). Music was recorded on
tapes on home stereo systems from records that friends lent them.

They rolled everything into bags and travelled on public transport.
When they arrived at a venue, they frequently found it to be cold, often
with a concrete or an uneven wooden floor. Such conditions would, of
course, have been detrimental to their health and would have made performing difficult and on occasions possibly dangerous, but the Company
at that point were committed to disseminating dance as widely as
possible.

The founders' memories of their first performances and some of the
early works give an indication of the formative period of the Company.
The founders in some ways retained a strong sense of ownership of the
Company, but there were difficulties at the outset. Jones also outlined
some of the complexities of the Company's relationship with Nadine
Senior. One of the Company's early public performances (discussed

---

[25] When Greater London Arts tried to modify their policies by promoting traditional African,
African Caribbean and South Asian work, companies such as Phoenix (cited as an example,
although they were not from London) were not eligible for funding because their work drew
on Western dance techniques. As the dance critic Jann Parry suggested, such a policy was
problematic because it encouraged the funding of works that evoked the past, rather than
innovative work concerned with contemporary issues (1988).

above) was at the National Youth Dance Festival in Glamorgan in September 1982, and at this Festival someone asked whether it was Senior's company. Hamilton said it was not. Senior, however, insisted that the Company acknowledge her involvement within that public arena (1997). The evidence of the programme suggests that this insistence was accepted, as Phoenix is not listed as a separate company. The members' names are listed together with the other dancers under the label of Harehills Youth Dance Theatre.

Sources and self-definitions

Location

The Company were clear about their aims and the importance of their location. As Edward Lynch said, '*The aims were to perform, and to create our own work. We always stressed that we came from Leeds. Leeds is where it's happening. Leeds has got the best dancers*' (1997). This comment is interesting when considered in the dance context of the late 1970s and early 1980s, when the majority of contemporary dance activity took place in London.

A choreography that took its inspiration from the Leeds area, in which the founders went to school, was *Speak Like a Child* (1983). Choreographer Darshan Singh Bhuller described it as being '*about when I was a kid in Harehills and Chapeltown and about these people too because they are out on the same street as I was ... It's about all the energy around here and about playing around and enjoying yourselves*' (Ferguson, 1983).

James said of this work that it was the second piece done with an outside choreographer and '*it was a lot more male dynamic. It was very physical and enjoyable to do and perform. People in the Company were more inspirational than anyone else*' (James, 1997). James's observations indicate the close connection the Company members had with each other, and their preference for powerful movement. In an interview for *The South Bank Show*, Fitzmaurice spoke about wanting the Company to extend their repertoire to more sensitive movement, which may have been part of the impetus for the involvement of some of the outside choreographers (in Evans, 1984).

An issue for the Company in relation to experience is that many people who were in the Company or involved with it and based in Leeds, had limited exposure to the dance world outside Leeds. This affected their views of themselves and their development. Their connections with LCDT opened up their visions but there was an inward focus to Phoenix despite their heavy touring schedules (Jones, 1997). One reason why this is important was that arts outside London tended to be marginalised, particularly at that time.

It is clear from statements such as Bhuller's above, from the interviews with the founders of Phoenix, and from the commentary about the Company on *The South Bank Show* (Evans, 1984) that the localities of Harehills and Chapeltown were formative in the early lives of the artists who grew up there. Carl Hylton, in a research paper, identified the difficulties in obtaining funding for local artistic initiatives by African and African Caribbean artists. He also highlighted the desire for artists to 'retain control of the creative processes and outcomes' (1996: 4) and for a permanent space dedicated to the arts.

Most of the African Caribbean community in Leeds live in the inner-city areas of Chapeltown and Harehills. The area 'suffers from high unemployment, low incomes, low levels of skills and educational attainment, poor housing, derelict buildings, a lack of confidence and a fear of crime, and a poor public image' (Gregg, 1998: 1).[26] It is also an area of prostitution and drug dealing and was one of the locations of the inner-city uprisings in 1981. The artist Prafulla Mohanti described the Leeds of the 1980s as 'a city of contrasts. Some lived in great Victorian mansions in Headingley while many were crammed into back-to-back houses with outside lavatories and no proper washing facilities' (1985: 72).

At the same time, it has 'a strong community spirit and wealth of active community organisations. It has a wide range of cultural and ethnic influences that make it an exciting place to be' (Gregg, 1998: 1). The Leeds Urban Initiative and Action Plan (1998) was designed to bring support to the area with European funding. The scheme identified particular groups as needing specific support, and these included young African Caribbean men. Hylton suggested that, as with other regions in Britain with a significant African Caribbean population, the Leeds community was dealing with issues of racism and unemployment. Various organisational strategies were devised to deal with these issues – for example, advocacy work in relation to housing, education, health and dealing with the police; providing additional education in the form of Saturday schools; and 'individual and collective approaches to Black art forms' (1996: 4). 'Art performs a duel function in our society, that of reflection of what exists, and creates fantasies of what is possible' (Connor, in Hylton, 1996: 5).

---

[26] As an example of crime in the locality, two murders in Harehills and Chapeltown were reported in the national news in articles that also noted high unemployment in the area, drug trafficking, gang wars and gun-related incidents. However, both articles also emphasised the positive aspects of the area (Wainwright, 1996: 27; Herbert, 2000: 3).

Hylton identified black arts expression as concerned with the self-expression of African or African Caribbean community cultures and issues, both past and present. In that sense, he viewed the art work as functional. He quoted David Hamilton, who suggested that contemporary dance, when combined with reggae and jazz as stimulants for creativity, has links with African peoples' folk traditions. Hamilton (1997) also suggested in an interview that the training for ballet and contemporary dance made it difficult for black dancers to express their culture (this comment is similar to one made by the artist Jonzi D).[27] Hamilton was highlighting the complexity of dance training and the creation of work for artists who wish to make culturally specific work. These ideas come from both an Afrocentric position and a political perspective that evolved with the Civil Rights Movement in the USA in the 1960s, which have both had an impact on dance.

In the early years of Phoenix an array of art forms and organisations in Leeds were initiated and led by black practitioners.

> The Black communities are particularly concerned to affirm their right to define and determine the parameters of quality and the essence of their cultural expressions. The official validation of these expressions will be achieved when the arts funding establishment creates space for Black communities to lead the process of defining, assessing and evaluating their art and the cultural contexts in which they are located. (Blackman and Bryan 1991, quoted in Hylton, 1996: 12)

This position, which endorses separatism, echoes that of the separatist women's movement. The stance endorses binary categories of black and white, just as the earlier movement endorsed the categories of men and women. If it may be strategically useful, as Spivak (1988; see also Morley and Chen, 1996) has argued, to adopt the category 'woman', it may also be strategically useful to adopt the category 'black'. There are, however, problems with such divisions because of the fixity of such categorisation and the limitations of identity politics, outlined by Brunsden (in Morley and Chen, 1996).

Hylton's description of the arts activities in the Chapeltown area of Leeds, however, highlights the need felt by African Caribbean arts practitioners to set up their own structures and to retain control of their

---

[27] This is a contentious point. Several of the early Phoenix dancers enjoyed the physicality of ballet at the Yorkshire Ballet Seminars. Moreover, ballet classes are an accepted part of contemporary dance training, and Phoenix have had ballet teachers taking class at different points in the Company's history.

work so that they had the means to explore their self-expression. His study locates a sample of African and African Caribbean arts in Leeds in the context of Black arts in the UK. In this sample, he discusses Phoenix Dance Company and RJC (Reggae, Jazz and Contemporary) Dance Theatre:

> Phoenix Dance Company is one of the most successful dance compa-
> nies in the country, with ten talented dancers, but lacks Black man-
> agement representation and uses European contemporary dance
> forms in preference to African-inspired dance forms such as reggae
> which was its early creative force. In comparison, RJC Dance Theatre
> [...] formed in 1992 by three former key members of Phoenix Dance
> Company [...] Leo Hamilton, Edward Lynch, and Donald Edwards, [is]
> committed to discovering and creating contemporary dance modes
> through the use of choreographic African music forms such as reg-
> gae and jazz. Equally important is the fact that at RJC Dance Theatre
> African–Caribbean artists remain in control of artistic direction of
> the company. (1996: 7)

The comparison between these two companies in this context is made because of matches in ethnicity and personnel and has also been used by dance critics (see Chapter 6). Such a comparison is problematic and reinforces racism. The two companies are quite different. Phoenix is no longer a small-scale contemporary dance company; although reggae was part of its early repertoire it was by no means the only aspect; and the Company were quite clear that, although their backgrounds influ-enced them, that was not their key identity. RJC, however, was founded as a company of Black British artists and had an agenda to explore the expression of that identity. In some ways the Phoenix members viewed that aim as going back to roots which, on reflection, they felt they had had when they began Phoenix but which was not apparent in the Company in the late 1980s and the 1990s.

Hylton says, 'Invariably the call for autonomy, whether formulated in terms of gender or in this case ethnicity and culture, can sometimes be misunderstood' (1996: 13). He argues that separate creative spaces enable African and African Caribbean artists to work out their own agendas and to be able to respond to issues affecting black communities. In this way, he states, an important link is established and maintained between the artists and the audience and community. The distinctions between art and community are blurred. So, for example:

> African and Caribbean dance is originally a social form. It needs, even more than other forms of dance, roots in a culture. Therefore it is essential that a proper structure of grassroots activity is maintained. Otherwise the 'flagship' becomes disconnected from the fleet and floats away. (D. Bryan, quoted in Hylton, 1996: 13)

Black arts were considered an affirmation of the cultural identity of people of African Caribbean origin, which had the potential to enrich and transform British cultural life.

Another view of Leeds and its culture is illustrated by Caryl Phillips (2002), a well-known novelist from Leeds, who discussed how the divisions in the city, through racism, are evident in football and the city's club, Leeds United. Phillips describes Leeds as a city marked by geographical boundaries that separate along the lines of class and cultural background. There was an established Jewish community as a result of migration from central Europe before the migrants arrived from the colonies of the Caribbean and the Indian subcontinent in the 1950s and 1960s. There have been tensions between the white working class and the new migrants and their more established families. For people of the African Diaspora, as evidenced by research by Caryl Phillips and Carl Hylton, Leeds offered both a potential for cultural expression and a place of racial tensions.

The South Bank Show of 13 April 2003 focused on Caryl Phillips, who offered further insights into what it was like to grow up in Leeds as a young black person. He said it felt like not having a home when he received questions such as, 'Why don't you go back to where you come from?'[28] He suggested that there needed to be a radical rethink of British history.

Identity

The identities that the founders of Phoenix discussed in interviews with me were of being Black British and working class, and of having the sense of a bond shared with each other as young men, which they termed a 'brotherhood'. Donald Edwards, in a discussion about how the group identified themselves, said:

> *If asked where we're from, I sometimes say the Caribbean, other times British, but I don't feel British even today. I've seen too many things my parents have gone through and I've gone through, even see it now. Things*

---

[28] To counter such racism, Leeds Racial Harassment Project was set up in 1995.

are not as bad as they used to be; but whereas people used to be more open about it, nowadays it's more hidden. We were born here and have a dual heritage culture but British society does not accept us as people. (1997)

David Hamilton said, '*Our parents are from the Caribbean but we are not just Caribbean; we are here and we're Black British – that's important*' (1997). Edward Lynch also said that 'Black British' was the term he used to identify himself. The comments from Edwards and Hamilton indicate the tensions of racism within Britain that they have experienced and the shifts in experience and identity between the first and second generations in this country. The difficulties with which the founders were confronted were typical of those facing young Black British men. 'The problem for black youth – young men and women – lies very much in their relations with the mainstream white community; policing, education, schooling and employment' (Sutcliffe and Wong, 1986: 21–2). Many writers, including Stuart Hall and Paul Gilroy, have also discussed these issues. In addition, Okwui Enwezor has identified similar difficulties for African American males. In a review of the exhibition *The Black Male: Representations of Masculinity in Contemporary American Art*, he said:

> The evacuation of young black males from the public sphere has proceeded on every front. As dropouts from the educational system, as victims of suicides, homicides and the penal system, as casualties of the incredible shrinking welfare state, as fatalities of the crack economy, and the AIDS emergency; and as targets of new and more virulent forms of racism, the social obsolescence of the black male youth has been quite systematic. (1995: 67)

Those artists in Britain and America from the African Diaspora who have achieved recognition of their work can counter such a bleak context and begin to shift the perceptions of and understanding of representations of people of African heritage. This is one element of the work of Phoenix Dance Company. From the quotations given above from interviews with the founders of Phoenix, it is clear that they identified themselves as people with a dual heritage, which they termed as Black British. So what does this term mean and what are the issues related to it?

Such identification could be viewed as part of identity politics – that is, as Kadiatu Kanneh articulates, 'claiming radical identity on the basis of belonging to a specific community [which] has often been condemned as an unsophisticated belief in the authentic self' (1998: 180). Kanneh, however, while stating that borders between cultures, races and sexes do not withstand analysis, suggests that:

> The political consequences in terms of racial identity and racism are profoundly different. Black politics – in terms of organising against racism, gaining positive, collective empowerment, recognising certain aspects of experience or identification – do need to employ certain essentialist categories in order to have any kind of strategy or existence [...]. Black is not always determined by negative racism, but can also be constructed through positive empowerment. It is also a category that is variously determined by historical circumstance, geographical positioning, gender, class or sexuality. (1998: 181)

Kanneh's argument gives legitimacy to the use of the term 'Black British' and offers a context for its use by the founders of Phoenix.

The value of a critique of essentialism is discussed by bell hooks, who argues that such a critique allows an acknowledgement that class mobility:

> has altered collective black experience so that racism does not necessarily have the same impact on our lives. Such a critique allows us to affirm multiple black identities, varied black experience. It also challenges colonial imperialist paradigms of black identity which represent blackness one-dimensionally in ways that reinforce and sustain white supremacy. This discourse created the idea of the 'primitive' and promoted the notion of an 'authentic' experience, seeing as 'natural' those expressions of black life which conformed to pre-existing pattern or stereotype. Abandoning essentialist notions would be a serious challenge to racism. (1990: 28)

Her argument articulates the trap that identifying something as Black British can create. Although the points she puts forward are significant, I think that, as Kanneh says, such identification can sometimes be strategically useful. It can also be viewed as part of a process in which, as hooks suggests, 'one constructs radical black subjectivity' (1991: 20).

The question of the terms that I use to discuss this Company was briefly mentioned in the Introduction. What is evident in Phoenix's work is their contribution to a dance lineage that has tended to marginalise the contributions of people of African descent. Through discussion of their work, it is possible to reconsider perceptions of and influences on British contemporary dance.

In postmodernity, reconsiderations of ways of thinking about diversity, identity and agency are manifested. The concept of agency is complex, but one aspect of it is the resistance to codes and structures of gender and cultural difference. Within dance performance there are opportunities to play with notions of identities through physicality and to present resistance to preconceived ideas of gender and cultural difference. The Company established themselves as a contemporary dance company. However, the response to their work throughout their history has frequently been about the composition of the company, as initially all the dancers were male and of African Caribbean descent. They have been viewed as a 'black dance' company and positioned as signifying cultural difference. At times, the Company has attempted to embrace this term in its publicity, but at others to question it as a descriptor. The dilemma both for the Company and for spectators is to find ways of valuing the particular, without physical signs of difference being read as otherness and as a site for discriminatory readings. Unfortunately, there are many examples, particularly in the media, of attempts to acknowledge and value difference but which reinscribe it. This is certainly the case with the use of the term 'black'.

The dancers in the 1980s were grappling with a sense of their own black subjectivity. One dimension of such subjectivity is class. Donald Edwards suggested that the Company were:

Always happy to say we were working class. It gave us an incentive, a drive; working class people tend to work [...] there is an honesty and integrity in what you do and what you are about. When we went into schools, the vast majority of kids were working class. (1997)

He also suggested that they were promoting black people positively and providing an alternative to some of the stereotypes of them, for example as drug users. He commented that it was not only the negative stereotypes that were confining but also positive stereotypes, such as black people as excellent athletes. Edwards, however, assumes a commonality in his reference to class, which is more problematic than his comments would suggest.

In his discussion of Gramsci's analysis of class, Stuart Hall suggests that, although classes may have aspects in common, there are also conflicting interests, so that class unity has to be created (in Morley and Chen, 1996). When discussing the 'class subject', Hall, from Gramsci's analysis, elucidates how the moments of unity are worked towards and

are in an ongoing process rather than constituting an arrival at a specific point of unity. Such understanding clarifies:

> how ethnic and racial difference can be constructed as a set of eco-
> nomic, political or ideological antagonisms, within a class which is
> subject to roughly similar forms of exploitation with respect to own-
> ership of and expropriation from the 'means of production'. (Hall, in
> Morley and Chen, 1996: 437)

A current difficulty, however, in any consideration of class is that 'class
as a theoretical concept and object of analysis has disappeared from the
agenda' (Pollock, 2002: 5). As Stuart Hall points out, this disappear-
ance and 'conceptual silence' is a serious matter (Hall, in Pollock, 2002:
5). Earlier work, however, such as Ron Ramdin's study *The Making of the
Black Working Class in Britain* (1987), offers a thorough background of
the factors contributing to class positions in Britain of those from the
African Diaspora. He suggested that young black people under-achieved
at school, lacked employment and became disillusioned because of the
lack of opportunities open to them. 'As part of the black working class,
they were alienated, the direct result of the precise and cumulative effect
of British policy-makers. Black youths understood through hard experience that colour was the major determination of their alienation'
(1987: 458).

   This was the context in which Donald Edwards, David Hamilton and
Villmore James created Phoenix Dance Company. Being young working-
class men, there were few expectations of their abilities and few choices
of employment. Their success, therefore, was particularly impressive.
However, while they identified themselves as working class, such identification was problematic. The inclusion into the British working classes
of the new migrants and their descendants was fraught with tension. As
Ramdin pointed out in a later study:

> The substitution of black for white labour would in time weaken
> working-class solidarity and increase the racist tendencies of white
> workers, who would increasingly become an integral part of the
> growing middle classes in postwar Britain. (1999: 163)

Ramdin's analysis comes from an outmoded Marxist view of class structures, but nevertheless he articulates a context which had repercussions
that the founders experienced on the streets, in their work in schools
and sometimes at after-show gatherings.

In one of the early works, *Forming of the Phoenix* (1982), choreographed by David Hamilton, each dancer introduced himself. They set up scenes of the everyday, of meeting each other, slapping hands, arrivals and departures. *Forming of the Phoenix*, as the title suggests, tells the story of how the Company began and, with evident parody, highlights individual characteristics and styles of each dancer. Hamilton is introduced as the person who initiated the idea of the group, with skills in modern dance and martial arts; Villmore James is introduced as the comedian of the group, and Merville Jones as the ballet dancer; Donald Edwards is seen skanking – performing his version of a Charlie Chaplin walk; and the toasting or rapping commentary, by Edward Lynch, gives the verbal context of the Company's beginning. Hamilton said of the piece that 'on the surface it's about how the group was formed. The interaction of the people makes up the group. Behind that is the core of the idea which is, like the mythical bird itself, taking from itself to develop, it dies and everything takes place within itself' (in Holgate, 1997).

In this work, the performers dance to *New Chapter of Dub* by what was then Britain's top reggae band, Aswad. After a career of fourteen years, eight albums and twenty-two singles, Aswad reached number one in the British popular music charts (Gad and Forde, 1988). As Gad and Forde point out, 'Reggae is very rhythmical, jazz was probably the nearest form to it – but even jazz musicians did not understand the rhythm of reggae [...] Kids of West Indian parentage [...] began to be inspired by reggae' (1988: 14). Reggae music was certainly a significant influence for the founding dancers, as it was in the 1970s and 1980s for many young black people in Britain (Ramdin, 1987: 461).

There is a continuous process of renewal and rejuvenation for the Company, incorporating a diverse range of music and movement vocabulary. Although rejuvenation is certainly a theme for the Company, the struggle has been for agency, rather than being driven by funders and critics. The legend of Phoenix was partly created by *The South Bank Show* TV documentary (Evans, 1984) and *Forming of the Phoenix* (1982). This legend is a story of five socially disadvantaged young men in eighties Britain, making good. Their style was described as 'high-spirited, athletic, fast, funny and fantastically dangerous' (King, 1985: PA).

One aspect that Phoenix represented on stage and in recordings was that of black masculinity. This was an element of their identity, which they were exploring (not necessarily consciously) and which was being read by audiences and critics. Henry Louis Gates, Jr, states in the preface to the book *Black Male: Representations of Masculinity in Contemporary Art*, which accompanied an exhibition at the Whitney Museum of

American Art, that the most long-lasting stereotypes of black men have been those connected with 'lust' and 'brutishness' and that there are many, 'images of blacks as beautiful bodies or as savage criminals' (in Golden, 1994: 13). This inheritance is part of the context in which Phoenix were working; although this exhibition was held in America, many observations in the book are relevant to considerations of black men in Britain. Thelma Golden, the exhibition's curator, said that she decided to begin the exhibition's coverage with 1968 because that was an important year in America, not least because it was a time of transition from the Civil Rights Movement to Black Power. The latter

> brought with it codifiable images of black masculinity. The black leather jackets, dark sunglasses, big afros, and bigger guns made visual the myths of uncontrollable aggression and rampant sexuality. Consequently, the collision of race with gender is one of the theoretical underpinnings of this project. (1994: 20)

What Golden identifies here in terms of representation, stereotypes and issues of gender and ethnicity are key elements when considering Phoenix Dance Company. In interviews, the Company members did not directly address issues of black masculinity, but their references to the racism that they and their families experienced, the limited opportunities available to them, and their support for one another (their 'brotherhood') were all aspects of their identity as young men of African Caribbean heritage (Edwards, 1997; Hamilton, 1997; James, 1997; Jones, 1997; Lynch, 1997). In addition, responses to their work from audiences and from some of the critics were in relation to the images of black masculinity that they were creating on stage.

In *The South Bank Show* (Evans, 1984) the dancers make clear that dancing is a central, integral part of their lives and that they do not separate their club experiences from their stage and touring experiences. They enjoy dancing and want to share that with a range of people through workshops and performances on tour. Their work is an example of Cooper Albright's consideration of the ways in which 'the performing body physicalizes the autobiographical voice to produce a representation of subjectivity which is at once whole and fragmented' (1998: 182). The subjectivities that Phoenix embodied were a powerful reminder that the descendants of the African Caribbean settlers had a good deal to contribute to British dance.

Windrush and after

The founders of Phoenix experienced at first hand their parents' hopes and dreams in England and their memories of and connections with the Caribbean. The arrival of the *Empire Windrush* on 22 June 1948 at Tilbury, carrying almost 500 Caribbean people, became 'a symbol of postwar immigration' (Phillips and Phillips, 1999: 2):

> a period when the establishment of a black British population, and ensuing conflicts such as the Notting Hill riots, became a central issue of political and social life in Britain. (Phillips, 2003: 10)

At that time, immigration from the Caribbean was only beginning, but this group played an important part 'in shaping a new British identity' (Phillips and Phillips 1999: 3).

The focus on the arrival of the *Windrush* as a means of prompting a review of the contributions of people from the Caribbean specifically, but also migrants to this country generally, over the past fifty years yielded performances, television programmes, books and many events. Much of this material had not previously been widely available and it offered people the opportunity to reconsider their perceptions.[29] One of the events held was the Windrush Gala Performance, which celebrated the contributions to Britain of people from the African Diaspora (Knowles, 1998).[30]

The Second World War was the catalyst for migration from the Caribbean to Britain. As the Caribbeans considered themselves to be British, they felt the need to defend the Empire when it was attacked (Phillips and Phillips, 1999).[31] At first, immigration began slowly. Workers were encouraged to move to Britain to meet the demand for labour after the war. In the mid-1950s the need for staff in the health service and transport was such that recruitment took place in the Caribbean. The people who migrated here were British citizens from Britain's colonies. Most people arriving in this country were in their twenties, with skills to offer. Their ideas about Britain were drawn from a colonial education system in which Britain was honoured as the

---

[29] Ron Ramdin in *Reimaging Britain* (1999) discusses the increasing contributions to British culture of artists from the descendants of Africans and Asians.

[30] Phoenix performed *Take My Hand* (1998), choreographed by Warren Adams and Andile Sotiya.

[31] At a talk given by Peter Fryer, author of *Staying Power: The History of Black People in Britain*, at the Nelson Mandela Centre, Chapeltown, Leeds (1995), I met some of these ex-servicemen and was intrigued by the generosity and pride with which they recounted parts of their stories. The experience renewed my anger at the distortion of Britain's colonial history with which I had been brought up through my education and the media.

'mother country'. As mentioned earlier, they viewed themselves as British and were shocked to be received with prejudice by many of the white population (Fryer, 1984; Edwards, 1997; Ramdin, 1999).

In the late 1950s and early 1960s, racist attacks were accompanied by journalism that sensationalised events. There were various calls for immigration controls, but against this prejudice were some people who acknowledged the underlying issue. Tom Driberg, then Labour Party chairman, said to the Trades Union Congress in 1958:

> People talk about a colour problem arising in Britain. How can there be a colour problem here? Even after all the immigration of the past few years, there are only 190,000 coloured people in our population of over 50 million – that is, only four out of every 1,000. The real problem is not black skins, but white prejudice. (in Fryer, 1984: 380)

The seeds of the institutional racism that MacPherson later identified in his report, *The Stephen Lawrence Inquiry* (1999), were sown in the legislation of the 1960s when black settlers were classed as 'immigrants'. The subtext of the first Commonwealth Immigrants Bill in 1962 was that black people were a problem and the solution was to restrict the number of them migrating to Britain. The legislation that followed throughout the 1960s and 1970s followed this pattern of discrimination against black people.

Two-fifths of the black people in Britain in the mid-1970s were born in Britain, but still many suffered from unemployment, inadequate housing, schooling with low expectations and police brutality. This context set the scene for resistance to a discriminatory system. In the USA, the Civil Rights Movement had made black people's concerns very visible. In the 1960s and in the 1970s, black militants in Britain also began to make issues known. In 1981 and 1985 there was unrest in British cities, and public and parliamentary debates about these events which focused on ethnicity and the role played by young black people in the disturbances. One of the triggers for the conflicts was the unemployment rate, which, for ethnic minorities, reached twenty per cent in 1983. This was at a time when unemployment for whites was ten per cent (Braham, Rattansi and Skellington, 1992: 58).

Events in 1981 have been portrayed in the media as a series of riots at a time when young black people protested and resisted the racism to which they had been subjected. The activities were particularly sustained in the cities where the old slave ports had been – London, Bristol and Liverpool – but some had also taken place in Leeds. Many of the reports and responses to these events took a tone of incomprehension.

They ignored the context of the prejudice, discrimination and racism that this second generation had witnessed their parents suffering and had experienced themselves through their treatment at school and, for many of them, from the police. The events were a response to racist attacks. Fryer (1984) suggests that arson attacks were common by 1981. One took place in Chapeltown in Leeds. A petrol bomb was thrown into the house of a disabled Sikh woman, who was burnt to death. Nationally such attacks were rarely reported and sometimes did not even appear in the local news. Police generally denied that racism was a factor in the attacks. The uprisings, however, had a psychological impact both locally and nationally through media reporting. Moreover, there were lasting physical scars in the form of burnt-out and boarded-up shops on the main Chapeltown road. These events may well have contributed to the alacrity with which Phoenix was supported by the Arts Council so that the funding body could confirm their lack of prejudice through their promotion of a group of young people who were located in an area that had been disrupted because of racial tensions.

The work of Phoenix read against this turbulent cultural context is a powerful statement of the founders' ability to fulfil their creative aims and to build a successful enterprise in a very short time. Various people helped them to realise their potential in the early days. On reflection, this may have been partly, although not necessarily consciously, because those people wanted to help young Black British men to succeed and wanted to prove that there were opportunities in Britain, so that circumstances could be better for those born in Britain than for their migrant families.

Philosophy, aims and influences

Donald Edwards, David Hamilton and Villmore James started the Company because they wanted to dance and make dances. '*We were young; we did what we had to do. It was more of a creative process. We wanted to express ourselves, so we did*' (Hamilton, 1997). Their philosophy of dance is revealed through David Hamilton's comments: '*Meaning was important. Phoenix did not just mean a dance company. Making mistakes, that was important, it wasn't just dance, it was part of life*' (1997).

Hamilton talks about wanting to express himself and of the steep learning curve with which the young performers were confronted. A significant means for Hamilton in his quest for expression was the use of reggae music as an accompaniment to some of the dance works, notably *Forming of the Phoenix* (Hamilton, 1997: 2). Paul Gilroy analyses how reggae music drew together people of the Caribbean who had very different cultural and political histories. He pointed out:

Once its own hybrid origins in rhythm and blues were effectively concealed, it ceased in Britain to signify exclusively ethnic, Jamaican style and derived a different kind of cultural legitimacy both from a new global status and from its expression of what might be termed a pan-Caribbean culture. (1993: 82)

The role of music for Hamilton was an important aspect of his creation of dance works that were expressive and had cultural significance. He said:

The Pentecostal Church is the underlying root because of the traditional African way of worshipping. It did not die but manifested itself in the spirit. [This explains why in] *carnival, jazz, hip-hop, the rhythm is driving and is an echo of something deep within ourselves.* (1997: 2)

Hamilton identifies the Pentecostal Church as being an important influence. Many of the new settlers to Britain were practising Christians, and when they experienced exclusion from the existing congregations in the 'motherland' they set up their own churches. As Sutcliffe and Wong suggest:

The black churches are, in terms of organization, resources and numbers, the single most important institution in the black community. For this reason alone their language would be of interest [...] the Churches are theatres of language performance. And their language, aesthetics and spirituality show a clear debt to Africa. (1986: 15)

Part of the language that Sutcliffe and Wong identify is that of call and response, in which the preacher uses his whole body to communicate and to create a rapport with the congregation, who are not passive but rather actively participate (1986). It is the influence of the Pentecostal Church, a sense of spirit and reggae music that were foundations for Hamilton's work. In her wide-ranging study, Dixon Gottschild discusses spirituality and dance, stating that 'people of African lineage continue dancing the spirit' (2003). Moreover, Jones identified the work of the early Company, saying, '*black dance is soulful; it comes from the heart, it has spirituality behind it*' (1997).

The influences identified above were significant not only in relation to the founders' contributions to contemporary dance but also to the organisation of the Company. The Company worked to some extent as a co-operative, using their own talents together with those of young choreographers who had trained at the London Contemporary Dance School. This was unusual, because a dance company is usually organised hierarchically with the artistic director as its leader.

During the 1970s in Britain, a number of co-operatives were formed as ways of organising housing, food, transport and artistic practices. Such co-operatives were an attempt to find politically effective ways of organisation that countered individualism and lessened involvement in the political and economic structures of capitalism. X6 was one of the best-known dance co-operatives in Britain. It formed in 1976, located in an old warehouse site in south-east London on the banks of the Thames. Ludus Dance Company, a dance-in-education company based in Lancaster, also operated a co-operative structure that has continued to be its means of organisation; as Linda Jasper and Jeanette Siddall comment, Ludus's survival 'is testament to the collective commitment and vision that has sustained the company in artistic climates unaccustomed to longevity' (1999: 83). Phoenix Dance Company also survived for over two decades; but although a co-operative structure was the initial organisation of the Company, it was short-lived. The interviews with the founding Company members show that in many ways David Hamilton was the accepted artistic leader, and this is further reinforced by the fact that his name is given as the contact on an early publicity leaflet. Jones credits Hamilton with the initial idea and suggests that Edwards, James and Lynch tended to follow his lead (1997).

So what were Phoenix's early aspirations and who were their role models?

> We looked at London Contemporary from a very young age. When we were at Harehills, LCDT was The Company. We were technically minded because we knew what an arabesque was or certain technical moves. We'd go to the theatre and see productions. Namron [Norman Murray] was there. We had videos of him dancing. He was one of the teachers who came to teach class to the Youth Group when I was there. It was like wow! Look at him, isn't he amazing? That was the role model that everyone carried. (Lynch, 1997)[32]

The young dancers sought to achieve Namron's physical skill and dance expertise. Namron, like the founders, was of African Caribbean heritage. He was both a founding member and one of the youngest members of the London Contemporary Dance Group (later to become LCDT),

---

[32] Namron was a colleague of mine for several years when we both taught at NSCD. I learnt a good deal from him about the early years of London Contemporary Dance Theatre and Phoenix Dance Company. I also watched him rehearse the latter Company.

which gave its first performance with members of the Graham Company at East Grinstead in 1967 (White, 1985). He was a member of LCDT for seventeen years and was a role model to many of his students. The dancer Kwesi Johnson, who was taught by Namron at NSCD, said that he was inspired by Namron's 'determination and passion, and his desire to pass his passion on to the people he was teaching' (2003: 15). Namron's wide experience and commitment to developing performers was invaluable to Phoenix in the early days (Adewole, 2003). He assisted the Company by teaching classes and sharing his knowledge about how a company was run (Namron, 1997). He also took the role of their rehearsal director for three months before travelling to Jamaica (where he was born) to be with his family after leaving LCDT. On return-ing to Leeds he became one of the founding teachers at the Northern School of Contemporary Dance in 1985. He taught some of the dancers who joined Phoenix, and continued to be an inspiration to many dance students and dancers[33].

Campbell reported that Namron had been one of the first teachers to offer technique classes at Harehills (1997). Villmore James remembered

> *Namron coming to Harehills when I was about eleven or twelve and recog-nising a performer, not just a black performer. For many years the Company wanted to be recognised as a company, not as an all-black company. We wanted to be known as performers.* (1997)

An important influence for Lynch was Michael Jackson, whose dance and music made him a megastar in 1982, with his album *Thriller* claimed as the best seller in the history of popular music (Mercer, 1994). Lynch said:

> *I toured with a band from the age of eleven. It was a family band called Big L and the Reinforcement. We played at the Albert Hall. I did that at the same time that I was dancing at school. The music side, the social side and the culture side all came from the music for me; it was passed down to me and I took that music into what we did.* (1997)

Members of the Company were also later influenced by their experi-ences on tour. For example, Donald Edwards said:

---

[33] Namron also choreographed *Steal Away*, an expressive solo accompanied by music by Michael Tippett and performed by Donald Edwards in the premiere production of *Language, Life, Respect* (1998) at the Northern School of Contemporary Dance in February, 1998. This was one of the productions from RJC, the company founded by Donald Edwards, David Hamilton and Edward Lynch in 1991 after Edwards left Phoenix.

When we toured to Australia, we saw Aborigines and we created a piece around that. In Spain we saw Flamenco dance and used that in a reggae section; we liked the way the dresses were flicked and the matador. (Edwards, 1997)

American culture was also influential on the young Phoenix, not only through the Graham technique (initially from America) and the dance videos of American companies, but also through American popular culture. Paul Gilroy further suggests that 'meanings around blackness drawn in particular from black America' were important for creating a new culture for those of African Caribbean descent (1993: 82).

An example of influences of American culture is that of *Nightlife at the Flamingo* (1983), set in an imaginary American nightclub in the 1940s. Choreographed by Edward Lynch, the work is energetic and exuberant, integrating popular culture with modern dance. It was noted as one of the most popular pieces in the early repertoire and contains a fast-moving duet reminiscent of the work of the Nicholas Brothers. The dance is a mixture of lindy hop, tap and modern dance creating rhythmic connections between each other. The atmosphere is highly charged with having a good time, which is emphasised by unison, and on occasions rhythmic clapping.

Although there is also an element of rivalry and competition in the work, this can be read as a positive view of black masculinity. The dancers are skilful, communicating strongly with each other and the audience and reaffirming a popular dance culture that has wide appreciation. The inspiration for the work, the Nicholas Brothers, were acknowledged as one of the greatest dance teams ever known; their career spanned over sixty years. They performed at the Cotton Club in Harlem, a showcase for top African American artists in the 1930s. However, although African Americans were employed both as artists and as support staff, they were not allowed in as audience. On a documentary programme about the dancers, it was suggested that when people talked about Fred Astaire and Gene Kelly they did not mention the Nicholas Brothers because of racism (1992).

In a film of the brothers, we can see them dancing in a nightclub, with tables at the back occupied by observers who are engaged in the action. The duet in *Nightlife at the Flamingo* is modelled on a duet previously performed by the brothers, with spins, jumps and razzmatazz showmanship. There is dancing on the table and a sense of unstoppability[34].

---

[34] As dance historian Ramsay Burt commented, it was possible that Lynch had viewed the film *Stormy Weather* (1943) in which Katherine Dunham appeared, and which was available as an off-air recording at the Yorkshire Dance Centre together with videos of Nederlands Dance Theatre. It was also possible that Nadine Senior had access to such recordings in 1980–81 (personal communication, 2 September 2004).

5. *Nightlife at the Flamingo*, 1983. Choreographer Edward Lynch; dancers
    David Hamilton, Villmore James; photographer Terry Cryer

Edward Lynch, who was also one of the dancers as well as the choreographer, said that he wanted the dancers to 'just dance to the music without counts [....]. That's how I saw it. American dancers went to the disco and just went to enjoy it' (in Evans, 1984). The film of the work shows dancers in a dance hall in the 1940s, mostly African Americans, juxtaposed with the Phoenix dancers in a local club.

Lynch talks about a happy atmosphere, and not training for dance but just doing it (in Evans, 1984). In this statement he links social and theatrical dance, which is an important element of some of the Phoenix repertoire. However, he ignores the dance rehearsals, which involve numerous repetitions of dance repertoire, and the training systems to which the dancers were committed – for example, David Hamilton studied karate. By talking in this way, Lynch reinforces the stereotype that black dancers dance naturally and rhythmically. He has internalised the stereotype and, therefore, does not acknowledge that learning dance is part of a process, from either a social setting or a more formal dance training, or perhaps both. As Brenda Dixon Gottschild points out, however, 'The "inborn-sense-of-rhythm" stereotype is so entrenched in the Euro-American imagination that it still holds sway in the most learned of settings'. It is, therefore not surprising that Lynch held the views quoted above. Dixon Gottschild furthers her argument by giving an example of a white choreographer, Doug Elkins, who was 'taught by black adolescents to dance and feel rhythmic subtleties the way they had been taught to do ... [this] helps explain the "nurture" part of the debate: Whites can be nurtured to dance black' (2003: 63). This perception has been developed only in recent years, but was less recognised in the 1980s when the dancers were forming their Company and their artistic concerns.

The Company were aware of the factors that had enabled them to dance, and were committed to making dance available to other young people. They wanted dance to be accessible, particularly to those who would not otherwise have the opportunity to be involved in the art form. Education, mainly through teaching dance classes and workshops, was an important and valued element of their work.

A video[35] of a schools performance by Phoenix organised by Suffolk Dance shows a large audience of children, from several different schools and wearing a variety of uniforms, looking intrigued and excited by the Company's presentation. The video is edited, and opens with the dancers performing contemporary warm-up stretches, followed by

---

[35] The video is undated, but Scilla Dyke, an animateur in Ipswich, Suffolk, from 1983, who later became the Director of Suffolk Dance Agency (Jasper and Siddall, 1999) and editor of *Animated*, suggested that the work was undertaken in the early days of her career in Suffolk.

travelling jumps across the diagonal of the space, progressing to impressive barrel jumps. At one point David Hamilton is shown speaking to the audience, but there is no sound of him speaking. Most of the music accompanying the dance is reggae. The company are dressed in practice clothes of loose trousers, t-shirts and sweatshirts. Another section of the video shows the company travelling again diagonally across the space but this time in a leader-and-follower formation. Hamilton leads the movement and the others do the same movement in their own style.

The movements were the content of typical contemporary dance classes influenced by Graham technique as it was taught in the UK during the 1970s and 1980s. The material is likely to have come from Hamilton's year of study at the London Contemporary Dance School and from the workshops and classes that the founders had attended. These sessions had been led by dancers from LCDT and Ross McKim from English Dance Theatre when they toured in the region and worked with local students. Another source of inspiration may well have been the classes and workshops available at the youth dance festival in Glamorgan. Their ideals of making dance accessible frequently overtook their skills. They were obviously inexperienced teachers when they began touring and teaching workshops, having only their own experience to draw upon. Scilla Dyke, who helped to establish Suffolk National Dance Agency, beginning as an animateur in 1983 (Jasper and Siddall: 1999), said that the group learnt as they went along, with more experienced teachers sometimes teaching alongside them and at other times making suggestions for teaching approaches. This enabled them to be more effective with groups, because they were not skilled at reading the physical needs of mixed-ability groups and adjusting their material accordingly[36].

They provided workshops in many schools and performed to diverse audiences in a variety of venues. An early publicity leaflet describes the company as 'an all male contemporary company with a special commitment to bring dance to young people, especially those living in under privileged and inner city areas'. This statement indicates not only the chosen dance style of the company but also a political ideal to share their understandings and benefits from dance with others like themselves.

There were also issues, about their teaching of workshops, which were not so positive. Jones thought that some of the teaching did not take the requirements of the group sufficiently into account and said that some of the teaching was inappropriate and '*brutal*' (1997). Edwards said that, because they were close in age to the students, they had an informal approach and at first did not really understand about professionalism and following clear guidelines (1997). Clearly, their

---

[36] Personal communication with Scilla Dyke, 14 February 2000.

inexperience was sometimes problematic. Lynch describes their early
work as '*follow the leader rather than education work. We were young; we did
not think of the dangers or safety*' (1997).

The Company experienced many pressures in the early years. They
toured intensively, suffering many injuries. Although they had the benefits of increasing recognition and tours abroad, they also felt they were
exploited by promoters and venues (Edwards, 1997). Pauline
Fitzmaurice, their administrator, felt that they had been given a good
deal for the Australian tour (1987), for example, as they were an
unknown group and the promoter was taking a risk in booking them.
She suggested that when the dancers considered the fee they were not
taking into account the overheads and expenses of a tour (1988). The
scale of their success had been a surprise to everyone. They had sold out
while Trisha Brown, a leading choreographer from New York, had
attracted only small audiences. The publicity material produced for the
company is a useful source of information. It was an important turning
point to be billed on the same posters and brochures as Brown.

The Company worked extremely hard in the early years, and some of
their diaries evidence the intense programme to which they adhered.
The diaries of one of the founders note that in 1985 from the first week
of January to the last week of March the Company worked six days a
week with only Sundays off. They then had one week off before a three-
week tour in Spain sponsored by the British Council, after which they
had a three-week holiday period, then worked on a new piece, *Blood
Wedding* (1986), with David Glass for another three weeks.

In the middle of June 1985 a week of Northern performances was
scheduled, but the performances further south in Swindon were can-
celled. The Company worked in London at the Battersea Arts Centre
from 12 July 1985, and rehearsals were booked in for July and the
beginning of August, after which the Company had their main break.
Preparation began again in September and continued throughout the
year; until December, each week was booked. The usual schedule was
one town or city per week. This is a fairly gruelling timetable, as touring
is very taxing and there were no understudies to cover if a dancer was
ill or injured (see Cope, 1976). A 1986 diary illustrated a similar pattern. Such a timetable did not allow very much time for the dancers to
reflect or to re-energise themselves. In fact, David Hamilton said that he
left '*in order to take stock*' (1997), which suggests a need for time away
from such an exhausting schedule. Hamilton's departure signalled the
end of the early phase of the Company's history. Chapter 2 investigates
the cultural and historical contexts in which the Company emerged and
developed.

Chapter 2:
Historical and Cultural Perspectives

Phoenix Dance Company emerged in 1981 at an historic moment for contemporary dance in Britain. In this chapter I investigate the complex set of circumstances that contributed to the particularity of its composition and development. I examine a disparate range of material within two specific frameworks, the first of which is historical. After the 1990s, consideration of dance history shifted to include insights from cultural studies and an understanding of the diverse contributions that formed contemporary dance. It is this shift with which I engage in this book and which I argue provides the potential for Phoenix Dance Company to be acknowledged as a significant part of British dance history. I consider aspects of the history of dance in Britain that set a context or had an impact on the specific development of the Company as it emerged in the 1980s and continued to develop in the 1990s.

The second framework considers some of the cultural circumstances in Britain in the 1970s when the founders of Phoenix were growing up, and in the 1980s when the Company was creating and touring work. An important factor here is the infrastructure and cultural policies of the Arts Council and of those dance organisations that had a significant impact on Phoenix's dance production. Although the Company did not engage overtly with the debates of the Black Arts Movement, nonetheless the movement was an important context in relation to their dance practices, their subjectivities and the reception of their work. A legacy of this movement is the use of the label 'black' as a descriptor of art forms: for example, black music, black theatre and black dance. This last term has engendered much debate, some of which will be considered in this chapter.

These two frameworks offer a way of analysing the multifaceted narratives of Phoenix Dance Company, although each section has more complexity than can be fully engaged with here. I am introducing these varied and multi-layered strands of recent British cultural history together with a close analysis of this particular Company, in which discursive, institutional, cultural and aesthetic issues are woven together in an impelling and evolving dance practice.

Ethnocentricism of dance historiography

There are many examples of texts that focus on the work of white British and American artists and ignore the important contributions of black British artists and African American artists.[1] Many dance books available in the 1970s and early 1980s either were from America or dealt primarily with ballet[2] and did not fully consider the cultural and political contexts of the dance work discussed.[3] Some of these books are well illustrated with photographs, which offer important information about specific styles and periods – for example, *The Magic of Dance* (Fonteyn, 1980). Others, which may or may not have illustrations, take a more scholarly approach and offer a detailed analysis, sometimes of a specific era, from archives, critics' writings and other scholars' works – for example, *Sharing the Dance: Contact Improvisation and American Culture* (Novack, 1990).

Joann Kealiinohomoku, in her well-known essay 'An anthropologist looks at ballet as a form of ethnic dance' (1970: 1983), criticises the evolutionist approach and Eurocentrism of certain dance texts. These include *World History of the Dance* (Sachs, 1937), *The Dance Through the Ages* (Sorell, 1967), *The Book of the Dance*[4] (Kirstein, 1942) and *The Book of the Dance* (DeMille, 1963). Her argument makes clear that dance from specific cultures needs to be assessed appropriately rather than by European values. Moreover, as Andrée Grau (1993) and Theresa Buckland (1999) both point out, several writers including Suzanne Youngerman (1974) and Drid Williams (1974 and 1991) have subsequently critiqued dance writing from an evolutionist perspective. Such texts tend to make generalised statements about 'primitive man' and the role of dance in early history. They then proceed to discuss indigenous dance briefly, often without specific information about the particular group of dances or their location, and cursorily discuss social dance as a context for the history of Western theatre dance. This format usually traces ballet from the Courts of Louis XIV in France to the present day and traces modern dance from the innovations of Isadora Duncan in

[1] Some texts have tried to popularise dance history and to provide a context for dance practice. One such example is Jan Murray's book *Dance Now* (1979), which contains a chapter entitled 'Ethnic Dance' in which Murray mixes the work of 'Britain's black group, the MAAS Movers' (130) with information about dance from several different cultures.
[2] Some texts, however, dealt with specific British dance companies – for example, *Twentieth-Century Dance in Britain: A history of the major dance companies in Britain*, edited by Joan White (1985).
[3] In contrast to the generalisations about African dance in *The Magic of Dance*, Georgina Gore (1995) has researched and written specifically about the role of dancing in Olokun worship in Southern Nigeria. Her work is an example of the specificity of research and writing required when discussing a culture to which one does not belong. Other examples include the work of Peggy Harper, 'Dance in a Changing Society' *African Arts/Arts d'Afrique* v.1(1) pp. 10–13, 76–77, 78–80 (1967) and Judith Lynne Hanna, *To Dance is Human* (1979).
[4] This book was criticised for its Eurocentric approach by Cynthia Novack in *Women and Performance* (1992). She also described how she explored her ambivalence towards the text and photographs in her choreography *Artifacts* ((The Empire After Colonialism)).

America and Europe. Examples of such texts are *History of the Dance in Art and Education* (Kraus, 1969), *The History of Dance* (Clarke and Crisp, 1981) and *Dancing Through History* (Cass, 1993).

There has been a gradual shift from such an approach, however, and some more recent writing applies the methods of cultural studies to dance. Norman Bryson suggests that a 'paradigm shift in dance history' (in Desmond, 1997: 75) would provide the potential for some valuable insights. Such a shift also provides a means of analysing the historical accounts of Phoenix Dance Company and a context within which to read such a narrative. Certain texts demonstrate the potential of this paradigm shift. For example, Jane Desmond's (1991) study of Ruth St Denis offers a close reading of St Denis's choreography *Radha* (1906), in relation to the cultural contexts of the time, and draws on theoretical approaches from Said and Foucault. This current study of Phoenix is also concerned with discussion and analysis that draws on more complex cultural contexts than have frequently been applied to dance history topics.

An example of this more recent approach is Lynne Emery's *Black Dance in the United States*. As Katherine Dunham acknowledges in the foreword, a complete study of dance forms of people of African descent had not been carried out in America until this publication in 1972. Dunham was an African American pioneer of concert dance, establishing her own dance technique and numerous choreographies.[5] She praises Emery's use of a range of documentation and her contextualisation of the concert dance, which is the book's primary focus. Emery was inspired to write this key text, aimed at the general reader as well as the specialist, after reading Malcolm X's autobiography and noticing that the dance literature with which her black students could identify was scarce (such a scarcity was also, as I noted in the Introduction, a motivating force for the current book).

Emery's book was published during a period of dramatic political and cultural changes. The Civil Rights Movement with its goals of inclusion and recognition for African Americans challenged the lack of value attached to America's black citizens. As Powell has said, the changes made

> black peoples and their cultures pivotal. The relative affluence of the U.S.A. before the oil crisis, the ever-expanding and influential mass

---

[5] Dunham's work is documented both in her own writings – for example, *A Touch of Innocence* (1959) and *Island Possessed* (1969: 1994) – and in those of more recent dance history scholars, such as 'The body possessed: Katherine Dunham dance technique in *Mambo*' (Fischer-Hornung, 2001), 'Katherine Dunham's *Rite de Passage*: Censorship and sexuality' (Burt, 2001) and 'Katherine Dunham's floating island of negritude' (Burt, 2004).

media, the burgeoning youth culture, political unrest, and a social atmosphere of moral leniency, formed a backdrop for the emergence and rise to prominence of a partially autonomous black culture [...] blackness became a cultural lightning rod that attracted controversy, commentary and acclaim. (1997: 127)

It was in this context that Emery's book was both written and read. At that time in America there was a curiosity and drive to investigate, document and distribute the wide range of culture from the African Diaspora, which had been undervalued and generally unacknowledged.

In 1981, the year Phoenix formed, Walter Sorell wrote *Dance in its Time*. His aim was to write a history of dance within the context of the artistic developments and significant events of specific eras. For example, he discussed the work of dancers who were dancing in a 'free and antiballetic style' (329), such as Ruth St Denis and Maud Allen, in the contexts of influences upon their work and developments in Europe at the beginning of the twentieth century. This was in contrast to the chronological accounts of dance history and books highlighting the achievements of specific dancers, choreographers and companies. In this book of 469 pages, he has only one page on African Americans and five references to the inspiration drawn from Africa within modernism. In this one page he traces the history of performers of African descent, from slavery through jazz, to the entertainment of Josephine Baker and Bill Robinson, and to the significant contributions to modern dance of Katherine Dunham, Pearl Primus and Donald McKayle. He also acknowledges the achievements of Arthur Mitchell. Although the intention of his book is more critical and politically aware than many dance history texts, it still marginalises the achievements of people of African descent and reinforces a Eurocentric approach.

The late 1980s saw more consideration of the contributions that African American performers had made to the development of performance culture in general and concert dance in particular. Richard Long in *The Black Tradition in American Dance* (1989) contextualises the account of performers and performance in musicals, films and dance theatre by acknowledging the cultural, economic and political isolation with which people of the African Diaspora had to contend. He also raises the contentious issue, which has continued to be debated, of the term 'black dance'. He chooses to use it to locate work that draws on elements that can be traced to African descent but not merely because of the presence of an African American performer in a dance work.

Almost at the same time as Long in 1990, Edward Thorpe published *Black Dance*. Thorpe's approach is less specific than Long's, as he is concerned with writing an historical outline tracing some of the same areas as Emery does. The book ends with the chapter *Black Dance in Britain* in which Thorpe cites Phoenix as being perceived as a black dance company because the dancers are black or 'mixed race', despite the Company's own perceptions. Thorpe does not examine the term 'black dance' but suggests that 'Merely by being Black dancers and being where they are, the company represents a symbol of hope for the future of dance in Britain' (1989: 185). Thorpe does not give any detail about what he means by this statement, but I would suggest he is implying that members of the Company, as they have stated, are role models because they are successful artists and because they developed their work in Leeds rather than in London (Edwards, 1997; Jones, 1997). Thorpe's response is similar to that of several dance critics and of the Company's audiences. The issues such a response evokes will be discussed in Chapter 6. Clearly, there have been some shifts in perception between the 1980s and the 1990s in terms of both the changes in the Company and the evolving cultural contexts.

In contrast to some of the books discussed above, Brenda Dixon Gottschild in *Digging the Africanist Presence in American Performance* (1996) investigates popular performance, everyday life and theatre dance, aiming to 'excavate the subtextual Africanist components, correspondences, influences [...] that are essentials in defining and shaping Euro-American endeavour in the United States' (1996: xiii). This book is groundbreaking in its detailed consideration of the previously unacknowledged influences, achievements and contributions of African Americans and the importance of African American culture. Her two later books, *Waltzing in the Dark* (2000) and *The Black Dancing Body* (2003), also raise issues of African American contributions to dance culture. Other writers who have contributed to a reconsideration of the role of black artists in dance cultural history, as Helen Thomas (2003) points out, include Burt (1998), DeFrantz (2002) and Perpener (2001).

In a discussion about dance history and cultural studies, Amy Koritz (1996) argues that it is important both to retain dance history as an autonomous subject and to pursue the intellectual benefits of including dance scholarship within the interdisciplinarity afforded by cultural studies. She questions the reasons for the neglect of dance within this arena at a time when the body has been the focus of a range of scholarly work. Koritz suggests that this may be because 'dance uses bodies to transmit and represent complex codes in a manner that explicitly distinguishes them from the lived experience of the nondancing body' (91). She also suggests that the lack of investigation into dance points to an entrenched binary opposition between body and mind, where the body stands for the material 'real world' and the mind stands for concepts and abstraction. For dancers of the African Diaspora, this was not the only binary opposition with which they had to contend; they also had their work framed and discussed within the context of 'black' and 'white'. This has certainly been a complex issue for Phoenix, and I would argue that it is evident from the brief overview of the historical texts above that this binary opposition in many of the books was an aspect that resulted in the work of those of the African Diaspora being ignored or marginalised. Only recently has a theoretical arena emerged in which it is possible to analyse work of such companies as Phoenix and fully to acknowledge the contributions they have made. However, in the 1980s when Phoenix were becoming established, the contrast between 'black' and 'white' was clear in the investigations into the conditions for 'black dancers'.

Readings of dance history

In a television programme, *Eye to Eye: Breaking the Mould* (1989), Margot Fonteyn dances whilst a male narrator repeatedly identifies her as the 'greatest dancer of our time' (Leoandro, 1989). The image of the dancing Fonteyn cracks open as though it were made of plaster and a black dancer emerges, proceeding to dance through architectural classical columns. This cameo begins the documentary of Carol Straker's Dance Company and the situation of black dancers in England in the 1980s. Straker began her company, which had its first public performance in September 1988 at the Hackney Empire, London, in order to encourage dancers from the African Diaspora to stay in Britain. Several of these dancers went to America to study or dance with the Alvin Ailey American Dance Theatre or Dance Theatre of Harlem, where there were more opportunities. Richard Webb, a dancer from Leeds, noted that it was encouraging to be in a class with more black people. The programme also offered anecdotes about the prejudice that the dancers had experienced in Britain. Despite such difficulties, there were increasing opportunities for dancers as contemporary dance evolved in this country.

The historical summary that follows highlights those key developments in the art form that were significant in relation to the formation of Phoenix at a time of dance expansion in Britain. Key to the growth of dance then was the establishment of the London Contemporary Dance Theatre (LCDT) and the London Contemporary Dance School (LCDS). To some extent, as mentioned in Chapter 1, these two were the models for the work that later developed in Leeds. As Merville Jones said, '*In those days, if you wanted to be a dancer you went to London Contemporary'* (1997). This comment gives some indication of the founders' focus on both the School and the Company as a standard to which they aspired.

Phoenix looked to LCDT as a model for their work, rather than rebelling against it as was the case for many of those dancers who had studied at LCDS, which had become an institution of contemporary dance. Whereas the founders did not have a conventional three-year dance training to rebel against, these artists wanted to reconsider their training and to discover their own forms and approaches. These approaches evolved in a new context, because British theatre dance history was dominated by ballet until the 1970s. Modern dance as a theatrical practice did not become established in Britain in the first half of the twentieth century as it did in France, Germany and America.

With the establishment of contemporary dance in Britain during the 1970s, a struggle began to gain serious consideration from the critics for the art form. This situation was quite different from that in America, where, for example, the dance critic John Martin had championed the modern dance pioneer Martha Graham and indeed educated audiences since the 1930s. The modern dance tradition in America was identified by Susan Foster (2000) as an 'initiative undertaken by white, bourgeois women at the turn of the century, [which] constructed a new expressive practice focused at the site of the individual dancing body' (28). These artists sought to overhaul body and soul in order to liberate individual creative impulses from the stranglehold of societal norms and aesthetic values (Foster, 2000). Although the LCDS and LCDT were important for the development of Phoenix, the work was based on Graham technique and imbued with Graham's philosophy, which was specific to her identity as a 'white, bourgeois woman' (Foster, 2000: 208). In addition, the technique was acknowledged to be more suited to a female body than to a male, although undoubtedly many male dancers used it effectively. So for the founders, although the Graham technique was a valuable resource, it is arguable that for them there were limitations in its application and there were other elements to their movement style in the early choreographies.

Whereas in America modern dance had evolved in the 1960s and was sufficiently established for artists to break away from established conventions, in Britain modern dance had barely found its place. Nevertheless, a number of the young dancers from Leeds in the late 1970s and early 1980s aspired to the training that the LCDS offered. The practicalities they had to deal with resulted in difficulties that they found hard to overcome. The aspiring dancers were young and unfamiliar with London. It was taxing for them to manage their lives in the city, away from home, at the same time as undertaking intensive contemporary dance training. Of the founders of Phoenix, only David Hamilton went to the School (for a year) and of the four women who joined the Company in 1989 three of them, Seline Derrick, Chantal Donaldson and Dawn Holgate, trained there. The fourth dancer, Pamela Johnson, trained at the Northern School of Contemporary Dance in Leeds.

From the early stages, LCDT offered a significant context for aspiring dancers. For those dancers seeking role models of dancers of African descent, William Louther was an important artist who was acknowledged for his flawless technique and superb artistry. He danced with the companies of Martha Graham, Alvin Ailey and Donald McKayle and joined LCDT in 1969 (Emery, 1988). He danced Alvin Ailey's *Hermit Songs* in 1969 for the company and in 1970 choreographed and danced *Vescalii Icones*: 'This was rightly hailed as a remarkable realization of the religious themes of Maxwell Davies's score, in which Louther gave a performance of genius' (Clarke and Crisp, 1989: 46).

LCDT not only provided inspiring role models but also acquired important works, which contributed to a diverse repertoire. For example, the company acquired Talley Beatty's *Road of the Phoebe Snow* (1959). Beatty was a dancer with the Katherine Dunham Company who later formed his own company. This work had previously been danced in London by the Alvin Ailey American Dance Theatre and was described by the critic Clive Barnes in 1965 as 'one of the great achievements of jazz dance' (in Emery, 1988: 287). In a review in 1969 he described the dance as 'a fine tense work, strung out tautly on the music by Ellington and Billy Strayhorn, and somberly evocative of life, youth and death in the ghetto' (in Emery, 1988: 287). The fact that the company had this work in their repertoire indicates their success and the range of the dance work that they performed.

Several people who choreographed for LCDT later did so for Phoenix. For example, Darshan Singh Bhuller, a contemporary of the founders and who trained at LCDS, made a work entitled *Beyond the Law* for LCDT (1981), which 'was an angry comment upon the race legislation in South Africa' (Clarke and Crisp, 1989:146). His first work for Phoenix was *Speak Like a Child* (1983). Choreographer Tom Jobe contributed *Run Like Thunder* (1983) and *Rite Electrik* (1984) to the LCDT repertoire. The former was 'an obvious crowd pleaser with its bright disco-frantic dances catching the energies of the score by Barrington Pheloung, LCDT's musical director' (Clarke and Crisp, 1989: 164). Jobe later contributed to the Phoenix repertoire with *Tainted Love* (1990), which was reworked as an excerpt for *19: Rewind and Come Again* (2000) and *Even Cowgirls Get the Blues* (1991). In 1970 John Percival, dance critic of *The*

Times, noted that LCDS and LCDT were unique in the encouragement of creativity and choreography, both by providing study as part of the training and by providing dancers with a forum for their own works (Clarke and Crisp, 1989). By 1971, with 53 full-time students and 150 regular part-time students, the School offered an alternative to the classical ballet training that had been dominant in Britain until then.

Despite its successes, LCDT struggled with financial constraints, which affected development in terms of obtaining suitable buildings and the repertoire. Jan Murray, dance critic for *Time Out*, said:

> All of the 18 new works mounted by LCDT this past year [1975] have been staged on a total budget of £15,000. Compare this sum with the £70,000 reportedly lashed out by the Royal Ballet to refurbish a perfectly acceptable production of *Romeo and Juliet*, and with the £150,000 spent on Festival Ballet's new *Sleeping Beauty*. (In Clarke and Crisp, 1989: 103)

Murray's statement shows the continuing dominance of ballet in Britain, even though contemporary dance was building new audiences. Despite financial limitations, the company introduced innovations. Between January and March 1976, the company undertook their first residency, sponsored by the Arts Associations of Yorkshire, Lincolnshire and Humberside. Nine dancers, a choreographer, a musician and two technicians worked together in venues that included Bradford and Bingley College, Hull University, York University, Lady Mabel College near Sheffield (where Nadine Senior studied) and Bretton Hall College near Wakefield. In 1977 there was another residency in Yorkshire. Earlier, Robert Cohan gave lecture demonstrations to contribute to the general public's education in contemporary dance and to develop an audience.

These residencies offered members an opportunity to create audiences and find out more about them. It also meant that a contemporary dance audience was being created in Yorkshire five years before Phoenix was founded. In order to encourage young men to attend, the company offered free classes if women brought their boyfriends. This was an effective strategy, as some men then applied to the school. The fact that LCDT needed to employ such a tactic indicates the predominance of females in contemporary dance as well as in ballet and the uniqueness of an all-male company such as Phoenix.

In 1980, a year before Phoenix was founded, LCDT was faced with a financial crisis that led to a fund-raising letter signed by key names in the ballet establishment, including Ninette De Valois, Marie Rambert, Margot Fonteyn and Frederick Ashton:

> There is no comparable contemporary dance organization in the world; its twin enterprises, London Contemporary Dance Theatre and London School of Contemporary Dance, have a unique international reputation. The work of the Trust is vital to the artistic life of Britain and brings immense credit to us abroad. It needs and deserves your support. (Clarke and Crisp, 1989: 140)

The support of these key figures from the ballet world is a measure of the standing and respect that LCDT held only thirteen years after Robin Howard had invited Robert Cohan to begin a contemporary dance company and school. The prominence of LCDS and LCDT meant that they were an obvious focus for aspiring dancers, as they were for the founders of Phoenix.

By 1986, however, despite the company's success, there were difficulties with funding that mirror some of those that Phoenix later experienced. Clarke and Crisp reported that it was 'disheartening to see how so distinguished a history of achievement should still be darkened by the ever-present problems of funding' (1989: 180). Such difficulties were particularly shocking because the company had a worldwide reputation:

> It is no exaggeration to say that the Contemporary Dance Trust, as umbrella for a school, a teaching system, a performing troupe, a manner of creativity, had altered the way a nation thought about dance – and had extended its influence into Europe. (Clarke and Crisp, 1989: 187)

Because of the work of the school and company, contemporary dance had become accepted by the general public and was also an important experience for young people in schools and colleges; for some it offered 'a means of transcending the bitter fact of their social and economic situation' (Clarke and Crisp, 1989: 187). This potential that dance offered was certainly an important aspect for Phoenix and one that they took account of in their performances and in their education work.

LCDT was not the first modern dance company in Britain; in 1966 Ballet Rambert, under the artistic direction of Norman Morrice, had persuaded Marie Rambert to change the repertoire from classical to modern. Throughout their histories the two companies have had a close relationship, with personnel moving from one company to the other. At times, however, there was competition between the two. The Rambert Company also had a school, and in the later development of Phoenix some of the dancers had been trained there. Ross McKim, a dancer with LCDT and later director of English Dance Theatre, became a director of the Rambert School. Coincidently, he was also one of the first outside choreographers for Phoenix, contributing *Reach* in 1982 soon after the Company formed, and was one of the LCDT members with whom they undertook dance classes and workshops.

As contemporary dance was developing, so too was experimental work. On 14 August 1972 Richard Alston's new company, Strider, performed at the Place, only five years after LCDT began. This was also the year of the first professional choreography, *Relay*, by Siobhan Davies, one of the first students at LCDS. In the 1970s some artists had survived by finding empty buildings and living in them temporarily while claiming unemployment benefit. For many this was the only way they could continue their work, because paying for living expenses and developing choreographic work, which initially did not attract funding or payment, meant that low living costs and social security payments were essential for survival. This was certainly the case for Phoenix in the early years of their existence. As Grau and Jordan point out, '[...] until the 1980s, the welfare state unofficially supported experimental dance, in the sense that dancers on unemployment benefit were able to support themselves and continue their creative work' (2000: 8).

Contemporary dance work that was considered experimental emerged not only from some of the groups based in London but also from the innovations at Dartington College of Arts. There was a link between Dartington, which provided a base for Jooss[6] and Laban, and the establishment of what was termed 'modern educational dance'. In 1963 an American modern dance course for teachers was established at Dartington and taught by Flora Cushman, who choreographed for and taught at LCDT when it became established. In 1973 major changes were made to the course by Mary Fulkerson, an American dancer and choreographer who was the main movement tutor in the Theatre Department. She introduced release techniques, brought over colleagues to teach and to choreograph, and instituted the International Dance Festival. One of the key people who taught both at the Festival and sometimes on the main course was Steve Paxton, who was the main instigator of contact improvisation.

---

[6] Kurt Jooss's Company was based at Dartington from 1933. Together with Sigurd Leeder, he developed the Jooss–Leeder technique, which fused classical and modern dance (Winearls, 1958).

Phoenix also performed at the Festival in 1983. The dance historian Ramsay Burt, who lived in Leeds at the time, observed:

Dancing has become a recognised way up for black kids in Chapeltown, some of whom have got into professional companies. LCDT and Rambert regularly do workshops in a Chapeltown school when on tour. Phoenix appears to model their movement style on LCDT. (1983: 21)

Burt also discussed their choreography. For the performance at Dartington, the Company danced Ross McKim's *Reach* (1982), David Hamilton's *Forming of the Phoenix* (1982) and Donald Edward's *Ritual for Death* (1982). Of this last work Burt said, 'It was a very violent and competitive piece [...]. One moment had a dancer hurling himself through the air into the midriff of another standing dancer [...] It was the sort of dancing I would expect to be revolted by' (1983: 21). The Company's commitment, however, meant that Burt appreciated the impact of their choreography and performance. The Company's style, modelled to some extent on LCDT, as Burt noted, contrasted with that of many of the other performers at Dartington who were influenced by more experimental approaches and release techniques.

The development of experimental work resulted in various festivals in the 1970s and 1980s. One that has become established is Dance Umbrella. Phoenix performed at this festival in 1983, 1985, 1988 and 1995. The 1985 performance was their official festival debut, but in 1983 the Company performed in the Final Fling Programme finale (Rowell, 2000). Initially, the aim of the festival was to provide a show-case for emerging British dance. The aims then shifted to developing audiences and to providing a forum for work from artists from the USA and Europe, but on many occasions it was funding that dictated what was possible.

There is a sense of following parallel stories when reading about LCDT and Dance Umbrella, both of which had a significant impact on the development of contemporary dance in Britain. In addition, the 1970s was a time of experimentation and expansion, whereas by the early 1980s a lot of energy had dissipated and it was more a time of establishment. Whilst the 1960s and 1970s had been about the influence of the Americans, the 1980s were about the achievements and contributions of European dance artists, and in the 1990s the focus was more towards British dancers locating themselves within a European dance culture. This shift can be seen in the changing pattern of artists attending the Dance Umbrella Festival (Rowell, 2000) and in texts such as *Europe Dancing* (2000).

The historical frameworks above provide a context within which a company of young male Black British dancers developed. There were very few opportunities for these artists to dance in ballet companies in Britain, but with the emergence of contemporary dance in the 1970s more prospects emerged. These shifts in dance culture were made within the wider context of changes in Britain.

Social and cultural contexts in Britain

Writing in 1987, Lauretta Ngcobo stated, 'A few years ago there was nothing called Black British Art and Culture. Today there is' (viii). Indeed, in 1976 Naseem Khan had written a report for the Arts Council entitled *The Arts Britain Ignores*. Several organisations contributing to the emergence of less marginalised arts were created in response to ongoing racism in the 1970s. For example, the Tara Arts drama group evolved as a direct reaction to a situation in Southall in 1976 when an Asian youth was stabbed. Some artists also incorporated race politics into their work: for example, the poetry of Linton Kwesi Johnson and the visual art of Rasheed Araeen and Keith Piper (Baldry, 1981).

A new genre of music emerged with reggae and the development of British reggae and Two Tone at the end of the 1970s. These styles were identified with the anti-racist struggle both because of their lyrics, which related to black people's lives in Britain, and because they were played at the concerts organised by Rock Against Racism and the Anti-Nazi League. As we have seen in Chapter 1, the founders, particularly Hamilton, were inspired by reggae for some of their dance works. The Rock against Racism Movement used the art school network to launch itself. During 1977–78, Rock against Racism organised about 200 events, including a major rock concert for 100,000 people at Victoria Park in the East End of London, and at this point, as Robert Hewison argues, 'Racism [was] used as a symbol of the capitalist crisis' (Hewison, 1995: 201).

For marginalised groups at this time, access to the mainstream arts institutions was a key issue (Baldry, 1981). Similarities emerged in the late 1960s between the cultural practices of the black British community, the gay movement, feminism and the community arts movement. Such initiatives were usually based in specific communities, frequently as part of community work projects that aimed to widen the base of participation in the arts by involving people in a range of artistic expressions, often collectively. Such work challenged the 'high' and 'low' art categories, the accepted canons and the divisions between professional and amateur, and tended to be organised co-operatively rather than hierarchically (Moore-Gilbert, 1994).

One of the contexts relevant to the development of Phoenix is the community arts movement, which developed in the 1960s and 1970s to make art more accessible to the majority. The aim was to eradicate elitism in the arts, though the movement appealed to, and was embraced by, those who attended the dominant art forms. 'The public funding agencies could defuse criticism by funding the community arts as an *additional* (and rather small) category. This kept the dominant cultural aesthetic entirely in place' (Lewis, 1990: 113). In addition, Lewis put forward the contentious viewpoint that 'Most working-class people were as alienated by the community arts as they were by the traditional' (Lewis, 1990: 114). There were tensions between community arts adherents and those who aligned themselves with other groups, including those who identified as Black British. The community arts movement was broadly committed to challenging capitalism and changing conditions for people through access to the arts; other groups were concerned to make strategic shifts in society in relation to issues of race, national identity, sexuality and gender. For example, in 1978 the magazine *Black Phoenix* was founded. The first issue

> directly linked the struggle for acceptance of black art to the larger fight for acceptance of black people: *Britain is our Home and we will not accept our Secondary and Inferior Roles in this Society.* Its claim about the way art was organized was accurate and direct: 'the English chauvinistic art promotion pattern ignores the art activity of black people in the country, or relegates it to ethnic pigeon-holes'. (In Sillars, 1994)

However, funding new initiatives raised complex issues, particularly for the Arts Council. One of the criticisms of the Arts Council was of the tendency for funding to be largely for companies and events based in London. Together with local authority funding, the establishment of nine Regional Arts Associations between 1966 and 1973 sought to address this imbalance. By the end of the 1970s these Associations were significant to the development of the arts in England. In 1973 a community arts working party was set up to consider:

> The extent to which the Arts Council should be directly involved in the subsidising of arts work; also to consider the relationship between experimental work and community arts projects, whether a

distinction needs to be drawn between these two fields of activity. (Arts Council 1973, in Laing, 1994: 29)

Britain in the 1980s

Community arts were the main area of discussion about 'aesthetic boundaries' in the Arts Council (Laing, 1994: 45). A focus of the community arts was on developing participation, rather than passive experience of the arts, and this approach matched the Council's aim of making education a central focus (Braden, 1978). The relationship of Phoenix to the local community of Leeds and specifically the African Caribbean community has been important to the Company, with varied success at different periods of their development. Seline Derrick (née Thomas), a dancer with the Company, lamented the loss of connections with:

> *our black community [...]. Leeds is our community. I went past a primary school that I used to go to, and I looked up and saw that in the windows they had a RJC poster and they had other posters of other companies that had been to the school; and it's predominantly black or Asian, and I thought, why isn't there a Phoenix poster up there? Have we come so far that we can't even see where we've come from and they can't reach out to us and say, oh we remember that?* Dawn Holgate [Education Director with the Company] *said that she had a five-year plan to introduce Phoenix back into the black community.* (1998)

This statement raises issues about gains and losses as the Company increased in size and status. While it was small-scale, the dancers were more located in the community, even though they did a good deal of touring. Once Neville Campbell had left, the Company members also struggled with the loss of a background shared with the artistic director, because neither of the two following directors, Margaret Morris and Thea Barnes, had a Leeds background. Indeed, a significant part of both their careers had been in America, whereas the founders' context was the local community and the increasing focus on black artists.

One organisation engaging with the support of black artists was the Black Dance Development Trust. Although the organisation made a 'substantial contribution to dance' (Bryan, 1993: 4), its focus on 'Afrikan People's dance' resulted in contemporary dancers feeling excluded, and engendered ongoing debates about definitions of 'black dance'. Some of the debate about the arts in relation to the community and wider contexts were documented in the magazine *Artrage*. The publication focused on the work of black artists and the issues related to their work in Britain, and the Greater London Council (GLC) sponsored a number of structures supportive of black artists. At a conference sponsored by the GLC entitled 'Black Artists, White Institutions', held at the Riverside Studios in London on 4 November 1985, Colin Prescod[7] gave a keynote address. He reported that 'Black youth' had been protesting about the inadequate schooling they were receiving, the lack of job opportunities and the harassment from police. He put these protests in context:

> From the colonies in Asia and the Caribbean, out of populations that were even then, in the 1950s and 1960s, struggling for 'independence', came hundreds of thousands of ambitious Black workers. Ambitious not for themselves directly, more so for their children. By the 1970s the children had begun to become young adults, and it was this 'Black youth' which first led the call 'out of the ghettos'. (1986: 32)

The founders of Phoenix were examples of the 'Black youth' whom Prescod describes. The 1985 conference aimed to move 'towards achieving a significant Black intervention into mainstream arts' (Solanke, Hilaire, Woodley, 1986: 2). A difficulty that the conference faced, however, was the limited representation from institutions, and many of those who did attend were not in positions of power within the institutions. Solanke, Hilaire and Woodley reported that the main response to the black artists was apologetic and sometimes patronising. There were, however, recommendations from the conference concerning programming, education and marketing, which focused on better representation and opportunities for black people within the institutions. As Bart Moore-Gilbert states, the necessity for such recommendations was evident from

> the increasing frustration and disaffection of the black British population (especially its youth) at the often blatant hostility shown towards them through the decade [which] were to come to issue in the rash of inner-city riots of the early 1980s. (1994: 6)

It is particularly inspiring that this was the time when the three founders formed Phoenix, against this backdrop of negative media

---

[7] Prescod is the film director of *Blacks Britannica* (1978) and *Struggles for the Black Community* (1983).

images of urban disturbances and limited opportunities. For David Hamilton the process was part of an evolvement of being young and having the drive to put their ideas into practice. *'We did what we had to do. It was more of a creative process'* (1998). In this comment Hamilton makes clear that he did not think of dance or starting a dance company as a job or a career but as something that he and the other founders needed to do. These young men, together with many of their contemporaries, were gaining a 'heightened sense of "black British" identity in reggae, dub and rap' (Hebidge, 1979; Hewison, 1995: 202). This sense of themselves, however, was in a context of change.

Britain was in a state of crisis in 1981, reported *The Guardian* (Petridis: 2002). One illustration of this was the uprisings throughout the country. The government, led by Margaret Thatcher, was unpopular. Unemployment was the highest since the 1930s, inflation rose to over twenty-one per cent and the recession resulted in many closures in industry (Hewison, 1995). At the beginning of April the police in Brixton, London, began a 'stop and search' policy. Over six days, 943 people were stopped, most of them black. Disturbances broke out in Brixton on 10 April and again on 10 July. The spirit of the times was encapsulated by the punk band The Specials in their number one hit *Ghost Town*. Their political agenda was evident in the lyrics: 'Can't go on no more, the people getting angry [...]. Government leaving the youth on the shelf [...] no job to be found in this country'. The radicalness of the band was not only in their politics but also in their musical agenda, as they produced ska, which had been the forerunner of reggae and was popular in Jamaica during the 1960s (Petridis, 2002). The songwriter Billy Bragg describes 1981 as

> one of those cusp years. It was the end of punk but it was also the beginning of a more engaged politics of the 1980s as a response to Thatcherism [...]. The demise of Thatcherism and the events that led up to the fall of the Soviet Union has left us in a post-ideological political landscape. It would be very difficult for young bands to make political music these days. (in Petridis, 2002: 4)

Bragg's comments offer insight into the cultural context of the year in which Phoenix Dance Company formed. There were significant changes in Britain after the urban disturbances in 1981 and it was a time when black British consciousness began to emerge. At the same time, television's Channel 4 expanded cultural programming and supported several black media initiatives, which resulted in black independent media organizations such as

> Black Audio Film Collective, Ceddo Film/Video Workshop, Retake
> Film and Video Collective, and Sankofa Film and Video Collective,
> among others. This resulted in the creation of an important, London-
> based, black media arts scene in the '80s and '90s: a scene [...with]
> roots in the race politics and in the ideologies of postmodernism and
> cultural studies. (Powell, 1997: 223)

The discussion above of some of the key aspects of the 1980s provides a
lens through which to view the issues relating to Phoenix Dance
Company in addition to the historical contexts and issues raised earlier.

Cultural contexts and cultural policies in Britain during the 1970s and 1980s

There are many cultural contexts relevant to the work of Phoenix
Dance Company. This section briefly considers aspects of cultural heritage as they relate to the contexts in which Phoenix Dance Company
were performing and to the legacy of the Black Arts Movement. This
movement emerged from the Civil Rights Movement and the Black
Power Movement in America, when African Americans resisted the vestiges of colonialism and racism and demanded that their cultural heritages be acknowledged. These challenges impacted British cultural life
and had an impact on terminology and the ongoing debates about
'Black arts' and 'Black dance'. The establishment, in the form of the
Arts Council in this case, began to put structures in place to try to gain
insight into arts provisions for culturally diverse groups, and the reports
discussed here are one example of such processes. The frameworks that
offer insights into the cultural dynamics with which Phoenix engaged
and/or that impacted upon their artistic practices are like interconnect-
ing boxes. The contexts discussed here, however, do not fit neatly inside
each other; rather, they offer insights into the complex factors that
interplayed in the emergence and development of Phoenix.

In a conference entitled 'Whose Heritage?' held in Manchester in
1999, Stuart Hall gave the keynote speech. He noted that the term
'heritage'

> is bound into the meaning of nation [and that] deeply intertwined
> with the everyday life of all classes and conditions of English men and
> women were the factors of colonization, slavery and empire [...].
> 'Empire' is increasingly subject to a selective amnesia and disavowal.

And when it does appear, it is largely narrated from the viewpoint of the colonizers. (6)[8]

He also pointed out that people from the Caribbean and the Indian sub-continent had made a significant impact on British society and culture, which as a result had diversified. He suggested that the representation of these communities in British culture was complex, but that there was now a need for the mainstream to

> revise their own self-conceptions and rewrite the margins into the centre, the outside into the inside. This is not so much a matter of rep-resenting 'us' as representing more adequately the degree to which 'your' history entails and had always implicated 'us' across the cen-turies and *vice versa*. (10)

Hall indicates the blurring of boundaries between cultural heritages. Paul Gilroy argues that 'the polarisation between essentialist and anti-essentialist theories of black identity has become unhelpful' (1993: x). Gilroy maps the African Diaspora as a formation that is both intercul-tural and transnational; he terms it the 'Black Atlantic'. Focus on such issues has become more prevalent in dance. Andrée Grau, discussing a project that she is directing on *South Asian Dance in Britain: negotiating cultural identity through dance*, noted the difficulty of identifying the many overlapping components of specific cultural heritages (2001). One of the issues in such discussions is the legacy of colonialism that manifests as racism.

Racism

In Frantz Fanon's notable text *Black Skin White Masks* (1952:1973),[9] his application of psychoanalysis to the unconscious workings of colonial-ism and racism offers an investigation of these processes. For example, he describes an incident on a train in which a young girl said, 'Mama, see the Negro! I'm frightened'. In his analysis of the situation, he artic-ulates how he had experienced himself as an object. He explains, 'I took

---

[8] It is arguable that the British honours system, which features the word 'empire' (for example, Order of the British Empire), is an example of the disavowal Hall is discussing. The refusal of the OBE by poet Benjamin Zephaniah, who is of African descent, highlighted the legacy of the Empire and the 'selective amnesia' that Hall described (Ullieri, 2004).
[9] Fanon's work has continued to be important to considerations of racism. In 1995 his work was the basis of an art event and discussion programme at the Institute of Contemporary Arts and a book entitled *The Fact of Blackness* (1996), which is the title of the chapter in *Black Skin White Masks* from which the example above is taken.

myself far off from my own presence, far indeed, and made myself an object' (1973: 79). He says that for him this experience was 'a haemorrhage that spattered my whole body with black blood [...]. This example offers insight into the damage to subjectivities that racism causes. As Griselda Pollock explains:

> Racism interrupts and recasts the formation of subjectivity negatively. Colonial culture does not positively mirror back the subject's body to itself as the basis for ego formation. Instead it turns on the racialised other a gaze which s/he can only experience for her/himself as *coloured* – as thus a negatively devalued *object* [...]. (Pollock, 1999: 256)

It is clear from some of the interviews with Company members that there were ongoing issues about racism either directly involved with their membership of the Company or more indirectly in relation to opportunities open to them in dance, as the following examples demonstrate. Donald Edwards said that sometimes when the Company went into schools to run workshops, '*kids shouted down the corridor* [at them] "*you black so and so*"' (1997). A dancer told rehearsal director, Norman Douglas that while touring in Glasgow he had '*been hassled because I'm black*' (1998). Warren Adams, a young dancer who danced with the Company in 1997, replied to a question about his choice of contemporary dance rather than ballet by saying, '*I'm a black dancer, aren't I? How many black dancers are there in the Royal Ballet?*' (1997). Dancer Gee Goodison made the point that if a critic or an audience member didn't know his name he would rather be identified as '*that guy with the wicked arabesque*' (1998) than by the colour of his skin. So while on the one hand the Company is viewed as a symbol of success, on the other hand it has constantly had to engage with the overt or covert effects of racism. As Loomba points out:

> Race has [...] functioned as one of the most powerful and yet the most fragile markers of human identity, hard to explain and identify and even harder to maintain. Today, skin colour has become the privileged marker of races [...]. While colour is taken to be the prime signifier of racial identity, the latter is actually shaped by perceptions of religious, ethnic, linguistic, national, sexual and class differences. 'Race' as a concept receives its meanings contextually, and in relation to other social groupings and hierarchies, such as gender and class. (1998: 121–2)

Racism is both a contentious and a divisive issue in Britain. As Salman Rushdie argues in his essay 'The new empire within Britain', 'Racism is not a side-issue in contemporary Britain; it is not a peripheral, minority affair [...]. It is a crisis of the whole culture, of the society's entire sense of itself' (in Kanneh, 1998: 140). An example of this crisis is the frequent reporting of immigration issues and the tone with which such accounts are reported. These stories, together with changes in the law, affect those born in Britain as well as those arriving in the country, because the sense of who belongs and who does not is played out on this terrain (Kanneh, 1998). One aspect of such reports includes calls for more immigration controls, producing 'statistics and reports [that] are often highly selective and emphasize symbolic fears about the present or future' (Braham, Rattansi and Skellington, 1992: 24). In addition, the language used by some politicians and in some newspapers contained symbolism that deliberately evoked the fears of some British people. This was particularly evident in what became known as the politician Enoch Powell's 'rivers of blood' speech in April 1968 (Gilroy, 1987), which suggested that there would be conflict because of immigration. Another example of the symbolism in language in the late 1970s was the term 'the enemy within', which was used even though 'in many cases [the person was] no longer an immigrant but born and bred in Brixton, Handsworth, Liverpool and other urban localities' (Braham, Rattansi and Skellington, 1992: 24). A well-known example is the statement Margaret Thatcher made in 1978 when she was leader of her party. She suggested that 'people are really rather afraid that this country might be rather swamped by people with a different culture' (in Skellington and Morris, 1996: 65). David Goldberg suggests that in this statement 'race is coded as culture' (1993: 73), with no reference to biology or superiority. The result, however, is equally exclusive and damaging.

The examples above are also examples of 'institutional racism', a term that received a good deal of news coverage after the publication of Sir William MacPherson's report about the police investigation into the death of Stephen Lawrence (1993). The concept can be traced to the Black Power Movement in America in the 1960s, after which it was taken up by social scientists. The term has two features: 'First, the production of racial inequalities by normal bureaucratic and professional administrative processes, and secondly, the irrelevance of the subjective consciousness of the individual officials, professionals and politicians involved' (Braham, Rattansi and Skellington, 1992: 111).

Black Arts Movement

The 1970s, when the founders were studying dance at school, and the 1980s, when they were establishing Phoenix, were the two decades in which the Black Arts Movement was prominent, following the Civil Rights Movement of the 1960s. Discussing the Black Arts Movement, Kimberly Benston argues that it can be seen as a 'continuously shifting field of struggle and revision in which the relations among politics, representation, history, and revolution are productively revalued' (2000: 3). This open perspective is in contrast to fixed and predetermined notions that have been attached to both the Black Arts Movement and the term 'black'. Benston's comments of critical accounts of work in the 1960s and 1970s also apply to current critical writing. He suggests that 'work is measured against a privileged notion of "blackness" which is posited as external to [...] the Euro-American "mainstream"' (2000: 4). (This, I would suggest, is a feature of some of the critical writing about Phoenix, which is discussed in Chapter 6.)

A conference in 1985 entitled 'Black artists, White institutions' included a discussion of Black Arts in London and the committee structures related to that area. Parminder Vir, Ethnic Arts Advisor to the GLC said:

> We need to define Black Arts as a political concept that comes out of our experience of living in racist Britain. If we are saying that community arts need to strengthen Black representation within its structures then these committee divisions may not be necessary. I think it is time to review the two committees and think of one which sees Black arts as part of mainstream arts. Within the mainstream however it is crucial to recognise that Black arts starts from a disadvantaged position in terms of access and lack of adequate facilities. (In Owusu, 1985: 3)

The issues raised in this discussion have been ongoing within the Arts Council's initiatives for cultural diversity.

Identifying some of the difficulties for the Black Arts Movement, bell hooks says: 'Opposition is not enough. In that vacant space after one has resisted there is still the necessity to become – to make oneself anew' (1990: 15). She says the process of becoming subjects evolves as

> one comes to understand how the structures of domination work in one's own life, as one develops critical thinking and critical consciousness, as one invents new, alternative habits of being and resists from that marginal space of difference inwardly defined. (1990: 15)

The insights that hooks draws on when writing as an African American come from a longer process than for those of African descent in Britain. Her engagement with the issues is from a sense of self that is proactive and productive in relation to racism, rather than being one of defensive resistance.

In Britain there were a number of initiatives that located the contribution of artists of African and Asian descent. In 1988 'The Essential Black Art' exhibition was organised by Rasheed Araeen at the Chisenhale Gallery, London. In 1989 Araeen curated another exhibition, 'The Other Story' at the Hayward Gallery, London, which celebrated the contribution of black artists to British art during the post-war period. The press reaction, however, was 'indifferent, patronising and in some cases blatantly racist' (1990: 9). This was the context for the Arts Council's commissioned report *Cultural Grounding: Live Art and Cultural Diversity: Action Research Project* (1990). Both exhibitions examined 'black art', which emerged 'as a result of the experience of the Diaspora, racism and black struggle' (Dexter, in Araeen, 1988: 3). Araeen argued that the issue was for work by 'AfroAsian artists' to be acknowledged as part of contemporary culture, and that the term 'black art' had been used so widely as to be rendered meaningless (1988). There are some problems with 'The Other Story'. For example, the title suggests that there is one challenge to the story of the art canon rather than a number of interventions by, for example, feminists. The exhibition of twenty-four items included only four by women, so the canon in relation to women of African or Asian descent is reinscribed rather than challenged.

'Black dance'

The term 'black dance' has been widely debated in America and Britain. Susan Manning suggests that it began to replace the term 'negro dance' between 1967 and 1969, as 'artists and critics responded to the ethos of the Black Arts Movement' (2004: xiv). In 1983, the Dance Black America Conference and Symposium was held at the Brooklyn Academy of Music and a follow-up forum was held by the Dance Critics Association. The topics at the conference included 'What is Black Dance?', 'Is there a Black Aesthetic in dance that is different from "White Dance?"', 'Roots: is there a loss of identity (roots) when a Black choreographer attempts a universal (non-ethnic) statement?', 'Dancers, choreographers, companies: what problems arise when a Black modern dance company or ballet company tries to be regarded as a modern dance or ballet company?' and 'Critics: what is the responsibility of the white or black researcher or critic or educator whose subject is Black

Dance?'. These questions were ones that Phoenix either directly or indirectly confronted as it developed and negotiated its identity with its audiences, critics and funders.

A company that preceded Phoenix, MAAS Movers, had also wrestled with some of these issues. As a result of Naseem Khan's influential report (1976), which made clear the inequalities of funding for 'ethnic' minorities, the Arts Council funded MAAS, the Minority Arts Advisory Service, which provided networking and facilitation for Black British people involved in the arts. One of its initiatives, which was also funded by the Greater London Arts Association, was MAAS Movers, a company of ten dancers. It was formed in 1977, following an acknowledgement that there were few opportunities for young black dance artists (Adair, 1992). As Emilyn Claid points out, MAAS Movers was instrumental in 'opening up an awareness of black dance politics and the many different emerging black British artists' (Claid, 2006). The company did not survive, partly because of inadequate funding and partly because its members were divided about the type of work they wished to produce. Some of the company who were trained in Graham technique wanted to create a repertoire of modern dance works and avoid the label of 'black dance'. Others wanted to draw on their African Caribbean heritage as an inspiration for their dance works (Thorpe, 1989). This is an interesting dilemma because it was one with which Phoenix was to grapple, particularly when it received funding from the Arts Council and found conflicting expectations about the Company's repertoire.

A decade after MAAS Movers began, there were debates about prospects for black dancers in Britain. It is evident from the history of the Dance Umbrella Festival that British Black and Asian artists were under-represented, and indeed the festival had been criticized for this. The *Parallels in Black* season in February 1987 held at The Place in London was a response to this criticism and fitted the criteria of Dance Umbrella, which was committed to experimental and innovative work. However, few black dance artists in Britain were working in an experimental way at this point, and the securing of funding was an aspect of the creative choices being made. Greater London Arts were prioritising work under the label of 'Black Arts', but this did not include artists who happened to be black but chose to work in the Western European tradition. As the American dance writer Elizabeth Zimmer pointed out, the group of artists in 'Parallels in Black' 'each drew in unique ways on [...] black heritage' (1987: 97), but she suggests that if they had not been such outstanding artists the combination of their ethnicity and postmodern work might have relegated their work to the sidelines. Bebe Miller, who later worked with Phoenix, was one of the six artists in this season (Powell, 1987; Zimmer, 1987; Rowell, 2000). Following this initiative, several conferences in the 1990s investigated 'Black Dance'.[10]

The Arts Council of England commissioned the report *Advancing Black Dancing* (February 1993), by David Bryan, to chart the views of those engaged with 'Black dance in Britain in the 1990s' (Hoyle, in Bryan, 1993: 3). This report followed the closure of the Black Dance Development Trust (BDDT), a national organisation involved with the development of 'black dance' for the five years it existed. The report identifies the difficulties of defining the meaning of the term 'black dance'. Evans suggests that the term 'becomes more and more pejorative in the face of this accelerating era of innovation' (2000: 15). There was an interest in fusion, which continues today, from several artists, including the Jamaican Carl Campbell, who founded Company 7; RJC; the Nigerian Peter Badejo, of Badejo Arts; and the Nigerian Bode Lawale, director of Sakoba Dance Theatre. There are also practitioners, including Kwesi Johnson and Jonzi D, who are directly influenced by urban contexts. These practitioners do not share just one black experience, and have varied views about the term 'black dance'. For Lawale, the term is 'degrading, it's disrespectful. They [people] don't say "white dance" choreographer' (1999: 15). These comments give some indication of the controversy that has been attached to the term. The working definition of 'black dance' that the researchers put forward was as follows:

> Black dance must continue to cherish, represent, reflect and advance the cultural heritage and aspirations of various black communities. To have Black dance without Black music would be a travesty and therefore a disengagement with the kernel of African culture. For Black dance in Britain to advance it must be allowed to establish its distinct identity. Part of that identity will involve the continued interpretation of Black experiences and cultures as they evolve. Consequently the development of the African traditional and African modernity has to be advanced by Black dancers, Black choreographers and Black dance companies. (Bryan, 1993: 12)

---

[10] For example, a meeting for practitioners was held at the Nottingham Playhouse on 8 March 1993, with a subsequent report by Shaila Parthasarathi. 'What is Black Dance in Britain?' was held at The Nia Centre, Manchester, on 21 August, 1993 and jointly organised with The Blackie, Liverpool, with a report by Yvonne Schumann, Tamalyne Kuyateh and Bill Harpe. These conferences were in response to the publication of David Bryan's report for the Arts Council, *Advancing Black Dancing*, published in February 1993. Hilary Carty gave an overview of 'Black Dance in England' in which she considered changes since the 1940s (2003).

The writers of this definition argue for recognition of the specificity of artists from the African Diaspora, and the importance of being in a position to develop a range of dance practices. In order to achieve this development, the establishment of a national organisation for black dance was recommended with a view to developing an infrastructure for 'black dance'. This development was to be achieved through communication networks, improved training and educational involvements, and improved access to venues and touring opportunities.

There were concerns that the training of young black dancers often prepared them inadequately for the demands of working with a company. Irie! Dance Theatre, based in south-east London and founded in 1985 by its artistic director Beverley Glean, was instrumental in setting up an accredited training course for African and Caribbean dance with Birkbeck College, London University, in an attempt to address this issue. Jackie Guy, the course co-ordinator and former artistic director of Kokuma, an international African and Caribbean dance company, developed a unique technique that 'fuses the authentic, ritualistic and dynamic energies of traditional African and Caribbean dance with modern contemporary dance techniques which draw on black British culture' (in Haslam, 1998: 13).[11]

There was contention, noted in the report, that the BDDT had mainly focused on traditional African dance groups. It was acknowledged that there was a valid historical reason to focus on African culture because

> European colonisation dislocated and relocated African people throughout the world, e.g. South America, North America, the Caribbean and Europe. The presence of African people has led to cultural innovation and new cultural expressions, most notable in the realms of music, e.g. Blues, Jazz, Reggae and Calypso. (Bryan, 1993: 12)

As the writer Diana Evans (2000) pointed out, despite black people having lived in Britain from the 1500s it was not until the formation of Ekome National Dance Company in Bristol in 1976 that traditional African Dance was presented. By 1984, however, Adzido Pan African Ensemble of twenty-eight dancers, funded by the Arts Council, had become the example of 'Black British' dance that was promoted and that reinforced stereotypes of Black arts. This became a difficulty for artists who wished to experiment with forms (Evans, 2000). It was acknowledged that contemporary as well as traditional expressions of

---

[11] This course is no longer running.

African culture were important and that, if the same degree of innovation in music was to be achieved in 'black dance' in Britain, 'then forms and styles that both draw on the past and are embellished by the present Black experience are essential' (Bryan, 1993: 12).

The report also noted that inadequate funding affected the development of artists. In addition, there was a good deal of ignorance about the work, and when venues booked 'black dance' they frequently expected to attract black audiences, which would then allow the venue to meet its equal opportunity requirement. When this was not the case, the group was considered a 'bad investment' (Bryan, 1993: 15). These issues illustrate the lack of an adequate infrastructure to support the work of black dancers. In addition, it is apparent from the venues example that the imposition of policies that try to redress inequality issues is not always effective.

The *Advancing Black Dancing* report also stated, 'Some companies, in their frantic pursuit of acceptance, abandoned identification with their Black heritage and history, by aspiring to be contemporary dancers who just happen to be Black' (Bryan, 1993: 18). It is appropriate at this point to reflect upon the connection between such discussions and reports and the policy documents of Phoenix Dance Company. Phoenix is described in the business plan of 30 October 1992 as having established 'the first black contemporary dance company in Britain' (3). The labelling of Phoenix in relation to identity is a theme that occurs throughout this study. To some extent the founders' views of themselves as dancers did not adhere to the Arts Council's notion of their identity. This was not a label that they initially embraced, although they were clear that their cultural heritage was integral to who they were and how they danced. When they were in control of their artistic pursuits, they viewed contemporary dance as an empowering medium through which they could potentially gain cultural equity. The dance of the early Company could be viewed as being aligned with the community dance movement, and their work encapsulated a level of fusion of dance styles and experiences that could be termed 'intercultural' as Patrice Pavis defines the concept: that is, 'The hybridization is very often such that the original forms can no longer be distinguished' (1996: 8). The founders, however, viewed themselves as contemporary dancers. Such descriptions as a 'black contemporary dance company' came from the funders and the management of the Company at specific times in its history.

Hilary Carty[12] (1996), Dance Director of the Arts Council of England, reviewed a conference entitled 'Ancient Futures' organised by

---

[12] Hilary Carty is Black British.

Irie! Dance Theatre with the Albany Theatre in Deptford (coincidentally, one of the first performance venues for Phoenix). She found that it offered an opportunity to share issues and suggest possibilities for the future. She suggested that in the 1980s there were a number of acclaimed, nationally touring companies that might be termed 'black dance', but because of a lack of infrastructure there had been a decline in these companies. Of the speakers at the conference, Carty noted that Margaret Morris, the artistic director of Phoenix at the time, spoke 'about press perspectives and the challenges of running a black dance company without sharing its cultural background'.

Thea Barnes, Artistic Director of Phoenix from 1997, pointed out during a discussion about 'black dance companies':

> *Using terminology that consistently defines artists by categories of difference is inappropriate at a time when even the boundaries between art forms are becoming blurred. What we need to emphasise is the fact that dance is diverse. We need to report and write about the genre and dance [...] in a way that knows and understands what denigrates and separates, whilst avoiding the pitfall of saying nothing at all [...Barnes] believes that the term 'Black Dance' is used by artists of African and/or Caribbean lineage attempting to subvert an identity given to them by a racialised society to reclaim their dignity, form a sense of camaraderie and to establish their difference because they want no part of a system which ostracises them. People band together to combat things.* (1998: 69)

The term 'black dance company' has been contentious throughout Phoenix's history. Discussion of the term continued throughout the 1990s in a variety of forums. On 23 October 1999 a Black Dance Focus weekend, organised by the Association of Dance of the African Diaspora, was held in London. A number of choreographers experimenting with fusing contemporary dance styles and African Caribbean dance discussed dance making in Britain, and it was noted that 'British choreographers of the African Diaspora are immersed in a continuum of shifting cultural aesthetics' (Barnes, 2000: 24). Barnes argues against the categorisation of artists under the label 'black dance', which she considers has had the effect of ghettoising their work (2000). As Thomas DeFrantz argues, an ongoing problem for companies from the African Diaspora is 'a voyeuristic exoticism of black bodies that placed the dancers outside the emergent mainstream of American classicism' (DeFrantz, in Doolittle and Flynn, 2000: 180). Although DeFrantz is discussing ballet in America, I would suggest that a similar dynamic is to some extent also apparent in contemporary dance in Britain. The discussions about black dance were within the larger framework of the Arts Council and Government policies.

Arts, education, funding

In 1997 the Labour Party produced a cultural manifesto, *Create the future: A strategy for cultural policy, arts and the creative economy*. There was a pledge of support for the arts and the cultural industries and recognition that cultural diversity was an important aspect of British life. The role of education was acknowledged as key in developing future audiences and artists. Nonetheless, despite apparent promotion of the arts, the National Campaign for the Arts (1997) reported that the changes to the education infrastructure and resources had resulted in a negative effect on the arts. The Ofsted inspections (organised by the government to establish and maintain standards throughout England's state schools) and league tables (which ranked schools according to specific criteria, including examination successes) had created pressure on the school timetable, which frequently meant less time for the arts.[13]

The implications arising from effective arts programmes in schools are indicated by Justin Lewis, who, following Bourdieu, suggests that the appreciation and understanding of art is linked to class and education and that, therefore, the role of education in the dominant aesthetic-value system is the key to understanding it (Lewis, 1990: 9). It is apparent from Chapter 1 that the founders benefited from their education, which played a role in their success, but the infrastructure of the 1980s was dismantled in the 1990s.

Lewis also suggests that when decisions are made about the arts, and in particular about public funding, considerations of value are the key criterion as to whether an activity is subsidised or not. Lewis argues that 'a system of value is unavoidable [...] it is inscribed within the practicalities of public funding' (1990: 7). Of course, a key issue here is who makes the decisions and who benefits. In a 1986 document for the Greater London Council, Alan Tomkins argued that specific forms of art such as opera and painting had been 'extensively colonised by a dominant class group' (1990: 88).

Lewis summarizes his argument as follows:

> Artistic value is an arbitrary aesthetic system. It is based upon and inscribed within social positions. It is not an 'essence' that lurks within the artistic object, to be discovered by those who somehow

---

[13] This was despite support from 'out-of-hours learning' schemes and the New Opportunities Fund, which were established in an attempt to provide resources for the arts.

naturally 'recognize' it. There is a dominant system of artistic value, which is instrumental in evaluating what receives public funding and what does not. This system is based upon levels of cultural competence, gained through education, as well as inscribed within the education system. (1990: 11)

Lewis argues that a consideration of where public funding goes and who benefits from it illuminates the fact that aesthetic value is given to some artistic activities and not to others. Those subsidised are usually linked to institutions such as galleries, concert halls and theatres. Within art forms, some activities are more likely than others to be subsidised; so, for example, the type of dance subsidised would be ballet and contemporary dance and rarely tap dancing, break dancing or ballroom dances. Occasionally, a regional arts association will fund such activities.

Audiences

A table from a British Market Research Bureau survey for the Arts Council (1986) shows that contemporary dance had the smallest audiences of any art form, including ballet. As with other art forms, the audiences are mainly from professional and managerial classes and most have received further education (in Lewis, 1990). Lewis also makes the point that those who attend arts events and activities tend to do so for more than one art form. Linda Jasper and Jeanette Siddall confirm these findings in relation to dance, but they also note that audiences were usually white and aged between twenty-five and forty-four (1999). These factors are relevant to the development of Phoenix, because within the value system that Lewis describes, the founders, as working-class young men from the African Diaspora practising contemporary dance, are potentially disadvantaged in relation to audiences that 'tend[ed] to be white' (1990: 16). Lewis states:

It is difficult to tell how much this is simply due to the disadvantaged position of black people in social class and educational terms. Do black people abstain from arts attendance because they tend to be working class or because of the dominance of white cultural forms? (1990: 17).

A report entitled *Attitudes Among Britain's Black Community Towards Attendance At Arts, Cultural and Entertainment Events* (1990), commissioned by the Arts Council, gives some insight into several of the issues that Lewis raised. The study was based on the assumption that African

Caribbean and Asian people rarely attended arts and entertainment events, because they were rarely seen at mainstream events. The research, however, showed this assumption to be flawed, because the communities evolved their own entertainment structures. Entertainment and the arts are important aspects of these communities; but in order to encourage them to attend events, good marketing strategies were identified as necessary.

Sharon Donaldson, a dancer and choreographer with Phoenix, endorsed this:

> *I don't remember my mother taking us to the theatre as kids, but we would go to churches and the carnivals and the cinema [...]. You have to entice people into the theatre [...]. You can't expect people to sit there and know nothing about a programme. You've got to actively go out there and seek them.* (1998)

People in the Arts Council study 'cited lack of adequate publicity, the high cost involved and their perception of "arts" as irrelevant, as basic reasons for not attending arts events' (Francis, 1990: 18). In addition, they thought that it was important to have events that were specifically targeted at certain communities, partly because 'the history of arts provision has been largely concerned with the establishment of "flagship" organisations [...]. The fringe movement evolved mainly as reaction to this strategy' (Francis, 1990: 29). Another important factor affecting attendance at performances was the range of provision in the regions, which was much less than in London.

In 1990 in Leeds, where Phoenix has its base, there was a population of 8193 people from the Caribbean, which was 1.3 per cent of the local population (Francis, 1990: A3). One of the important contributions that Phoenix makes to the local Leeds community is the provision of excellence within contemporary dance, in terms of both performance and education. In a discussion about dance practice and performance, Nikki Crane of South Humberside Dance Project suggests that it is easier to encourage people to participate in dance activities than to get them to watch dance performance. Most people have participated in dance at some point or another, even if only at a party. The codes for dance, however, are unfamiliar and may discourage people from attending performances. The median age for attendance at contemporary dance performance is thirty-four, whereas for ballet it is forty-nine. Contemporary dance appeals to a younger audience who are also likely to be participants of the form.

Dance animateurs and dance agencies have been highly successful in targeting specific groups with a range of dance activities. Females are usually in the majority, but styles such as hip hop have attracted males. Attracting a dance audience is a different matter. 'Groups such as Phoenix Dance Company or the English Dance Theatre have attempted to do this by playing at non-dance venues such as community centres and schools' (Lewis, 1990: 97).

This observation suggests that Phoenix Dance Company chose venues at schools and community centres in order to attract a particular kind of audience. Their aims, however, were much more specific than this. Through their workshops and performances, they had a mission to involve young people who would not usually have access to dance. These venues, particularly the schools, were the ones to which they had access because initial contacts were made through their old school, Harehills Middle School.

Another way of attracting audiences is by showcases, performances where the participants present their skills and thereby inform friends and family of aspects of dance culture. An example of this approach is when a company offers an educational package and either the participants have the opportunity to perform in a performance comprised of all participants, or the workshop members perform a work in the same programme as the company. Phoenix has offered both these opportunities as part of its educational programmes. A significant aspect of these programmes was the Company's commitment to education. This evolved from the dancers' recognition and acknowledgement that an important input to their own professional lives as dancers (and for some as choreographers) was their creative experiences in dance classes at school and later with the Youth Group. As David Hamilton noted, *'Phoenix was an example of what the potential in dance in education could mean'* (1998). This potential was then subject to Arts Council policies and procedures.

Phoenix Dance Company and Arts Council policies

In relation to Phoenix Dance Company, we can consider a number of difficulties inherent in the Arts Council's policies and identified by Su Braden in her book *Artists and People* (1978):

> [The] so-called cultural *heritage* which made Britain great – the Bachs and Beethovens, the Shakespeares and Danes, the Constables and Titians – is no longer communicating anything to the vast majority of Europe's population [...]. The greatest artistic deception of the

twentieth century has been to insist to *all* people that this was *their* culture. The Arts Council of Great Britain was established on this premise [...] *People make culture* and it is in this continually developing movement that money should be invested, rather than in the Arts Council's notion of trying to make people cultured. (Braden, 1978: 153–5)

Clearly, the Arts Council's approach had the effect of marginalising the work of people of African Caribbean heritage. This was the context in which the founders established Phoenix Dance Company in 1981 as a small-scale local initiative without public funding, when most of the focus was still on arts initiatives and events in London.

In 1984 the Arts Council of Great Britain (ACGB) published *The Glory of the Garden*. This report was commissioned because of changes in society and the pressures on funding which made a thorough review of policies necessary. The ACGB decided to give priority, for five years until 1989, to five main areas: art, dance, drama, music and education. The report recommended an increase in the responsibilities of regional arts associations. It also acknowledged that dance was underfunded, with low salaries and limited time to create new work. Companies were operating on shoestring budgets. There was recognition of the need for stronger companies and stronger links with the regions. New monies were allocated to address these issues, 'to strengthen the support given to Black and Asian dance' (ACGB, 1984: 15) and to develop educational outreach. At that time only one dance company, the Royal Ballet Company, had a permanent home for rehearsal and performance; the remaining companies all toured. There was an acknowledgement of the need to build on the existing touring structure and to strengthen regional companies.

Within the context above, the report made specific comments about Phoenix Dance Company:

One company to whose development the Council attaches particular importance, Phoenix Dance Company, provides a good example of the considerations which underlie much of the Council's approach to its strategy. Phoenix is an exciting company of young Black dancers, formed as a result of the outstanding dance-in-education work at Harehills School in Leeds. The company's artistic achievements over the past few years bear eloquent testimony to the talent which can emerge in the regions; but that talent cannot develop its potential to the full without adequate funding. Phoenix has been an occasional project client of the Arts Council and of the Yorkshire Arts

Association. Its work is in a category which is of great potential importance, and in order to provide the basis of stability necessary to its artistic growth, the Council now intends itself to fund it on a more secure basis, perhaps by a three-year franchise. At the end of the franchise period, it may be appropriate to devolve the company's entire funding to the Yorkshire Arts Association. (ACGB, 1984: 15)

It is clear from these comments that Phoenix fulfilled one of the key objectives of the Arts Council – to give support to what they termed, without definition, 'black dance'. It also allowed them to support work that emerged from the regions, and they had stated that they wanted to 'strengthen existing regional companies' (1984: 15). The decision to fund the Company because of these priorities had long-term implications that will be discussed later.

Further reports from the Arts Council were significant for the Company. In 1989 the Arts Council of England (ACE) produced a report entitled *Towards cultural diversity*. Nearly ten years later, the Arts Council produced another document, *Cultural Diversity Action Plan* (ACE, 1998), in which it acknowledged that there had been significant changes to British culture. Specifically, cultural diversity, which had been marginal at the time of the 1989 action plan, played a key part in the cultural activities of Britain by 1997. Ethnic minorities made up 5.5 per cent of the population. Of this number, nearly half were born in the UK and most were under the age of twenty-five (1997). The Plan noted a commitment by ACE to enhance the infrastructure so that there was more appreciation of the cultural diversity of Britain, to improve access to arts practice and to ensure better resources for artists.

The Arts Council's Green Paper on cultural diversity, *The Landscape of Fact* (1997), was a preparation for its policy on cultural diversity. It defined 'Black Arts', which for convenience was shorthand for 'African, Caribbean, Chinese, and Asian Arts' (1997: 22), as

an ongoing continuum that is in a constant state of change and development. Its heterogeneity needs to be acknowledged and reflected in policy. At certain levels, 'Black Arts' is affected by varieties of cultural roots – social, religious, generational and community influences. At others, the use of the category should seriously be challenged. In order, however, to allow the various strands of 'Black Arts' to develop with the maximum freedom, urgent attention needs to be given to overall strategies for sustaining and developing them. (1997: 22)

Most responses to the Green Paper were supportive. One important item noted was the absence of Black and Asian arts managers and administrators and the need to provide access to opportunities in the mainstream for such people and for artists and audiences. A difficulty commented upon was the tendency for terms such as 'Black Arts' and 'cultural diversity' to imply a homogeneity that does not exist. It was further noted that there was a lack of training structures for African Peoples' Dance, South Asian Dance etc and that 'arts education – particularly higher education – is still marked by a Western European cultural bias, and alternatives are inclined to be marketed as exotic' (Arts Council, 1997: 16).

Naseem Khan noted that, after her 1976 study had highlighted issues of cultural diversity, twenty years of Arts Council policies had focused on disadvantage. This had the unfortunate outcome of marginalising as 'the other' the arts and artists that they were intending to benefit. In addition, the arts and artists were viewed as homogenous, ignoring their complex differences and needs. ACE's 1998 Action Plan was created to address those issues.

In another report commissioned by the ACGB, *Black Theatre in England* (1988), its author Elizabeth Clarke listed a number of theatre companies and details of their policies, form and style, the content of the their work, the needs fulfilled and opportunities taken, their potential growth and sources of funding.

She stated:

> Sooner or later the National Theatre, the RSC and other such centres of 'excellence' will have to decide why the definition of 'excellence' is automatically exclusive of the black British input [...]. If the London scene is bleak, the regional scene as far as black theatre goes is even bleaker. (1988: ii)

This point was endorsed in relation to all the arts in the report by Francis (1990) mentioned earlier. Clarke's report recorded that Yorkshire Arts 'recognises that the loudest cry in Black Arts in the region is not from drama but for dance' (1988: 81–2). This is significant in relation to the funding for Phoenix, as it indicates that at that time there was activity in the region that was acknowledged by the Regional Arts Association. Of course, it also raises other complex issues in relation to the categorisation of the Company.

Nevertheless, various reports reflected a growing recognition of the importance of acknowledging that 'every social practice has a cultural dimension' (Thompson, 1997: 226). This point is reinforced by an initiative by the Arts Council and the British Council entitled *Re-inventing Britain: Identity, Transnationalism and the Arts* (1997), which brought together well-known academics and artists. Homi Bhabha argues for culture to be defined as an activity rather than an identity, so that an 'Indian dancer is no longer restricted to Indian forms or the Argentinian musician to tango' [...]. This disconnection of cultural identity and ethnic origin speaks to the self-image of many non-European artists across Europe (1997: 6). This is important, he argues, because it offers a way out of the marginalisation of African dance forms and of ballet being viewed as the dance language of the nation. It is evident from such perspectives that in the late 1990s and early twenty-first century there have been moves towards a blurring of boundaries, which have offered opportunities to artists from a range of cultural heritages.

The latest initiative of the Arts Council relating to cultural diversity was termed *decibel*. One of the regular publications from this initiative noted that by the 1980s 'the ideal of retention, authenticity and purity so important to their parents ceased to have the same sort of force' [for the next generations] (2003: 2). There was, however, a recognition that 'the arts play an integral role in helping us understand the world and our different communities' (2003: 14). It is this role that Phoenix has continued to develop through the various phases of its development.

One of these phases is the focus of the next chapter. After David Hamilton left the Company, Neville Campbell, a contemporary of the founders, accepted the position of artistic director. As we have seen, the infrastructure and cultural policies of the dance organisations and the Arts Council had a profound effect on Phoenix's artistic practice. In Chapter 3 the focus is on the long-term implications of funding and the institutionalisation of the Company.

Chapter 3: Phoenix Plus: An Emerging Repertory Company

This chapter traces two key transitions of Phoenix Dance Company in relation to institutionalisation and issues of gender from 1985 to1991. The Company changed considerably during this period. It became a revenue client of the Arts Council of Great Britain in April 1985 and hence became accountable for both artistic and financial decisions. It therefore developed from a small-scale company, initially run with a loose peer-group structure, to an established, funded, hierarchical company that toured internationally. This was also the period in which the founding artistic director, David Hamilton, left and Neville Campbell, the new artistic director, took Phoenix into an important phase of growth and development. The employment of women in what had hitherto been an all-male company was another important transition for the Company. I argue that these changes profoundly shifted the Company's identity. The significance of these developments and their impact on the perception of the Company by its audiences, the critics and indeed the members themselves will be considered from readings of the archives.

Becoming a revenue company: 1985

When Phoenix became a revenue company, the funding allocation of £63,000 from the Arts Council ensured the Company's financial security and enabled it to extend its work. It became a limited company in July 1985 and a registered charity the following month (Holgate, 1997: 11). An indication of the financial position before funding is the fact that the dancers were not Equity members and had not been receiving Equity's minimum wage.

The Company consisted of seven directors: five dancers and two administrators (Pauline Fitzmaurice and Jo Stenholm – CD, September 1985). The *Morning Star* described the group as the 'greatest success story of dance in our time' (King, 1985: PA). Stephanie Ferguson, a critic who has continued to follow the Company's work, commented, 'Although polished and professional, they have not lost any of their streetwise slickness and their performances are still raw and powerful, an explosion of pent-up inner-city energies' (1985: PA). Such comments acknowledging the Company's achievements are likely to have informed the Arts Council's decision to fund the Company, which was

6. *Square Won*, 1985. Choreographer Edward Lynch; dancers Merville Jones, Edward Lynch; photographer Terry Cryer

building on its success at a time when 'The budget for ethnic arts[1] grew from four hundred thousand pounds in 1982–3 to two million pounds in 1985–6. This increase proved to be a powerful stimulus to black theatre, benefiting companies such as Temba, Tara Arts, Black Theatre Co-operative and Talawa' (Hewison, 1995: 238–9). As we have seen in Chapter 2, in the 1980s the Arts Council was attempting to support cultural diversity, as is evident from the budget increase, although some of the terms which were used then, such as 'ethnic' and 'black', are problematic. Phoenix received funding because of the strategy that the Arts Council had laid out in the 1984 report *The Glory of the Garden*. The benefits to the Company of receiving funding from the Arts Council were clear in terms of extra resources and publicity, but there was also an artistic cost, which will be explored in this chapter.

The Company's new-found success and funding award entailed structural changes. On 22 September 1985 (BM), the proposed management committee met.[2] It is interesting to note that there was a high level of dance expertise on this committee, which was not the case in later years, and several people at this meeting later became members of the Board for the Company. The personnel were white British and Americans, and at the Board meeting on 6 September 1987 the Chair stated that he had received a letter from Jane Nicholas concerning the absence of any black or Asian people on the Board. This comment seems to support the view that one aspect of the Arts Council's decision to fund the Company was to meet targets in relation to ethnicity at all levels in its client organisations.

The discussion that followed focused on whom to approach and on connections that could be made through existing organisations. The tension between the Company and the Arts Council is evident in the subtext of the Board meeting's minutes and notes. The indicative climate is illustrated, for example, in a document outlining the composition of the Company, Equity contracts, the agreed touring, holidays and rehearsal periods. The document has a statement in brackets that reads, 'Of course, the Board reserves the right to alter, reverse or negate any of the above at any time!' (BM, 6 September 1987). I read the exclamation mark to emphasise that control lay with the Board, which had obligations to the Company's funders. The implication of this position is that decisions might not always have been in accord with what the Company desired or would have wished to prioritise.

At the 6 September meeting, Jane Nicholas explained the Arts Council's policy in relation to Phoenix as a revenue client. The intention

---

[1] This is the term used in documentation in the early 1980s.

[2] See Appendix 2 for a list of personnel.

was to devolve the Company to the Yorkshire Arts Association (as it then was) but for the Company to retain a national profile. Devolution was scheduled for April 1988. It was the first dance company ever to be devolved, and Nicholas suggested that the Company needed to institute a management committee as a first step towards being in line with other revenue clients (CD, 30 October 1987).

In Linda Jasper and Jeanette Siddall's study of dance management, choreographer Wayne McGregor discussed the requirements for effective management: 'Dance management must be about respecting the individual artist's choices' (1999: 32). Unfortunately, the Board minutes indicate that this was not always the case for Phoenix Dance Company. At the meeting on 22 September, the Company, including the dancers, the two administrators, the costume designer and the technician, were simply observers. The Company was asked about an artistic vision for the future, and David Hamilton described 'how the dances choreographed by the Company members originated, the different methods of teaching and [...] learning by experience' (BM, 22 September 1985: 2). In this encounter it appears that Hamilton was required to explain his work. This was previously unnecessary because the Company had shared a culturally specific perspective that informed their experiences. As Gurmit Hukam, a contemporary of Darshan Singh Bhuller and Neville Campbell who later became rehearsal director for the Company in 1985 and 1990, explained, '*David was the serious driving force, but there was huge loyalty and commitment from all the members at that time. They had a kind of shared vision about what Phoenix was*' (1998). This statement reinforces the particularity of the Company's commitment to their work and to each other. It also gives an indication of the shift the Company made in order to internalise some of the values and structures required by the Arts Council. In this process, Hamilton had to translate his creative experiences into a language that was both understood by and acceptable to the Arts Council officers.

Language influences our understanding and perception of our lives and, therefore, how we use it and the context in which we use it are significant. The requirement for Hamilton to explain his work could be interpreted as an example of 'colonial discourses [that] form the intersections where language and power meet' (McLeod, 2000: 18). This process is also evident in Hamilton's creation of an artistic policy that was also involved with language and power. His resistance to providing a policy that fitted the Arts Council's criteria may be viewed as an attempt to avoid internalising values that were disempowering (McLeod, 2000).

The significant changes in the Company at this time contributed to the loss of Phoenix's unique identity. Moreover, I would argue, from the context above and from a reading of the 1985 minutes, that the structure required by the Arts Council seems inappropriate. This view is reinforced when the youth of the dancers and their ideals, which were embedded in the formation of the Company, are taken into account. There is a tension here between the requirements of an accountable government body and the creative self-management of a group of dancers who wanted to explore their own artistic interests and to share their skills in educational and community settings.

The Company at that stage was on a small scale. By granting it funding, the Arts Council gained political credibility and was able to satisfy its own agenda as stated in *The Glory of the Garden*. Unfortunately, the Council did not put any mechanisms in place to enable the artistic practices of the Company to develop and expand. The Board were the managers, and so the artists no longer directly managed their work and instead became employees of the Board. The initial vision and dance-making practices of the founders ceased at this point. They were angry about the effects of this imposed structure. The Arts Council, however, were not sufficiently reflective of their own practices and structures to support the Company's choreographic beginnings (Edwards, 1998; Barnes, 18 January 2001).

Some of the statements from those Phoenix dancers who shared the founders' background offer insight into the Company, which for the Arts Council became merely another 'product'. Martin Hylton said, '*Phoenix is home*' (1999). Some of his contemporaries at Harehills Middle School went on to train at the London School of Contemporary Dance and danced with Phoenix and Rambert Dance Company. He explained:

> *I always wanted to dance with Phoenix and wanted my career to be with Phoenix from the age of 19. Phoenix, as its title, gets reborn. Before, the Company was all male and had a different strength to today. Directors come and go and some* [directors] *are stronger than others.* (1999)

Hylton's remarks illustrate the importance of the Company to the dancers and to those with aspirations to dance with Phoenix. There were, however, tensions when some of the structures changed. It becomes apparent from the minutes (BM, 22 September 1985) how much the dancers had to learn about funded company structures. They had neither knowledge nor experience of such structures and were thus at a disadvantage in terms of retaining significant control over the direction of the Company. At the Board meeting on 22 September 1985, the role of company directors was explained as well as the duties of a management committee and the position of a rehearsal director.

On the surface, the recommendations made in *The Glory of the Garden* seemed to offer valuable support to the dancers; but it can be argued that it initiated a process of disenfranchisement. It can, of course, be claimed that the Company has become an international success; but this was at some cost to the founders. Janet Smith, who was mentioned in the same report, described her image of this process.

> There is a ladder propped up against the wall, which the dancers and companies climb with the aid of funding from the Arts Council, but when the other side of the wall is investigated, there is a heap of dancers and companies who have fallen, when their funding has been withdrawn, or they have been unable to meet the Arts Council's requirements.[3]

This process is also vividly described by David Dougill, writing in the *Sunday Times*:

> Devlin comments pungently on the recent demise of Janet Smith and Dancers, who were generally regarded as one of the most 'accessible' of contemporary companies. When the troupe was made a regular client in 1984, in that moment of elevation it was handed a poisoned cup. (Dougill, 1989: PA)

So the Company was not alone in the difficulties that the requirements of funding placed upon them. As African Caribbean men, however, for them there was a further dimension, which mirrors colonialism:

> Colonialism is perpetuated in part by justifying to those in the colonising nation the idea that it is right and proper to rule over other peoples and by getting colonised people to accept their lower ranking in the colonial order of things – a process we can call 'colonising the mind'. (McLeod, 2000: 18)

I would like to argue that this process affected the early Phoenix group in two ways. Firstly, as men from the African Diaspora living in Britain, they were subjected to the negativity of racism on a day-to-day basis.

---

[3] Personal communication with author, May 2001.

Secondly, as members of a Company funded by a government organisa-tion, they were expected to internalise the values of the Arts Council and to operate with a structure similar to that of the Council's other revenue clients. The effect of this was that the founders of Phoenix lost much of their autonomy and some of the specificity of their regional, social, cultural and historical conditions. As one of the dancers, Hugh Davis, said, '*In the early days it was a Company that was run by dancers and they did actually own it. Now the dancers do not own the Company*' (1998).

John Mcleod argues that internalising the interests and values which assume that the world, in this case dance, operates in a particular way is extremely disempowering for those 'colonised'. Such interests were also apparent in other areas of dance (2000). Joyce Sherlock suggests that in dance study and dance writing of the 1980s, 'the hegemony of upper middle class, white, male interests' (1988: 236) was dominant and, with the exception of New Dance, there was very little work 'criti-cal of the late capitalist economy of Britain' (Sherlock, 1988: 237).

In a study of Rambert Dance Company (formerly Ballet Rambert), Sherlock documented some significant factors about a dancer's life, based on interviews with the dancers. Some of the insights in her study are relevant for this analysis of Phoenix because of the issues raised about being a member of a repertory company. Sherlock found that, in contrast to the widely held belief that dancers begin their long training from early childhood, some of Rambert's female members had begun training in their teenage years. It is more common for male dancers to begin their dance training after childhood. There was agreement among the dancers that it was easier for men than for women to gain a place at ballet school and then to find employment, because there were fewer men in the profession. At the same time, however, there still remains a stigma attached to men involved in dance (see Adair, 1992, and Burt, 1995).[4]

The study identified two other issues. Firstly, there was a tendency to be totally involved with the company because of the amount of time spent touring together. Secondly, some women in the company found it difficult to combine motherhood with a career as a dancer. The study also discussed the fact that 'the cultural values of family background and the dancers themselves showed characteristics decidedly within a middle class view' (1988: 149).

The experience of the dancers and their involvement in the repertory is evident from the following observation:

---

[4] Men, however, are not a homogenous group and such a stigma may not have the same resonance for some gay men and African Caribbean men.

The dancers talked about the personal satisfaction of dancing a dance, which is quite separate from recognising its artistic or experimental qualities. The interpersonal dynamics of choreography came over as being fairly authoritarian in the company and this was contrasted by one dancer as being less personally satisfying than a 'Pina-Bauschesque'[5] experience she had had on sabbatical where there was improvisation, total sharing of ideas, constant changing up to the last minute, but an intense personal involvement which impressed her. (Sherlock, 1988: 148)

Sherlock's study offers a context within which to read the achievements of Phoenix. It offers insights into ways of working within a dance company in the 1980s. It also provides a model of contemporary dance in which most participants were white, middle-class women at a time when the decision-making roles of artistic director, musical director and choreographer were predominantly held by men (Sherlock, 1988; see also Adair, 1992).

Phoenix offered another model of a dance company. As David Henshaw commented:

it is a company which shouts its pride in black British culture [...] with talent, energy and vision [they] imprinted their mark on Western culture. They took the burgeoning British contemporary dance and made it speak distinctively of their own experience [...] their achievement for dance and for black dancers, is to be celebrated. (1991: 44)

The achievements and success of the Company which Henshaw identifies are obviously important factors in the Arts Council's interest in the Company.

The consequences of funding

The offer of Arts Council funding was a response to the growing professional recognition of the Company. The funding allowed the dancers to pay themselves more realistic wages and made their future more secure. They also, however, became accountable to an imposed template of professional arts management. To some extent the imposed structures of a

[5] 'Pina Bausch is one of the outstanding personalities of dance in the second half of the twentieth century [...]. Her [dance theatre] approach became a model and credo for a whole generation of choreographers, directors, and filmmakers. By rejecting harmonious and aesthetic dance she focused on the expressionism of movement.' (Bremser, 1999: 25)

management board and the expectations of the Arts Council conflicted with the Company members' approach to dance. It was specific qualities and viewpoints that gave the Company its unique identity in British dance.

The Company changed, however, from one in which making their own work and their commitment to each other were their main concerns, to one that was responsible for a significant amount of funding. The annual turnover for the Company in 1987 was £130,000; for six years it had managed to keep the books balanced, but had no reserves. In 1987 it was predicted that it would go into the red by £4,500. The main source of funding at this point was from the Arts Council of Great Britain. In 1986 and 1987 the Company received £65,000. The other funders were the West Yorkshire Grants and the Yorkshire Arts Association, from whom it received £12,000. In addition, in 1987 the Company received £5,000 from Leeds City Council (Leisure Services) to part-fund a new show and run a community project. The balance of funding came from touring, but it was noted that the Company was seriously underfunded (CD, 1987). Funding brought with it the pressure of expectations.

Within any institution there are work practices to be adopted. For dancers these include keeping fit and healthy and attending company class and rehearsals. Venues and audiences also expect cancellations of performances to be the rare exception. Initially, however, during a period of adjustment, the Company continued to operate on a more personal level, attending to issues as it suited the dancers individually rather than considering what was required of them professionally. They were gradually adjusting to what was required of them, but in the process there were complaints about cancellations of workshops and performances. Between March 1985 and March 1986, there were nineteen cancellations, often because of injury (CD, 1986). As a small company the dancers were frequently overworked and, therefore, susceptible to injury.

They were issued with targets to meet, whereas previously they would have set their own. For example, the Director of Dance and Mime stated that the Company should aim to give a minimum of sixty-five to eighty performances in England each year, of which at least fifty should be outside Yorkshire. The Company were expected to produce at least one full-length evening's programme of new work per year (30 October 1987).

Sometimes, however, the dancers did not look after themselves adequately, given the demanding nature of their profession. As Emilyn Claid, a choreographer who made two works with the Company, pointed out, once they received funding they were required to '*be disciplined and*

*have their bodies in shape, which was never thought of before that money.
They did their thing and everybody loved it'* (2000). The Company's status
as an Arts Council client highlighted the issue of the cancellations,
which were considered unacceptable. For example, the Director of
Canon Hill Park, Birmingham, wrote to the Dance Director, Arts
Council of Great Britain, to complain about a late cancellation; this
resulted in a meeting between the Dance Director, the administrator of
Phoenix and artistic director David Hamilton (CD, 19 March, 24 March,
31 March 1987).

Neville Campbell suggested that the Company had a poor reputation
with venues and venue managers. The dancers' youth, together with
their lack of formal dance training and administrative training, meant
that they did not always meet professional expectations (2000). Jane
Dudley, however, in an interview on *The South Bank Show*, described the
dancers as 'totally disciplined and totally professional' (1984). The
dancer Rick Holgate suggested that they were not '*a technically accomplished company at that time [...] but there was something special about
them'* (1998).

Another area of contention was their teaching assignments.
Campbell said that their workshops sometimes '*push*[ed] *children beyond
their physical capabilities'* (2000).[6] The young dancers and their expertise were, however, likely to have been viewed as a novelty in a context in
which many of the teachers had a limited knowledge of contemporary
dance and where classes were offered to girls more often than to boys or
to mixed sexes. Nevertheless, their funding was under threat because of
these difficulties; moreover, according to Campbell, David Hamilton was
frustrated by trying to dance, rehearse and choreograph with contemporaries who were not always willing to respond in a professional manner. Hamilton's decision to leave may have been further influenced by
the lack of control of the Company's direction following the introduction of a management board. It is, however, not always easy to remember why certain decisions were made, and Hamilton did not clarify the
details of his decision. He later commented, in an interview for Radio
Leeds, that he left because it was time for a change and he thought each
individual should have the room to grow and were perhaps holding
each other back (1988).

It seems clear from minutes of the Board meetings and from some of
the interviews that there were tensions between the dancers and the
Board from the outset. There are benefits, however, that an effective
board could provide:

---

[6] This point was also made by Merville Jones when I interviewed him (1997).

Boards of directors can provide objective views, fresh insights and encouragement. Quarterly board meetings are useful milestones for the works: an opportunity to reflect on what has been achieved, identify the major challenges and check the financial position [...]. Sometimes, however, it might appear that board members are amateur players in the arts who waste time with pet theories and push irrelevant and vested interests instead of letting the professionals get on with the job. (Jasper and Siddall, 1999: 53–54)

It is clear from this statement that there are disadvantages as well as advantages in working with a board, and Phoenix had a complex and sometimes tempestuous relationship with the various Boards throughout their history.

They also had to be accountable for their financial decisions. By April 1987 the Company had a deficit of £20,000, partly explained by the cost of moving to their new space at the Yorkshire Dance Centre and by increased salaries. The minutes indicate that, following this deficit, the ACGB required quarterly figures, which is an example of further control from the funders that may not have been of benefit to the Company (BM, 26 April 1987). One of the issues here is that 'Accountability to funding bodies is labour intensive and there is considerable paperwork involved' (Jasper and Siddall, 1999: 52). Initially, Pauline Fitzmaurice, the administrator, was uninformed about funding applications. She was the dancers' ex-drama teacher rather than an experienced dance company administrator. Dick Matchett and Peter Brinson from the Gulbenkian Foundation, however, were impressed by Phoenix's early performances and suggested to Fitzmaurice funding for which they were eligible (Fitzmaurice, 1996).

Another example of conflict between the Company's needs and the ACGB requirements was the production of an artistic policy:

The Arts Council wanted an artistic policy but it was difficult to get a wording which David would accept and that they would accept. There was no division in the work between education and performance, but the Arts Council expected that. Part of me felt if they had taken us on, that was their problem. They had to make some adjustment. But they saw it as a process of maturity and that it was their job to guide the Company through. There was an unspoken belief that the way big companies operated was the way a company should operate. There was a breakdown in communication. We could not get them to understand that the reason why Phoenix was special was because we did operate in a different way; and that if they insisted on change, that would result in more conventional work. (Fitzmaurice, 1988)

This statement by Pauline Fitzmaurice clearly indicates the difficulties and mismatch between a small co-operative Company, with its unusual beginnings, and a funding institution that wanted to support the Company to fulfil its own policies and objectives but lacked insight into the institution's own structures and practices and their political implications. The assumption that the institutionalisation of the Company was a process of maturity ignores the Company's specificity and, I would argue, is an example of institutional racism. There is an echo here of European colonisers assuming that those they colonised needed 'educating', with little recognition of the particularity of the people's own understandings. It is not surprising, therefore, that despite resources, achievements and the positive beginnings of the Company, it was in disarray by 1987.

David Hamilton's final performance with Phoenix Dance Company was on 23 May 1987 at the Civic Theatre, Leeds. At this point Phoenix was a small-scale touring dance company, employing dancers for every week of the year. The Board of directors numbered twelve, six being directly connected to dance (CD, 30 October 1987). There were six dancers: Donald Edwards, Villmore James, Edward Lynch, Colin Poole, Douglas Thorpe and Gary Simpson. Not only had the Company been successful on their British tours, but also their Australian tour in 1987 was well received. A reporter, Terry Owen, quoted Hamilton as saying:

We are one of the few dance companies in the UK with that background [West Indian reggae culture]. We have been able to take the reggae music and dance we grew up with out of the disco and put them into a theatrical context without losing what you could call their natural setting. For our black audiences in England, the recognition of their cultural identity can be a very powerful force. (1987: PA)[7]

This indicates the specificity of this group of dancers and the place they had established for themselves within British contemporary dance in six years. Phoenix offered an important role model to audiences and to those who participated in their education workshops. The Company understood that a 'sense of ownership [was created] through knowing the dancers and knowing the themes; it goes deeper than an immediate response; they've made contact and go away with a much deeper

[7] This quote is from a review in the Company archive that had no source information.

experience' (Jasper and Siddall, 1999: 115). Although Hamilton had a clear artistic vision and commitment to education, and the Company's work was commended by the critics, his approach was not necessarily shared by the Board or the funders (Jones, 1997).

Towards the end of the 1980s, issues of finance and funding were affecting all areas of the performing arts. On the one hand, public subsidy in the form of grants and guarantees was generally falling in real terms; on the other, business sponsorship was proving to be a welcome source of new funding, particularly to London-based and so-called 'national' companies (Dunlop, Moody, Muir and Shaw, 1995: 2). The funding context for Phoenix, therefore, had changed from when they first received support from the Arts Council. The move towards business sponsorship put an extra pressure on companies generally but particularly on contemporary dance, which was viewed as a less attractive proposition than ballet because of its small audiences. By 1989 sponsorship funding was beginning to decrease, and throughout the 1980s 'audiences for contemporary dance continued to decline, whilst those for classical ballet remained stable' (Dunlop, Moody, Muir and Shaw, 1995: 2). It is clear, therefore, that as a contemporary dance company Phoenix was likely to encounter financial difficulties and, as the critic David Dougill pointed out, 'The constant need to money-grab, to chase and please sponsors, [was] suffocating the magic of dance' (1989: PA).

Though discussing a later period, Deborah Baddoo's observations are particularly pertinent to such a climate. She suggested that 'Black dancers need advocates who can translate from their bodies into the language of funders, promoters, marketing personnel and project partners' (2003: 32). The translation, I would argue from the evidence above, was inadequate in relation to Phoenix, so that the strength of their specificity was undermined rather than enhanced. Baddoo's comment underlines the potential mismatch between artists' approaches to their work and those of the supporting agencies, and this is one of the main arguments against business sponsorship. Nevertheless, despite such difficulties there were important developments in dance that provided a positive context for Phoenix's development.

In an overview of dance with considerations for development for the twenty-first century, Jeanette Siddall[8] of the Arts Council of England outlined some of the achievements for dance in the 1980s, which

> saw growth in animateurs and companies, the first Dance Umbrella
> Festival, the birth of Dance UK and the Foundation for Community

---

[8] Jeanette Siddall was dance officer for ACGB in 1989, progressing to be a senior manager in ACE before becoming Director of Dance UK in 2001 and then Director of Dance, ACE in 2003.

Dance, and the establishment of degrees in dance. [In addition], access, education and finding new ways of engaging audiences have been integral to artistic developments. (2001: 3)

In this context, the Arts Council and the dance profession acknowledged the need for a more formal infrastructure. To this end the Arts Council established a number of dance agencies throughout the country, following the report *Stepping Forward* (1989) by Graham Devlin. The aim was to build stronger professional input in regional areas and to enhance local dance activities (Jasper and Siddall, 1999). The report also identified the need to 'develop a nucleus of strong companies with clear identities to work on the middle scale' (Devlin, 1989: 13).[9] Arguably, under Campbell's directorship Phoenix gradually became one of these companies.

International acclaim and a new artistic director: 1987

The Australian tour in 1987 helped to establish the Company's international reputation. They had extended their national touring to some European countries, but Australia was the furthest they had travelled at this point in their history. The Board minutes show that the tour was considered a success. One reporter commented on the fact that they had been dancing together since their early school days, and clearly saw that as a significant factor in their style and choice of choreographic works (Anderson, 1987: PA). The four works they performed on that tour were *Forming of the Phoenix* (1982) and *Primal Impulse*[10] (1985) by David Hamilton, *Running* by Jane Dudley (1985) and *Alpha/Omega*[11] (1987) by Donald Edwards. It is clear from this list that the tour mainly offered the Company's own choreography, and it was this to which the press positively responded.

Pauline Fitzmaurice asked Neville Campbell to rehearse the Company for the important Australian tour, and during rehearsals Hamilton decided to leave. Campbell went on tour with the Company to Australia on 28 December 1986 and continued to work with them throughout January. The tour was initiated because a festival organiser, David Blenkinsop, who had visited the Harrogate Festival where Phoenix performed, had noticed them and booked them eighteen months in

---

[9] The sustained funding by the Regional Arts Boards contributed to the continued growth of several companies and organisations, of which Phoenix was one example (Siddall, 2001).

[10] This is the title from the 1985 programme, although in Holgate's Choreochronicle the work is listed as *Primeval Impulse*.

[11] Not listed in Holgate's Choreochronicle.

7. *Primal Impulse*, 1985. Choreographer and dancer, David Hamilton; photographer Terry Cryer

advance. The Company received good publicity and drew bigger audiences than the internationally famed Trisha Brown; as Fitzmaurice stated, 'No one would have expected that' (1988). The schedule they agreed to, however, was a punishing one, which Jane Nicholas said would not be allowed under British Equity rules (BM, 18 January 1987).

When they performed at the Battersea Arts Centre later that year, they were publicised as a group that had 'come a long way since they were first seen at BAC back in 1982. They're now well known as one of the most innovative and exhilarating contemporary dance groups around' (BAC publicity, July 1987). They offered 'a glorious finale' to Aberdeen's first dance festival in October 1987 in which the writer in the *Evening Press* considered that they 'put on a powerful performance [which] demonstrated just what has made Phoenix one of the country's top contemporary companies' (26 October 1987: PA). These reviews demonstrate the popularity of the Company nationally and the potential for a successful international reputation. The Company, however, was in a period of transition.

The decision was taken to ask Neville Campbell to 'caretake' the Company (BM, 29 March 1987). Although Campbell's background was similar to that of the founders in that he went to Harehills Middle School and Intake High School, he had had more extensive dance experience. The Company received little response to the advertisements for a new artistic director. Only two applications were received, perhaps because dancers, choreographers and directors were unwilling to relocate to Leeds from London, where the main dance activity was based. In a discussion about the poor response to the advertisements, it was suggested that a shortage of funds was also an issue (BM, 18 March 1987).

At the Board meeting that followed the annual general meeting, the difficulty of finding a new artistic director was discussed. The management had considered Campbell as a possible candidate, but they agreed to set up a shortlist of potential candidates. Jude Kelly suggested that a 'big name' as the new artistic director was both desirable and possible: someone who had very high standards and would be able to extend the company.[12] The post-holder would be required to dance in addition to being artistic director. The Board members endorsed the view that the new appointment should be consistent with the Company philosophy as it existed then (BM, 18 March 1987). It is questionable whether in fact this happened, as it is evident from the comments below about conflict between the new director and the Company almost from the outset.

---

[12] One person suggested for the new appointment was Darshan Singh Bhuller, who was eventually appointed as artistic director in November 2002.

The administrator Pauline Fitzmaurice explained that the group of dancers wished to remain all-male and had stated a preference for a black artistic director, although they did not want a political appointment (BM, 18 March 1987). It is interesting to reflect on what was meant by this statement. What did being an all-male company mean to the dancers? In my interviews, the founders spoke of their relationship to each other as that of a brotherhood. This term is deeply connected to their experience of masculinity, and evoked African Caribbean culture and attempts to reinforce their masculinity against attacks, either overt or covert, from the dominant Eurocentric culture. The term describes important social and psychic sustenance and a sense of community. The popularity of the Company was certainly linked to its composition as an all-male company, and that was also part of their identity, which understandably they did not want to lose. As Merville Jones explained, '*We always knew all five of us would be there for each other; we're brothers at the end of the day*' (1997).

What were their reasons for wanting a black artistic director and how were they defining that term? Their request was made at the time of the Black Arts movement when there was some recognition of separatist companies. This is complex in relation to Phoenix, however. On the one hand, they viewed their source as contemporary dance and wished this to be acknowledged. On the other hand, they used reggae and aspects of their heritage as their inspiration and source and were deeply connected to their own community, which inevitably influenced and played a large part in their work. It could be argued that the founders' apparent desire for a black artistic director emerged from an anxiety about the true essence of the Company, and that their disenfranchisement that had begun with the receipt of funding from the Arts Council had continued with the appointment of Neville Campbell. The dancers, however, had also suggested that Campbell (who did not identify as black) might be a possible candidate. Before he became artistic director, moreover, the Company had asked him to make work for them. They went to Darlington and worked at a centre that Campbell had managed to get free of charge, where he choreographed *Boo Bam* (1983) and *Black Sweet Angel* (1983). These were his first choreographies and became part of the Company's early repertoire (Campbell, 2000). Campbell's narrative is a good illustration of the importance of free or low-cost resources to the Company's early development, also mentioned above.

Neville Campbell studied dance at the London Contemporary Dance School, after which he was a dancer with English Dance Theatre and Moves Afoot and then dance artist in residence at Strathclyde. He was artistic director of Phoenix from 1987 until 1991. He then pursued a freelance career as a choreographer and teacher and undertook roles as artistic director of Tumbuka Zimbabwe Dance Company and Scottish Dance Theatre.

Campbell was an ambiguous figure in relation to his ethnicity, as one of his parents was white European and the other was from the African Diaspora. He was asked to apply for the post of artistic director but was reluctant to do so, as he recognised that his appointment might be problematic unless the dancers were enthusiastic, and he wanted one of the founders to take the position. After the interview, however, he was offered the job. Although initially hesitant, he said in retrospect, '*I am glad I took it. I had a great time*' (2000). In an interview with Ramsay Burt in 1989, Campbell said that his work tended to be politically orientated. 'I'm interested in social issues, things I find disturbing or have anxieties about. I generally do pieces inspired by things like news items or a movie I have seen' (in Holgate, 1997: 22).

By September 1987, Campbell was attending Board meetings as artistic director for the Company and Merville Jones had taken a job as a contemporary dance teacher at the Hammond School in Cheshire. As his colleague Gurmit Hukam explained, from the outset 'Neville's vision was [for the Company] to be among the big established companies [but] I don't think he felt he had a free hand because of the legacy he inherited' (1998). The minutes now become much more formal and indicate a change of organisation in the Company.

Neville Campbell had an informal discussion with the dancers in Salisbury in September 1987, which was documented and served as information for the Board. Campbell said that he considered it important to hear the dancers' concerns about working with a new artistic director after six years of working with Hamilton. Campbell had just finished rehearsing two new works for the repertoire and thought it an opportune time for such a discussion. The dancers had obviously discussed some issues amongst themselves earlier and shared ideas about the evolution of Phoenix, their way of working and aspects of the repertoire that evolved from it (CD, September 1987).

Further discussion covered technical training. The dancers had found Campbell's approaches too demanding. They wanted to keep some approaches to working and style from Hamilton's direction and wanted to continue to choreograph their own work. Accessibility to the audience was another issue that they felt strongly about. Phoenix attracted audiences even when a very limited budget for publicity was available. The dancers wanted to retain their appeal for non-theatre audiences in small-scale venues, although they acknowledged that middle-scale venues offered larger floor space, which 'promotes high unrestrained energy' (CD, September 1987: 2). These remarks indicate the beginning of changes of direction for the founders.

Neville Campbell's ambition was to reach audiences in the larger venues, and he developed the Company's technical prowess. Moreover, differences between Hamilton's and Campbell's choreography were identified in an interview with Campbell that Ramsay Burt conducted in 1989. The early work tended to be constructed around the dancers' physical qualities and incorporated their dynamism and vigour, and Hamilton conveyed the 'emotions of the people performing' (Burt, in Holgate, 1997:21). With Campbell's arrival, this style was modified to express political and social issues of contemporary relevance. The change of direction of the Company, and to some extent its ownership, is apparent in this comment from Campbell:

> The boys[13] asked me many questions in relation to the funding body's perspective on Phoenix. What did they want to fund? A resource for Yorkshire and, an exciting small scale touring company, why? This was territory that was unfamiliar for the dancers and yet it was influencing the direction of their work and their experiences as dancers (CD, September 1987: 2).

These questions highlight the complex issues that resulted from the Arts Council's decision to subsidise the Company on the grounds that it fulfilled their funding criteria, partly on the basis of the dancers' ethnicity. The dancers further questioned 'how the Arts Council viewed Phoenix in relation to their Artistic Policy on ethnic minorities'. Seemingly, Phoenix, by not promoting itself as an African Caribbean company, was perhaps missing potential opportunities. Nonetheless, although they did not promote themselves as black, they did feel that they were working towards a black consciousness by performing (CD, September 1987: 2).

Despite dilemmas over the identity of the Company, Nadine Senior thought that Campbell 'raised the company to another level altogether by the stature of the choreographers [he commissioned] and he took it to a level that the original Phoenix didn't want it to go to. It became a more sophisticated company' (1998). Senior alludes to the Company members' desire to retain ownership and direction of their work and of the artistic enterprise which they had created.

---

[13] The use of the term 'boys' is interesting here, as it appears to follow the dance tradition in which male dancers are frequently referred to as boys but also separates Campbell from the dancers in his role as artistic director. It is not clear from his comment whether he sees himself as one of the 'boys', although he danced with them.

8.   *X3*, 1987. Choreographer Neville Campbell; dancers Douglas Thorpe,
     Gary Simpson, Robert Edwards; photographer Terry Cryer

Two reviews written in September 1987 highlight some of the issues for the Company of the transition from Hamilton's directorship to Campbell's. Emma Manning, writing for *The Stage*, says, 'whatever the technical refinement, the Phoenix dancers' pace and daring make them one of the most exciting small dance companies around' (24 September: PA). What made them exciting? I would argue from the discussions I have had with the dancers, artistic directors and some members of audiences from the early 1980s that, as discussed in Chapter 1, it was the dancers' commitment to the expression of their subjectivities and their sense of a shared cultural heritage that they communicated to their audiences. The strength of this commitment transcended technical abilities and training. The dancers were physically skilful, but with Campbell's arrival the dancers' technicality became more central to their work – hence the notes in the Board meeting minutes about the dancers' concerns that the classes were too technical.

Campbell's training informed his vision of contemporary dance and gave him a broader dance context. It was his training, however, that contributed to the differences between himself and the dancers, despite similar backgrounds, in relation to dance in general and the Company specifically. Hamilton's departure meant a diminishing of the connections to specificity through cultural homogeneity and reggae music. A significant aspect of the Company's sense of ownership had already disappeared as a consequence of the Arts Council's directives and requirements. Campbell's arrival furthered the dancers' dispossession. He envisioned a contemporary dance company with a diverse repertoire, which could develop into the middle scale.

The Board meeting held on 30 October 1987 to discuss the devolution of Phoenix Dance Company was attended by the Company administrator and the new artistic director, Neville Campbell. Previously the dancers would have attended and discussed issues for themselves, but now they were represented. The Arts Council were to assess the Company over three years and continued to send representatives to Board meetings when appropriate. It also assessed the Company's performances as part of national dance provision and was involved with senior appointments within Phoenix. This, of course, meant that a good deal of the control of the Company was with the Arts Council.

A history of the Company, included in one of the business plans, is illuminating. Key features highlighted were that it was a national company, performing in small theatres, arts centres and community venues, and touring for at least thirty weeks of the year. Three foreign tours had been undertaken to Italy, Spain and Australia, with aid from the British Council. It had grown from a company of three dancers to six dancers, one technician and two administrators:

> Phoenix's work had a wide appeal, particularly with young people and those whose involvement with dance was slight. Most of the repertory was internally created and varied from high-energy excitement through philosophy to dramatic themes, often with spiritual meaning. Much of the work was naïve, but the effect of watching these dancers who had grown up together and now worked together was quite unique. (BP, 1987)

This document does not have an author's name on it, and although it comes from within Phoenix the patronising tone of the text is similar to that in comments from both the Company's supporters and their critics. Was the term 'naïve' used because the early work did not easily fit into the genre of contemporary dance of the early 1980s? One important factor was that the choreographers were still very young and relatively inexperienced for national exposure. Another factor may have been that by 1987 there were expectations of the Company's repertoire and touring commitments, which lent a different perspective to the early work.

There has been a tension in the Company's history about the Phoenix style. At first this was identified as 'spontaneous' and 'high energy' and there were concerns that something vital would be lost if their technique developed. Campbell suggested that *people undermine and underestimate the company* [...] *always have done*' (in Holgate, 1997: 22). He asserted that he thought the Company would be strengthened with more technique and that this in turn would develop spontaneity. He also said he would like terms such as 'rawness', 'high energy' and 'physicality' not to be applied to the Company (in Holgate, 1997). Clearly, he was challenging the categorisation of Phoenix, which inhibited their development as a contemporary dance company with a diverse repertoire.

As mentioned earlier, an important factor for the Company was its location. Clement Crisp, writing in the *Financial Times*, acknowledged that the recognition of Leeds as a 'significant centre of dance' was an indication of changing 'attitudes and patterns in British life' (14 March 1988). He is, of course, referring to the situation in which London as the cultural capital of Britain is also the centre for dance. There has been much more development in the regions since the 1980s, but London still remains the dominant focus. The Company, however, was acknowledged as an asset to Leeds. For example, *The Observer*'s reporter Michael Coveney described it as 'an extraordinary troupe of black dancers which emerged from the Harehills area in 1981 and is now fully established on the national and international circuit' (1990: 59).

Clement Crisp, however, was not only concerned with the city but was also referring to the educational authorities and the fact that their progressive attitudes encouraged the conditions in which dance flourished and allowed the founders of Phoenix to prosper. He argued that 'Phoenix Dance Company is the proudest result of this system: the company has, during the past six years, shown itself one of the most vivid and exhilarating modern troupes in Britain' (1988: PA). He also suggests that the group is a co-operative drawing on experiences they have in common. But, as indicated earlier, at this point the collective enterprise was already well on the way to being dismantled and formalised into a more hierarchical structure.

On 18 June 1988 the working group for Phoenix met to discuss staff structure. A consultant suggested that the Company approach any changes through appraisal, comparing themselves against the market position and their peer groups. Another suggestion was to institute a less subjective management appraisal. In addition, it was suggested that it would be useful to consider the question 'This is where we are; where do we go from here?' through shared discussion or through the consultant. It was noted that much of the communication within the Company was informal and that, for example, detailed weekly call sheets, with get-in and call times, hotel, class times etc. needed to be instituted. The consultant considered that it was well run when compared with peer-group companies but that some aspects, such as office work usually done on the road, needed reorganisation. Nonetheless, it was also acknowledged that there was a need for all members to feel involved. The finance system was also addressed and the issue of wage differentials, which was controversial, was unresolved at the end of the meeting (CD, 18 June 1988).

It is clear from this document that there was a significant change in the running of the Company in 1988. The operating structures were being considered not only by the members of the organisation but also by a professional consultant. So although it was necessary to have structures in place for the smooth running of the Company and for its accountability to its funders, such changes were another move away from the dancers' involvement with how it functioned. They were placed in the position of executing the selected repertoire for a contentious amount of pay and having less input into the ethos of the Company.

Repertoire

Eleven works are listed in the 1982 repertoire in the Dance Choreochronicle (see Appendix 1) compiled by Dawn Holgate (1997) from the Phoenix archive. Only one of those works, *Reach*, choreographed by Ross McKim, was made by someone outside the Company. That pattern is repeated until 1989. The other external choreographers were:

- Neville Campbell, who choreographed *Black Sweet Angel* (1983) and *Boo Bam* (1983) before he became artistic director in 1987
- Veronica Lewis, *Traffic Variations* (1983)
- Darshan Singh Bhuller (a contemporary of the founders), *Speak Like a Child* (1983)
- Jane Dudley, *Running* (1985)
- David Glass, *Blood Wedding* (1986).

Between 1982 and 1986 the Company choreographed thirty-two works, only seven of which were choreographed by people from outside the Company.

When Neville Campbell became artistic director, he made eight works for the Company between 1987 and 1991. Villmore James choreographed *Leave Him Be* (1988) and Donald Edwards choreographed *Revelations* and *The Path* in the same year. There were also works by eight outside choreographers, though some of them, such as Darshan Singh Bhuller and Philip Taylor, had close connections with the Company. Of the twenty-four works in total, twelve were made from inside the Company.

This overview of the repertoire provides a context to assess the significance of these early choreographies. As the Company developed and changed, the focus on creativity and making work as a significant aspect of the Company's philosophy shifted, and the approach to choreography became much more typical of any repertory dance company. The impact of these changes on the founders is evident in a 1991 interview in *The Voice*, a newspaper specialising in African Caribbean perspectives, with Donald Edwards, who said:

> We've evolved rep which is more mainstream, so we're now exposed to a different type of audience – we've lost the local punters who can't afford to pay the big theatre prices. We've also lost the jazz, reggae and blues element. The programme now is more European contemporary dance based. I used to enjoy the fact that I could express my culture through dance – the philosophy and things that we used to dance

9. *The Path*, 1988. Choreographer Donald Edwards; dancer Villmore James; photographer Terry Cryer

about stabilised me and created some happy moments. I think we need the black element again in the company, we need that balance. (Anon, 1991: PA)

This clearly expresses the sense of disempowerment that the founders experienced as they found that they no longer had control of the Company. Phoenix gained a prestigious Digital Dance Award, which made it possible for Aletta Collins (*Gang of Five*, 1989) and Emilyn Claid to work with the Company. Claid spoke of the process of making *Breakdown in Draylon* (1989) with the Company:

Neville thought it would be really good for them to work with outside people [...] so he brings in two white women to work with them, kind of knowing that was fairly provocative. The process began with massive improvisation and lots of talking and listening to music and some wonderful times with these guys going into their world [...]. They did rebel in the studio. Someone took all his clothes off and put a hat on his dick and improvised, there was snickering going on, but at the same time, I had to laugh. (2000)

This indicates a way of working that was very different from the one in which the group had a shared understanding of an approach to the work. Edward Lynch, however, said that he was

proud of doing that work with Emilyn. We were very professional. Working with Emilyn was brilliant ... [we] knew her through Extemporary [Claid was artistic director of Extemporary Dance Theatre]. *I liked her work. What she did with us was from her perspective, looking into yourself, emotions.* (1997)·

Villmore James described the work as focusing on '*an old person looking back on his life – love affairs, neighbours. We used text in the workshops preparing the work, but it wasn't in the final piece*' (1997).

These comments suggest that the Company rose to the challenge that Claid set them. Nonetheless, there were tensions, which Claid alludes to when she speaks of rebellion in the studio, not only because of the way the dancers were asked to work but also because the choreographer was a white woman and there was therefore a complex interplay of gender and ethnicity in the working process. However, as Gatens points out, 'The crux of the issue of difference as it is understood here is that difference does not have to do with biological "facts" so much as with the manner in which culture marks bodies and creates specific conditions in which they live and recreate themselves' (Gatens, in Barrett and Phillips, 1992: 133). The interaction, therefore, between Claid and the dancers was located in a context of the particularities of their expertise and the elements of their working practice.

Campbell suggested that some of the dancers had sexual and ethnic prejudices against some of the choreographers employed. Nonetheless, the remarks from Claid and Lynch suggest that in many ways it was a productive and successful working process. It was also, however, a difficult phase because of the sense of loss of the Company's identity as dancers. Another area of loss was in their connection to the local community. It is interesting, then, that a report of this period documenting the achievement of the Digital Dance Award states that 'contacts with the community are growing, and we are beginning to identify a role for ourselves in the region' (CD, 22 October 1988). This statement is curious, coming seven years after the foundation of a company whose primary identity was within the community. It appears, therefore, that developments within the Company were problematic.

The above factors contributed to a turbulent year for the Company in 1989. In February, less than a year into Campbell's directorship, an emergency Board meeting was called in response to his resignation. He gave two reasons for his decision. The first was his concern about the dancers' behaviour, which he considered unprofessional. The second was the underfunding of the Company, which resulted in a lack of implementation of his artistic policies. The first point reflects the tension between the dancers' aspirations for the Company that they founded and Campbell's desire to build its profile. In addition, Campbell was an inexperienced artistic director and the dancers found his dictatorial style difficult (Johnson, 1998; Thorpe, 2006). As a result of this meeting, three dancers left, and Stephen Derrick, Rick Holgate and Booker T. Louis joined Phoenix.

Company aims

In 1989 the aims for the Company included expanding, raising its national profile, extending and improving its repertoire, developing the dancers creatively and technically, and reviewing its education and outreach work (Holgate, 1997). The education and outreach policy stated, 'The Company want to encourage the idea of dance being essential to everyone. To advance the contemporary dance field by expressing the importance of physical, intellectual and creative ability and energy' (CD, October 1988). The Company aims, however, were made within a difficult climate in contemporary dance. As David Dougill reported in the *Sunday Times*, four ballet companies took three-quarters of the Arts Council's dance budget and retained buoyant audience numbers. However, mainstream contemporary dance, represented by Rambert and LCDT, had lost a third of their audiences developed during the dance expansion of the 1970s, and they were under pressure to meet education, outreach and touring targets (PA, 1989).

In 1989 Phoenix performed a programme that balanced guest chore-ographies with those by the Company and toured to middle-scale ven-ues for four months of the year. In this transition period, a core of six dancers continued to perform in small-scale venues for six months of the year. Campbell's aim was to increase the profile of the company and 'improve the Phoenix "product"'.

It is clear from the stated artistic aims that the role of the Company was social and political as well as aesthetic. Fundamental to the Company's approach at this time was the concern to

> present non-elitist, high quality contemporary dance to as wide an audience as possible; offer work opportunities to young black dancers; provide opportunities to young people to experience dance through an extensive programme of education/outreach work in the community. (CD, June 1990)

In addition to having these aims, the Company was also committed to maintaining fulltime employment for the dancers, offering opportuni-ties to choreograph within the Company, and choosing choreographers, musicians and designers who would encourage development as well as enrich the repertoire. The Company also aimed to work towards com-pleting one small-scale and one middle-scale tour each year.

There was a recognition that the Company needed to provide the means for members to develop their skills and expertise for their own benefits and for that of the Company. As a middle-scale touring com-pany, Phoenix had two main advantages. Firstly, the Company had a reputation for producing work that was 'accessible' and attracted an audience, which was more diverse than other dance audiences, includ-ing as it did a significant number of people who would not normally attend dance performances. Secondly, few companies were producing work on the small or middle scale at the time (CD, June 1990). However, in a letter to the Chair of the Board of Phoenix, the Assistant Director (Arts) of Yorkshire Arts expressed concern that the Board had agreed an expansion of Company touring from small scale to middle scale without adequate preparation with the funding bodies (21 June 1989). In addition, changes were noted in relation to the appointment of a new executive post of administrative director. This person would be responsible to the Board for the direction of work and overall planning in consultation with the artistic director, who would have overall control of the Company. The ensuing relationship between the Board, the artistic director and the administrative director has been complex in the Company's history.

The 1989 business plan indicates some of the issues and problems that were to beset the Company for the next ten years. The artistic director acknowledged a difference between its artistic vision and the views of the funding bodies and the public. He suggested that a misunderstanding of what it meant for Phoenix to be 'accessible' and 'entertaining' prevented the Company developing into a contemporary dance company of national importance. In order to counter this difficulty, it was suggested that the introduction of nationally and internationally renowned choreographers, together with internal choreography, would challenge preconceived ideas of what was 'suitable repertoire' for the Company. In addition, there was to be more emphasis on performing in traditional theatres, on media work and on increasing the funding and potential sponsors of the Company 'as a major influence in modern contemporary dance' (1989: 2). The previous perceived difficulties of the Company over reliability and professionalism were indicated by an acknowledgement that it was necessary 'to establish and confirm the image of the Company as a fully professional, reliable and efficient unit' (1989: 2).

Another indicator of the changes in the Company at this point was the recognition of a need to extend and develop the repertoire. 'Choreographies included in the repertory three years ago are no longer appropriate to the existing level of ability [...] there is a clear identifiable "Phoenix personality" created by the company's ability to draw from differing dance forms' (1989: 2). Despite the difficult climate, Campbell's artistic direction transformed Phoenix 'from a small-scale company of five to a middle-scale company of ten, performing all the year round' (Brown, 1991: 11).

Phoenix Plus

In an effort to broaden Phoenix's artistic horizons, [Campbell] brought in female dancers and outside choreographers who dealt with non-black issues in their work. His moves freed Phoenix from the narrow scope of its minority origins, turning it into a British contemporary dance company. (Craine, 1991: PA)

Debra Craine thus labels British contemporary dance as a form that does not embrace specificity, and suggests that specificity was a restriction rather than a strength for the Company. This certainly was not the view of the founders, nor indeed of the dancers who joined the Company later.

In April 1989 Chantal (Sharon) Donaldson (now Watson), Dawn Donaldson (now Holgate), Seline Thomas (now Derrick) and Pamela Johnson were invited to join Phoenix for a six-month project called Phoenix Plus (Holgate, 1997). The four women had also attended Harehills Middle School and therefore knew the founders from their shared school experiences. Although the project was a success, there was uncertainty about funding to expand the Company permanently. The administrator Pauline Fitzmaurice said, 'It will be a tragedy if we have to lose the girls.[14] They are not just four females, but four special dancers who fit into Phoenix and enrich the company. They have the right feel and special quality in performance we need for the future' (in Ferguson, 13 December 1989: PA). Fitzmaurice thought that it might be necessary to 'look to private sponsors, but that can limit us, [because] we have to give them what they want instead of doing the things the company should be moving towards' (in Ferguson, 13 December 1989: PA).

The Phoenix Plus project raised issues about gender for the Company and their audience. At this point, it is pertinent to refer to Judith Butler's studies in relation to gender. She argues that 'gender is a matter of repeated performance of cultural norms, not an expression of inherent nature, whether one is a "real" woman or a drag queen' (1990: 32). It was the repeated norms that were evident on stage in 1989 when the four women joined the Company. In addition, it is important to acknowledge in relation to the dancers' subjectivities that 'identifications are multiple and contestatory; that is, they are "incorporations" of negotiations with multiple "vectors of power" that include sex, gender, race, class, sexuality and so on' (1993: 33). So for both dancers and audiences it is the interplay of these elements of power that are present in performance.

Despite the acknowledged benefits of the Phoenix Plus project, however, there were difficulties with the way in which the women were introduced. Edward Lynch thought that after the initial project it would have been better if Phoenix had continued to be a male company, and then perhaps after the third project to have made the different

---

[14] This comment not only follows the tradition in dance of referring to women as girls, but also reinforces Fitzmaurice's position as the dancers' ex-teacher who taught them as pupils at Harehills.

10. Studio Photograph, 1985: Pamela Johnson, Dawn Donaldson (Holgate), Sharon Donaldson (Watson); photographer Terry Cryer

composition of the Company permanent:

> *I say we lost a lot. They had trained, their backgrounds were different, it was more contemporary, been to LCDS or NSCD, nothing cultural, issue-based – classical, abstract dance, physical theatre: that's what they brought as Black British dancers.* (1997)

The sense of disenfranchisement that leaks through this statement by Lynch was a source of tension within the Company and created difficulties as it evolved. This was the final break with the founding Company, whose initial gender composition had been an important factor in the way Phoenix operated and the repertoire it presented. The shift from an all-male company to a male and female company made it less unusual in the sense that this is the familiar composition of a contemporary dance company; all-male companies are rare. Indeed, as Ann Cooper Albright posits, 'the legacy of women-centredness [...] in modern dance was inextricably linked to the marginalization of this body-centred art-form' (1997: xiv).

The significance of incorporating women into the Company in such a context was clearly multi-layered and complex. For instance, one aspect of this layering is the gender conflict and sexism within black communities that Michelle Wallace articulated in her study, *Black Macho and the Myth of the Superwoman* (1970). Although Wallace is discussing conditions in the United States, similar concerns are prevalent in Britain; and as hooks points out, such circumstances have not improved. She suggests:

> While it obviously serves the interests of white supremacy for black women and men to be divided from one another, perpetually in conflict, there is no overall gain for black men and women. Sadly, black people collectively refuse to take seriously issues of gender that would undermine the support for male domination in black communities. (1992: 101)

It is in this context that the tensions between the men and women and Phoenix were played out. Neville Campbell has defended his actions:

> *I thought expansion was the only way forward for this Company [...]. I chose four females that the guys all knew well. And the guys treated the girls in the most appalling way [...] all respect to the girls; they stuck it out.* (2000)

He also said that he had to bring in women who could stand up to the men (the men had threatened to resign if the Company did not stay all-male) (Campbell, 2000). It is significant that the four female dancers who Campbell chose to join the Company had had school experiences similar to those of the Company's founders. An important difference, however, was that they were trained at the LCDS and NSCD, where they not only developed their technical and creative skills but also had the opportunity to engage with critical thinking about the art form. In addition, they had completed a number of professional engagements with different companies before joining Phoenix. For example, Pamela Johnson had danced with DV8; Chantal Donaldson was a dancer with Extemporary Dance Theatre; and Dawn Donaldson danced with Images Dance Company and Extemporary, joining Phoenix in 1989. This, of course, means that their experience of the dance profession, in terms of working with a range of dancers, choreographers and artistic directors and accommodating different working styles and expectations, was wider than that of the founders whom they were joining.

Campbell suggests that the Company had been stagnating before three of the dancers left (Hamilton, James and Jones) and the Company took on new dancers. Pamela Johnson, however, says:

> *It became very easy for certain people in 1989 to turn around and say, well, the Company has gone as far as it could go, which is why it expanded. I remember hearing that quite a lot in 1989 but now I don't know how true that is. The guys don't think that, do they?* (1998)

Johnson's comment illustrates the complexity of interpreting some of the key changes and events in the Company, particularly the contentious employment of women. In addition to the women, three new male dancers joined in 1989: Stephen Derrick, Rick Holgate and Booker T. Louis. At that point, Donald Edwards, Edward Lynch (two of the founders) and Douglas Thorpe were senior members of the Company, so that a more hierarchical structure was established, contrasting with the peer-group structure with which the Company had begun. Campbell thought that the impact made in the early years had lost strength, and the Company was ready for a new direction and development. This viewpoint is confirmed by Donald Edwards, quoted in *The Voice*:

> *The all male Phoenix had its advantages, but after seven years it was time for a change. There's only so much that you can dance to with other men – ideas get stale. The addition of the women has been great. It's brought a new outlook, balance and dimension to the company.* (Anon, 1991: PA)

Because the tour was so successful, the Arts Council funded the Company to make the female dancers permanent members. Phoenix was then a middle-scale company with ten dancers, and was reinventing itself. These changes were evolving in a 1990s context in which there was a move away from the separatist politics that had emerged from the Civil Rights Movement and the Women's Liberation Movement. Moreover, the Company developments raised some other issues. From 1981 until 1999, a significant number of the dancers had a dance background from Harehills Middle School, with some also having gained experience at Intake High School and/or the Northern School of Contemporary Dance. This provided a common link in terms of understanding and mutual background in Leeds, which, despite tensions, provided a sense of community and shared aims and must have contributed to the Company's strengths as well as its difficulties.

The *Sunday Times* critic David Dougill wrote an article entitled, 'The Phoenix flight lacks destination' (13 September 1987). In an interview with Ramsay Burt (1989, in Holgate, 1997),[15] Campbell agreed with the statement in that title and said that the Company was in a state of flux. He said that he had no plans to bring in women at this point; however, the Company received funding for the Phoenix Plus project in the same year. He also said, 'Whether it stays all-black is another question, but that's not an issue, it's not a policy I or the dancers have made' (in Holgate, 1997: 23).

It is pertinent at this point to question Campbell's decision to employ women in 1989. He said that at first everyone, including the Board, was against such expansion, but he thought it to be '*the only way forward* [...]. *I was tired of its single petty-mindedness about its being all-male. I've never been into all-male environments*' (2000). This comment highlights both his frustration about working with the dancers and his own sense of cultural and ethnic ambiguity, which meant that he did not share their sense of brotherhood and did not appear to respect their perceptions of themselves. His difficulties over how to develop the Company before he decided to employ the women, I would suggest, stem from several factors, including his scepticism about all-male groups. His ambition for the Company appeared not to take its specificity into account. Instead, by bringing in technically trained women and well-known choreographers whose work demanded technical expertise, he placed the male dancers in a position where their weaknesses were exposed, rather than working with their strengths. Although the male dancers were

---

[15] This is the date given in Holgate (1997), but the interview may have been earlier. The date for the Dougill review is stated in the interview as 13 September 1988, rather than 13 September 1987 as printed on the copy of the review in Company documents.

able to fuse a range of movement vocabularies, they perhaps had become complacent in relation to their artistic project. Campbell recognised that bringing in technically proficient women would threaten the public admiration and affection for the men, and he implied that the presence of the women would force the men to '*just get on with their jobs and be professional*' (2000). It is clear from Campbell's statement above that his concerns were different from the founders', and this transition must have been a difficult time for the Company.

Phoenix Plus, as the project was called, was appreciated by the critics. John Percival, writing in *The Times*, commented, 'Phoenix Plus is so much better than the old plain Phoenix that it would be criminal not to keep it going' (in Holgate, 1997: 17). Campbell, as well as choreographing for the Company himself and commissioning members of the Company to choreograph, also brought in guest choreographers. Philip Taylor from Netherlands Dance Theatre had studied at Intake High School, but Gary Lambert from Rambert Dance Company and Michael Clark, who had trained at the Royal Ballet School, were obviously from very different backgrounds. So the potential for the style of the Company to diversify still further was introduced at this juncture. According to David Dougill, writing in the *Sunday Times*, this was timely because there had been a danger of the company being stereotyped as a 'high energy' company (22 October 1989: PA). Some of these developments were recorded in a TV documentary, *Phoenix Plus* (1989), directed by Roger Keech and produced by Mike Murray for BBC North East Leeds.

In the autumn season of 1990, critics expressed concern that the repertoire did not match the dancers' technical ability, and this has been a theme that has returned at various points in the Company's history. A point to note here when considering the Company's technique is one that John O. Perpener III makes when discussing Talley Beatty:

The breathless urgency of his dancers' virtuosity becomes a visual metaphor for the consummate technical proficiency of black dancers, as if Beatty were saying through them, 'Yes, we can dance better than anyone else and do it twice as fast'. (2001: 187)

It is arguable that the dancers in Phoenix, under Campbell's direction, were also motivated to prove that they were better than other dancers and that the critics and audiences expected virtuosity and were dissatisfied with works that did not focus on such physicality.

In 1990, Aletta Collins's *Gang of Five*, which she created for Phoenix, won the prestigious Bagnolet Grand Prix de Danse (an international

11. *Gang of Five*, 1989. Choreographer Aletta Collins; dancers Gary Simpson, Edward Lynch, Donald Edwards, Douglas Thorpe, Robert Edwards; photographer Terry Cryer

choreographic competition) and the Bonnie Bird Prize for New Choreography. This work was created in 1989 and Campbell described it as 'about a group of men, how they behave towards each other, the one-upmanship as they struggle to out-do each other'. Balford Henry, who interviewed Campbell while the Company was on tour in Jamaica, suggested that this work offered a familiar and local angle. While the Company were on the island, they gave master classes at the Jamaica School of Dance (17 March 1991).

The critics acknowledged the Company's development. Ann Nugent, writing in *The Stage*, said, 'Director Neville Campbell has achieved the transformation remarkably, finding dancers and three choreographers who complement each other to such an extent that the results may perhaps constitute the beginning of a challenge to the London Contemporary Dance Theatre' (18 October 1990: PA). Allen Robertson in the *Daily Mail* said, 'thanks to the vision of artistic director Neville Campbell, Phoenix [...] can hold their own next to any other dance company in this country' (12 October 1990: PA).

In 1991 the Company repertoire was well received. For example, David Henshaw said of the season at Sadler's Wells, London, that the Company invited comparison with LCDT; there was a wide range of 'interpersonal dynamics. Lingering moments, gentleness and sensitivity are developed, and not only in the male/female interactions' (Henshaw, 1991: 44). It is notable that the company with which Phoenix is compared is the one that set the standard to which they aspired. The dancer Melanie Teall (who joined Phoenix in 1995) saw the Company when she was at college in 1991. '*I couldn't believe the audience were reacting the way they were. I hadn't been to a dance performance where people stood up and cheered*' (1998). She was inspired by their performances and decided she would like to work with Phoenix.

Reviewing the Company, Stacey Prickett commented:

Michael Clark's *Rights* showed off the company admirably [...]. The flesh-revealing stylised leotards maximised the physicality of the dancers [...]. Precarious balances, expansive body lines, and intricate footwork were interwoven with manipulative duets and trios [...]. Clark's deconstruction of classicism displays the body as both sensual and explosive. Meanwhile [the] text presented a political commentary drawing on associations outside the dance. (1991: 36)

Prickett does not question the representation of the dancers in pink, satin, skimpy costumes, but from my perspective such a choice of costume appears to epitomise the lack of reflection on the dancers' subjectivities. As Rick Holgate said, '*I felt really uncomfortable wearing the costume* [...] *leotard which was pink and beige, cut up the crutch, everything hanging out*' (1998). Chantal Donaldson suggested that she had gained from the process of working with Clark and thought it '*a wonderful process*'. However, Clark's drug addiction affected the outcome, which she considered was a compromise (1998). So although the working process was one in which the dancers developed their dance expertise, the work as a whole raised issues that, unfortunately, can only be indicated here.

In addition to commissioning choreographers from outside the Company, Neville Campbell also commissioned Pamela Johnson's first choreography, *Subject of the City* (1991). 'The performers use each other's bodies like building blocks to create pictures, dissolving and reforming in an almost gymnastic clarity' (Robertson, 1991: PA). Ann Nugent's sense of the Company working together at this time was that they were 'united in their sensual plasticity, musical awareness and versatility' (Nugent, 1991: PA). The rehearsal director, Heather Walker, confirmed this unity, commenting, 'When they got on stage they worked as one; it was remarkable' (1998). The connections that the Company presented on stage came from the depth of understanding that they had with each other. As Rick Holgate articulated, '*As individuals we got on really well with each other. The rapport on stage felt so good; you could trust everybody physically, movement-wise, and there was enjoyment in the Company. It was superb, absolutely superb*' (1998).

For some reviewers, the Company's development led to an acknowledgement that 'Phoenix has made a refreshing contribution to British modern dance' (Anon, 1991: PA). For others it had 'lost the raw dynamic spirit of its early days and replaced it with a smoothly accomplished sophistication. They are all beautiful dancers but there is some loss of character of identity in this transition' (Thorpe, 1991: PA). This is a theme that haunted the Company in reviews over the next ten years.

There were mixed reports of the dancers' experiences of working with Campbell to achieve the high-quality repertoire. Sharon (Chantal) Donaldson said, '*You knew where you were with him. [Also] he was a great teacher*' (1998). She also said, however, that when she started asking questions in order to become more informed about the Company, her relationship with Campbell deteriorated; and that he was unable to realise his artistic ambitions because of financial restrictions. She suggested that as '*the Company grew stronger as a unit, he felt threatened and isolated*' (1998). Pamela Johnson thought that '*he broadened the scope of the Company* [but that] *he was very dictatorial and too close to the guys that he knew*' (1998). This latter point, she suggested, created difficulties in

12. *Subject of the City*, 1991. Choreographer Pamela Johnson; dancers
Dawn Donaldson, Booker T. Louis, Seline Thomas (Derrick), Stephen Derrick;
photographer Andy Snaith

his role as artistic director; and she thought that if Lynch and Edwards had not continued to dance in the Company, perhaps it would have been considered a new Company (1998).

Johnson raises an important point here, because the early Phoenix that Donald Edwards, David Hamilton, Villmore James, Merville Jones and Edward Lynch established was a dancers' company. Although David Hamilton was acknowledged as artistic director, the dancers developed the Company according to their artistic visions. When Neville Campbell directed the Company, this was not the case, even though he was also one of the dancers. In an interview with Debra Craine he suggested that the dancers were unprepared for the Company's change of scale. He said, '*I didn't feel the dancers were ready for it* [...] *I don't think they coped very well. I was unhappy in the job because of the unwillingness of the dancers to go further, and I couldn't work with dancers who wanted to dictate policy*' (9 October 1991: PA). Campbell's comment encapsulates a key tension for the Company relating to the dancers' perceptions of their roles, which contrasted with the expectations of the artistic director and the management. In effect Phoenix did become a different Company but, because the name did not change and many of the dancers had education and training experiences in common, this was not acknowledged.

One of the factors creating tensions between the men and the women in the Company, in addition to the founders' sense of loss, was the fact that Campbell

set up competition between the two sexes and he put the women on a pedestal'. He said, 'This is what you're trying to get to, fellas' [...] it led to mistrust [...] people began to rebel against what he was trying to do. He had some great visions, but the way in which he went about them wasn't great. (Dawn Donaldson, 1998)

Chantal Donaldson also mentioned the rivalry that her sister describes (1998). Campbell's divisive tactics had repercussions that continued to reverberate throughout the Company in the following years and are discussed in the next chapter.

Heather Walker thought that 'the women were very strong, very intelligent, and quite formidable; you had to admire their professionalism and their abilities. They were a stunning group' (1998). The four women were widely acknowledged, both within the Company and by critics, as proficient dancers. However, Walker's observation offers insight into the complexities of their roles and tasks within the Company. They had to contend with male colleagues who remembered them as schoolchildren. As Pamela Johnson elaborated, '*The humour picked up exactly where it left off. The sexual innuendoes, childish humour, I responded. If I could go back and change anything in my life right now, I wouldn't have responded*' (1997). In addition, the expectations of the women were extremely high. I would suggest that they had to be strong, be formidable and develop their professionalism in order to achieve success despite the confrontational situation they met in the Company.

Issues of training

As mentioned above, a key difference between the men who founded the Company and the women who joined Phoenix in 1989 is that the women had undergone formal dance training. The dancers might have adopted or internalised various attitudes and expectations as a result of their training. In 1993, Dance UK organised a conference entitled *Tomorrow's Dancers: Training Tomorrow's Professional Dancers.* The papers indicate concerns about dance training in Britain in the 1980s and early 1990s. Some of these issues are elaborated in a paper by Tony Geeves, 'The difference between training and taming the dancer'. Geeves argued that there was a need to 'remodel' approaches to teaching and to reconsider body metaphors such as the 'body as instrument' and 'body as machine', which dehumanised the dancer (1993: 11). He also suggested that teachers should not teach by terror but consider the psychological as well as physiological needs of their students. He asked, 'Are we training our students to understand and develop their own technique or are we taming them so that they are conditioned to respond to a recognised stimulus?' (1993: 13). That Geeves asked such a question, and that the conference was organised at all, would seem to imply unease within the profession about some of the training practices. So although the women had undoubtedly benefited from their training, they are also likely to have internalised some of the narrow approaches prevalent in the dominant forms of dance training of the time. As the dancer and choreographer Nigel Charnock commented, 'what happens during the training is that somehow the reason that you wanted to dance gets trained out of you' (1994: 14).

For the men who founded Phoenix this was not their experience, as they had not been exposed in the same way as the women to such concepts of the body, and perhaps had greater artistic freedom as a result. Thus the men's lack of exposure to the prevalent dance training systems both was a significant strength and arguably became a weakness. In addition, apart from Hamilton's year in London, the men had remained located in the city of their childhood. In the long term, the men's limited search for a range of artistic inputs may have restricted them and they perhaps became a parody of the critical constructions to which they were vulnerable. So their appeal and success emerged because of their 'rawness' and 'energy', for which one could read 'naturalness' – part of the defining trope that 'black people innately have rhythm'. This is clearly a complex topic with many layers, and can only be mentioned here.

The employment of the women in Phoenix created tensions both professional and cultural. One of the issues of the wider context for the women of Phoenix, as bell hooks explains, is that the:

> White female body always appears to be a signifier of 'natural' beauty. The Black woman, on the other hand, is treated as this figure whose beauty is somehow constructed, artificial, devoid of inherent beauty. This is still a major issue for Black women in terms of the development of our sexual identities. (In hooks and West, 1991: 117)

This context is a significant one for the women dancers in Phoenix. So much of the focus for dancers, particularly women dancers, is on their looks as well as their skills. For black women, therefore, 'the burden of representation' (Mercer, 1994) is potent. One of the difficulties that Phoenix encountered is identified by Judith Williamson: black artists, because they have been marginalised, are frequently in a position of being 'representative' and speaking 'for the black community' (in Mercer, 1994). Kobena Mercer termed this situation the 'burden of representation'. The specificity of the artists is eroded under such a burden, but it is this expectation to be representative that emerges in critics' writings about Phoenix and is evident in such labels as 'the black dance group'. But paradoxically the founders had embraced that role and appreciated the acknowledgement of their success within their immediate black community.[16] The specificity of Phoenix's art practice is lost when such labels are applied to it, as the work of the Company is only viewed through the lens that this label offers, rather than the diversity of Phoenix's dance practice being acknowledged. For the women of Phoenix this 'burden' had implications in relation to sexism as well as racism. The four women who joined Phoenix, however, were extremely successful in establishing their expertise in the dance world as members of the Company, in interpreting other choreographers' works and, for Chantal Donaldson and Pamela Johnson, in creating their own choreography. They succeeded despite the fact that, as black women engaged

---

[16] Personal communication with choreographer Beth Cassani, who was at school with some of the founders and who also teaches Company class for Phoenix (2006).

with an art form in which the body is central, they were susceptible to misrepresentations and misreadings in relation to issues of female presence and its associations with sexuality. Through making their own work, such artists have opportunities to undermine such limitations to their subjectivities and present themselves in powerful realignments, which I would suggest the women of Phoenix worked towards.

The employment of four women with an educational background similar to that of the founders but who had also received a formal dance training was paradoxically both divisive and yet a significant development for the Company's future. The dilemmas that this change engendered are located in the complexities of racism and sexism, which have been ongoing concerns for the Company. The next chapter will consider some of these complexities.

Chapter 4: Diving into the Fire: Shifting Identities

This chapter focuses on the development of the Company from 1991 to 1996. It considers in detail events during 1992–93 when major conflicts, paradoxically predicated on the Company's strengths, were played out in various ways. I argue that this period included significant transitions that highlighted issues of gender and ethnicity. In order to analyse these transitions and conflicts in relation to the dancers' perceptions of themselves and the dominant modes of dance management, I examine Company documents that include Board minutes, reports and other papers.

By 1991 some of those documents were describing the Company as a middle-scale company operating for fifty-two weeks of the year. The Company comprised a new artistic director – Margaret Morris – an administrative and technical team and ten dancers.[1] Most of the dancers had similar cultural backgrounds and training, which had an impact on their engagement with dance and their expectations of the Company. Margaret Morris and the dancer Clare Connor had neither the dancers' cultural nor educational background. The loss of the shared sense of specificity in terms of heritage and history, which had been fundamental to the Company's original identity, was a profound change for Phoenix. Indeed, the appointment of Margaret Morris exacerbated the complex tensions around gender and ethnicity with which the Company were already engaged.

A sense of loss: The Company's changing identity

The appointment of four women dancers in 1989, and Margaret Morris's appointment as artistic director two years later in 1991,[2] had significant implications for the Company's identity in the early 1990s. As discussed in Chapter 1, a significant aspect of this identity was the fact that for eight years it had been an all-male Company. The dancers

---

[1] The 1992–93 tour listed the dancers as Stephen Derrick, Booker T. Louis, Chantal Donaldson, Dawn Donaldson, Pamela L. Johnson, Ricardo Goodison, Seline Thomas, Ricky Holgate, Clare Connor and Martin Hylton. Only three of these dancers (Connor, Derrick and Holgate) did not attend Harehills Middle School; but Stephen Derrick studied at the Northern School of Contemporary Dance and so shared a Leeds background with the other dancers. Five of the dancers studied at this institution (Derrick, Goodison, Hylton, Johnson and Louis; the last two dancers listed also studied at LCDS). Ricky Holgate and Clare Connor both came from the South of England and both studied at the London School of Contemporary Dance, as did four other dancers (C. Donaldson and D. Donaldson, Johnson and Louis).

[2] Morris was appointed as artistic director on 30 September 1991 (Stevens, Company Press Release) and began her position in January 1992 (Funding Application YHA, 1992–93, 1).

also shared a specific cultural and geographical background. Although new opportunities emerged from the appointment of women, there was also a significant loss, which reverberated throughout the Company for many years after the early personnel changes. The four women dancers were from Harehills Middle School, and Dawn Donaldson had also been a student at Intake High School. Margaret Morris's very different background could, however, be said to have introduced unforeseen circumstances for the Company.

In 1992 the Company submitted a business plan to its funders, Yorkshire and Humberside Arts (YHA), which included a SWOT (Strengths, Weaknesses, Opportunities, Threats) analysis. This document provided a snapshot from the point of view of their client. Key internal strengths of the Company were considered to be certain aspects of its identity that were defined and recorded in the 1992 business plan (BP, 1992: 15) as:

- Unique history of the company
- Predominantly black and Leeds-based with continuing commitment to its roots
- The image of the company: accessible, street-cred, attractive to young audiences in particular
- Role as ambassador for contemporary dance developing new audiences
- Dancers do education and outreach work.

These five points were fundamental to the dancers' perceptions of themselves as practitioners of dance throughout the 1980s to this point in 1992. These were also the strengths that the Arts Council noted in *The Glory of the Garden* (1984). The Company's popularity with audiences continued to grow, but their specificity was also, paradoxically, the site of perpetual struggles with modes of management that seemed to acknowledge diversity. This apparent acknowledgement was undermined by a lack of understanding from the Arts Council, and sometimes from the Company Board, of the implications of encouraging a group that did not fit the norm for a dance company. These institutions, which the dancers had to navigate, lacked insight into their own practices. Instead, the Company, particularly the founding dancers, became disenfranchised as a client of the Arts Council. In order for the Arts Council to account for the public money for which it is responsible, there are procedures to follow, which are based on a normative model. This model, of course, was not appropriate for Phoenix because it was not a 'typical' dance company – hence the ongoing discord once they were awarded funding.

In addition to the list of the Company's specific strengths, some external opportunities were highlighted in the SWOT analysis. These included the fact that the Northern School of Contemporary Dance was based in Leeds and that there was a need for cultural ambassadors for Leeds and the North (BP, 1992). These opportunities were important for the dancers not least because of their connections both with NSCD and Leeds. The analysis also identified some external threats, including economic recession and the 'perception of middle scale venues as white, middle class and non-street cred' (BP, 1992: 16).

It was noted that Phoenix's presence in some of these middle-scale venues was 'eroding the company's image' (BP, 1992: 16). These remarks indicate the wider role that Phoenix played at both local and national levels. They also illustrate the difficulties of success for the Company. Performing in larger venues, while allowing them to expand both their repertoire and their audiences, raised concerns that they were losing their community and local connections and some of the strengths through which they had initially gained their success. The comment also raises the wider issue of companies locating appropriate venues and vice versa. This was acknowledged to be an area that needed to be addressed industry-wide in an action plan that emerged from a seminar held at the Institute of Contemporary Arts on 26 February 1996, attended by marketers, programmers, administrators, animateurs and artistic directors (including Margaret Morris) from companies (Marchant, 1996).

Notwithstanding the difficulties the Company faced, its artistic objectives in 1992 included the establishment of yearly choreographic experimental workshops for Company members. Performances of the outcomes of some of these workshops were held at the theatre at NSCD and sometimes included students from the NSCD itself[3] (BP, 1992: 18). This was one example of the Company's attempts to keep some local connections in Chapeltown, where NSCD was located. It was difficult, however, for the Company to develop these connections at the same time as undertaking its heavy touring schedule.

Phoenix Dance Company was no longer run by the dancers but directed by the management and the Board. The 1992 business plan (BP, 1992: 21) noted that 'Clarification of the role and responsibility of the Board of Directors and its sub-committees' was necessary. This implies an understandable tension between the Board and the dancers; the Board had to ensure that the funders' requirements were adhered to, and these requirements threatened the dancers' sense of place within the Company. For example, one of the dancers was asked to leave the

---

[3] I saw some of these works from 1993–99 while I was a staff member at NSCD.

Board meeting on 24 September 1992 because there was a lack of clarity about staff attendance at Board meetings. This was clarified at a further meeting, when it was agreed that dancers were able to attend as observers. In addition, one of the dancers attended as the Equity representative.

The moment of the dancer's ejection from a Board Meeting encapsulates the disenfranchisement that the dancers experienced. The very structures put in place for the advancement of the Company were not necessarily in the dancers' interests. A meeting held on 2 March 1992, attended by the YHA advisers, the Company management and the YHA dance and mime officer, focused on the Company's artistic policy. Under a heading of cultural identity, it was noted that the key issues were perceived to be cultural. This was explained as meaning that Phoenix 'is primarily a black company but it is a Contemporary Dance Company' (CD, 2 March 1992: 1). This statement highlights a key tension within the Company's identity. There was deep ambivalence throughout the Company's history about its relationship to blackness, not least because of the potential trap such a relationship held in a post-colonial context.

These notes also illustrate some of the changes that continued to take place within the organisation of the Company. Morris explained at the meeting on 2 March that a policy statement was being written and ideas and feedback were being sought from the dancers. The notes from this meeting imply that this may have been the first occasion on which dancers had been involved in feedback. For the founders, however, such involvement would have been integral to the operation of Phoenix. These notes also show how far the Company had moved from its early beginnings. Morris had to strategise in order to counter the dancers' sense of disempowerment and to find ways of involving them in developments. This is in stark contrast to the early evolution of the Company when the dancers' creativity and decisions drove its direction.

There were other changes that caused unease within the Company. The introduction of two white employees, Margaret Morris as artistic director and Clare Connor as a dancer, led to questioning by the dancers of their status and identity as a Company. In a discussion about funding at the meeting on 2 March 1992, it was noted that, as the Company was no longer exclusively black, the dancers were concerned and confused about the reasons for receiving funding. The notes suggest that there was an attempt to reassure them, and the reasons for funding were given as being related to artistic standards, sound management and development. The Company at this time was acknowledged to be a good one, with accessible programming and tremendous potential.

The uneasiness about the transition the organisation was undergoing is evident from the notes of the discussion, which record that the

Company had no role models: in fact they had become the role models. The artistic director suggested that the dancers were yet to become fully rounded artists. She said that they were being nurtured and were gradually becoming familiar with the new directions (2 March 1992). This last point illustrates aspects of the transition from a small-scale to a middle-scale company. The latter demanded more from the dancers, and Margaret Morris was appointed to lead the Company in meeting these demands. Not only was there negotiation concerned with being part of an institution with growing prestige, but also 'It was felt that the Company like other Black British artists were finally moving towards a non-denial of the Black British experience' (2 March 1992: 2).

This conclusion was reached by the eight participants in the meeting: one man and seven women, all of whom were white. Although their perception may have been accurate, it also, in hindsight, sounds patronising. It seems that during Morris's directorship there was overt acknowledgement of what was recorded in these notes as the 'Black British experience'. Undoubtedly, this was partly because of the pressure she was under, from funders, critics and audiences, to justify her position as a white director who was also female, and whose professional dance experience was primarily in America. She was the exact opposite of what the Company was famous for – that is, being black and male – which created identity problems that she had to unravel and try to solve.

In many ways it seems that, although Phoenix had established itself as an internationally recognised Company, it was haunted by the sense of loss of important aspects of its emergence . As mentioned in the previous chapter, the dancers experienced this loss in the choice of repertoire and in the organisation of the Company, which was answerable to the Board. At the Board meeting on 27 July 1991, the role of the Board was questioned. This was an ongoing problem for the Company, both in establishing how the Board should function in order to facilitate Phoenix to its full potential and also in arriving at an appropriate composition of members on the Board.

A brief review of the Company, reflecting on the 1991–92 period for the 1992 business plan, described Phoenix as being true to its name. The mythical bird had survived the fire, and so too had the Company. There had been significant changes in staff, including new support staff. There had been no artistic director from May 1991 to January 1992, and the first white dancer had been hired (the description as stated in the review, p. 4).[4] There was also a redundancy because of financial pressures. The year had clearly been a stressful one, and it was noted

---

[4] Clare Connor was appointed in June 1991 when Gurmit Hukam was acting artistic director. There had been a white apprentice before this appointment.

that it was only because of everyone's dedication that it had been a success.

The minutes of the 24 September 1992 meeting indicate that some of the issues with which the Company was dealing in a context of British contemporary dance were ones with which other companies were also struggling. The issues included the need to receive adequate funding, finding sponsorship, the demands of touring, and constant pressure on staff to achieve almost impossible goals. In addition to the above, Phoenix was frequently associated in people's minds with its early character, and funders, sponsors and audiences continued to desire something of the success of the early 1980s as the Company developed. Margaret Morris was placed in a difficult position and asked the Board to clarify their agreement with her artistic policy. She had been appointed because she had experience of middle-scale and large-scale touring, not because she understood black culture. She stressed the importance of agreement about the Company before deciding how or if it should move on. She also pointed out that consensus within the Board was important. The tension thus expressed obviously raises questions about the suitability of Morris's appointment, discussed below. It also highlights the problems that she had to solve and the complexity of her task.

This was a time to review and reflect on the Company's achievements and future direction. The business plan (30 October 1992) identified policy tensions eleven years on from the creation of the Company. It pointed out that there were conflicting expectations from stakeholders, who included staff, the Board of directors, funding bodies, audiences, venue managers, the professional dance community, community and education dance workers and agents, and the local Leeds community. They all had views about what the Company should or did achieve. These policy tensions were noted (1992: 3) as:

- Autocratic vs. democratic management
- Black vs. multicultural company
- Mainstream vs. linked to the community
- Small scale vs. middle scale
- National vs. international.

It is clear that these tensions had arisen partly because of the expectations of the Company as a funded institution. The Company attempted to keep connections with the small-scale community and national roots. At the same time, funders expected it to develop and tour in the middle-scale, mainstream and international arenas. The issues of management and identity of the Company in relation to ethnicity were complex and ongoing.

The Company brought in outside management consultants, Robin Hoyle and Tessa Gordjiecko (of Novus Training Ltd, which was funded by a grant from the West Yorkshire Management Development Scheme), to provide a framework for discussing and resolving the issues noted above within the financial year. Some of the difficulties, it was acknowledged, had come about because the expansion of Phoenix had evolved sometimes without clear policy decisions (BP, 1992).

The mission statement in 1992 was as follows:

> Phoenix Dance Company aims to share the spirit of dance across the divisions of a multicultural society. To perform vital, exciting and relevant contemporary dance. Staying true to its roots and to the name Phoenix, it will be unafraid of renewal, rejuvenation and change. (BP, 1992: 1)

In the context of what has been written above, this appears to be an attempt to minimise the internal tensions. Nonetheless, there were divisions within the Company as well as in the diverse society of which it was a part. The notion of staying true to its roots and having gone through the fire is one that is emotionally charged. It is also theoretically problematic, because it alludes to the ghost of essentialism and authenticity that has continued to haunt the Company. Stuart Hall offers a model of production of identities, which 'denies the existence of authentic and originary identities based on a universally shared origin or experience. Identities are always relational and incomplete in process' (Hall and du Gay, 1996: 89).

A lack of acknowledgement of this process by funders, critics and audiences meant that the Company's aspirations to fearless change were tempered with the actuality, which was often painful. The early 1990s were another period of dispossession and identity crisis for the Company.

The ghost of essentialism and authenticity hovers around the name, the myth and the founders. On the front page of the business plan (1992), Hamilton says:

> It's there in the name, Phoenix. The bird diving into the fire. The fire is the actual learning process. That's when you burn and when you're most alive. Every time you go on tour is like in the fire, every time you are on the stage you are in the fire, when you choreograph you're in the fire. The spaces in between are life. The fire itself is those particular points along the way when you learn. (1992)

The Company began with the vision, ideals, spirit and passion that shine through in Hamilton's comments. But by 1992 the Company was an institutional structure, driven as much by funders' criteria, venue and audience requirements and the hierarchy of the management system as by artistic desires and vision. It was noted that, because the Company was already overstretched in terms of personnel, its only option for the future was to limit its activity (BP, 1992).

Despite the positive tone of the 1992 business plan, there had been financial difficulties. In July 1990, almost a year after the Phoenix Plus project when women first joined the Company, there was a financial crisis because the funding offered by the Arts Council was not sufficient to sustain the middle-scale Company. The Board endorsed all the plans for development submitted by Neville Campbell, the former artistic director, up to this point and, therefore, sought further funding, which it seemed would be forthcoming. In May, however, all bids from all departments of the Arts Council were frozen until September. Acknowledging the serious implications of this for Phoenix, the Arts Council and Yorkshire Arts Association attempted to secure funding from the Arts Council's contingency funds. It was deemed necessary to consider alternative plans in the event of failure to secure such funds. At this point, it seemed that without the extra funds the Company would have no alternative but to cease trading. A publicity campaign was planned, but in the interim the Company was assured by the Arts Council of Great Britain and Yorkshire Arts Association that funds would be forthcoming and the contingency plan was, therefore, unnecessary (BM, 1 July 1990).

The Company then struggled with a deficit of £25,000, which had arisen mainly because of redundancy payments to the previous administration. This was referred to as 'the execution of management restructuring as requested by the funding bodies' (FA, 1992–93: 1). As a result, the Company was without administrative support for four months, which was obviously a strain for all the staff. Although Phoenix was established at the time of Margaret Morris's appointment, it is evident from the outline above that there were a number of tensions and difficulties which she inherited.

Artistic direction: The appointment of Margaret Morris

Several major changes occurred in 1991 and 1992. The most significant was the appointment of Margaret Morris, a white woman, as artistic director. As well as joining what had until 1989 been an all-male company, she shared neither locality nor cultural experience with the dancers, whose artistic identity had been, up to this point, tightly bound up with the shared understanding derived from their background.

Margaret Morris was born in Wales, spent most of her professional dancing career in New York, and toured internationally as a soloist with the Murray Louis Dance Company from 1982 to 1989. She had been on the faculty of the Nikolais Dance Lab in New York and at the Laban Centre in London, and had taught and choreographed throughout the USA, Canada and Europe (programme, *Catch the Spirit Tour '92–95*).

The 1992 business plan noted that Morris had 'toured internationally as a dancer, choreographer and teacher [and had] just returned from New York to her native Britain' (2). This comment indicates that the funders and the Board were keen to develop the Company both nationally and internationally, and therefore sought to appoint someone with a background that would make that possible. The attributes of the Company that had initially been highlighted for support in *The Glory of the Garden* (1984) – that they were black and based in the regions – no longer seemed to be a significant consideration for the funders or for the Board.

In an interview (June 1996), Margaret Morris told me that she had been naïve when she first took the job. In an interview with Ismene Brown, she said, 'I was very naïve as to how people perceive blackness' (1995). She had not considered the issues in relation to racism that might be involved. Within a year of arriving in the post, Morris set up a retreat for the Company, where the resentment amongst the dancers became clear. In discussions during the retreat, it was apparent that for the dancers two key factors were important: that they brought their British–African–Caribbean experience to the stage, and that the Chapeltown experience of a close-knit community and cultural homogeneity in terms of school backgrounds provided an important perspective to their work. Margaret Morris, however, suggested at this time that the dancer David Hughes, who was white, would have fitted in well with the Company because of the shared school experiences. A dancer with the Company, Martin Hylton, confirmed this view when he said, '*no-one would dare say he couldn't dance with Phoenix because he was white*' (1999). This statement makes it clear that interpretations of the Company solely in relation to ethnicity are inadequate and that any analysis of Phoenix Dance Company should consider the impact of the community location out of which the dancers emerged.

Another white dancer and choreographer (also a pupil at Intake High School) who worked well with the Company was Philip Taylor. He choreographed two successful works for them: *Haunted Passages* (1989, revived 1995) and *Sacred Space* (1991). The dancer Rick Holgate said, *'he brings out the qualities in Phoenix dancers that critics like to see* [and] *which show the diversity in the dancers'* (1998). Another dancer, Booker T. Louis, reinforced Holgate's viewpoint, stating that although the Company had a reputation for being *'stylish, energetic, exuberant, his choreography is a contrast to those terms and it is good for people to see the other side of the coin, that we do have a lyrical, subtle side'* (1998). These observations reinforce Morris's statement and indicate some of the complexity of issues of identity for the Company. I suggest that, in addition to considerations of ethnicity, gender is also an important factor that aids understanding and insight into the Company.

The transition created by the employment of women was difficult for the Company. The men who founded it felt the loss of the project which they had set up and which focused on their shared interests and bonds, developed through an all-male group. Although they could see benefits from the new appointments, the change was a management decision taken by the artistic director and the Board rather than by the dancers, who previously had made such decisions. There was also a challenging transition for Phoenix caused by employing people who did not share the Harehills and Chapeltown background. Morris, however, was concerned that the Company could become quite isolated and inward-looking if it employed people only from that specific community. She suggested that there was a 'need to have different points of view artistically' (1996).

Morris thought that the Company was overcome by its success and could not keep up with what was required of it. She also thought that Phoenix fitted conveniently into those Arts Council policies that were concerned with devolving work to the regions, developing initiatives for men in dance and increasing the potential for black dancers (1996: 2; ACGB, 1984). As a result of these kinds of cultural policies, she suggested that, instead of letting the Company evolve in its own time, ACGB should accelerate the pace. The dancers were then in a position of having to fight for the right to perform contemporary dance. From discussions with the dancers, Morris believed that they perceived that their experiences in a racist society had become part of their dancing (1996).

It was a complex task for Morris to both support and nurture the dancers' development when her understanding was limited by her own cultural background. The dancers' experiences of racism and their understanding of their performances from this perspective was not something that she shared. In addition, when she was speaking on behalf of the Company, she was frequently perceived to be 'the wrong colour' (1996). Yet in her role as artistic director she had to find a way of both leading and representing the dancers in public forums. Her position was a difficult one not least because some of the dancers wanted an all-black Company; and although the Black Arts Movement of the 1980s no longer had the same impact, there were legacies of those philosophies that leaked into expectations of the Company. Morris was attempting to lead a contemporary dance company without ignoring the political tensions of their perceived identity as a 'black company'. Her view was that she could fight racism from her position as a white woman.

Many theorists have stressed that whiteness has been an unmarked category (Dyer, 1997; Frankenberg, 1993; Phelan, 1993). As white people, Dyer explains, we 'see ourselves and believe ourselves seen as unmarked, unspecific, universal' (1997: 45). Indeed, as Dyer demonstrates and as is clear in *Being White* (1987), a video made on the same topic, as soon as the category of whiteness is interrogated it tends to disappear into other categories of, for example, class or religion. In her study *The Social Construction of Whiteness* (1993), Ruth Frankenberg argues that whiteness is a 'neutral category whereas other cultures are specifically marked "cultural"' (197). She also argues that there is content to whiteness to the extent that it 'generates norms, ways of understanding history, ways of thinking about self and other, and even ways of thinking about the notion of culture itself. Thus whiteness needs to be examined and historicized' (Frankenberg, 1993: 231).

This view has gradually been acknowledged in recent studies, including those of Richard Dyer and the collected writings in *White? Women* (1999). Dyer argues that 'white as a symbol, especially when paired with black, seems more stable than white as a hue or skin colour' (1997: 60). There are, however, a number of paradoxes connected with whiteness. Although it is evident that we all possess 'raced identities' (Brown, Gilkes and Kalowski-Naylor, 1999: 5), it can be difficult to address the issues associated with being white without being confined by guilt or admiring 'the other' and thoughtlessly expecting those disempowered by the use of white power to find solutions.

It was paradoxically under Morris's directorship that the Company was defined within the policy documents as a contemporary dance company that was 'black'. She, however, stated, '*you cannot put a colour to art*' (1996). In an attempt to deal with the very complex area of categorisation and binary oppositions of black and white, Morris tried to transcend the limitations of such a position. In this attempt she also sought reference points from America with which she was familiar. She referred to Alvin Ailey, a well-known African American choreographer and the artistic director of the Alvin Ailey Dance Company, who refused to use the term 'black' in relation to his company and his work. He did not want his company to be limited by such a label. Indeed, as the dance critic and author Brenda Dixon Gottschild points out, the mission for the Ailey Company was based on the premise of ethnic diversity (2003: 75). Clearly, Morris was searching for a role model for Phoenix to help in negotiating this difficult area of categorisation.

Morris thought that the Company had enormous potential and that the challenge was for it to be open to change. Her professional experience enabled her to develop the hitherto minimal Company policies and to introduce structures in which the dancers could develop artistically (1996: 2).

> Whilst holding on to the importance of the history and the development of Phoenix, she [Morris] believes it is important to move ahead. Phoenix remains true to its name, diving into the fire and coming out renewed, informed and strengthened by what has gone before, and inspired to move forward to new challenges and triumphs (BP, 1992: 2).

This statement is an indication of the attempts Morris made to build on the successes of the founders, but also of her determination to develop the Company artistically.

The establishment of an effective working relationship with the Board was one aspect of Margaret Morris's role as artistic director – hence the concerns mentioned above in Board meeting minutes. There were, however, many other issues she needed to consider in relation to running a company. It was important that as a director she was able to take risks when choosing the repertoire in order for the Company to develop. As Richard Alston, the choreographer and artistic director of Richard Alston Dance Company, pointed out, 'no artist wants to fail – but they need space to take risks – and they need support' (in Marchant, 1996: 6). There are also many difficult decisions to be made. As Matz Skoog, the artistic director of English National Ballet, observed, 'Often you have to make repertoire-planning decisions very far in advance, potentially committing the company to an irreversible artistic decision for years to come' (2001: 4).

There is a range of roles in dance companies. Those such as Phoenix, which have the stability of funding and offer longer-term contracts for the dancers, are in a position to offer the dancers training experiences and opportunities for development. Janet Smith, the choreographer and artistic director of Scottish Dance Theatre, comments:

In an ongoing company dancers can take on different roles and responsibilities, and become involved in decision-making processes. There is the opportunity to contribute to the creative process and look beyond to how the company works and plans for its future. (In Siddall, 2001: 6)

Whereas for most dancers in companies such opportunities would offer career development, for Phoenix this was where they had started; they had made decisions and plans for the future from the beginning. Janet Smith also stated, 'Dancers discover and develop talent as teachers and facilitators that feeds back into the studio and empowers them to take on other roles' (in Siddall, 2001: 6). Phoenix began teaching and facilitating as they evolved the Company, so for them the roles were always part of their working practices.

In 1991, Tom Jobe, a choreographer, had been working with the Company during the period when they had been without an artistic director. The dancers expected him to be appointed as the new artistic director (Johnson, 1998).[5] The appointment of Margaret Morris was, therefore, a shock for the dancers. They were:

> brought into the auditorium at Northern School [where] the Chair of the Board [...] told us that they had decided to appoint Margaret Morris. Who? Margaret Morris. There was total disbelief. We had never heard of her at all. (Johnson, 1998)

Sharon (Chantal) Donaldson, who had been ill at the time of the interview, was descended upon by the entire Company after the meeting at the Northern School of Contemporary Dance. They went '*straight round to my house [...] really upset. They thought that the Board had not listened to them. We were pretty angry as a Company*' (1998).

As Dawn Donaldson, her sister and fellow dancer, pointed out, it was odd that the Board appointed Morris when she had not seen the Company perform and was unfamiliar with their background.

> We felt she didn't understand us [...] but she had a job to do and she set up a lot of good standard practices in the Company which we hadn't

---

[5] Although Tom Jobe was shortlisted for the position, it seems possible that the interviewing panel discovered his HIV status and subsequently decided not to appoint him. Jobe died in London on 8 December 1992, aged thirty-nine, less than a year after Margaret Morris took up the position of artistic director (www.artistswithaids.org/artforms/dance/catalogue/jobe.html, accessed 1 March 2007).

experienced before. She was naïve but there were some good things about her. (1998)

The lack of knowledge about Morris and her lack of knowledge of the Company, however, were not the biggest shocks for some of the dancers. For Pamela Johnson, who paradoxically is probably the most aware of feminist politics of any of the members of the Company, it was the fact that

> *a woman got the job that really shocked me. Phoenix has always been really strong and gutsy and grounded and the character of this woman was very lovely, nice and communicated everything on the same level, 'Is it alright if we do this?' etc.* (1998)

Morris's style of communication caused some problems for the Company. As Pamela Johnson explained:

> *When I became passionate about something, my voice raised or […] one of the guys might go into patois. She had absolutely no insight into this, she didn't understand this and she* [interpreted] *it as an attack on her, then she just closed off and that was a problem.* (1998)

To what extent this was an issue about Morris's way of communicating and to what extent it was about ethnic and class backgrounds is open to interpretation. From what Morris had said in her interview with me and in articles published in the press, it appears that she was both unprepared for the complex issues raised initially and in a difficult position in relation to people's expectations of both her and the Company. For example, an article in *The Times* of 9 October 1991 reports her saying:

> *I have no intention of changing the company's image. I see it as essentially a black dance company […]. Those are its roots coming out of a certain culture in Leeds, which has made it what it is. Now it's growing into middle-scale work and touring internationally. As with all art forms, as you grow you need to open out your receptiveness to other cultures and to other experiences.* (PA)

There is no reflection here of the complexities of managing such a company from a background not shared with its members. Nor is there any evidence of insight into the inevitable losses in the 'opening-up' process that Morris envisaged. The lack of awareness displayed in her state-ment, together with her approach to communication, created tensions in the Company. Morris, however, was negotiating difficult terrain: leading a group of people who had been marginalised but who were participating as internationally acknowledged artists. In this shift it was inevitable that some of their frustration would lead to anger, and Morris had the complex task of managing emotional pressures, nurturing the artists, meeting her own desires for the Company and satisfying the fun-ders' requirements for its development.

In a discussion about language, bell hooks argues that speech is not only about communication but also about power:

> An unbroken connection exists between the broken English of the displaced, enslaved African and the diverse black vernacular speech black folks use today. In both cases, the rupture of Standard English enabled and enables rebellion and resistance. By transforming the oppressor's language, making a culture of resistance, black people created an intimate speech that could say far more than was permis-sible within the boundaries of Standard English. The power of this speech is not simply that it enables resistance to white supremacy, but that it also forges a space for alternative cultural production and alternative epistemologies. (1994: 171)

It was evidently important for the dancers to continue to use the range of communication with which they were familiar, even if that was diffi-cult for the artistic director (patois was explored in one of Barnes's choreographies, *Unbroken* [1997]).

As has already been stated, the dancers at first thought that Morris was an inappropriate choice, as did some other people within the dance world. For example, the choreographer Emilyn Claid (who made work for the Company in 1989 and 1993) thought, 'Maggie was completely the wrong choice [but] you don't want to take on a job and then think you are the wrong person for it. You want to do the very best job you can. She was sensible not to stay longer' (2000).

The opinions about Morris's suitability appear to be concerned with her insight into and understanding of a Company whose identity was connected to their educational background and their African–Caribbean–British heritage. In addition, at that time the expectations about her ability to lead such a Company made her job more difficult. Discussions about cultural background and the identity of the Company were very explicit at this time, and it was agreed that 'In terms of performance, Phoenix is primarily a black contemporary dance company' (BP, 1992: 5).

This is a change from when Campbell was director, when he had explicitly argued that the Company was a contemporary company and that the skin colour of the dancers was irrelevant. In an interview with Judith Mackrell, dance critic for *The Independent*, on 12 September 1990, he identified Phoenix as '*first and foremost a modern dance company. I'd be appalled to think we were ever funded because of the colour of our skin*' (PA). The appointment of Morris had forced the dancers into a position where they examined what they had in common, which was more than their school background and love of dance. Their parentage, cultural background and commitment to self-expression as Black British people were brought into focus when confronted with a white female director whose key dance experiences had been in America. (This tension between experiences of American and of British contemporary dance was also an issue when Thea Barnes became artistic director.)

The dancers seemed to acknowledge that Morris brought to the Company a number of strengths, which they gradually began to appreciate. '*I think it's because of Maggie and her practices that the dancers are now so involved in policy procedures in the Company which is such a rarity in any dance Company on this scale* [middle]' (Johnson, 1998).

Indeed, Johnson stated, '*who we are as a people* [...] *our points of view are in the artistic and procedural policies of the Company*'. This, Johnson suggests, is because Morris:

> was white and female and middle class and outside of the culture that we understood. She had also been outside of Britain for many years. She couldn't come in and say you are this and you are that. She didn't want to change Phoenix; she wanted to carry Phoenix on [so] she wanted to get to know who Phoenix was. (1998)

This comment illustrates some of the difficulties for Morris in leading the Company. It also indicates the way in which she attempted to learn from the dancers and give them space to develop as artists. One of her strengths and achievements, in addition to developing the repertoire, was the set of structures she put in place for the dancers' development in terms of appraisals, training opportunities and strengthening the choreographic time for the dancers (BP, 1992).

Although it is clear that Morris had the expertise to develop the Company's skills, create good working practices and exploit the connections she had in the dance world, her ethnicity meant that there was a complex relationship that she and the dancers had to negotiate. There is an inevitable ambivalence for white people who are theorising racism, or attempting to undermine it, of both combating the stereotypes and being drawn towards them, which is the other side of racism that Stuart Hall (1997) identifies. It is, of course, impossible to work outside this dynamic, because it is woven into society.

In *White* (1997), Richard Dyer's discussion of culture and representation offers some examples of white people's behaviour that is linked with a 'desire to be black' (45). He suggests that white people's desire to acquire a tan is linked to this wish, which is also indicated in the fascination with specific dance and music styles. He describes dancing with a black friend in black venues in New York in 1980. In one dance there were two lines of dancers who faced each other, and dancers took it in turns to dance between the lines. Dyer recounts that he 'never felt more white than when I danced down between those lines. I know it was stereotypes in my head; I know plenty of black people who can't dance' (6).

He suggests that the notion of whiteness could be associated with 'tightness, with self-control, self-consciousness, mind over body' (ibid.). Dyer, in that dancing moment, recognised that he hated dancing between those lines because, despite his love of dancing, he acknowledged that 'I had not the kinship with black people that I wanted to have' (ibid.). In this revelation, Dyer identifies an important dynamic that operates within studies such as this one concerned with Phoenix Dance Company. His example is pertinent not only because this study is obviously based on dance but also because, when people are represented, they are represented through their bodies, raising issues about embodiment. As Dyer (1997) argues:

> Concepts of race are concepts of different kinds of bodies. What makes whites different, and at times uneasily locatable in term of race, is their embodiment, their closeness to pure spirit that was made flesh in Jesus, their spirit of mastery over their and other bodies. (25)

In her study *The Black Dancing Body* (2003), Dixon Gottschild makes clear that 'race theory based on body types stands on shaky ground' (103). She also argues that it is not that certain bodies cannot do specific dance forms but rather that cultural preferences establish 'what we like to *see*' (103). Both Dyer and Dixon Gottschild argue that cultural perceptions are embodied, and it is this embodiment that is evident in the Company style and cultural form communicated through the bodies of the Phoenix dancers.

Company style and cultural form

For two of the dancers in the Company, Martin Hylton and Booker T. Louis, there was a distinction in style that was difficult to articulate.

> *For me, dance in the North, Leeds, almost had its own style [...]. It is not as clear as saying American dancers are like this, English dancers are like this. You can see it, feel it, but to name it is difficult.* (Hylton, 1999)

Booker T. Louis said:

> *I think the Company has a definite style [...]. I'd find it very hard to describe but as different artistic directors have come over the years, the style has changed slightly, slight additions, not necessarily subtracting from what is already there but additional qualities have been added to the so called Phoenix style.* (1998)

The dance style of Phoenix Dance Company in the early 1990s was informed by several elements. One such was the educational experience they had shared at Harehills Middle School, based on movement experimentation using Laban's movement principles. Another was the contemporary dance training at either the Northern School of Contemporary Dance or the London Contemporary Dance School, where the students learnt both ballet and contemporary technique (mainly Graham technique). A third was the dance activity they had shared with their families at home and with their peers in the clubs. The dancers would have absorbed some of this kinaesthetic understanding unconsciously, whereas other elements would have been consciously learnt.

In her study *Digging the Africanist Presence in American Performance* (1996), Brenda Dixon Gottschild discusses elements of movement from the African Diaspora that have been absorbed into European and American dance, frequently without acknowledgement. She developed these ideas further in *The Black Dancing Body*:

> In some sense, we can say that dance of all kinds is about the literal and/or metaphorical play and balance between freedom and control, improvisation and set sequences, technique and inspiration, tension and release [...there] is a basic difference between Europeanist and Africanist perspectives with regard to those paired opposites. The place in the body where they are most clearly located and easily

observed is the torso. The vertically aligned torso is the center of the Europeanist ballet body and stands in contrast to the articulated Africanist torso where chest, ribs, belly, pelvis, buttocks can move independently, and sometimes 'dancing to a different drum'. (2003: 37)

The Phoenix dancers had access to both these aesthetics through their education, dance training and cultural background. It was these factors that they were identifying as a Company style, and which they had a sense of but found difficult to identify. In addition, because some elements had been absorbed from an early age through their education and others had been absorbed from their families and peers, it was difficult, although not impossible, for dancers without such a background to work with the Company. As Gottschild makes clear, this issue is about far more than just skin colour, and many elements of movement style can be both absorbed and learnt by people from different cultural backgrounds (1996 and 2003).

The tensions in the Company over identity and style were apparent in the subtext around the departure of dancer Clare Connor,[6] who was white (BP, 1992). The Board meeting in December 1992 was very formal and a number of sub-committees were set up to consider different aspects of the Company. A Board member asked for the reasons for Clare Connor's resignation. The artistic director stated that she had personal reasons, 'but she had also been aware of the policy tensions with regard to the racial make-up of the performing company' (BM, 12 December 1992: 3). These tensions were alluded to by the dance critic Stephanie Ferguson, who observed, 'somehow the addition of Clare Connor destroys the symmetry of the famous line-up' (14 September 1991: PA). Some of the dancers also talked about conflict in the Company in relation to Clare Connor, and about the audience's reaction to the Company composition:

There were personality clashes; the major problem for her was the Company. As a performer she was fine, but people didn't like the idea. It didn't look right. It was like having a black swan. If you were going to have white dancers, you had to have more than one. (R. Holgate, 1998)

---

[6] I attempted on many occasions to interview Clare Connor, via telephone and email, but unfortunately she did not wish to contribute to this research. My understanding of her reluctance, after speaking to some of the dancers who danced with her and to people who knew the Company at the time, is that her experience in the Company was difficult and it was not a period that she wished to revisit.

This comment is particularly interesting because it is made by the other dancer in the Company who did not share the educational and Leeds background of the majority of the dancers. For Holgate, it seems that skin colour and the identity of the Company, based on being black, was important. There was also concern from audience members in relation to aesthetics.

However, Heather Walker, who worked with the Company temporarily from 1992 as rehearsal director, said that, after 140 dancers had been auditioned in London without anyone suitable being found, perhaps Clare Connor did 'fit in' (1998). Walker said, 'On stage you didn't notice she was white; she moved the way they moved. She was in *Spartan Reels* and she fitted in just fine, she really did. She was a good dancer' (1998).

The Board were concerned about the dancers' views and the tension that had arisen after Morris's appointment. One of the Board members approached the Equity representative and suggested that there appeared to be significant differences between the management's and the Company's perspectives regarding Phoenix's identity. The representative acknowledged that this was the case and that it was difficult to represent the range of views at meetings. It was agreed that the Board member would meet the Company. The discussion covered four main areas: the Company members' views of the identity of Phoenix; the role of Phoenix and how it was fulfilling its mission; the artistic and staffing policy of the Company; and personal and professional development. It was apparent from the ensuing discussion that a good deal of frustration was present. The discussions were recorded as follows:

> Phoenix as a Black Contemporary Dance Company is a reality. To think otherwise is to deny the existence of its predominantly Afrikan (sic) Caribbean membership. There was the feeling that stereotyped views of Blackness were inhibiting members of the Management and their acceptance of Phoenix's true identity.

Blackness was described as the dominant perspective and ethos within Phoenix and it was said that it should remain so, even if there were to be a change in the composition of the Company (Morrison, 1992: 2).

It was acknowledged that there was a lack of clarity about the Company's mission and that there was general disharmony about its direction:

> The work of Phoenix must speak to the Black British experience from a perspective which is culturally relevant. Any approach which does

not recognise this as a starting point leaves the dancers feeling spiritually and psychologically empty. (Morrison, 1992: 3)

It is important to note here that any dancer in a repertory company may have difficulty with dancing material that feels irrelevant to them in some way, but clearly there is also a culturally specific issue which the dancers were stressing at this point. It is interesting also to note that the training heritage of Laban and Graham that the dancers drew on in their work does not appear to have been questioned. During the meeting with the Company:

> It was stated that Phoenix had a responsibility to present positive images of Black people on stage. In this regard they also needed to consider how the Company contributed to raising its profile within the Black Community. Clearly, the Company saw itself as ambassadors, advocates and vanguards of a cultural perspective which is generally missing from the dance stage. (Morrison, 1992: 3)

This statement raises important points that relate to the Company's subsequent development. The Company wanted a definition of its uniqueness, supported by an appropriate artistic policy and staff who agreed with the Company's ethos. The dancers also felt that the composition of the office staff should reflect that of the Company on stage: that is, they wanted staff of African Caribbean rather than white European heritage (Morrison, 1992).

The extent to which there was now a gap between management and Company is clear in the following statement:

> The present repertoire engendered feelings of cultural and political oppression. When we complained about its soullessness we are told that the Management cannot give us our souls. We have to find ourselves in whatever we are given to do. (Morrison, 1992: 4)

Brenda Dixon Gottschild explains 'soul' as representing

> that attribute of the body/mind that mediates *between* flesh and spirit. It is manifested in the *feel* of a performance [...]. Soul, the term and the concept, has been irrevocably linked to and associated with African American expressive performance styles. (2003: 223)

She also suggests, 'For African American performers, soul is the nitty-gritty personification of the energy and force that it takes to be black and survive' (2003: 223). This is also true of African–Caribbean–British performers such as Phoenix, which was the point that the performers were trying to explain to the management. Although the dancer's job is to communicate expressively to the audience, which is what the management were discussing, the dancers were commenting on their difficulty in finding expression in repertoire with which they could not identify.

The dancers felt that the time for professional development was limited, but it was only in their choreographic development period that culturally relevant material was available. This material they considered substantially different from the repertoire that they were dancing during the rest of the year. They thought that the management and the Board needed to take responsibility for the situation (Morrison, 1992). There appears to have been a tension here between the Company and their experience of the management and the Board, and also a lack of opportunities to represent their views, although there was a representative from the dancers on the Board.

The issue of identity was pursued in a meeting of the YHA[7] advisers with the dance officer and artistic and administrative directors of the company. The directors stated that the dancers perceived themselves to be a contemporary dance company first and black performers second, providing positive role models. It was noted that there was an imbalance in having a white administration and Board and a black performing company. A retreat had been planned to discuss some of these issues further.

Repertoire 1991–93

In the previous chapters, issues about choreographic identity have been raised in relation to specific times and artists. The arrival of Margaret Morris as artistic director created an opportunity to expand the repertoire to include works from American choreographers in addition to choreographies from British artists. The Chair of the Board of Phoenix Dance Company, Graham Devlin, in a publicity statement announcing Margaret Morris's appointment in 1991, said, 'Her American

---

[7] Yorkshire Arts Association (YAA) was formed on 14 January 1970. On 6 August 1991 YAA became Yorkshire and Humberside Arts (YHA). On 22 June 2000 YHA changed its name to Yorkshire Arts Board (YAB) and on 1 April 2002 YAB transferred to the Arts Council of England (ACE) and became Arts Council England, Yorkshire, although YAB was not formally removed from the Companies House register until 17 February, 2004 (Schindler, Arts Council England, Yorkshire, 2004).

experience will open up new horizons for the company and her talent for selecting and nurturing choreographers will be invaluable to us' (in Stevens, 1991).

This statement highlights two issues that were fundamental to the establishment of Phoenix's repertoire at this time. Most of the repertoire in the 1980s had been produced by the Company or by British choreographers who were closely linked with the founders' back-grounds and shared a Graham-based technique. Margaret Morris, how-ever, introduced American choreographers, including Donald Byrd, Bebe Miller and Danial Shapiro and Joanie Smith. This change of direc-tion was what the Board and funders thought appropriate for the Company's development. It resulted, however, in confusion for the dancers, as their success had been based on their production and per-formance of work that to some extent drew on their cultural specificity.

In many ways it seems that, although Phoenix has established itself as an internationally recognised Company, it is haunted by a sense that important aspects of its emergence have been lost. The choreographer Emilyn Claid, in an interview that I undertook with her, identified some of the dilemmas that the dancers faced. They were aware that they were becoming world-famous but still had not left Leeds:

> They are in this incredible double bind of being successful in a white world, knowing that they have never left where they came from. There is another level that they are dealing with in terms of confi-dence. No one is actually making them feel good. (2000)

So although at first the dancers had danced because they felt it was an integral part of their lives (indeed, David Hamilton made it clear that he did not distinguish between dance and life), this integration was gradu-ally eroded. The expectations of the funders and the employment of artistic directors who had visions of national and international success meant that the dancers lost their autonomy. In addition to this, as Claid notes, they were not being nurtured and encouraged as artists.

Emilyn Claid had had connections with the dancers in the Company since 1984, when she made a work for the National Youth Dance Company, and later through her teaching at the Northern School of Contemporary Dance. As we have seen in Chapter 3, Neville Campbell then commissioned her to make a piece for Phoenix, *Breakdown in Dralon* (1989). He also commissioned Aletta Collins to create *Gang of Five* (1989).

Although this was not the first time white women had choreographed for the Company, the significance of Collins's and Claid's work with the

Company was that they drew on the dancers' strengths. Claid's observation above shows her insight into some of the dilemmas facing the Company in relation to their history and ethnicity, and she did her best to work with the dancers using an empowering approach that minimised their loss of autonomy.

When Margaret Morris was artistic director, Claid made another work for the Company, initially entitled *Windrush* and then retitled *Shoot No. 526* (1993). The work was not about immigration to Britain, and she decided that the first title was influenced by the exposure of Windrush on the news and was rather romantic (Claid, 2000). The second title reflected her sense that 'Really, it's a film. Stark scenes about people and feelings, human things, sketches from a life – young to old, an inevitable pattern? ... perhaps' (programme note, *the spirit of a new & exciting dance future*, 1993–94: 5).

Her experience of working with the Company four years after making *Breakdown in Dralon* (1989) with the dancers was fraught with tension.

> I picked up this terrible gender war going on between the women and men. I would go into the studio and find the four women sitting together [...] completely furious with the men and the situation and the Company, unable to work. Another day, I would be working with the women and the men would be in the studio playing football at the back, with no regard for what is going on. (2000)

Claid identified the sources of this friction as the disempowerment of the dancers once they had accepted funding, and the lack of preparation for the transition from an all-male company to one comprising women and men. In addition, her methods of working required the dancers to improvise and deal with personal issues, and at that point they were not prepared 'to reveal anything about themselves at all' (2000).

Ricky Holgate identified some of the difficulties for the Company. '*I don't think we were used to expressing ourselves on a level that Emilyn wished us to [...]. It was daunting*' (1998). He did, however, appreciate Claid's attempts to draw work from them that related to their backgrounds and the journey they had taken as a Company. This way of working was one of Claid's particular strengths as a choreographer. It is possible that if the piece had not been made when the Company were without leadership because Morris was off sick, there may have been more opportunity for them to come to terms with it and make a valuable addition to the repertoire. As it was, unfortunately the piece was only performed a few times.

Sharon Donaldson's perspective of the working process supported Claid's interpretation:

> *She opened the can of worms and she got it all. That was not because of Emilyn but because they did not get the chance to air their grievances [...]. In that situation she was dealing with, a lot of personal things were beyond the women coming in 1989. I guess it is all the cultural stuff that we were dealing with. (1998)*

Here Donaldson refers to the conflicts with which the dancers were struggling. The first was that of the gender composition of the Company and the uneasy transition, particularly for the founders, from an all-male company to a company of women and men. The second is that of ethnicity and the tension for Phoenix of holding on to a sense of their shared histories and cultural specificity in the light of requirements from the funders and of working with the artistic direction of a woman who did not share their backgrounds.

Creation of dance works was an integral aspect of the early Phoenix; and as the Company evolved, opportunities were given to dancers to contribute choreography. Pamela Johnson had two works in the repertoire, and her first work, *Subject of the City* (1991), continued in the Company programme. In her interview she said she thought that she was in a privileged position in relation to her career in dance. Unusually, she did not audition as a dancer until the age of thirty. '*Everything has been a stepping stone; it's been there*' (1998). She did not anticipate a career in dance but rather came to it because of her involvement at school. At that time she viewed the London Contemporary Dance Theatre as a role model, and in particular one of the dancers, Darshan Singh Bhuller, who had also been a pupil at Harehills Middle School (Ferguson, *Yorkshire Post*, 1991: PA). Before training at the Northern School of Contemporary Dance, she had been a founder member (at sixteen years of age) of Sabata, a company involved with dance in education in the region. Other members of Sabata were Seline Thomas, Hugh Davis and Robert Edwards (all of whom danced with Phoenix at some point).

In 1993 Johnson had her second opportunity to choreograph for the Company and produced *Face Our Own Face*, which was constructed around a large metal sculpture of the outline of a woman. A comment from the writer Hilary Robinson is interesting in relation to Johnson's choreography. She says, 'when it comes to the very physical activity of making art, many women turn to their own bodies or images of women's bodies as a vehicle for making images, for making meaning'

13. *Family*, 1992. Choreographers Danial Shapiro and Joanie Smith; dancers
    Donald Edwards, Seline Thomas; photographer Steve Hanson

(1992: 18). This is the case to some extent with this work of Johnson's. *Face Our Own Face* was partly inspired by bell hooks's essay *Black Looks: Race and Representation* (1992). The author's dedication for the book was printed in the programme:

> To all of us who love blackness who dare to create in our daily lives space of reconciliation and forgiveness where we let go of past hurt, fear, shame and hold each other close. It is only in the act and practice of loving blackness that we are able to reach out and ...'
> (Programme note, *the spirit of a new and exciting dance future*, 1993–94: 6)

Johnson was concerned to challenge both representations of women in dance and perspectives of blackness. As a cultural producer, she was creating, as Jacqueline Bobo described in her study *Black Women as Cultural Readers*, 'alternative and more viable images' (1995: 26). One of the starting points for Johnson's work was the struggle for power in the relationship between her mother and father. A key element was that she specifically brought aspects of Black British experience to the stage. For example, the work began with a portrayal of a club scene, which Johnson had to navigate carefully in order to avoid stereotyping. The process of making the work was a journey of discovering perceptions of black women and how they viewed themselves, and attempts to shift negative images and to create more positive ones. Johnson wanted to create a work with which audiences of African Caribbean heritage could identify and which would challenge white audiences to reconsider their assumptions (Adair, 1995).

Sharon Donaldson also made works for the Company and, together with the three other women (D. Donaldson, Johnson and Thomas) from Harehills Middle School who initially joined Phoenix, offered perspectives that were informed by gender, formal dance training and experiences in other professional companies. Donaldson said that she thought the women '*did enhance the Company tremendously and brought them in another direction*' (1998). Johnson thought the experience that the women brought to the Company meant that '*we looked at practices and procedures a lot more than the guys did*' (1998).

Phoenix produced a range of choreography both from choreographers within the Company and from those commissioned to make work for them. There were, however, many criticisms of the choreography, despite this range. An issue that emerged in several critics' reviews was the perception of a Company with a high technical standard, but which often danced choreography that did not enhance their abilities.

For example, Clement Crisp, critic for the *Financial Times*, pointed out when writing about the 1991–92 season, 'What it cannot boast is a clear choreographic identity [...] the abiding image of this evening is of strong dancers whose gifts are the hostages of their repertory' (11 October 1991: PA). Crisp's comment reveals his own perceptions and expectations of the Company and also highlights the complex issue of the Company's repertoire.

He also stated in November 1992, after watching a performance from their tour at Sadler's Wells which included Aletta Collins's *Gang of Five* (1989), *Family* (1992) by Danial Shapiro and Joanie Smith, *Spartan Reels* (1992) by Bebe Miller and *Sacred Space* (1991) by Philip Taylor:

> As an ensemble of dancers it must be ranked very high for the rhythmic alertness, the fine flash of step and limb, the clarity of dancing. Though the repertory has, from the first, been uneven – and sometimes dire – Phoenix style has come to the rescue. (1992: 13)

He suggests that the Company's 'repertory [...] needs to rise to the level of the dancers' artistry. I would love to see them challenged by great choreography, by revivals of major dance pieces. They merit nothing less than the best' (1992: 13). Jayne Dawson, writing in the *Yorkshire Evening Post*, thought the Company were in good form for their tenth anniversary tour and described them as 'one of the best modern dance outfits in Britain' (18 September 1991: PA).

Despite such praise, it is also evident from other comments from the critics that there were concerns about the Company in 1991 and 1992. Information from Company archives about problems with the repertory allows the critics' views to be read in another way. Campbell's *Heavy Metal* (1991) had to be dropped because of injury. Taylor's *Sacred Space* (1991) had to be suspended for part of the year because of the costs of music rights. These issues give insight into some of the reasons for difficulties with repertory that are not solely connected with artistic choices. The Company also undertook a range of education and outreach work both in Britain and in the USA. An education team of ex-Phoenix members taught and performed in preparation for the performance tour (BP, 1992: 4). There was, therefore, a connection at this stage between previous members of the Company and the current Company. Although in-house choreographers were encouraged, it was also important for the artistic directors to commission suitable choreographers who would develop the dancers' strengths and appeal to audiences. In 1992, Bebe Miller created *Spartan Reels* for the Company.

14. Choreographer Bebe Miller in the studio rehearsing *Spartan Reels*, 1992, with dancers Claire Connor, Dawn Donaldson, Ricky Holgate, Sharon Donaldson; photographer Steve Hanson

I was invited to review the world premiere of this work. This was my first introduction to Phoenix behind the scenes. I watched the Company in rehearsal and had an opportunity to speak to Miller about the working process. She was interested in choreographing for people she did not know and who had a different background to her own. She was surprised to discover in making *Spartan Reels* that she wanted to explore the different dynamics of the men and women, and choreographed dances that reinforced traditional views of male and female behaviour. She also realised that Phoenix had a good deal to offer but were constrained by expectations of 'the old Phoenix'. I would suggest that this work and Miller's approach to choreography were a challenge to the Company (2 September 1992).

John Percival, writing in *The Times* (12 November, 1992: PA), comments that this work

> is a more demanding assignment for the dancers, but one to which they bring the same irrepressible confidence of communicating with their audience [...] it is the liveliness and invention of the movement that make this the evening's most satisfying choreography.

Allen Robertson, writing in the *Daily Mail*, also received the work positively. He observed that Miller

> uses devices from social dances but overlays them with sharp, often playful motifs full of the pace and drive of modern urban living. The outcome is something like 21st century quadrilles. The dancers grab Miller's choreography and really run with it. Never have they looked so joyously alive nor so completely professional. (18 November, 1992: PA)

Robertson describes Miller as 'a black choreographer based in New York' (1992: PA). It is clear from Company documentation and from the critics' writings, particularly at this point, that the issue of 'blackness' and identity was a recurring theme. I think this was not least because Maggie (as she was called) Morris was a white artistic director directing a company of black dancers which, as mentioned above, had been defined both by the critics and sometimes by the Company themselves, although not initially, as a 'black dance' company. This raised many questions from the press about which voice Morris was speaking with when she spoke for the Company.

15. *Spartan Reels*, 1992. Choreographer Bebe Miller; dancers Booker T. Louis, Seline Thomas; photographer Steve Hanson

The tension between what Morris viewed as suitable for a dynamic contemporary company and what the Company and those close to it could deal with is apparent at this point. The funding application to YHA in which the artistic and educational aims of the Company were outlined included a note about choreographic work for 1992, stating that the Company had invited Bebe Miller from New York to create a new work for the Company. She is described as 'a prominent black woman choreographer whose energetic style seems well suited to the Phoenix dancers. Her work often deals with "black" issues' (FA, 1992: 3). I do not think this was how Miller perceived her work. As Dixon Gottschild pointed out, Miller had been 'inside the downtown dance scene and its aesthetic criteria for some time' (2003: 74). This scene was predominantly made up of white artists who worked experimentally, and Miller's own company comprised both black and white dancers (Parry, 1992). Jann Parry discussed the dilemmas confronting the expectations facing black artists in Britain and suggested that Miller, in common with some other African American artists, dealt with such expectations by 'distancing herself from choreographers who draw on African or black American dance traditions. She preferred to be seen as a female choreographer "who happens to be black"' (1992: 54).

Phoenix, however, sometimes took this approach to their identity and at others sought to embrace their African Caribbean heritage. The description of Miller in the Company documents mentioned above indicates the confusion about identity and categorisation that was prevalent at this time and also the gap between the management's and the dancers' perceptions of what was appropriate for the Company.

Miller's work was received positively, but the dancers 'found it difficult to adapt to Bebe's style of work, and during the choreographic process there was much illness among the company' (BP, 1992: 10). It was also noted, however, that the Company became more familiar with the work in performance and felt 'free to play with the movement style and characterisation' (BP, 1992: 10). The dancers' experience of contemporary dance and performative presence at this point was limited to that informed by LCDT and their own aesthetics. Bebe Miller and Emilyn Claid, however, required the dancers to work with a presence with which the dancers were not familiar. In the work, Miller humorously exposed the competition and tension between the women and the men as they gathered in opposite corners of the stage from one another. Miller created images of vibrancy and community with an air of poignancy and nostalgia, which is particularly evident in the powerful line dance in one section of the work, performed to haunting vocal lyrics (Adair, 1995).

Miller has been described as a choreographer who

> extracts a high degree of input from dancers, whether they are part of her company or merely the living materials she is working with on commissioned pieces. Miller treats them as individuals whose virtual duty is to make her movement their own. (Bremser, 1999: 157)

Such an approach is demanding for dancers who are not working in this way most of the time. I think it is fair to say that the dancers did not understand Miller's radical postmodern style, which demanded skills and approaches with which they were unfamiliar and to which they were not particularly open.

Booker T. Louis, a dancer with the Company from 1989, said about the process:

> *Initially, I didn't like it because it was a new way of working for me; it was very experimental [...]. I do not like* [the process] *where you are practically making the piece yourself, where you are experimenting and the choreographer is taking ideas and moulding. I do not like working that way and that is the way Bebe was going.* (1998)

There is also an issue of ownership here to which Louis may have been reacting. When the dancers were creating their own work and had more of a sense of their control of the Company, they did not need to be concerned about whose work was credited. In a situation in which the dancers might feel disempowered, the question of whether or not they received credit for their work became more crucial. So it may have been not only the process but also the 'taking of ideas' to which Louis objected.

Comments from Heather Walker illustrate the dancers' professionalism, because although some of the Company did not enjoy the creative process, that was not obvious in performance. Walker said, '*We worked on Spartan Reels, which I don't think the dancers loved, but I really enjoyed learning the piece and I thought they did it wonderfully*' (1998).

There were parallels between the difficulties the Company experienced in relation to their creative process with Miller and those they experienced with Claid a year later. Both choreographers expected input from the dancers and both choreographers used the tension between the men and the women as an aspect of choreographic explorations.

Another work in the repertoire in 1992 was *Family* by Shapiro and Smith, which became a firm favourite. Allen Robertson, writing in the *Daily Mail* (18 November 1992: PA), describes it as

16. *Face Our Own Face*, 1993. Choreographer Pamela Johnson; dancers
    Sharon Donaldson, Dawn Donaldson, Seline Thomas; photographer Steve Hanson

a domestic comedy of squabbles and loving designed to take place round a big over-stuffed armchair. The whole family uses it as a springboard, a tumbling mat, a vault, a diving board and a home base [...] it is good-natured and fun.

In contrast, however, Judith Mackrell, writing in the *Independent* on 13 November (1992: PA), found that the

inflated energy and cheerfulness of this piece seem wincingly fake. To begin with, it's choreographed around a chair – an overused prop that virtually guarantees imaginative decline. And though it's presented as an exploration of the tensions of family life, there's nothing in the way the dancers vault over the chair, plump on each other's knees or bare their teeth that suggests any recognisable drama.

Some of the observations from critics, report writers and the dancers themselves suggest that there was a perceived notion of what was or was not suitable for Phoenix and what would enhance their style. Such perceptions contributed to Morris's struggle to convince everyone that she could and would direct the Company into a successful future.

In a meeting on 10 September 1992 between the artistic director, administrative director, funding officers and attached advisers, various issues were raised in relation to artistic policy and future plans for the Company. Generally, the choreographic developments were well received and the two new pieces by American choreographers Bebe Miller, and Danial Shapiro and Joanie Smith, were perceived to have been challenging for the Company. Heather Walker found that the Company were wary of her: 'It was as though, because I was white, middle-aged and female, I couldn't possibly know what they were thinking and what they were feeling; but yet we were all dancers, and so I did' (1998). Walker's comments indicate an important aspect of the profession in terms of their common experiences of the discipline required to attain and maintain physicality and to achieve strong performances in a range of choreography. They also indicate, however, the 'colour-blindness' that Williams (1993: 142) and Frankenberg (1993) identified. For many white people, one of the ways of dealing with the racism that results from inequality and prejudice is to take a position of denial. Patricia Williams, who gave the Reith Lectures (1997) for the BBC on the topic of racism, describes the phenomenon as adopting a view of 'I don't think about colour, therefore your problems don't exist' (1997: 2).[8]

Whiteness and the privilege that it entails is an issue of power; as Brown, Gilkes and Kalowski-Naylor point out, feminist approaches have supported the view that '*anyone* in a position of power has a responsibility to think about the consequences of how that power is exercised' (1999: 5). It is important to acknowledge that being white 'marks boundaries of social inclusion and exclusion, and is constituted in opposition to its subordinated "other", the "not-white", the "not-privileged" (Lewis and Ramazanoglu, in Brown, Gilkes and Kalowski-Naylor, 1999: 23). Indeed, as Dyer argues, 'the point of looking at whiteness is to dislodge it from its centrality and authority, not to reinstate it' (1997: 10). It was important for the Company's development that the funders, the Board and members of the Company who were white had some insight into the way whiteness conveyed power. The dancers who were marked by their blackness did not have the choice of ignoring the implications of that. As bell hooks explains through the concept of a critical black gaze, there are ways in which black people have an understanding of whiteness through their close observations of white people because that is where the power lies in a system of racial inequality (1992). Indeed, whiteness provides access to privileges even when, for example, gender and class disempower people (Brown, Gilkes and Kalowski-Naylor, 1999).

The issue of perceptions of the Company's identity was reiterated at another meeting, on 10 September 1992, of the arts advisers for Yorkshire and Humberside Arts attached to Phoenix Dance Company. It was noted that both the artistic director and the administrative director, Liza Stevens, thought that the dancers still felt unclear about the nature of the Company, its cultural identity and the reasons for receiving funding. Advisers suggested that perhaps a guest could be invited to speak at

---

[8] Some key works in both literature and theatre offer significant insight into issues of ethnicity. For example, Toni Morrison in *Playing in the Dark* (1993) discussed the centrality of black representation to the construction of white identity. This is an argument also put forward by Said in his study entitled *Orientalism* (1978). In the bestseller *Black Like Me* (1977), John Howard Griffin documents his experiences in the segregated southern states of America when he changed his skin tone from white to black. (I can remember reading this book when I was younger, and it had a profound effect on me.) In more recent times the play *The Colour of Justice* (1999) based on the transcripts of the Stephen Lawrence Inquiry (1999) contributed to ending the silence around whiteness and provided insight into racism in Britain.

the next staff meeting, addressing issues of Black British dance/culture: for example, Maggie Semple[9] or Derrick Anderson.[10]

At this point in the Company's history, internal communications were being attended to and Phoenix was the subject of a good deal of monitoring. An audience survey carried out during the autumn tour of 1991 and the spring of 1992 indicated that most people in Phoenix's audiences were middle class and under forty-five years of age, and 92 per cent described themselves as European. Only 4 per cent described themselves as Caribbean, African or Asian; 76 per cent were female. These figures correspond with the national figures for attendance at contemporary dance performances, except that the percentage of females attending Phoenix performances was higher than the national figure of 59 per cent (McCann Matthews Millman, 1992).

The same organisation also carried out telephone research, interviewing contacts at venues about how the Company were perceived by current and potential bookers. The purpose of this research was to inform the Company's shift from the small to the middle scale. One comment summarises a viewpoint that echoes the critics at that time (1991–92):[11]

> One of the problems is that it looks like any other contemporary company [...] the energy and the buzz had gone the last time [...]. Mainly the fault of the repertoire [...] this year's first piece was made for LCDT, and the second piece didn't exactly set the world on fire. The repertoire has to come first. Has to be one that suits the company and gives them identity. The original Phoenix members have formed a new company, and I think this will be a problem for the company. People will remember the first company. There was a great deal of enthusiasm. It was nothing to [do] with dance, and everything to do with sex [...] they really brought things alight. (12)

---

[9] Maggie Semple was Head of Education at the Arts Council in 1992. Her perception of the issues that Phoenix faced is evident from her article 'African dance and adzido' (1992). Although the article was discussing a company that specialised in African People's Dance, Semple's comments about the inappropriate reviews of their work raised wider issues, which were applicable to some of the reviews of the Phoenix repertoire. She also said, 'I suppose I lack patience – I want to see a period of time when Black companies can choose a variety of images to present their work. I long for an abstract image or a picture of a beautiful black face which would attract audiences just as much as the present publicity' (27).

[10] Derrick Anderson was Deputy Director of the Yorkshire Arts Association, and the Artistic Director for Kokuma (1986).

[11] From the Company documents, it appears that this survey was completed at much the same time as the audience survey, although the report itself is undated.

This viewpoint also echoes that of the report writers discussed below. All the respondents, however, perceived that the Company had a very good reputation and were very much respected (McCann Matthews Millman, 1992).

The comments above crystallise the complex issues with which the Company struggled in terms of identity and repertoire. The spirit that the founding Company imbued was repeatedly sought by the dancers, choreographers, directors, funders, critics and audiences. Indeed, the title of the 1992–95 tour was *Catch the Spirit*. It is arguable that the spirit could not be caught because it was specific to the founding dancers and the time and place in which the early work was formed.

Brenda Dixon Gottschild argues that spirit and soul are '*embodied*, meaning that their location and means of expression for all human beings are in the flesh; secondly, through the soul power, the body manifests spirit' (2003: 222). She suggests that spirit is 'manifested in the *resonance* (fullness, depth, power and reverberation) of performance and rooted in African danced religions' (2003: 223). She also suggests:

> One of the reasons the black dancing body exhibits such a palpable, tangible, almost material sense of spirit/soul is its heritage. *Danced religion* and *dancing* divinities reside in African and African American history as well as in the Africanist collective memory. It is *not* a matter of biology, *not* genes, but a *cultural unconscious* that lives in the spirit and is reconstituted – re-membered – in the muscles, blood, skin and bone of the black dancing body. (2003: 224)

Clearly it is this 'cultural unconscious' that the dancers wanted to access in the repertoire and to which the audience responded. It was also what the choreographers from the Company shared with their fellow dancers and drew on for their creative projects. This is evident, for example, in works such as *Forming of the Phoenix*, choreographed by David Hamilton (1982); *The Path*, choreographed by Donald Edwards (1988); *Nightlife at the Flamingo*, choreographed by Edward Lynch (1983; 1989); and *Face Our Own Face* (1993), choreographed by Pamela Johnson. There was no place for this 'cultural unconscious', however, in the organisation of the Company.

Policies and developments

It is clear from the documentation of Board minutes, reports and questionnaires for 1991 and 1992 that frameworks were put in place to monitor the Company and to assist future developments. In addition, the dancers' welfare was being addressed through attention to their resettlement fund and training opportunities. The price of this for the dancers was a further erosion of their place within the Company.

The minutes from the Board meeting of 24 September 1992 identified difficulties that repertory companies were experiencing at that time over identity, policy, role and future. Chris de Marigny, then editor of *Dance Theatre Journal*, reported that Rambert Dance Company and London Contemporary Dance Theatre were both having problems, and he suggested that the black/white issue (the term in the minutes) should therefore not be the Company's only concern. He outlined three competing views of the Company:

> Those who would like to revive the small audience/close contact/ street influenced company, for which the present organisation is totally unsuitable. [The potential for this approach for the company really ended in 1987 when Campbell took over, although some small-scale work was still carried out then.]
>
> Those who see Phoenix as at least equal to Rambert and LCDT [the two main repertory contemporary dance companies at the time]. Phoenix may be doing better artistically and at the box office, but this role would be dangerous as the company is seriously under-resourced, under-staffed and the staff over-worked. Phoenix may be the most sponsorable company in the country, but there is no-one there to go and get the sponsorship [...]. The alternative would be to look at the schedule and reduce it to fit the staff available.
>
> Those who would like Phoenix to tour internationally. Organising foreign tours is problematic, time-consuming, costly and the risks are great. We need to find out who will cover the cost of the risk. Economics of foreign bookers are also deteriorating so international touring may not be appropriate for the company at this time. (BM, 1992: 3)

These minutes indicate that some of the issues with which the Company were dealing were ones with which other British contemporary dance companies were also struggling. The issues included adequate funding, sponsorship, touring demands and staff who were constantly attempting to achieve almost impossible goals. In addition, Phoenix was frequently associated with its early beginnings, and funders, sponsors and audiences continued to desire something of the success of the early 1980s as the Company developed.

The agenda of developing the Company into a well-established middle-scale company was a difficult one to carry out. The term 'middle-scale' was defined by the Arts Council in relation to small-scale companies and required touring programmes to larger theatres, but this in turn increased pressures on companies to put on programmes that they did not have the resources to provide. In addition, the Arts Council was no longer funding venues, so there was more pressure for companies to generate good box-office returns. In such a structure, Phoenix was in effect competing with the larger and better resourced companies, Rambert Dance Company and LCDT. It was understandable that Margaret Morris stated at this meeting that it was important to have agreement about the Company in order to decide where or if it wanted to move on.

The documentation for the Company from 1993, when Margaret Morris had been in post just over a year, is more professional than previously and clearly indicates the shift in direction for the Company and the changing roles for the dancers. For example, both the Company's mission statement and Margaret Morris's artistic policy show a concern with acknowledging and promoting the specificity of the Company in relation to cultural heritage. These statements also make clear the commitment to embodiment of that specificity within the repertoire.

The Company's mission statement stated:

> Phoenix Dance Company is dedicated to being a world class contemporary Dance Company: *invigorating, challenging* and *exciting* our audience. Phoenix is committed to producing work that broadens the audience's perception of – and embodies – a Black British experience. (March 1993)

Morris's artistic policy, May 1993, stated:

> Phoenix Dance Company presents modern dance that is distinct, ground-breaking and accessible. As a repertory company in which the performers are British people of Afro-Caribbean descent we aim to produce work that is inspired by this background as well as others. Through such work Phoenix energises new audiences with a passion for dance and throws dance to the forefront of artistic expression in modern multi-cultural society.

The development of the ideas evident in these statements is an indication of the debate about Black Arts in the 1990s, which had evolved from perspectives on this topic in the 1980s. It was also in 1993 that RJC Dance Theatre emerged after successful completion of a West

Midlands Arts Dance Development project, Spectrum, the aim of which was to 'develop a contemporary black dance vocabulary relevant to people of today' (Edwards, 1997: 10). This project was undertaken by the early Phoenix dancers Edward Lynch, David Hamilton and Donald Edwards, together with Martin Robinson and Douglas Thorpe who had also danced with Phoenix, and Joe Williams, Artistic Director of Kuffdem Theatre Company. When RJC was set up, its aim was to develop 'a coherent, recognisable and relevant structure for Black British Dance' (RJC Touring Information, 1996). This is another example of the concern with 'black dance' within the infrastructure of the Arts Council and regional agencies. At a time when Morris was attempting to widen the perceptions of Phoenix, some of the Company's founders were engaged in focusing on Afrocentric movement in RJC (that is, movement rooted in African and Caribbean societies, which influence current modern dance forms such as Hip Hop, Soul and Jazz) (Edwards, 1997). As we have seen, there were many parallels between the beginnings of the two companies, as well as obvious differences. An important similarity is the deep connection with African Caribbean heritage that the founders of both companies valued. In addition, although both companies were supported to some extent by government funding, the artists thought that this limited their development either through influence or through restrictions on funding. As Donald Edwards said in relation to the early Phoenix, '*Slowly the funders exerted their influence on the Company, affecting a change in philosophy and approach which took it away from its cultural roots*' (1997: 26).

He also despondently refers to plans for a work to be toured in 1998, *Language, Life, Respect,* which is described as reflecting

> *the difficulties experienced by both the original Phoenix Dance Company and RJC in gaining recognition for this fusion of cultures* [but] *this programme may never be developed due to lack of funding. This demonstrates the lack of understanding of the funding bodies of the artistic vision of RJC and its commitment to the fusion of western and black cultural dance and music.* (1997: 11)[12]

The sense of disempowerment evident in these two statements reflects the problems that emerged for the dancers because they were funded

---

[12] The work was toured and received an enthusiastic review from Kevin Berry in *The Stage* on 5 February 1998. He said, '*Language, Life, Respect* is varied, fluent, and intelligently paced [...] and there is still that astonishing capacity to excite [...] When Leo Hamilton is on stage he dominates. He performs *Break These Chains*, his own work, with muscular clarity and great ambition' (RJC, archives).

when their work fitted the criteria of the funders' current policies, rather than being supported as artists who contributed significantly to the development of British contemporary dance, as discussed in the previous chapters.

It was this legacy that Morris was negotiating as she attempted to lead Phoenix. In her artistic policy, she is trying to acknowledge the Company's heritage and at the same time to avoid the dreaded 'b' word, as Thea Barnes is later to label any references to the word 'black' (in Mackrell, 1997). It is used, however, in the mission statement, which highlights the ambivalence about the Company's understanding of its cultural heritage. Morris's attempts to clarify this identity do not really succeed, if the writings of critics are taken as an indication of the response to the Company.

It was not only the critics, however, who used the term 'black' in their writing in such a way that it is arguable that the artistic achievements and development of Phoenix were fixed and limited. The funders also used the category 'black' in their documentation for companies. For example, Yorkshire and Humberside Arts sent out comparators for the companies to fill in, and the question on personnel reads, 'Total number of dancers in company of which how many are black?' (1993). Another way in which YHA monitored companies was by using report writers. The role of report writers was to give independent feedback to the regional arts board officers to help them make decisions about funding and development work. There were also national assessors and report writers for the Arts Council of Great Britain (ACGB).[13] The writers were selected from people who were knowledgeable about the art form. They submitted reports to the funding body which were considered in relation to the company's progress and their comments were also forwarded to the company. There were occasional meetings of the report writers with the YHA Dance Officer to discuss the Company's progress.

At a meeting on 21 April 1993, it was noted that the Company needed to 're-establish its uniqueness and that the move to the middle scale had perhaps lost its initial identity (no training, young people off the streets of Leeds, black)' (1).

It is clear from this statement that, while Morris and the Company were attempting to evolve artistic strategies that encompassed cultural identity but were not limited by it, the report writers wanted the Company to retain what they perceived to be its identity in the early 1980s. This desire for the 'lost identity' was also apparent in many critics' writings in the late 1980s and 1990s.

---

[13] The Arts Council of Great Britain (ACGB) was dissolved in April 1994 and became the Arts Council of England (ACE) (Dunlop, Moody, Muir and Shaw, 1995).

Despite any sense of loss that some stakeholders voiced, as discussed earlier, certain achievements had established Phoenix as a key company on the contemporary dance landscape. The main achievements listed in the 1993 business plan are as follows:

- Establishing the only regionally based contemporary dance company in England
- Major contribution to emergence of an Afro-Caribbean presence in mainstream cultural life in the UK
- Establishing Phoenix as a full time repertory company
- Establishing a secure base at the Yorkshire Dance Centre
- Successful expansion from small to middle scale touring company on both the national and international circuits
- Creating a positive, high profile role model for young people of all cultures
- Developing new audiences for dance
- Developing young choreographers
- Successful re-organisation of policies and structures within company
- Acceptance into Dancers Resettlement Fund Scheme
- Significantly increasing amount of revenue/annual funding received over the last 4 years.

The first points made are significant achievements within the climate for contemporary dance in Britain in 1993. Most contemporary dance companies were based in London and offering few opportunities to people of African Caribbean descent; and few of the companies offered full-time contracts, as they usually operated for only a certain number of weeks of the year. It was quite common for dance companies to rent space for rehearsal rather than to have their own space, and that created extra travel for the dancers and more administration.

The first in the list of ways to pursue this policy is particularly grand: 'fulfilling our role as British ambassadors for communication across cultural boundaries by presenting world class contemporary dance within the British and international forum' (artistic policy, March 1993). This is a very big claim, but it is made in a context in which such companies as the Royal Ballet have been used as cultural ambassadors and where the British Council champions many artists in their projects across the world.

In August 1993, Morris reported that by the end of the year the Company would have travelled from Argentina to Hungary as well as having worked locally. The Company's reputation was evident from the fact that it was the only British Company to be invited to the 'highly acclaimed Cannes International Dance Festival and the only Company internationally to be invited back two years in a row' ('future of Phoenix' CD, 1993:1).

In May 1993 the artistic director reported that Phoenix was in a

> critical position owing to lack of funding. The high level of injury and illness in the company is directly related to lack of funding [and without increased funding] the only option would be to radically reduce the repertory so that each piece only has a maximum of 5 dancers. (BM, 22 May 1993: 3)

Despite this grim prediction, Morris was to report in the summer of 1993 that the

> Company has consolidated its position on the middle-scale circuit and almost completely eliminated a large deficit. As a successful and popular contemporary repertory company Phoenix are ambassadors for the Yorkshire Dance Centre, Leeds and Yorkshire throughout the world. ('future of Phoenix' CD, 1993: 1)

As well as encompassing the achievements charted above, 1993 was a year in which a consultation was put in place to develop internal communication and policy-making structures. The consultants identified several problems, including lack of communication between groups within the Company and between the Company employees and the Board. In addition, it was acknowledged that there was a breakdown in trust and some major tensions over policy. Work was carried out with the Company in order to proceed with the developments that were needed, but it was acknowledged that the Board must work more effectively if any improvements within the Company were to be supported (CD, Stevens, 1993).

It was suggested that when people bought tickets to see a Phoenix performance they were thinking about certain characteristics, including a high-energy approach, a male company and black dancers. It was acknowledged that the company had slotted into the 'international mainstream' but possibly at the expense of some loss of identity. Morris talked at the meeting of wanting to continue to bring international choreographers in to make work, but also to balance this with the development of the company's own choreographic work (21 April 1993:1).

The regional arts board appraisal, which is 'a snapshot in time, taken every five years, in keeping with ACE Guidelines' (BM, 21 July 1994: 4), identified key points in the report, which were intended to encourage discussion. These included the need for Phoenix to reconsider its priorities because it was attempting to do too much, and the need for the budgeting process to include planning to avoid deficit. The YHA acknowledged that the Company had already discussed the main issues (BM, 21 July 1994).

The Company was concerned by the interpretation of its work by YHA and spent time to re-state Company policy and core activity. One of the Board members commented that the Company 'is promoting black British culture both at home and abroad' (BM, 21 July 1994: 5). The Company had decided to cut back education work unless further funding was secured. The Board, however, considered that Phoenix had a significant role to play in the development of opportunities for black dancers. The issue of developing black dancers was also acknowledged to be a national one, and a Board Member reported that discretionary grants for dance trainees had been introduced. There was a concern, however, that some of the trained black dancers were unemployed. A Board Member stated that 'the company [...] recognises the issue of race will be continually under discussion and contradictions will inevitably arise' (BM, 21 July 1994: 6). The Company was also committed to developing black audiences, although it was concerned to reach other audiences as well.

In response to comments from YHA about the Company's role and profile, Phoenix responded:

> The report also appears to have assumptions about the company regarding race issues. We will continue to discuss all of these issues on an internal basis; however impetus for debate must come from within the company, rather than in response to external pressures in order that company members can develop their own artistic and political approach, listening to, but not being influenced by outside opinions. (1994: 4)

This statement indicates the difficulties that the Company faced in negotiating the needs of the dancers and the artistic development of Phoenix while recognising the expectations and perceptions of the funders.

The changes the Company had undergone were only too apparent when a founder dancer applied for the position of assistant artistic director and was not appointed. Despite his relevant experience with another company in addition to Phoenix, it was decided that lack of formal training would not allow him to facilitate the dancers'

17. *Covering Ground*, 1994. Choreographers Danial Shapiro and Joanie Smith; dancers Stephen Derrick, Sharon Donaldson; photographer Steve Hanson

development. There were few applicants for the job; one reason was thought to be that Leeds was less attractive than other locations to some potential candidates. It was noted, however, that other companies were also experiencing problems in recruiting, because people who might otherwise be interested in the job were seeking work abroad or setting up their own companies (BM, 24 May 1994: 3).

In 1995 it was clear that the Company certainly had a progressive role in supporting and promoting the development of black dancers, choreographers and teachers, in attempting to increase their black audience, and in taking positive action when possible to support the training of black technical staff and administrators. It was committed to using live music and commissioning composers and designers, working creatively in the community, and developing as a middle-scale mainstream company.

The Company pursued its education and outreach policy through a range of activities, which included:

- going into schools
- education and outreach packages with performances
- lecture demonstrations and discussions
- targeting outreach work at those communities who rarely have access to the arts
- holidays courses for those from twelve years of age up to professional level
- occasional large-scale educational projects
- open rehearsals
- an open class for professional dancers and third-year dance students
- work experience for students in administration, marketing and technical/stage management.

On 13 July 1996 Maggie Morris announced her decision to leave after the following season. She had considered a plan that allowed for an overlap with the new artistic director so that the change in leadership would be as smooth and supported as possible. Morris was keen that the new appointee would not have to endure the steep learning curve that she had had to undertake when joining the Company. She was complimented on her development of the Company. (Although the beginning had been a battle, the dancers acknowledged that she had managed the Company well and provided opportunities and structures that allowed it to evolve successfully – see earlier comments.) At the same meeting, Thea Barnes (who was later to become the artistic director) was welcomed as the new assistant artistic director (BM, 13 July 1996).

18. *White Picket Fence*, 1996. Choreographer Darshan Singh Bhuller; dancers Dawn Donaldson, Ricky Holgate; photographer Steve Hanson

At the time when Morris resigned and Barnes began her new appointment, there was a breakdown in communication about the lease of YDC. Alternatives were considered, including leasing another site (the Company, however, remained at YDC through to 2001 and beyond). Phoenix toured to Jamaica, but international touring became increasingly difficult financially.

The General Manager explained that 'contemporary dance was not perceived as a box office "banker" by theatres'. Such companies, therefore, were being removed from schedules to satisfy guidelines from theatre boards to minimise financial risk. 'Whilst Phoenix's box office returns are good they are still hard to market and so amongst the first companies to be cut' (BM, 5 October 1996: 3). The result of this strategy meant that Phoenix had managed to balance its books from 1993 to 1996 only because it had successfully secured sponsorship. Core costs had increased with inflation but revenue funding had either decreased or remained at a standstill. This meant that without sponsorship the Company had a significant shortfall (BM, 5 October 1996). Many of the issues that Phoenix confronted continued to be concerns for the next artistic director, Thea Barnes, and are discussed in the next chapter.

Chapter 5: Rewind: A Retrospective

This chapter traces the interface between cultural institutions and their policies of arts management on the one hand, and creativity in relation to the particular historical and social circumstances of Phoenix Dance Company on the other. The earlier chapters were written in retrospect, but the research for this chapter was undertaken while the Company was engaged in its professional tasks. Here I argue that many of the Company's previous difficulties with inadequate funding and with expectations of the repertoire from funding bodies, critics and audiences are the legacy that Thea Barnes, its artistic director from January 1997 to January 2001, attempted to overcome in order to lead it into the twenty-first century.

I have structured this chapter so as to allow Barnes to enunciate something of the theoretical complexity of the issues confronting Phoenix both before and during her directorship. As a dancer, choreographer, teacher and scholar, Barnes brought many skills to the Company and was both rigorous and perceptive in her research of its past, in order to lead it into the future. It was during this period that I had most direct contact with the Company. As mentioned in the introduction, Barnes facilitated my research by giving me access to Company documents, rehearsals, classes, auditions and educational initiatives. In addition, we had frequent conversations about developments within the Company and plans for the future. Barnes was aware of the difficulty of achieving her vision, in which she aimed for recognition of the Company's artistic achievements, free from the restricted expectations of ethnicity. Jean Fisher, in the *Third Text* in 1995, wrote about a similar dilemma for visual artists, which she considered to be a problem of

> how to express one's worldview, with all the multiple cultural inflections that inform it, without betraying either one's historical or geographic specificity or art, and without being caught in the web of signs that are all too consumable as exotic commodity. (6)

This quandary has recurred in the artistic decisions surrounding Phoenix Dance Company throughout its history. Its artistic directors have all negotiated the complexities of artistic decisions from specific backgrounds and viewpoints, and some of these negotiations have been discussed in previous chapters. Many of the questions with which the

Company has been confronted have been related to the 'web of signs' to which Fisher refers, and specifically concerned with issues of identity.

Thea Barnes's desire to develop the Company artistically meant that she wanted to create a repertoire that would be diverse and would allow the Company a fluid rather than a fixed identity. A step towards this aim led to her decision to create a retrospective programme of excerpts of popular works from the Company repertoire.[1] This work enabled Barnes to stay within the budget and to satisfy artistic goals.[2] She came from a background of dancing in American dance companies, where she suggested there was more familiarity with the concept that the 'black dancing body' (Gottschild, 2003) could dance a range of material. Her decision to present a retrospective was both pragmatic and visionary. There was insufficient budget for new work, but the retrospective also provided the ground from which to depart from the past work of Phoenix and to take a new direction in which the repertoire deconstructed what the 'black dancing body' was symbolising in performance (Barnes, 2 September 2004).

Contexts for 19: Rewind and Come Again

The programme, entitled *19: Rewind and Come Again* (dancehall slang for 'encore!'), toured from September 2000 to April 2001. The '19' of the title referred to the nineteen years of the Company's existence, and the programme was designed for

> the dancers to physically embody the history of the company, so they would come to have this tradition in their bodies and then put new ideas into the next show when we'll be looking forward. By giving them the chance to be steeped in Phoenix's history, they will then have the opportunity to spearhead the company's future with really diverse dance. (Barnes, in Hutchinson, 17 November 2000: PA)

---

[1] Two examples of dance texts that demonstrate the implications of arts policies on artistic choices are *Ballet Russes and its World* (1998), in which Lynn Garafola presents a reading of business records of the company, and Susan Foster's *Dances that Describe Themselves: The Improvised Choreography of Richard Bull* (2002), in which she demonstrates how funding policies limited choreographic experimentation.

[2] Part of Barnes's vision was for the dancers to continue to benefit by retaining their fifty-two-week yearly contracts, but this entailed difficult financial decisions. The Arts Council only provided the Company with part of its funding requirements and the Company was responsible for raising the remaining funding. When the next director, Darshan Singh Bhuller, was appointed, the dancers lost this financial security and were employed on nine-month contracts (Barnes, 18 September 2004).

The aims that Barnes articulates here align with some of the principles set out in *The Policy for Dance of the English Arts Funding System* (ACE, 1996). For example, the policy acknowledges that 'the past must be honoured; diversity of form, aesthetics and activity is a strength. It provides choices for artists and audiences, enriches the art form and makes dance relevant to more people' (7). The programme Barnes created, *Rewind*, effectively acknowledged the past. It also, by the choice of works incorporated, gave performers, audiences and critics an opportunity to appreciate fully the wide range of aesthetics Phoenix had engaged with during its history.

Thea Barnes's statement also voices a concern to build on the achievements of the Company without the restrictive expectation from audiences, critics and funders that it should adhere to preconceived notions of the Phoenix repertoire. This artistic freedom to which Phoenix aspired is a position that is taken for granted by some artists. For example, Jean Fisher comments that such a position 'is the luxury traditionally afforded the white male artist, whose authority or identity have historically been more or less assured, freeing him to deal with more abstract levels of existence' (1995: 6).[3]

So although it is frequently taken for granted that white artists offer artistic contributions that are universally significant, this is rarely the case for artists who are considered to inhabit a culturally different position. Nevertheless, such artists may wish to create work that is culturally specific, as in the example Susan Manning gave in her essay on American modern dance in the 1930s:

> African-American choreographers were intent on choreographing visions of blackness. And so the underlying representational trope remained: whereas the white body could represent a universal body, the black body could represent only a black body. (1996: 193)[4]

This representational trope is still evident today and is one context that affects the work of Phoenix Dance Company. Indeed, several contexts have impacted on the Company's work either directly or indirectly.

---

[3] This position is, however, constrained by factors such as sexuality and physical ability, so that a white gay man and/or a disabled man would not necessarily feel free to explore 'abstract levels of existence'.

[4] Mark Franko suggests that Manning's interpretation of the 'modern dancer as universal subject' (2002: 93) and her discussion of the representation of the African American body did not fully acknowledge the political context of the 1930s. He states, 'Given the antiracist politics of the CP-USA [Communist Party] in the thirties and the "ethnic Americanism" of the Popular Front, "speaking for" oppressed African Americans was not construed as appropriating identity from black subject positions' (2002: 93).

A further example is the context of funders, with which dance artist Brenda Edwards is concerned. *The Policy for Dance of the English Arts Funding System* stated that 'artists are the key decision-makers on whether, and how, their work should be categorised by the funding system' (7). However, although this may have been the intention, Edwards in 2004 does not find it realised. She posits that although the Arts Council of England has given priority and a high profile to what it terms 'cultural diversity', application of that term may not be beneficial to the artists it is targeting. Edwards also suggests that several issues are not adequately addressed under such a label: for example, the lack of opportunities for black women artists. She argues that ACE has power because of economics, and artists are required to confine themselves to the boundaries that the funders create. Furthermore, she suggests that sometimes the 'institutional powers appropriate change' (2004: 16) within organisations, resulting in 'cultural meaning [being] lost' (2004: 16). She gives Phoenix as an example of this process.

This viewpoint highlights one aspect of the complexities of Phoenix's identity that Barnes was attempting to address with *19: Rewind and Come Again*. The Phoenix dancers, predominantly from the African Diaspora, have frequently been considered by critics and audiences to represent the 'Black or Black British people [who] make up 2.2 per cent, with Black Caribbeans the largest black group at 1.1 per cent' of ethnic minority groups in Britain (Commission for Racial Equality, 2003). Although this is an important aspect of the Company, which this study addresses, I would argue that what is possibly more significant, as is apparent from Fisher's comments, is that the Company is acknowledged for its artistic strengths rather than defined by its ethnic composition. However, as we have seen in previous chapters and will be clear in the next chapter, the tendency for Phoenix to be discussed only in terms of ethnicity has been problematic for the Company throughout its history.

Barnes had a strong vision for Phoenix that evolved from her experiences in two key contemporary dance companies and her understanding of dance education. She began her professional career with the Alvin Ailey Dance Company, later becoming a member of the Martha Graham Dance Company for eleven years. Highlights of her career include Martha Graham's ballet *Song*, created especially for her talents; performing on Broadway in *Treemonisha* and *The Wiz* and on television in Ailey's *Memories and Vision*; and Graham's *Clytemnestra* and *Diversions of Angels*, for *Celebrate! 100 Years of Lively Arts at the Met*. Thea Barnes taught at the Laban Centre, London Contemporary Dance School and the Northern School of Contemporary Dance, Leeds. She also regularly contributes to dance journals.

Her experience at NSCD gave her insight into the specific issues that arose because the Company was based in Leeds. She wanted to lead the Company into the future with strong dancers, diverse choreography, effective education and informed audiences. This was at a time when there were a significant number of new dancers joining the Company. A group of dancers had begun working with Phoenix at similar times and were ready to leave within months of each other to begin new careers. Dancers' performing careers are precarious and short, as Jeanette Siddall outlines in *21st Century Dance* (2001), and they usually stop performing professionally in their mid-thirties.

Barnes perception of this transition of changing personnel was that it was an opportunity:

> *This season half the dancers are new, with varying movement experiences and training. Phoenix is a repertory company and thus the dancers' experience in and the potential for development of a number of movement styles is increased.* (Barnes, 1999: 35)

When Thea Barnes was appointed artistic director of Phoenix Dance in 1997, she evolved a perception and an analysis of the 'Phoenix Phenomenon', as she termed it, which crystallises key issues of this study. An important aspect of this phenomenon was the tensions between 'Phoenix Past' and the Company as it existed in 2001. This chapter, therefore, will also focus on Barnes's attempt to ease these tensions and to take the Company forward. Despite her optimism and clarity of vision, however, at the end of the tour of *Rewind* most of the staff were made redundant, and Barnes left the Company in January 2001.

The year 2001 thus saw the last performances of *19: Rewind and Come Again* and the ending of the Company that Barnes had directed. It was also when the *Eclipse Report: Developing strategies to combat racism in theatre*, following a conference on 12 and 13 June 2001 at Nottingham Playhouse, was published. Although this report specified theatre, many of the issues it raises are relevant and applicable to dance generally and to Phoenix specifically. This conference was an initiative of the Arts Council of England, East Midlands Arts Board, the Theatrical Management Association and Nottingham Playhouse Initiative. Many institutions analysed their organisational structures in relation to racism following Sir William MacPherson's 1999 report, *The Stephen Lawrence Inquiry*. This incident and the inadequate institutional structures to combat racism that it both highlighted and came to symbolise had far-reaching implications for British society and is, therefore, one of several contexts relevant to Phoenix Dance Company.

Stephen Lawrence was a young man of African descent who was murdered in the street in 1993 by five white youths. He was frequently referred to as 'the black teenager' in the voluminous publicity that followed his death. His 'blackness' and the issues related to this description of his identity received close scrutiny in a number of forums. The public inquiry into Lawrence's death was set up 'to identify the lessons to be learned for the investigation and prosecution of racially motivated crimes' (programme note, Norton-Taylor, 1999). This was after the Crown Prosecution Service had dropped the prosecution because of insufficient evidence, a situation that was found to be a result of police incompetence and corruption, and after a private prosecution previously brought by his parents had failed. The case and its implications were given wide publicity in the national press.[5] It became a symbol for a stand against racism, and the Lawrences, who were 'articulate and upwardly mobile, were just the "right" kind of black family to find support from the *Daily Mail* and middle England' (*The Guardian*, 1999: 69). Stephen Lawrence was certainly neither the first nor the last young person of African descent to be attacked and murdered in Britain. However, the fact that he was destined to become a respectable middle-class professional, together with his parents' articulacy about the crime, created an alliance amongst an extensive range of people who were deeply disturbed by the implications of racism within British culture.

[5] The following references, in date order, are a small sample of the articles written in relation to Stephen Lawrence's death and the implications that arose from the public inquiry and the MacPherson Report. They are representative of the range of publications, including national press, occupational publications and popular magazines, that covered the case. Understandably, much of the coverage was in 1999 when the Report was published.

Chaudhary, V. 'Lost dreams of an unspent life', *The Guardian*, 27 April 1996, p.23.
Dodd, V. '"The hardest thing is knowing they did it. I hope for a miracle": The Lawrences speak out', *The Observer*, 5 July 1998, p.3.
Editorial. 'A misguided and unfair report', *The Daily Telegraph*, 25 February 1999, p.29.
Bucky, S. 'Government pledges to repair race relations', *Financial Times*, 25 February 1999, p.1.
Jack, I. 'A family tragedy, a police force disgraced and a nation shamed', *The Independent*, 25 February 1999, p.1.
Travis, A. 'Stephen Lawrence's legacy: confronting racist Britain', *The Guardian*, 25 February 1999, p.1.
Turner, J. 'Time to act for Equal Opportunities', *Stage Screen & Radio*, March 1999, p.4.
Kirsch, B. and Purcell, M. 'Stephen Lawrence report "a new window of opportunity": National Conference NATFHE', *The Lecturer*, July 1999, p.13.
Castle, S. 'Lawrence family honoured for racism struggle', *The Independent*, 19 October 2000, p.10.
Neustatter, A. 'If I can change just one child, that will be an achievement', *The Guardian*, 27 June 2001, pp.8–9.
Williams, Z. 'Alone and unsupported', *Good Housekeeping*, April 2003, pp.50–52.

There was widespread acknowledgement that changes needed to be made within a range of institutional structures and organisations to eradicate racism. The transcripts of the inquiry were edited into a play by Richard Norton-Taylor entitled *The Colour of Justice* (1999), and a television programme entitled *Why Stephen?* was broadcast on BBC2 on 13 February 1999. The MacPherson Report was published on 25 February 1999. The implications of this report and the continued influence of its findings were evident in subsequent conferences and reports. The *Eclipse Report* is one such example, containing this key paragraph:

> Institutional Racism consists of the collective failure of an organisation to provide an appropriate and professional service to people because of their colour, culture or ethnic origin. It can be seen or detected in processes, attitudes and behaviour which amount to discrimination through unwitting prejudice, ignorance, thoughtlessness and racist stereotyping which disadvantage minority ethnic people. (In Brown, Hawson, Graves and Barot, 2001: 3).

The *Eclipse Report* considers factors relevant 'towards a national strategy' in relation to racism, equality of opportunity and positive action. It also includes an appendix of artists' and speakers' contributions. Tyrone Huggins, artistic director of Theatre of Darkness and also Chair of the Board of Phoenix Dance from 1997, outlines some of his concerns in this appendix. He also details his connection with Phoenix and his observations about issues of racism in relation to the Company. He first worked with the Company as a sound engineer in 1981, was a member of the Board for seven years, and took on the Chair after an eighteen-month break. He said that he was:

> honoured and pleased to be considered such a natural successor [of former Chair Graham Devlin] for such an eminent role in such a prestigious company. But I am not a fool. Also departing was the Artistic Director and soon to follow the General Manager. I ask you to imagine what might happen next? In the space of six months, Phoenix lost all of its experience at senior level, including the invisible colleges [informal networks] associated with those individuals, gaining instead two Black people with very different invisible colleges. (2001: 49)

Huggins's invisible college was made up of Black British theatre practitioners and a group of artists who were determined to provide a context
for Black British artistic practices. In addition, as the Chair of the Board
he needed to be involved with the informal networks of support for the
Company. He was aware of the glass ceiling that limited skilful performers from progressing, but he also thought there had been some changes
in the media, evidenced by the fact that there were more 'Black faces on
TV' (2001: 47), which provided an important context.

Huggins, however, did not consider the appointment of practitioners
from the African Diaspora as necessarily unproblematic. He was concerned that there might be difficulties for Phoenix with a black Chair of
the Board and a black artistic director and said that he thought 'this is
where it all falls apart' (2001: 49). In order to avoid that happening, he
called a funders' meeting but did not find any help forthcoming. He suggested that the dancers were satisfied with his leadership, but that there:

> were issues of authority unseen by white eyes. There is a phenome-
> non in which one Black person finds it difficult to accept the author-
> ity of another unused to the experience. This played itself out within
> Phoenix at all levels. I hunted around for practical support and
> received warm words and platitudes. (2001: 49)

Barnes's perception of the situation differed from this. Her invisible colleges drew on an international network of artists and educationalists
who were influential in the dance world. She did not view the tensions
as an issue of the internalised oppression[6] that Huggins expresses, but
rather to be about the structure of the Company in relation to leadership. She expected to have leadership of the Company with the Board's
support. She viewed the real issue to be about how to run a dance company, not that of the colour of skin (21 July 2004). There was a clash
between those views (see below). In 1999 Huggins informed his Board
and Yorkshire Arts that he did not think he could manage Phoenix, as
'the situation was becoming critical and my personal resources were in
excess of meagre' (2001: 5). Yet he was encouraged to continue and it
was not until March 2001 that he resigned as Chair. On 23 May 2001
Phoenix Dance Company ceased its activities, except for a small education component. Following Barnes's departure, the funders decided that
the Company needed to be restructured, and it was not until 2002 that
it reopened with a new artistic director, Darshan Singh Bhuller.

---

[6] Internalised oppression is, as Noam Chomsky articulates, a process of 'internalising alien
values and then convincing oneself that one is acting freely' (in Gottschild, 2003: 66).

To what extent this process was about the management system or about lack of support of the Company as a role model is, as Huggins suggests, impossible to trace; but as he pointed out:

> What is clear is that this process, driven by the funding system for its own inarticulate reasons, has led to 17 or so poorly paid and predominantly Black artists and practitioners being made redundant, while five or six highly paid and exclusively white consultants pore over the entrails of the dead bird, whose complexity of practical operation will never be summed up in all the reports prepared for all the processes of arts administration that the system can devise. (2001: 50)[7]

The disappointment that Huggins experienced in being unable to support the development of Phoenix dance effectively, and the frustration of dealing with a system that was inadequate to support him in his task, are apparent from his comments. His remarks, while honest, do not fully acknowledge his own lack of experience as a chair nor the pressure of his other commitments. Although he was experienced as an artistic director, his lack of practice in an administrative leadership role was perceived by Barnes to have contributed to the difficulties that the Company faced (2004).

It is also important to note here that the temporary ending of this narrative in 2001 had significant features that were similar to those in the relationship between funders and Company earlier in its history. Both in 1984 and in 2001, the Company's development was very much a result of the funders' agenda. Although the Company members also had agency throughout these years, this was painfully negotiated through the structures imposed upon them. Huggins's remarks highlight the tensions that the Company experienced throughout its history: of exercising agency in relation to the direction and practices of Phoenix, and yet at the same time being constrained by funders' agendas. Tricia Rose's argument in relation to black popular cultures is

---

[7] This was a very difficult time for the Company. The consultants whom Huggins mentions set up focus groups, one of which I attended on 20 July 2001 at the Northern School of Contemporary Dance. They gave an outline of the expectations for the Company's future and of changes in structure and funding. One of the main changes was for the dancers to be employed for part of the year rather than to have contracts for fifty-two weeks. Much of what was said at that meeting in terms of developing relationships between Phoenix and the local community as well as developing national and international profiles had clearly been on Thea Barnes's agenda, including the insight that the context had changed and that the Phoenix of the past was not necessarily that of the future. Thus Huggins's frustration mirrored my own sense of frustration which I experienced at the focus group over the way the Company had temporarily closed, the reasons for that closure and the implications for the future.

pertinent to these constraints: 'Cultural forms, expressions, and representations continue to be deployed, directly and indirectly, in the service of political agendas, not always those of our choosing' (1997: 260). There is a play of power in such deployment, which the Company members have had to negotiate.

As in the early 1980s, the structure with which the funders obliged the Company to comply in 2001 was problematic for the personnel, although in different ways. In 2001, the Company members were employed by the Board, who served in a voluntary capacity as legal directors of the Company. The artistic director and general manager reported directly to the Board, which also had to approve the yearly budget (Holgate, 1997). The structure was such that each Board member served for three years and could be elected for a further three. Members were then required to stand down for a year before re-election. The Board was self-appointed and attempted to ensure that the range of members covered legal, educational, organisational and general arts backgrounds. The Chair of the Board was chosen from Board nominations (Huggins, 2001).

There were difficulties with such a structure, as I observed during the time Barnes was artistic director. Firstly, the members had their own demanding careers, and their involvement with Phoenix was, therefore, limited. Secondly, because of the time commitment, it was difficult to recruit sufficiently knowledgeable members. Thirdly, the relationship between the roles of the Board and the artistic director was problematic. Concerning this last point, it seems that Barnes, with her experience of artist-led companies, expected the Board to support her lead and to facilitate her directorship and the vision that they and the dancers had chosen when they employed her. She was also concerned over members of the Board making artistic judgements when their expertise was in legal or personnel matters (12 January 2001). Despite many conversations, the Board required more involvement than Barnes anticipated. There were disagreements, and eventually the Board informed her that they had lost confidence in her artistic vision, which they had previously supported. Despite the complexities of changing personnel in the Company, tensions between the Board and the Company management, and limited resources, many critics continued to acknowledge the Company's achievements.

New directions for the Company, integrating past and future

The *Lancashire Evening Post* reported that Phoenix was 'one of the best things to come out of that city's [Leeds] virtual dance industry' (Upton, 2000: PA). The writer also noted:

> The resulting mixture of movement and textures would really defy anyone not to find something to enjoy here. There's an eclectic mix that leans heavily on predominantly Afro-Caribbean roots but also embraces the increasingly cosmopolitan make-up of the company [...]. Above all the works celebrate the liberating nature of dance and its unique ability to blend styles and culture. (Upton, 2000: PA)

This reflects what Barnes wanted to achieve with this programme. The writer acknowledges Phoenix's achievements and the diverse repertoire that the Company had performed in the nineteen years of its existence. This recognition is also evident in Val Javin's review in the *Huddersfield Daily Examiner*: 'It was a retrospective in that it charted precisely where this hugely successful company has come from but it also gave as an encore, a tantalising glimpse of what might lie ahead' (2001: PA).

In *The Guardian* (28 November 2000), Stephanie Ferguson, who had written many reviews of Phoenix, wrote, 'Phoenix had led the way for black British dance' (25). She also noted that many of the dancers who had originated in Leeds had recently left the Company; only Hugh Davis remained and the other performers were from Finland, Russia, Madagascar, Zimbabwe, South Africa and Jamaica. Despite Barnes's efforts to move away from the label of 'black British dance', many critics applied this category to the Company, as evidenced above. The other point that Ferguson makes concerns the dancers' heritage. As we have seen, a distinctive feature of the Company until 1999 was the dancers' shared background of dance education in Leeds, which was an unusual beginning for professional dancers. It is much more common for dancers to come from many countries, as was the case with the Phoenix Dance Company in 2000 who performed *19: Rewind and Come Again*.

Rewind consisted of excerpts from eight of the Company's popular works together with three new works inspired by early Phoenix works, which Ferguson describes. *Brawta* (Jamaican slang for a little extra) is a work for three couples:

> We're down at the dance-hall and it's a free-for-all as they let rip to the rap. This funky battle for dance supremacy is full of loose gyrations

and peacock struts, each contender slipping on a black coat before they go for it. Raw and fun it captures what early Phoenix was all about [...] *Key Club* [is] homage to the company's jazz heritage [and] *Strange Fruit* [is] a powerful solo for Sotiya, danced to Nina Simone's harrowing version of the song. (2000: 25)

Ferguson's observations suggest that the new works communicated some of the enjoyment and involvement of the early Company.

Yet Natalie Anglesey, writing in *The Stage*, thought that supporters of the Company might be concerned to discover that Phoenix had 'changed direction', which she linked to the use of multimedia and narrative (2000: 17). Nonetheless, she praised the dancers and their dancing, the popular works from the repertoire and the newly created pieces, saying that 'the dancers really come together [...and] show that this vibrant company is at its best when it can simply demonstrate the joy of dance' (2000: 17). Although this is a positive comment, the use of the word 'joy' also implies an expression of a 'natural' element to the Company's achievement rather than emphasising their professionalism.

In contrast to the positive tone of the above reviews in relation to the dancers, dancing and choreography, Ismene Brown, writing in the *Daily Telegraph* (26 September 2000), had serious reservations about the programme. She categorised the Company as follows:

Roots are also clearly a mixed blessing for Phoenix Dance Company. Once easily pigeonholed as the black boys' company from Leeds, now, 19 years after its birth, it is shifting uneasily in its niche, having added women, whites and mainstream contemporary dance to its original urban, streetwise laddishness, and now having only one Leeds dancer in its ranks. (Brown, 2000: 22)

Here Brown is trying to classify and fix the Company into categories. In doing so, she sacrifices accuracy; for example, the founders worked with a contemporary dance idiom as part of their approach to movement from the outset. Clearly, *Rewind,* with its retrospective aspect, lends itself to observations about the Company's identity and past, but this review, together with others by Brown,[8] has a judgemental tone that masks rather than reveals the choreography. For example, she says, 'the dancers, many from overseas don't dance together like a boisterous family, the way one remembers' (Brown, 2000: 22). Brown is lamenting the

---

[8] Other reviews by Ismene Brown are discussed in Chapter 6.

loss of the Company of her memory.[9] She is reluctant to acknowledge the strengths of the Company dancing in 2000, who were from very diverse backgrounds and inevitably danced with qualities different from those of the earlier companies, in which the dancers shared some movement experiences and knew each other from schooldays. Brown also had reservations, as Anglesey had, about the multimedia input:

> There's also an off-putting preachiness about the exhortatory videos and orotund declamations and some flatulent choreography parachutes on the greatness of Martin Luther King or Nina Simone. (2000: 22)

Anglesey considered that the narrative bordered 'on the pretentious [and that] ultimately this means less dance and a marked drop in pace' (12 October 2000: PA). Barnes's attempt to use mixed media and to urge the audience to shift their expectations of the Company was unappreciated by Anglesey and Brown. The outcome of the video and narrative was another example of constrained funding. The intention of the whole programme was timely and pertinent, but the quality of the video and the length of the clips between dances did to some extent undermine the energy of what I considered to be the excellently chosen excerpts of popular works together with the new works.

Ismene Brown was also dismissive of some of the excerpts: for example, *Longevity* (1994) and *Strange Fruit* (2000). She did not offer readers insight into the power of these two important works. *Longevity* was first choreographed by Gary Lambert for Rambert Dance Company and then reworked for Phoenix. It is a duet danced partly in silence and partly to Martin Luther King's famous speech, 'I have a dream'. The message of hope and transcendence of the text is embodied in the physical images on stage. Critic Kevin Berry, reviewing the performance in 1994, thought that the dancers 'radiate[d] a power coming from collective inner strength in a profound and quite riveting performance' (1994: PA). The other work that Brown considered 'flatulent choreography' was *Strange Fruit*, choreographed by Thea Barnes and Andile Sotiya (a dancer and choreographer with the Company), in which I would suggest the evocative lyrics are intensified by the deeply moving physicality of Sotiya's exquisite performance.

Barnes was particularly interested in the development of dance vocabulary. She invited David Hamilton to teach the Company ska- and

---

[9] The sense of loss of a remembered company which this critic articulates is also echoed in Nicholas Dromgoole's review discussed in Chapter 6.

reggae-influenced dance movements, particularly the rock step, in order for the Company to embody an aspect of the founders' movement. This became a fruitful exchange of experiences of popular dance. She also created several choreographies while with Phoenix, which is a difficult task when directing a company. When Hamilton made works for the Company, it was still small-scale. Campbell made a number of works at the transition time when the Company was growing. Morris, however, only co-choreographed one work. There is a conflict between the two roles, because a choreographer needs to be free to think of the work as it develops, whereas the director must have an overview of both what is currently happening within the Company and what needs to be organised for the future. Nevertheless, Barnes choreographed *Unbroken* (1997), *Four* (1998) and *The Last Word* (1999) and with Andile Sotiya co-choreographed *Key Club, Brawta* and *Strange Fruit* (2000).

Unbroken was an important departure for Phoenix. It was one of the few solos in the Company's repertoire and one of the few works to engage with narrative. Working with Sol B. River's text, it presented a dialogue between the movement and the text that extended beyond the fixity of the subject. It offered perspectives, experiences and juxtapositions between movement and text that allowed the fluidity of gender and ethnicity to be glimpsed. The solo embodied 'the spirit and conflict of man and woman and the journey of wisdom that brings about enlightenment' (*Essentially Phoenix* programme note, 1997). The work was performed by both male and female members of the Company; but although the critics responded well to the dancing, they were less convinced by the prose, which David Dougill, writing in the *Sunday Times*, described as 'part sanctimonious' (1997: PA). River's text, however, was powerfully evocative, and descriptions such as Dougill's diminished its strength. The rehearsal director, Norman Douglas, thought that the critics 'missed the point'. For him, when the solo was danced by a man, he read an aspect of the work as 'about how men are sometimes constricted and unable to communicate' (1998: 4). For Douglas the work was 'one of the most moving pieces I'd ever seen. It brought in lots of issues' (1998).

As well as developing her own work, Barnes wanted other choreographers to make work for the Company, but some, for example Bill T. Jones, were beyond the budget. She was also attracted to Henry Oguike's[10] work, which embodied a nonliteral approach to contemporary dance, as well as to the more theatrical dance elements that choreographers Jonzi D and Benji Reid offered. She deemed it important to consider the

---

[10] The director who followed Barnes, Darshan Singh Bhuller, commissioned Oguike to make a work, *Signal*, in 2004.

19. *Unbroken*, 1997. Choreographer Thea Barnes; dancer Booker T. Louis;
photographer Steve Hanson

aesthetics of dance vocabulary and the contexts within which the work was made and performed, for understanding and insight into choreography (12 January 2001). It was this perspective that she brought to *Rewind.* The last performance of this work was in Southend, coincidently Ricky Holgate's home town. On 12 April 2001 I watched the penultimate performance at Darlington Civic Theatre[11] and travelled back with the despondent dancers. Some, however, were relieved that the ending of the Company freed them to explore other possibilities. The narrative of Phoenix is a complex myriad of beginnings and endings, but each phase has been influenced by the dancers, the artistic directors, the Board, funders and critics as well as by other associates. So what expertise and specific qualities did Barnes bring to the Company before its demise?

Her credentials for her post with Phoenix were impeccable. Her early dance career as a performer with the Alvin Ailey Dance Company influenced her in many ways. Barnes explained that Ailey was not a symbol about being black, as was, for example, Martin Luther King. Rather, he was an inspiration for a utopian dream of the acceptance of difference. He was a role model and also provided a positive vision of African American women in his famous solo for Judith Jamison, *Cry* (1971). After this formative influence, Barnes then joined the Martha Graham Dance Company, where she performed as a soloist and principal dancer (Barnes, 9 November 1998).

Her association with these two companies is significant because of the influence of American contemporary dance in Britain. Indeed, it was members of the Graham Company, specifically Robert Cohan, who were instrumental in the founding of London Contemporary Dance Theatre. Barnes had considerable experience in choreography and performance (on Broadway and for film and television) and also had a wide range of teaching experience and a commitment to dance education.

In 1993 Barnes began working with Phoenix Dance Company as the rehearsal director, but only during the summer, when she was free from her teaching at the Laban Centre, London. She became the assistant artistic director in 1996, was interviewed for the position of artistic director in November 1996 and was appointed to begin the post on 7 January 1997. After discussions with the dancers and technical staff about the Company, she created a vision for Phoenix that she considered viable for the immediate future. She explained that:

---

[11] Darlington Civic Theatre was also an early venue for the Company, as they performed there in 1982.

When you come into a new contemporary dance company [as an artistic
director] *you can make choices that either toss what is already there or
take whatever is there to go to the new place or steer it in another direction.
I felt the way the dancers were, there was no way I was going to come in
and totally redesign the company without a real huge ugly fight.* (1997)

From the outset, Barnes faced challenges in her attempts to pursue her
artistic vision for the Company. She outlined her key aims as being:

*To broaden Phoenix's dimensions as a contemporary dance company; to
steer it into being eclectic and international, having a repertory that is
global in its perspective as well as connected to and recognised nationally.
Repertory takes on a different meaning in this context and allows for the
expression of diversity that communicates the range of experiences within
and outside Phoenix Dance.* (1 February 1997)

Thea Barnes's aims for Phoenix attempted to counter essentialist
notions of identity. Paul Gilroy argues that in order to break away from
such restrictive notions it is necessary to shift away from nationalist history. He suggests that 'essentialist theories of racial difference that are
currently so popular should be seen as symptoms of loss of certainty
around "race"' (2000: 8). In his book *Between Camps*, Gilroy argues that
'the time of race may be coming to a close even while racisms appear to
proliferate' (2000: 44).[12] His argument is based on developments in sci-
entific research and cultural perspectives that result in fluid rather than
fixed identities. It is clear from her aims stated above that Barnes was
determined to foster a Company that was not limited by traditional categorisations and that embraced the fluidities of which Gilroy writes. She
also intended '*The creative work of Phoenix Dance* [to] *take its inspiration
from diverse cultural experiences including drawing from the diversity of black
British experience*' (in Holgate, 1997: 36).

 Although she wanted the Company to be stimulated by its heritage,
she did not want it to be confined to its past and specific artistic expectations. These concerns were shared by other artists who were struggling
to have their artistic merits acknowledged rather than becoming an
example of cultural diversity. For example, Sanjoy Roy argues in a discussion of Shobana Jeyasingh's work, 'Jeyasingh the choreographer
fades into the background in favour of Jeyasingh the Indian woman

---

[12] In his book, *After Empire: Melancholia or Convivial Culture* (2004), Paul Gilroy argues for
British multiculturalism and an acceptance of the end of empire from those who are living in
denial.

living in Britain who engages with questions of migrancy, diaspora, race, tradition, hybridity and so on' (Roy, 1997: 4). In an unpublished paper, Barnes stated, 'Phoenix's particular kind of potential requires a forum that does not constantly remind and measure by its past' (1998). She considered that the Phoenix of 1981 provided an inspiring model, after the images of chaos, looting and uprisings in the cities in Britain at that time, and she had no wish to negate that legacy. She proposed, however, that although the past should be acknowledged it was important 'to be more concerned with developing a future' (in Holgate, 1997: 36). As Natasha Bakht pointed out in an article concerned with the difficulties of overcoming stereotyping, 'Essentially, we are asking for the freedom to be unpredictable' (1997: 9). These comments and arguments are concerned with artists' demands for recognition and cultural equity rather than being categorised under the label of cultural diversity.

It is a vision of cultural equity that inspired *Rewind*, and the video footage included in the programme locates the Company and is in line with the Mission Statement:

> By keeping its community and historical foundation intact, Phoenix Dance Company intends to encapsulate the diaspora of black British community and design its artistry to inspire and enlighten a diversity of community groupings. (1 February 1997, artistic director's report)

Barnes had given the issues raised by the term 'black' a good deal of consideration, and defined her perspective as follows:

> Black is a political stance and thus a belief in my right to be proud of my heritage. It is also a declaration expressed where needed to defend my particular cultural, political and social rights as a fully-fledged and empowered citizen in the society in which I reside. "Black" is not exactly who I am or an adequate label, category, or description of the art work I practice. (AD report, 5 May 1997)

She considered it necessary to change the Mission Statement, education policy and artistic policy in order to begin to put into practice the vision that she had presented at her interview. Moreover, this was a period of re-evaluation because the Company was changing. Dancers who had been with Phoenix since 1989 began to consider careers other than performing, as they had reached their physical peak. This in turn entailed hiring dancers, some of whom were at the beginning of their career and, therefore, did not have the experience and expertise of the departing dancers. As Niall McMahon, a teacher for the Company, pointed out, such a radical change might happen in any company 'where you have a flat period for five years where nobody leaves at all and then suddenly you lose half your company' (1998). In this context, Barnes reconsidered the Company's Mission Statement. She said, '*I wanted to change it* [the mission statement] *around so that it was said in a manner that we were of African descent, but that's not what we were about [...] did I open up a can of worms?*' (2 May 1997).

The Chair of the Board, Tyrone Huggins, wanted these ideas to go to an artistic committee. A meeting of this committee, however, was only attended by Gill Cooper (the general manager), Thea Barnes, Tyrone Huggins and all the dancers. Barnes believed that the meeting became an attempt to deal with various issues about the running of the Company that were not connected with artistic vision (1997). There appeared to be some resentment from the dancers that Barnes was African American. One of them passed a remark that made it clear that he felt it was not quite right that Barnes had the position of artistic director because, as Barnes explained, '*I'm not even British. Also my directness is sometimes quite abrasive*' (18 May 1997).

The tension that this dancer was identifying reflected the sense of loss of ownership of the Company for some of the dancers. This loss is part of the cultural memory of the Company, passed on with each new generation of dancers. So despite the differences in political awareness and the visions of Campbell, Morris and Barnes, the experiences of the dancers were in some ways similar. It was not the dancers' visions that directed the Company. In addition, the geographical location of the Company in Leeds and in Britain had always been an important aspect of its identity, but became less significant as dancers from different parts of the world were employed. The tension that the dancer mentioned in relation to Barnes not being British is also mirrored, however, within British contemporary dance. There is both an acknowledgement of the importance of the legacy of American contemporary dance and the international aspect of the art form and at the same time a desire to have the developments of British dance, dancers and choreographers fully recognised.

Despite such confrontations, Barnes was determined to be inclusive in her approach to the Company, and set up training sessions and discussions in which the members had the opportunity to debate and gain further insight into the controversial issues surrounding the Company's identity and artistry. A memo dated 6 July 1998 to the dancers from the artistic director and education director Dawn Holgate asked the dancers to consider the statements below, and their own viewpoints in relation to them, for discussion of a revised Mission Statement.

> To inspire and entertain through dance and to develop new audiences for dance whilst enriching and embodying the spirit of a black British experience
>
> [...] we are proud of our allegiance to Black Britain while at the same time reflecting and consistently affirming the diversity of that experience. (1998: 1)

Such discussions also took place when Margaret Morris was artistic director, but Barnes's perspective was more politically astute. Concerning her ambitions for the Company and her hopes for the employment of dancers, Barnes said, '*I want Phoenix to be a place where dancers of African descent can find a job [...] but if I cannot find the dancers who meet the criteria to do the work then I will look somewhere else*' (18 May 1997).

Barnes's political ideals were such that she wished to '*take positive action*' to provide opportunities for encouragement and training of 'disenfranchised' artists, administrators and technicians whenever possible. Her main aim, however, was to produce the best possible contemporary dance company, and to that end she was willing to employ dancers of any ethnicity, as was Neville Campbell (AD report, 1 February 1997: 5). She was concerned that the dancers should have a sense of the dance context in which they worked, and so she set up research time when they worked with professionals with varied experiences and expertise: for example, Rui Horta (April 1999). Another important element of Barnes's approach to the Company was her determination to have the education work and the performance work of the Company running in parallel. To this end she appointed the dancer Dawn Holgate to lead and develop the education work. Barnes's concern was to actively empower the dancers in their roles as educators and to provide opportunities for participants to engage with high-quality education provision through which they too were empowered. The interconnection for Barnes of performance and dance education is evident in her artistic vision, in which she stated, 'As a means to broaden the horizons of its artistry, the artistic vision of Phoenix is supported by a passion for dance education' (in Holgate, 1997: 37).

In an article in *Animated*, Barnes said that her inspiration for the Company was the forty-year-old Alvin Ailey Dance Theatre. Ailey was seeking a specific kind of '*dance theatre and [...] practices for making dance*'

(Barnes, 1989–99: 28). Barnes put in place a re-evaluation of the '*purposes and processes*' (Barnes, 1989–99: 28) of Phoenix from spring 1997 to the end of 1998. She suggested that it '*had to be done in such a way that Company members would be full, active participants in articulating agreements and shaping new operational methods*' (1989–99: 28). While its procedures were being transformed, the Company's educational aspects were being considered too. Phoenix was awarded an Education, Research and Development Initiative (ERDI), written and secured by both Barnes and Gill Cooper, the general manager, which provided the means to develop its approaches to education work.

Two dance education experts, Marion Gough and Loren Bucek, were employed to help Phoenix with the project. A think tank was formed in August 1997 and in December 1997 Bucek led a week of educational development and Gough monitored the research and development. The aims were to define, change and implement systems of accountability for the education work. I attended some of the workshops and realised how important it was for the Company to have time to reflect upon its development, and for the members to have the opportunity to work together without pressure at such a key transitional time. Performers, technicians, administrators and Board members all took part in the workshops. This research was an example of Barnes's vision of potential developments for the Company (Barnes, AD's report, 1997).

Awards such as ERDI were significant but insufficient. Although Barnes's vision for the Company was expansive, the resources for its realisation were not. She viewed the education work of the Company as fundamental to its development. Concerned about funding, she asked, '*If the education work stops, how will it be possible to educate audiences to accept what they are not used to or to develop new talent?*' (Barnes, 12 January 2001). The education work was particularly important for opening opportunities for cultural equity, as the Company's work attracted audiences and trainee performers who were not white, middle-class females, the predominant group involved with contemporary dance.

In her interview with me (April 1999), Barnes discussed the tensions and strains that were apparent in the Company. The difficulty with limited funding was an issue. The budget barely covered operating expenses, salaries and day-to-day operations, much less new work. Jasper and Siddall point out that 'creative management of resources is essential to survival on the small- and middle-scale [...and] the struggle with limited resources is constant' (1999: 52). Barnes's perspective was that it was not possible to run the Company as a middle-scale company with the resources available at the time. Further, Mark Baldwin, who was scheduled to choreograph for the Company, had received a better deal in Germany. The Company, therefore, needed another choreographer who would make work within the budget for the new season at short notice. This is one example of the pressures with which the Company were confronted because of limited funding and the difficulties involved in commissioning choreographers. The employment issues in relation to choreographers are highlighted in a report commissioned in 2001 by the London Arts and Yorkshire Arts Board, *Choreography as Work (UK)*. This found that Yorkshire-based choreographers were more frequently employed, but that they were regarded as having a lower status than those choreographers based in London. This is an interesting finding, because the issue of locality is both a strength and a weakness in the Company's history, as noted in earlier chapters.

History in the making

On 28 September 1997 Barnes telephoned me to let me know of some of the changes occurring in the Company. She wanted me to know of the events behind the scenes as they evolved. There were to be changes of management practice, and policy documents that clarified conditions of employment. Some dancers had complained about aspects of the way the Company was run, and the dance officer called a meeting with advisers. Barnes raised the question of whether the Company was a dancer-led Company rather than one led by an artistic director. At this point she thought that the Company was funded because the Arts Council could demonstrate that they were politically correct. She stated that Phoenix had initially been used to fulfil political agendas and ambitions and was still being used in that way. When the founders first received funding, they too had been concerned about the award's political context. The Chair, Tyrone Huggins, also commented that the financing of Phoenix was the result of a funding initiative (14 March 2001). From these comments it is apparent that the funders' agendas influenced the artistic outcomes and that tensions continued to reverberate throughout the Company. In addition, there were factors that affected the Company's productions but were beyond their control. For example, one person had a family bereavement, with the result that the technical requirements for the show had to be learnt in a single day and the show went up without a sound check. The Company were working with tight budgets, and each member of staff was under pressure with little leeway, as this example illustrates (Barnes, 9 April 1999).

In 1999 the Company had a £32,000 deficit, which they could clear only by touring some of the old repertoire. Touring was problematic, as it put a strain on the dancers. An example of the results of such strain was an injury to Pamela Johnson. In 1991, Johnson thought that she would stop dancing by 1995, but in fact she continued until 1999, which turned out to be detrimental to her health. As Barnes said, she was '*a casualty of the process of Phoenix*' (2003). When the Company went to Venezuela, Johnson injured her hip. Barnes commented, '*she should have taken a year out. She was exhausted, but because Phoenix didn't have a rotation system, she suffered*' (2003). This is a good example of the high cost to dancers of inadequate funding and of companies attempting to provide work on a scale for which they are not resourced. So the new repertoire used fewer dancers, in order to limit the pressure on the Company.

One strategy Barnes introduced was to commission duets rather than works for a group of dancers. In the programme before *Rewind*, she commissioned Jonzi D to create a duet. This was an inspired choice in a number of ways, not least because there was a direct link between this artist and the Company. Jonzi D was motivated to train as a dancer after a visit from Phoenix Dance Company to his London school. He then trained at London Contemporary Dance School, where he later became artist in residence. Although he appreciated the choreography classes, he found it difficult to break-dance at the same time as studying classical ballet and contemporary techniques, which made him feel 'as if my body was colonised' (in Phillips, 2001: 4). This is an interesting observation about the embodiment of dance techniques. For Jonzi D, these techniques did not feel enabling but rather limited his potential to improvise, and his perspective counters the commonly held belief within contemporary dance communities that technique is a pre-requisite for choreographic creativity. From the early 1980s he developed his skills as an MC and break-dancer (Adair, 1999).

The expansion of the repertoire by fusing hip-hop with contemporary dance is similar to the work of Rennie Harris in the United States, and indeed Jonzi D used a picture of this artist in his early publicity. Rennie Harris has interesting parallels with the founders of Phoenix, as, like them, he had no formal dance training. For him, hip-hop is the dance of life. 'We love what we're doing' (in Dixon Gottschild, 1999: 60), he says of his troupe, which is also what Hamilton said of the early Company. Harris was born in 1964, so is also a contemporary of the founders. Another interesting aspect of Barnes's choice of Jonzi D as a choreographer was her desire to expand the perception of Phoenix and its repertoire, and hip-hop offers an opportunity for that. As Rose points out, 'the global circulation of hip-hop music and culture has produced new black diasporan links' (1997: 267).

In terms of appealing to a wider audience, hip-hop is relevant because 'Since its beginnings in America [...] Hip-Hop has become the voice of inner-city youth, manifested in grafitti-art, turntablism, rap and break-dance' (Adewole, 1997: 3). Adewole also notes that Jonzi D's 'approach is an effective tool for moving any aesthetic of the fringe into the main-stream area' (1997: 3). The work Jonzi D created for Phoenix was *Us Must Trust Us* (1999), which was based on topics that the two dancers, Nicola Moses and Maria Ryan, wished to explore, and the idea of trust, which was powerfully communicated. The witty text, combined with hip-hop and contemporary movement vocabulary, was both humorous and poignant. By working with two women rather than two men, Jonzi D broke the stereotype of hip-hop as male culture. He is perceptive about the dangers of categorisation, as is Barnes; so although he clearly draws from his heritage as an African Caribbean male, as an artist he is not willing to be limited by it.[13] His choreographic skills and ability to empower dancers in the working process was evident in a rehearsal that I observed on 7 August 1998. I had watched several rehearsals with different choreographers during the period of this study, but the atmosphere at this one was noticeably both vibrant and informal, at the same time as intensely focused.

Although choosing appropriate choreographers and creating effective artistic programmes are obvious aspects of Barnes's role as artistic director, she also brought other skills, including her understanding of dance scholarship. Her own studies had given her insight into the political and cultural issues related to dance criticism and she also appreciated the role of dance history and the importance of dance archives. The Company, therefore, applied for a capital Lottery bid and received funding for equipment to set up a sophisticated archive project. The intention was for this to have a public forum through a photographic archive of a choreochronicle with selected photographs and a textual commentary (which I would have written). This was to be housed first at the Northern School of Contemporary Dance, and made available for public access in time for the Company's twentieth anniversary in 2001. The archive was also to provide the material for the anthology programme (which became *Rewind*) in which Barnes wanted to '*recreate and capture the ideas and energy of the first original members*' (2000). Unfortunately, Barnes' departure and the subsequent temporary closure of the Company meant that the archives were packed up and not easily accessible, so the choreochronicle was abandoned.

The *Report on the Archives of Phoenix Dance Company, Leeds*, written by Helen Wood of the Business Archives Council, detailed a number of key

---

[13] Interview with author, 12 August 1999.

20. *Us Must Trust Us*, 1999. Choreographer Jonzi D; dancers Nicola Moses and Melanie Teall; photographer Sarah Jones

points about the project. She noted the fact that in Britain there is a general lack of understanding and/or interest in archiving contemporary dance, unlike in the United States. The value of an archive was acknowledged to be in the unique historical records it provides, which may be useful for public relations activities, for informing young dancers about the Company with which they were performing, and for external researchers. At the time of the report, the archive was split across several physical locations, including a store distant from the main office. The resources included videos, CDs, lighting plans, costume designs, promotional material, reviews, photographs and so on. In addition, several people held material about the Company. The intention was to make copies of this material and to collect all the artistic-related records together. This data was then to be categorised against specific choreographic works. For example, all the artistic materials for *Unbroken* (1997) would be collected together to form a database, which would be easily accessible by all members of staff and eventually by external researchers. This was an ambitious and extremely worthwhile project which, unfortunately, was only partially realised.

The archive was necessary for *Rewind*, as it provided a range of material in accessible form about the choreographic works that were included in the programme. Barnes was eager for the founder members to be involved with the work and wanted them to reconstruct one or two of their early pieces. Despite encouraging early meetings, the founders decided that, as they would not have overall artistic control, they did not want to engage with the project,[14] and so Barnes chose three works, which she used as inspiration for three new works choreographed by herself and Andile Sotiya (Barnes, 9 December 1998 and 2 April 1999).

In *Brawta* the dancers each demonstrated their own quirky speciality, and there is an evident link with Hamilton's *Forming of the Phoenix* (1982), in which each dancer played a specific role. *Key Club* drew on the jazz dance expression of the early work, specifically Lynch's *Nightlife at the Flamingo* (1989). Some of the works in the early repertoire were concerned with specific cultural experiences, for example Edward's *The Path* (1980). *Strange Fruit* to music by Nina Simone followed this tradition.

Barnes's and Sotiya's ways of working with the choreographic diversity of the Company were impressive. They drew on its strengths and created vibrant new works, which both stood alone and were an important aspect of the collected choreographic overview of the Company. The rest of the programme was based on reconstructions of earlier works. In most cases the choreographer worked with the dancers on an excerpt of the work. The process of reconstruction raises a number of

---

[14] Personal communication with Donald Edwards, August 2004.

issues, which were debated heatedly at a conference entitled *Preservation Politics* held at the Roehampton Institute on 8–9 November 1997. As Ramsay Burt pointed out:

> Much of the most interesting debate about reconstruction and revival within the conference hinged upon the tension between notions of the originality and authenticity of choreography and the way these are embodied in performance by dancers. (1998: 32)

Dancers from a variety of different trainings, physicality and backgrounds may subtly alter the look and experience of a dance work. Also, 'The process of reconstruction draws attention to the sometimes uneasy relationship between the idea of the choreographer as inspired genius and the agency of the dancers who perform their work before audiences' (Burt, 1998: 31).

Barnes's perception of these issues meant that she was not attempting to achieve original or authentic extracts of the earlier works in the repertoire. Rather, she aimed to recreate them so that the Company embodied a range of styles and the audience had the opportunity to experience that range in one performance. Thus the dancers could be said to embody cultural equity through their performance. The agency of the dancers and their contribution to specific works was acknowledged by Barnes and by the choreographers she commissioned to rework their choreographies.

Educating audiences

Barnes's understanding of the legacy of the founders to British contemporary dance and the current Company was evidenced in the education initiatives she set up as mentioned above, in her writing and in some of the repertoire, including *Rewind*. She was active in various dance-related forums as a choreographer, dance educator and dance scholar. Her perception of the value of Phoenix's educational workshops was informed by the fact that lack of funding for vocational training had resulted in a mainly female, middle-class and white student population (Siddall, 2001). Although this group did attend the Company workshops, as mentioned earlier, the educational initiatives also attracted young people of African descent and, therefore, offered opportunities that might otherwise have been unavailable. In addition, the Company provided a role model, as is clear in the example of Jonzi D, and several of my students were encouraged by the creative example that the Company offered. The Arts Council of England recognised that

'mainstream education, the vocational training infrastructures and creation and dissemination processes are all based on western dance models' (in Siddall, 2001). The need for better opportunities for what was
termed 'culturally diverse dance' was also acknowledged. Although
much of Phoenix's work has been and is based on western models, the
Company also offers potential for other approaches, which were noted
as early as 1984 in *The Glory of the Garden.*

Thea Barnes set up a number of structures to shift perceptions of
Phoenix in order for the Company to have a diverse repertoire that
would be appreciated by a wide audience. She educated audiences
through after-show talks and dance workshops. In one talk (13 August
1999) that she gave at Ballroom Blitz, a large dance event held at the
South Bank, London, each year, she illustrated the range of the Phoenix
repertoire over the years through specific examples of works. Barnes
emphasised at the beginning of the talk that videos only give a partial
idea of the work and cannot properly capture the three-dimensional
kinaesthetic experience of watching live performance. Videos do, however, give a glimpse of works that otherwise would be represented only
in words and static photographs. She suggested that it was important to
look at Phoenix for what it is rather than through expectations of what
the Company should be. She also indicated that there was a lot of discussion by stakeholders that continued the ghosts of what they wanted
Phoenix to be (Barnes, 1999). Her analysis of the Company was that it
reflected a range of extraordinary experiences of different people and
how they chose to make dance. It was not a concept of how Phoenix
should be, defined by people outside the Company. Although a publicly
funded company necessarily has expectations and requirements from
stakeholders, what Barnes is challenging here is the racism and limited
perceptions that were apparent in the ghosts, which were to do with
'blackness' and which she vigorously refuted.

The seeds for *Rewind* were evident in this talk as Barnes described
Phoenix in the context of British dance and its role as a repertory company. The programme was created to show a mix of styles, the Phoenix
Phenomenon, and to overcome the limitations of resources. '*I only have
nine dancers and three tech crews on any one tour, with which it is just not
possible to support a diverse enough repertoire for the context to really realise
just how far we've come*' (Barnes, 1999: 84-85). She was interested in
how choices could be made about dances, and about expression rather
than producing what was expected. In order to deal with some of these
issues, she aimed for a retrospective show through snippets from the
beginnings of Phoenix to the current context, in the hope of '*killing
some of the ghosts. It is important to acknowledge that Phoenix is not just*

this one thing' (Barnes, 1999). She also spoke about her own process in which she and the dancers learnt two or three movements from a number of pieces and then manipulated them and hence embodied some of the vocabulary for the future Phoenix Company (Barnes, 1999).

Phoenix's identity crisis

Olivia Swift, writing in *Dance Now*, identifies some of the issues with which Barnes was concerned as an 'identity crisis'. There are some inaccuracies in her article, since Barnes was the fourth, not third, artistic director and in 1999 it was eighteen, not nineteen, years since the Company was founded. She also implies that the identity of a Company rests with the dancers, but that is unusual for a repertory company. For example, Rambert Dance Company and London Contemporary Dance Theatre focus more on repertoire and artistic direction. The unique beginning of Phoenix, however, has tended to create a focus on the dancers.

The article appears to be based on an interview with Barnes, although that is not specifically stated. Barnes argues that she wants to lose the 'black dance' image, which she calls the 'ghost of Phoenix past' (in Swift, 1999: 84). For Barnes it is important that Phoenix is 'probably Britain's only real repertory company, even though it has never really been recognised as such'.[15] But as Swift points out, being a repertory company is problematic, as it lacks 'a certain definite, long-term sense of what they actually are, rather than all that they can be' (1999: 85). She also suggests that diversity has 'proved to be [Phoenix's...] prize asset and its biggest hindrance' (1999: 85). There is, however, a significant difference between, on the one hand, Phoenix creating dance informed by the dancers' and choreographers' heritages and demanding recognition for their cultural specificity, and on the other hand the categorisation and expectations that funders and critics have imposed upon the Company.

An article written by Anne Sacks in the *Evening Standard* (16 April 1999) is a good example of some of the comment that Barnes was attempting to counter. Sacks raised issues about Phoenix's identity and said that they 'pose the question to which there is no answer: what is black dance? Is it dance by black dancers and choreographers? Is it a certain movement style, or is it dance inspired by black experience?' She then suggests that the style and content of Jonzi D's work *Us Must Trust Us* is black dance, as is *Cornered*, choreographed by two dancers with the

---

[15] Nevertheless, Rambert Dance Company and Diversions Dance Company are also recognised as repertory companies.

Company, Warren Adams and Andile Sotiya. This work 'deals with two men and the challenges they face being trapped, not only in a small space but in life itself. Their relationship plays a pivotal role in how they approach these challenges' (programme, *Phoenix Dance Tour 99*). These two works are, Sacks suggests, black dance because they are made and performed by black people. Although Sacks seems to understand some of what Barnes intended, she nevertheless attempts to define and categorise – hence the title of the article, *There are no black and white answers*. This in effect confines Phoenix and does not acknowledge its demand for recognition or the diversity of its repertoire or artistic practices.

In Paul Carter Harrison's introduction to *Black Theatre: Ritual Performance in the African Diaspora* (2002), it is clear that the issues concerning such performance cannot be summed up as Sacks attempts to do. Although Harrison is discussing theatre, several of his comments are pertinent to dance. He suggests that:

> it is commonly accepted in the African Diaspora that performance is not limited to an edifice, the technology of computerized sets, or the bounding of a script. An opportunity for performative expression can be located in the daily rituals of life, including 'sporting events and in circuses, in storytelling and in public events, in clothing and hairstyles.' In the African tradition, theatre begins with the incantative voice of the storyteller (griot), the poly-rhythms of the musicians, and the gesticulate responses of the body, all orchestrated to bring spiritual enlightenment to mundane experience. (2002: 8)

Both David Hamilton and Thea Barnes made work that drew on this concept of an African heritage connected to spiritual enlightenment. They both shared a deep sense of the potential meaning in actions that are not created for pure entertainment but with an ambition to have value to both the makers and the audiences. As Paul Carter Harrison argued, many artists from the African Diaspora faced the challenge 'to formulate a specific practice that can contextualize African-inspired values and overcome the trauma of dislocation and subjugation'. Although some of the works in the Phoenix repertoire are examples of such a practice, others have been concerned with what Jean Fisher termed 'abstract levels of existence'. Each artistic director of Phoenix worked in their own way with the Company for cultural equity, recognition and the means to create a diverse repertoire.

As we have seen, Barnes's credentials for developing a repertory company were exemplary and her vision was astute and far-reaching. It is possible, however, as she herself acknowledged, that her approach to

21. *Cornered*, 1999. Choreographers Warren Adams and Andile Sotiya; dancers Martin Hylton and Hugh Davis; photographer Sarah Jones

attaining her goals together with insufficient support meant that her dreams for Phoenix Dance Company were only partially realised. Some of the difficulties with which Barnes was confronted were also ones that the previous directors had faced, but as we have seen in earlier chapters the complexities of the negotiations were played out differently. Critics' writings have significantly contributed to the perceptions of funders and audiences, and the next chapter analyses some of the issues that critical responses to the Company have raised.

Chapter 6: Phoenix Reviewed

This chapter addresses the dialectic of creative arts and cultural criticism in the context of a historical and political shift in Britain and the 'Black Atlantic' (Gilroy, 1993). It looks at how dance critics reviewed the Phoenix Dance Company. The previous chapters have investigated Phoenix's historical archive, and it is within this context that the critical reception to Phoenix Dance Company is considered. Although some reviews have been included in earlier chapters, here the concern is with the key issues raised by the material. This critical writing in local, national and international newspapers and specialist dance magazines and journals raises important issues. The location of this writing in the media indicates the less established position of dance criticism and, in particular, of writing about the comparatively new art form of contemporary dance, in comparison with other art forms. In Britain, dance reviewers writing for the press are often termed 'dance critics' and the two terms are thought of as synonymous, whereas there is usually a distinction between critics and reviewers in critical writing on other art forms. A reviewer usually writes reviews from first impressions of a performance in a short time span, sometimes the same evening as the event or overnight. The term 'critic' is usually applied to those with an academic background writing with a more scholarly approach. As William Littler explains:

> The critic is more than a writer. Criticism is a branch of aesthetics and proceeds from a philosophy of art. The critic is someone with a broad historical knowledge of the art to which he addresses himself and some working hypotheses about its nature [and...] is able to put the particular dance event into a general picture [...]. (In Sayers, 1987: 44)

For the purposes of this study, however, I will use the term 'critics', because it is in common usage in Britain for writers who review work for a wide range of publications. Sally Banes, referring to both writers writing in daily papers and those writing more considered articles in specialist dance journals, considers the critic's role. She suggests that this is to describe, interpret and evaluate a dance work, as well as to provide a context for a work in relation to aesthetics and/or history. She suggests that 'the critic's job is to complete the work in the reader's understanding, to unfold the work in an extended time and space after the performance, and to enrich the experience of the work' (1994: 25). Although it is clear in the selected examples in this chapter that the intention of the critics was to fulfil their task as Banes defined it, some of the contextual information, descriptions, interpretations and evaluations are limited by the critics' own preconceptions. It is, therefore, in many cases arguable that the critics were only partially successful in their quest to inform their readers about the work of the Company.

The critical discussion in this chapter focuses on the language used by critics, and on their expectations of Phoenix Dance Company's work. I argue that it is evident in this material that there are tensions between the Company's artistic visions and aims, and the establishment's response. These tensions can be categorised into three periods: the beginnings of the Company with David Hamilton (1981–87); the transition and development period when Neville Campbell directed the Company (1987–91); and the paradoxical break with the past, at the same time as attempting continuity, with two directors who did not share the Company's history, Margaret Morris (1991–96) and Thea Barnes (1997–2001). I have selected specific examples of reviews in order to analyse some of the themes and issues that emerged in these periods.

Dance criticism

Dance criticism is significant for our understanding of dance, not least because it provides an important record of specific works in an art form that vanishes after it has been performed and leaves only representational traces. Although recent revolutions in technology offer some options for recording dance, dance companies frequently do not have sufficient resources to use them effectively. In addition, many companies still place little importance on archiving material.[1]

There have been a number of changes in dance criticism since the establishment of modern dance. Writing on ballet usually focuses on an appraisal of the performance and performer rather than of the choreography. This is because of the familiarity of both the ballet vocabulary and the ballet repertoire (except modern ballet works), and until recently dance critics in Britain have been more informed about ballet than about modern dance (Sayers, 1987).[2] Modern dance, particularly

---

[1] Dr Valerie Preston Dunlop was involved with an archive project at the Laban Centre, London, and acknowledged that few companies valued archives (personal communication, 3 June 2004). See also *The Report on the Archives of Phoenix Dance Company, Leeds*, discussed in Chapter 5.
[2] In Britain the leading dance critics write for national newspapers; for example, Judith Mackrell writes for *The Guardian* and Ismene Brown for *The Daily Telegraph*. In the USA, Arlene Croce writes for the *New Yorker*, Deborah Jowitt for *Village Voice* and Marcia Siegel for the *Boston Globe*.

at first, presented a newly evolving movement vocabulary and innovative choreography. The critics' role was to inform and educate their readers about modern dance. John Martin (1933, 1936) led the way with his pioneering writing in the 1930s, which focused on the emerging modern dancers, supported their work and offered insight into the radical new form. In the 1960s Jill Johnston (1971), dance critic for the *Village Voice*, wrote insightfully about the experiments of the Judson Group and provided an important record of a significant group of artists. In 1996 Diana Theodores wrote a study analysing the contribution of the New York School of dance critics – Arlene Croce, Nancy Goldner, Deborah Jowitt and Marcia Siegel – who 'created a turning point in the history of dance writing'. There was much questioning of the role of dance criticism in the 1990s and concern about issues of identity in terms of the work and who wrote about it.

These questions and concerns continue into the twenty-first century. The distinction between dance ethnography and dance criticism has become less clear since critics have begun to write about movement not solely in the theatre and ethnographers have questioned the 'authority of the Western observer' (Gere, 1995: 7). There have been challenges and questions concerned with critics' evaluation of works in relation to cultural difference (Gere: 1995). The cultural politics of criticism has, as Bruce Fleming comments, entailed the critic becoming to some extent a 'cross-cultural arts commentator' (1995: 37). Critics need to be aware of the political power they hold, as 'most international arts exchanges are political and economic investments' (Fleming, 1995: 37) and the critic then becomes 'part of an international political process' (Fleming, 1995: 38). In addition, for artists such exchanges and opportunities are important for their development and contribute to their profile (Siddall: 2001).

The archive raises some issues about critics' aesthetic judgements and about communicating those in writing. Although many of the reviews of Phoenix are problematic because of the categorisation of the Company, they nevertheless provide an important record of the performances that offer insights into perspectives and contexts of the particular times in which they were written. Dance criticism has been mainly descriptive. As Larry Lavender argues in his article 'Post-historical dance criticism' (2000–01), less attention has been paid to aspects of interpretation and evaluation. This has been partly because of the ephemeral nature of the art form, so that critics have considered description to be an important part of their role. Although other performing arts share the ephemerality of dance, a key difference is that most theatrical and musical productions have a text that can be referred to, whereas dance relies on the moving body. As Jane Desmond points out, 'dance leaves the fewest traces (most dances have not been recorded in any way), making historical reconstruction and analysis exceedingly difficult' (Desmond, 1991: 29). Hence the importance of dance criticism, which at least provides some record. The dance critic Marcia Siegel, whose writing provides significant insights into the works of key dance practitioners, argues for description that allows the 'dance to reveal itself on its own terms' (1995: 6). In her view, 'the dance is my best information' (1995: 191). This viewpoint is strongly adhered to within dance criticism. Nevertheless, Lavender argues that, despite difficulties of ephemerality, there are aspects to a work that are intrinsic to it and that can be beneficially discussed. Indeed, 'critics are widely expected (by the public at least) to judge the works they review' (2000–01: 92).

Critical descriptions of the Phoenix success story

The dancers of Phoenix were fortunate to have critical acclaim very early in their careers. For example, Jane King, writing in the *Morning Star*, considered that 'The swift rise to fame of Phoenix is the greatest success story of dance in our time' (1985: PA). Their success and unique background were also noted in reviews when they toured abroad.[3] Some of the descriptive terms used in the reviews, however, became limiting as the Company developed and sought recognition for its diverse artistry. In the early years, the Company was identified as 'the all-black, all-male'[4] company, and many of the early reviews discussed the Company in these terms. For example, an unidentified writer in Aberdeen for the *Evening Express* on 26 October 1987 noted, 'The all black, all-male group put on a powerful performance of four works showcasing its formidable talents'. There were also many comments on the group's physicality and energy. Alison Steel's description of a performance in 1982 is an example: 'The enthusiasm and vitality of this five-man black group leapt off the stage at Darlington Arts Centre' (PA). Jane King, writing in the *Morning Star*, described the Company's attributes as 'youthful enthusiasm, ravishing vitality [...] breathtaking

---

[3] The *Majorca Daily Bulletin* of Friday 3 May 1985 gave a detailed report of the Company and its repertoire. *The Western Australia Department for the Arts*, December 1987–January 1988 (issued with *Country Copy*) commented, 'The choreography is athletic and spectacular and combines a variety of dance forms such as reggae, soul and blues, jazz, ballet, break dance to tap and rock and roll' (PA).

[4] This term may have come from a Company publicity document (1987), which described the dancers as an 'all-male, all-black company'. It was not a description by which the founders wished to be limited, however, and in the late 1980s Neville Campbell rejected the term and its restrictions.

athleticism' (1984: PA). The specificity of the Company is noted above and the descriptions of the Company and their work that the reviews offer are typical of those of the early 1980s. Some early reviews facilitated readers' reflections on the dancers' skills and the impact on the audiences, whereas some critics had expectations of the Company that they considered to be unfulfilled. The following selection of reviews offer insight into such issues and also demonstrates the range of contexts in which the work of the Company was reviewed.

Lesley-Anne Sayers's study (1987) of twentieth-century British dance criticism found no published studies of dance criticism in Britain, other than a few articles that discussed specific aspects: for example, 'the relationship between dancers and critics' (4). Sayers cites the background of twenty-two British critics, six of whom were women and ten of whom had been educated at Oxford or Cambridge University. In addition, most British dance critics at the time of her study in 1987 were, and today are, white westerners. Although there are some cultural commentators from the African Diaspora (for example, Brenda Edwards) their writing is usually found in the specialist dance magazines or African Caribbean press. From the information above, I would suggest that dance critics in the 1980s, although not a homogenous group, did have aspects of ethnicity and class in common.

The situation in the USA, where dance criticism has a longer history, is slightly different. For example, the researcher and writer Brenda Dixon Gottschild, who is African American, has written both scholarly work and reviews for the press. Clearly, a critic's values are culturally specific. It does not, however, necessarily follow that a critic must share an artist's background in order to review the work effectively. To extend Stuart Hall's argument, one cannot assume that a critic from the African Diaspora will review a work of African–Caribbean–British artists more effectively than a European–British critic. As Hall suggests, such a line of argument is predicated on a racist view that suggests all black people are the same (in Morley and Chen, 1996). What is important, however, as Brenda Dixon Gottschild points out, is that critics are well-informed about any work about which they write (1996). Here the issue is of relevant information, knowledge and awareness of the issues, which tend to be invisible to the dominant socio-cultural group. The reviews that follow were mainly written in local and national newspapers. Writers in the local press may have a limited background in dance, and such writing may form only part of their role with the specific newspaper. Critics writing in the national press are likely to have more expertise in relation to the art form, but, as will be evident, they communicate their preconceptions as well as their insights. The critical response to Phoenix is informed by considerations of the body, skin colour, politics and aesthetics that contribute to readings of the work of dance-makers and performers of African Caribbean heritage discussed below.

Reading dance

The use of the term 'reading' makes it clear that there is potential for other readings of a specific work, rather than one correct interpretation based on the intentions of the maker of the art product. This approach to criticism using deconstruction emerged from Jacques Derrida's work. It is useful when considering Phoenix, because it considers ambiguity in relation to readings of a work that cannot be resolved, and suggests that 'indeterminacy of meaning is inescapable' (in Lavender, 1997: 33). Thus it offers the potential for more fluid interpretations of Phoenix's work. One approach to criticism that links with deconstructionism is intertextuality. Barzilai and Bloomfield explain as follows:

> Because all present texts, literary and critical (though this distinction itself is challenged) are permeated by past ones, no text is ever self-contained or sufficient unto itself. Every text is an intertext, or network of scraps and fragments, a set of relations formed with and by other texts. (1986: 160)

A key element of both deconstructionism and intertextuality is that it is apparent from both approaches that a work of art does not have a single fixed and stable meaning (Lavender, 1997). As Janet Adshead-Lansdale points out, 'The reader is [...] a co-creator of a mobile text, breathing new life into *a dancing text*' (1999:25). Although individual members of an audience will interpret works according to their own background and understanding, at the same time dance interpretation is based on specific cultural meanings, which are communicated to the public by critics, as Marcia Siegel (1998) and Janet Wolff (1995) argue. This is the approach of the four dance critics whom Theodores intro-duces in *First We Take Manhattan* (1996). Arlene Croce, Nancy Goldner, Deborah Jowitt and Marcia Siegel produced descriptive writing that was 'the means by which they pinpointed the physical look of the dance, [and] recalled the kinaesthetic experience of the dance' (1996: 42).

Contemporary dance is a cultural practice, producing images in time and space that are transitory, and it is those images and a kinaesthetic sense that the critics interpret and communicate. They are engaged in watching bodies in action in dance, and such observations, as Stuart

Hall has argued, are likely to raise issues of gender and ethnicity. Indeed, he says:

> It is difficult [...] to have images of bodies in action, at the peak of their physical perfection, without those images also, in some way, carrying 'messages' about *gender* and about *sexuality* [...]. Each image carries its own, specific meaning. But at the broader level of how 'difference' and 'otherness' is being represented in a particular culture at any one moment, we can see similar representational practices and figures being repeated, with variations, from one text or site of representation to another. (1997: 231–32)

The body

As Hall points out, gender and sexuality are key aspects of reading moving bodies, and a central dilemma of Phoenix has been issues of the body. This is an element of which the founders were aware in the readings of their work. Donald Edwards spoke of performing in skimpy costumes and that '*the black male bodies*' on stage became '*a selling factor*', which was exploited by both their costume designer and their administrator/publicist (1997). He said there were '*five black bodies, good vibrant bodies on stage, a bit like the Chippendales, people/women got excited by seeing that black body, how it moved, the energy that it gave off – that's just one of the things that we had to deal with*' (1997). The critics responded to this 'selling factor', and the adjectives chosen – such as those quoted below from Stephanie Ferguson, 'raw', 'powerful', 'pent-up' – all allude to a subtext of sexuality.

An issue here is the prevalent fantasies that Frantz Fanon analyses in his famous text *Black Skin White Masks*, in relation to black men: 'One is no longer aware of the Negro, but only of a penis; the Negro is eclipsed. He is turned into a penis' (1952; 1973: 120). For black performers such fixation affects responses to their work and can detract from the seriousness of their artistry. Dyer (1992) argues that, whereas images of white men tend to concentrate on areas of work or leisure, images of black men, despite the fact that they might be American or European, are frequently connected to hints of 'the jungle' and 'savagery'. Such findings are relevant to readings of Phoenix because it is within this context that their work is evaluated. Dyer also discusses the focus within western society on the body as a site of leisure, because people have the time and opportunity to develop a fit body. Men who develop their bodies concentrate frequently on building their musculature, which then becomes a '*sign* of power – natural, achieved, phallic' (Dyer, 1992: 114). But, of course, although muscularity may appear natural, an aspect of biology, in fact it is a result of dedicated exercise. Dancers frequently have developed musculatures through regular dance classes as preparation for performances. The cultural contexts in which these images and readings occur vary significantly from decade to decade.

As Ann Cooper Albright points out, however, the 'dancing body both enacts its identity and confuses these cultural markings through the combination of movement, autobiographical text, and visual image' (1997: xxv). So while there are difficulties with readings of specific images, performances and performers, there is potential for deconstruction. An example of a reading of specific images that offers another viewpoint in relation to black athletes comes from bell hooks:

> A young White man spoke up about the image of Black athletes on cereal boxes, saying it was the first time in his life he wanted to be a Black man [...]. I thought he had made a profound point, because for him to see this image as valuable, legitimate and worthwhile put it in a more humanizing light, meaning he could potentially be close to this image, an act which might be subversive, threatening even to White supremacy. This is why critical readings of popular culture are so important. Critiquing representations, we understand more fully the subtleties between subject and object and their concomitant power dynamics at a given historical moment. (1991: 39)

It is arguable that, as with the image of black athletes that hooks alludes to, Phoenix provided images to which to aspire. We have seen in earlier chapters that the dancers undoubtedly provided role models for young people of African Caribbean heritage, but what is less considered is that they had a profound influence on white people, of whom I am one example; and some of the critics have also been affected by their work. When critics are aware of the political context in which a work is made, rather then focusing solely on aesthetics, their work is obviously more informed. It is also crucial that they are informed about the criteria appropriate to a work with which they are not familiar, as discussed earlier (Dixon, 1991: 5). The need for recognition and the need for critics to use appropriate criteria are, however, becoming more widely acknowledged. As Ann Cooper Albright comments, 'More and more dancers and choreographers are asking that the audience see their bodies as a source of cultural identity – a physical presence that moves with and through its gendered, racial and social meanings' (1997: xxvi).

In relation to gender, Cooper Albright suggests that re-consideration of the ways in which the body is represented in motion is important, as is re-thinking the musculature (1997). Dancers do not merely represent categories but have the capacity to offer challenging readings, because 'dance can help us trace the complex negotiations between somatic experience and cultural representation between the body and identity' (1997, Cooper Albright: xiv).

Skin colour

Meanings of images may be considered differently because they are read in another context. When audiences go to Phoenix Dance Company performances, they view them in the contexts of current media images. So for example, in 1981 the news was saturated with images of young black men in urban disturbances, and the charismatic, vigorous performances of the new Company may have been read by some groups of the population as less threatening than images of the uprisings in Bristol, Leeds and London. Another consideration when reading the images of the early Phoenix is that, despite their successes as role models and as cultural ambassadors, on their tours abroad they were dancing in a context in which 'most definitions of "Britishness" assume the person who belongs is "white" and it is still not an inclusive term' (Alibhai-Brown, 2000). When images of Phoenix are being 'read', 'questions of cultural belongingness and difference' are components of such readings (Hall, 1997). Adrian Piper has created work, for example *Cornered* (1989), which shifts the fixed identification of race from the signifier of skin colour. Piper is African American but her skin tone allows her to 'pass' as white. In her performance, she asked a series of questions to the 'white' spectator, which gradually exposed 'the enormous difference while exposing the utter insignificance of the ground which legislates these differences – gene arrangement, the odd biology of blood' (Phelan, 1993: 8). The complexities of racial identity are such that Peggy Phelan comments, 'One cannot simply "read" race as skin colour' (1993: 8). Meiling Cheng, however, although agreeing with Piper's and Phelan's challenge to the equation of race with skin colour, argues that 'skin color *does* register visual information and implies social and psychic consequences' (in Jones and Stephenson, 1999: 210). These consequences are evident in critical writings about Phoenix.

Work such as Piper's, however, challenges stereotypes and narrow expectations. There were numerous stereotypes (a few simplified characteristics) applied to black people, which served to reinforce the power relations in the Empire between the colonisers and the colonised, and Hall (1997) argues that traces of these racial stereotypes have continued to the present day. Homi Bhabha (1983) in his discussion of the stereotype argued that the concept of 'fixity' was an important element of colonial discourse in 'the ideological construction of "otherness"'. There was ambivalence to the stereotype, which shifted between what was known and a need to repeat what could not be proven. So, for example, the focus in critics' writing on the dancers' 'rawness' and 'energy' emphasises a connection of 'the black body' with the 'uncivilised' aspect of colonial discourse. The example that Bhabha offers is the 'bestial sexual license of the African that needs no proof, [yet] can never really in discourse be proved' (1983: 18). This discourse and need for repetition of the stereotype is a lens through which many of the critics have viewed Phoenix's work and have, therefore, recreated stereotypes in their writing.

Politics

There have been challenges to the ways in which people of African heritage have been represented. These challenges have taken different forms in the late twentieth and early twenty-first centuries. In the USA the Civil Rights Movement of the 1960s 'challenged the "relations of representation" between racially defined groups in American society' (Hall, 1997: 256). This movement, and the influences of it in Britain, focused on shared identities and making visible those groups, initially African Americans, who demanded social equity. In the 1980s and 1990s the collapse of the dream of integration and civil rights resulted in a black underclass and a culture of drugs, guns and intra-black violence. At the same time, however, there was a growing requirement for respect for black cultural identity and an increase in black separatism (Hall, 1997). The Black Arts Movement in America and Britain was one manifestation of this requirement for a visible identity. As Fanon argued, much racial stereotyping and violence arose from the refusal of the white 'Other' to give recognition 'from the place of the other' to the black person (in Hall, 1997: 238). Although the history for African Americans and Caribbean British people is significantly different, some of the shifts in representations in the USA have influenced cultural perspectives in Britain, not least because of the pervasive distribution of American culture and particularly through music and films. Lola Young, in her study *Fear of the Dark* (1996), specifically analyses British films in relation to race, gender and sexuality and makes the point that there is far less critical work in Britain than in the USA on images of black people. Nevertheless, the critical responses to Phoenix have been written in the context established above and have informed audiences, funders and the Company Board.

Phase 1: The 1980s – from 1981 to 1987

The reviews and articles about the Company, or about dancers who at some point danced with Phoenix between 1981 and 1987, focus on their rapidly growing reputations and their achievements in a relatively short time span. A selection of early reviews from the archives, located in the local, national and international press, demonstrate a story of success, appreciation and rewards, as illustrated in an example from the Australian *Sunday Times* of 28 December 1986, in which the Company are described as 'one of the most exciting in the world' (1986: PA). The reviews frequently comment on specific performances and choreography with reference to the shared school background of the performers, their policy of teaching in the community and the early triumphs of the Company. In addition, many reviews comment on the wide range of the repertoire and the enthusiastic, energised performances of the dancers – reviews that raise the question of whether this emphasis on energy and physicality is descriptive or ideologically informed, based on racialised assumptions that imply 'natural' ability rather than trained professionalism. Phoenix's early press coverage focused on the educational experience through the teaching at Harehills Middle School and was mainly in the local papers – the *Yorkshire Post* and the *Yorkshire Evening Press*. There was, however, some coverage in the national press. In an article in the *Sunday Times*, entitled 'Youth in sport', Nadine Senior said:

> for the first time in their lives, these children realised there was something they could succeed at. I can't prove it, but it seems to me that an hour's hard technique work and creative thinking just doesn't go with smashing up telephone boxes. (NSCD AF, 1981)

In the same article, the writer made the point that many of these students were also successful at athletics, demonstrated by the fact that for four consecutive years Harehills dancers won city-wide competitions in athletics. These comments indicate the importance of the context from which Phoenix emerged. It is arguable that without the sports context and the focus on the school the Company might not have attracted the interest of the local and national press. Such coverage was, however, problematic, because it invoked a historical context of racism in which, as Kobena Mercer argues, 'African peoples were defined as having bodies but not minds [...]. Vestiges of this are active today in schools, for instance, where teachers may encourage black kids to take up sport because they are seen as academic underachievers' (1994: 138).

So, paradoxically, although the intentions of such teachers were to benefit the children, such encouragement also reinforced particular expectations of the young people. The success of the young dancers from Harehills Middle School who later became dancers in Phoenix emerged, therefore, from a context in which the teachers' and, later the funders' views, echoed preconceptions that associated black people with 'natural' physical prowess. As Kobena Mercer (1994) argued, however, there were benefits to such views, as sport was an area in which black people were allowed to excel, and it was their success that gained Olympic medals for Britain. In addition, some black sports champions, such as Muhammad Ali, have effectively used their status for a political platform.[5] The associations that Mercer articulates, mentioned above, can also be seen in many of the critical responses to the Company.

The debut performance of the Harehills Middle School Contemporary Dance Youth Group was reviewed in the *Yorkshire Evening Post*. The writer commented, 'The boys [...] contributed some remarkably athletic jumping and lifting' (NSCD AF, 1981), which reinforced a stereotype of physicality in relation to black masculinity, as Mercer identified above. Reviewing a duet between Merville Jones and Sharon (Chantal) Donaldson, the writer noted that 'Both dancers have an excellent sense of movement and line which made their duet special' (NSCD AF, 1981). For the Leeds Festival of Youth Theatres, Harehills produced a version of *Paradise Lost* in which it was noted that 'the Harehills high standard is maintained throughout' (*Yorkshire Post* 1981, NSCD AF). Many of the young dancers from the Youth Group, including Jones and Donaldson, later joined Phoenix. It is evident from these reviews, despite the reinforcement of particular representations as illustrated in the first comment, that these young dancers received a level of critical acclaim, unusual for young performers, even before they were dancing in Phoenix Dance Company.

On 18 July 1982, only eight months after Phoenix had formed, Nicholas Dromgoole reviewed the Company in *The Sunday Telegraph*.[6] Sayers suggests in her study on criticism that Dromgoole is an example of a critic 'whose values are clearly incompatible with the ideology of a great deal of Contemporary Dance' (1987: 198). Nevertheless, despite his bias towards ballet, he frequently wrote about contemporary dance. In the review quoted below, he noted that the dancers

---

[5] Phoenix Dance Company was later acknowledged for their excellence and chosen in 1996 to represent British dance at the Cultural Olympiad, Atlanta Centennial Olympic Games.
[6] Some of the writing in this chapter was included in a paper entitled 'Reviewing the reviews: Issues of criticism in relation to Phoenix Dance', presented at the *Dancing in the Millennium Conference*, 19–23 July 2000, Washington DC, and published in the Conference Proceedings.

looked impressively different. They danced with conviction and muscular ease, they had put together choreography that was musical and showed them off well and they had not forgotten that dance takes place in a theatre and has to please, impress and extend an audience's imagination. (quoted in Holgate, 1997)

This was a review of their performance as part of *Dance Days* at Battersea Arts Centre, organised by the Centre's artistic director Jude Kelly,[7] who had seen the Company perform in Leeds. This performance took place in London, the centre of contemporary dance in Britain; and the coverage in the national press, so soon after the formation of the Company, contributed to their success and became part of their publicity for future work. Clearly, this critic was entertained, but the observations raise a number of questions. What was it that he saw as different, and different from what? The term is ambiguous in relation to the Company's blackness and class. He appears to endorse their achievements, but can be read as confirming their difference from mainstream white culture. Here the issue is whether the Company are required to advertise their difference or whether they are allowed to speak in general from a specific place. Are the comments he is making about the artistic merit of their work, or is there also a subtext about 'blackness'? These remarks appear to illustrate the writer's perceptions as much as they give information about the Company at that time.

The Company certainly received local commendation. In 1982, an article in *Rendezvous* in which the dancers and their ages are given as David 20, Donald 19, Villmore 19 and Merville and Edward 17 commented that 'Phoenix seem set to attract still more attention as they prepare to embark on extensive touring from the end of this month' (21 October–3 November 1982: PA). This comment was made in the context of writing about the dancing at Harehills Middle School. The writer was impressed that many children at the school were from deprived backgrounds, and suggested that dance offered them a way out of the dole queue or the boredom of the streets. Such a remark emphasises an approach that in effect views dance as a means of social control, particularly for young people of African Caribbean heritage. Unfortunately, such comments undermine the engagement of such young people with the art form and the potential that they have, as in the case of Phoenix, to contribute to dance as artists.

[7] Jude Kelly was a member of Phoenix's first management committee in 1985 and Chair of the Board until 1987.

The Company not only received local, national and international coverage, but also attracted the interest of publications such as *Artrage,*
published by the Minority Arts Advisory Service (MAAS).[8] Karin
Woodley, writing in issue 7, observed that the Company's most interesting aspect was its rapport with the audience. Her observation about
Forming of the Phoenix (1982) and specifically Edward Lynch's toasting
was that it was 'an attempt to bring in an aspect of black street culture',
and that this contemporary dance company was 'as good – some say
better than the established ones, and incorporated "little bits" of our
own culture' (1984: 12). The context in which Woodley was writing in
the early 1980s was that of the Black Arts Movement, when black
artists were concerned with exploring the specificity that they brought
to a range of art forms. It was from this perspective that Woodley was
identifying aspects of this early Phoenix performance and the
Company's connection with its audience.

The Company's rapport with the audience is also indicated in *Leeds
Other Paper,* 28 February 1986: 'The entire audience whistled and
applauded'. This was at a Civic Theatre performance, which Duncan Lee
reviewed in the *Evening Post* on 18 February 1986. He noted that it provided 'a hypnotic climax to the evening and left last night's audience
calling for more' (PA). The Company's achievements, particularly in
relation to the range of dance presented, were noted by several critics.
The *Spalding Guardian* of 18 October 1985 observed that, following the
Thames TV *South Bank Show* in October 1984, Phoenix were recognised
as 'one of the most exciting and original young companies on the dance
scene' (NSCD AF). Stephanie Ferguson suggested that they were
'Pulsing with eighties dance trends [... and that] Phoenix are an
immensely versatile company (*Yorkshire Post,* 18 February 1986: PA).
Emma Manning noted in *The Stage* that 'whatever the lack of technical
refinement, the Phoenix dancers' pace and daring make them one of
the most exciting small dance companies around' (24 September
1987). This is one of the few comments implying that Phoenix lacked a
formal technical training, as most of the reviews focus on the 'athleticism' of the Company. Despite what might be viewed as a limitation,
however, Manning echoes many of the critics, as mentioned above, in
her perception of the exhilaration in performance with which the
Company was identified.

At this point it can be seen that from 1981 to 1987 the critics locally,
nationally and internationally wrote positively about the Company and

[8] MAAS, funded by the Arts Council of Great Britain and the Greater London Arts Association,
was set up after Naseem Khan's 1976 report, *The Arts Britain Ignores.* The organisation provided information and advice on the arts 'of ethnic minorities in Britain' (Rodrigues, 1984, 1).

its speedy success, unique background, repertoire and rapport with audiences. However, some reviews, despite their commendation of the Company, used language (discussed below) that detracted from the Company's achievements and raise questions about how critics reach their judgements.

The interpretation and evaluation of dance

The evaluation of Phoenix Dance has been complicated by a shift in dance aesthetics so that the basis on which judgements of dance works are made is open to debate. As Larry Lavender has argued, many dance artists have rejected the Kantian idea of a choreographic work as a valuable product, focusing instead as much on the process of making the work. Dismissing the idea of the individual artist as a genius removed from his or her social circumstances, they do not accept the 'paradigm of visual aesthetic quality as the basis for art critical practice' (Lavender, 2000–1: 94). There is also recognition that Kant's concept of 'disinterested aesthetic value' is based on a system that assumes certain hierarchical and universal concepts.

Lavender argues, however, that it is possible to discuss a work in terms of its 'referential identity' or 'objective properties' (2000–1: 96). In order to do this, though, it is important to recognise that appropriate aesthetic values need to be applied to a work. Lavender gives the example of ballet and contact improvisation, which have sets of aesthetic values that are very specific but different from each other. Therefore, to judge one by criteria that are specifically appropriate to the other would make no sense. This argument is particularly pertinent when viewing works that explore cultural values that are not necessarily embedded, or recognised to be so, in mainstream culture. In her book *Digging the Africanist Presence in American Performance*, Brenda Dixon Gottschild analyses the review by Robert Greskovic (a European) of Garth Fagan Dance (Garth Fagan is an African American) published in *Dancemagazine* (1991). Through examples, she argues that the language Greskovic uses and the criteria implied are inappropriate to the work of this important postmodern choreographer. For example, the work is judged by ballet aesthetics such as line and form, but Fagan deliberately does not work with upright centredness, which is a key element of ballet. As Gottschild points out, 'One of the easiest ways to disempower others is to measure them by a standard that ignores their chosen aesthetic frame of reference and its particular criteria' (1996: 140–1). These examples show the importance of critics and readers being aware, particularly when discussing work of artists with whom they do not share the same cultural background, that judgements have a subjective element. In addition, a critic who succeeds in informing others' perception and appreciation of the work gains 'aesthetic authority' (Lavender, 2000–1: 102).

The main task of criticism, Lavender argues, is to reveal an 'understanding of a work's "intrinsic aesthetic properties"' (2000–1: 98). However, he asks, 'In the absence of any universal standards for the evaluation of art, how can we justify an aesthetic judgement?' (2000–1: 98). An important aspect of evaluation is to enable others to observe in the work the reasons for the evaluation. This is the approach to criticism articulated by John Dewey and is at the core of much criticism. Such an approach is in opposition to the intentionalist argument, which holds that interpretation of artistic works relies on the intentions of the artist. Wimsatt and Beardsley, however, argued against this view in *The Intentionalist Fallacy* (1970) and considered art works to be independent units whose meanings are apparent in their internal structures, which supports Lavender's argument that these are the properties being evaluated. In her essay *Against Interpretation* (1963: 1982), Susan Sontag also argued for criticism to illuminate the work rather than to dilute it through interpretation. She questioned what type of criticism would be useful and suggested, as Siegel does, that effective criticism would be that which described the work well (1963: 1982). It is apparent from various reviews quoted in this chapter that many of the critics writing about the work of Phoenix were not sufficiently reflective of their own perceptions and did not adequately address the task of informing their readers about the dance repertoire of the Company.

Phase 2: The late 1980s and early 1990s

In a review dated 12 September 1990 (PA), Judith Mackrell outlined some of the key issues facing Phoenix within the context of British dance in the early 1990s. She began with the controversy raised by positive discrimination policies, through which many black dancers were seen to be 'patronised' and 'trap[ped]' by 'a set of unwanted expectations'. She suggested that Phoenix was 'a model minorities dance group – its membership exclusively male, working-class and black [presenting work that] conformed to a very black and very street-cred image, with an up-tempo jazzy style and heavy use of blues and reggae music. To some they were a flagship modern black company.' This description is reinforced by the reviews discussed earlier, and the Company's identity to which Mackrell alludes is considered in Chapter 5.

When Neville Campbell became artistic director in 1987, however, he considered that to grow artistically the Company needed to develop beyond such boundaries. As Mackrell said in her report, 'The dancers' energy and muscle power were impressive, but descriptions like "exuberant" stuck to them as doggedly as clichés about natural rhythm and the company seemed increasingly imprisoned in its own style of urban dance machismo'. Campbell made changes, which Mackrell cites, including enlarging the Company to accommodate four women and commissioning work by 'non-black choreographers'. He also broke 'the "unwritten policy" of maintaining an all-black membership and started to look for white or Asian dancers'. As we have seen in Chapter 3, Neville Campbell, whose parentage was both European and of African descent, was adamant that he did not want to receive funding as a 'black company'. It was, therefore, ironic to be included in the season entitled *Dance for the Sheer Joy of It* (18 September–13 October 1990), which Mackrell commented was 'by implication a season of black dance'. However, she also made the case for black dancers to accept such opportunities because they were poorly represented in dance, and suggested that it was not surprising, given the funding policies, 'that those companies who benefit from black/white segregation should exploit their minority status for every penny that it's worth'.

This review is an example of a critic using expertise to articulate and try to clarify an important issue of categorisation. Phoenix's identity and the Company's demand for recognition without being confined by inappropriate boundaries have been discussed in previous chapters. In the current chapter, the focus is on how the critics navigated this problematic tension. Mackrell accurately identifies the changes that Campbell made to the Company's operation and in response to the dilemmas raised by positive discrimination policies and funding policies. One of the paradoxes that the Company faced was the contrast between the generally positive comments about the dancing and the sometimes negative remarks about the choreography, even though the repertoire was very varied. This paradox raises the question about audiences' and critics' expectations. It seems that the dancers performed with a high level of skill and danced with the force and involvement that their viewers expected, but that the choreography was more problematic and raised issues about the Company's identity.

An overview of press reviews compiled by the Company for 1990–91, 1991–92 and 1992–93 noted that one of the common views expressed by critics was that the Company's repertoire did not meet its expectations and did not match the dancers' technical ability (PA). So, for example, Mary Clarke, writing in the *Dancing Times* of November 1990, said that the 'choreography was not remarkable' (PA). John Percival in *The Times* said, 'it desperately needs a repertoire that will show its increased potential to better effect' (PA) and Edward Thorpe in the *Evening Standard* in October 1990 thought that 'the material is not yet worthy of their talents'.[9] Paradoxically, in 1990 when the critics were lamenting the repertoire, the Company won the Grand Prize for Ballet Theatre at the International Choreographic Competition in Bagnolet, France. At the same time as regretting the choreography, however, the critics praised the dancing. Allen Robertson in the *Daily Mail* in October 1990 thought that the dancers' 'vigorous dynamism is livelier than ever'; Louise Levene in *The Independent* in the same month considered the dancers to be 'excellent'; and Mary Clarke in *Dancing Times* in the following month noted their 'young, lithe intoxication of movements' (PA).

Similar observations were made during 1991[10] and 1992,[11] although there were fewer criticisms of the choreography. Those critics who were concerned about the repertoire, however, were particularly insistent. For example, Clement Crisp, writing in the *Financial Times*, made the following comments in separate reviews in October 1991: 'what it cannot boast is a clear choreographic identity'; 'the abiding image of this evening is of strong, disciplined dancers'; 'Time and again the dancers rescued the dance from the banality and I wonder if it is not now time for Phoenix to seek a repertory enhanced by proven work from the greatest names' (PA). The stature of the Company that Crisp is implying was previously commented upon in October 1990 by Ann Nugent in *The Stage*, who observed that the Company 'may constitute the beginning of a challenge to LCDT' (which was at that time the key contemporary dance company in Britain). This opinion is important because it is an acknowledgement of Phoenix's status as a contemporary repertory company and releases it from the restrictive 'black dance' category.

By 1992, Allen Robertson, dance critic for the *Daily Mail*, acknowledged their aim of becoming a world-class company as realisable, writing, 'if you've seen them before you'll be surprised by how far they've grown in the past year. They now look set to take on the world' (1992).

[9] The repertoire in 1990 was *Human Scandals* and *Solo* by Neville Campbell, *Rights* by Michael Clark, *Manic* by Simon Rice, *Tainted Love* by Tom Jobe and *Shock Absorber* by Darshan Singh Bhuller. The quotes from Clark, Percival and Thorpe are from a Company document, which gave an overview of critics' responses to Phoenix for 1990–91.
[10] The repertoire in 1991 was *Heavy Metal* by Neville Campbell, *Subject of the City* by Pamela Johnson, *Even Cowgirls get the Blues* by Tom Jobe, *Interlock* by Darshan Singh Bhuller and *Sacred Space* by Philip Taylor.
[11] The repertoire in 1992 was *Family* by Shapiro and Smith and *Spartan Reels* by Bebe Miller. Clearly, programmes included earlier works.

Reading between the lines of selected reviews provides information about the writer's assumptions and views, and may often indicate more about the writer than about the performance.

Critical responses to the dance performance of people of African Caribbean heritage

From the specific reviews I have selected for this chapter, particularly those written by Judith Mackrell, Ismene Brown and Nicholas Dromgoole, I argue that the issue of the Company's African Caribbean heritage and the impact that it has upon their work and readings of their work is an ongoing consideration. Although the debates about approaches to dance criticism provide a wider context for this topic, specific aspects need further reflection. For handling feedback to choreographers, Liz Lerman pioneered an effective approach that enabled them to develop their work. This approach encourages those giving their reactions to be open and perceptive rather than judgemental. It is also relevant and useful for written critical response in the form of reviews and analysis of specific works (Adair, 1999). Lerman confronted racism in a debate when she questioned, 'What is white art?' and argued that 'white art means the privilege of never having to answer the question' (in Gere, 1995: 130). As we have seen above, and which Mackrell so astutely articulated, Phoenix was frequently in a position of being confined by the label 'all-black Company'.

Who is writing?

As mentioned above, the specificity of a writer's background and experience will have a bearing on their writing, but it is the critic's ability to be well informed and reflective on their preconceptions that will be significant if they are to produce insightful writing. So to follow Hall's line of argument (in Morley and Chen, 1996): a writer's ethnicity and gender may have an impact on their writing, but this is not necessarily the case. However, particular values and approaches have tended to be dominant. Marcia Siegel (1998) suggests, for example, that western critics work with hierarchies, although this is seldom admitted. She accepts that physicality is always experienced in relation to a context, which cannot be ignored, and that contexts are not universal. Although she considers that Laban systems offer a useful means to observe and analyse movement, she suggests that they have a Eurocentric bias. Critical response is written in the context of the dance canon, which is primarily Euro-American, and artists from other backgrounds such as those of African heritage are under-represented (Gere, 1995). Bruce

Fleming argues that there should be an 'insistence that the standards of white people of northern European stock not be used as a measure of value for all artistic products' (1995: 11). In addition, Brenda Dixon Gottschild has completed detailed research from which she suggests that what she terms 'Africanist aesthetics' have been ignored or denied. She offers numerous examples and suggests that Africanist attitudes pervade our society and many elements of postmodern art, including 'the radical juxtaposition of ostensibly contrary elements, the irony and double-entendre of verbal and physical gesture, [and] the dialogic relationship of performer and audience' (1995: 99).

A key issue in relation to Dixon Gottschild's research is that of power. Postmodern approaches are heralded as 'new' in Euro-American contexts without acknowledgement of the connections with African contexts. This lack of acknowledgement also occurred earlier in the twentieth century with modernist artists. Choreographer Jawole Willa Jo Zollar suggests that the liberal attempts to confront power issues within dance by using phrases such as 'culturally specific', 'multicultural', 'world dance' or 'black dance' are insufficient, and what actually needs to be discussed is racism. She defines racism as 'prejudice plus power, not individual power, but institutional power [...] African American people do not hold the power to be racist, not yet' (1995: 131). In a talk to the Dance Critics Association in Los Angeles in 1990, she used the Alcoholics Anonymous stepped-recovery approach to suggest recovery from racism in the dance community. Joan Acocella objected to this approach and suggested that 'a subtext of such public confessions is that we are all guilty' (1995: 135). Although Acocella reacted negatively to Zollar's confrontational approach, I would suggest that the extreme measures that Zollar employed indicate the depth of the trauma of racism and are evidence of the need to employ structures to systematically dismantle institutional racism.

Critics' choices of vocabulary

Clearly, critics have different understandings of the words they choose for their writing and the consequent impact on specific audiences. Some of the words chosen to describe the work of Phoenix have compounded many of the stereotypes associated with people of African Caribbean heritage in relation to physicality and sexuality, some of which have already been discussed. Others will be identified in this section. As we have seen, Phoenix's work is frequently labelled as 'black', focusing on the dancers' ethnicity; but as Bruce Fleming (1995) argues, the implications of the use of such terms is often disregarded. He argues that 'labelling of anything non-Western as "ethnic" is clearly a value judgement' (11). Moreover, Gere (1995) suggests that this term is mis-used, as does Joann Kealiinohomoku (1970: 1983). She suggests, 'By ethnic dance, anthropologists mean to convey the idea that all forms of dance reflect the cultural traditions within which they developed' (1983: 537). In her essay, using this definition, she argues that ballet is indeed a form of ethnic dance and that this term should not be used as a euphemism for non-western work.

Although in the late 1960s the seeds of contemporary dance had barely been sown in Britain, in America the form was well established and had a history of written critical response. In the context of the Civil Rights Movement it is hardly surprising that the critic Marcia Siegel reported that 'black dance is the most emotional issue in all dance' (1972: 137). She discussed the difficulties of being a white critic writing about black dance, and explained that there were few black critics and those that did exist at that time either could not or did not want to work in the white press. She also suggested that militant publications such as *The Feet* promoted black dance without sufficient attention to quality. In the 1970s she noted that there seemed to be an acceptance of blackness as the main reason for a company to exist, a factor that was accepted as key to its success (1972). She suggested that there were positive aspects of this development, such as providing a means to a sense of pride for black audiences. Much of the work she noted tended to be promoting black consciousness. She also remarked on a tension between these approaches to work and that of the established work of the Alvin Ailey Dance Theatre, which some viewed as too commercial. As Brenda White-Dixon noted (1991), 'The Black awareness movement spawned apprehension in some segments of the community toward schools that offered European-influenced dance techniques' (27).

As she comments, however, it is important to acknowledge that there were few openings for black dancers when Alvin Ailey, Donald McKayle and Arthur Mitchell were beginning in the early 1950s (1972). Phoenix also offers opportunities to black dancers, which even in the twenty-first century with shifting attitudes in relation to diversity are not as abundant as might be expected. Although there have been changes since the middle of the twentieth century, some of the issues that Siegel and White-Dixon reflected upon continue to be debated in current dance contexts.

As Mackrell notes, some of the positive adjectives used to describe the Company, such as 'exciting' and 'energetic', tend to label the group in a specific way. For example, in a review of a performance at the Royal Hall, Harrogate, in 1985, the critic Stephanie Ferguson identified the dancers as:

young, gifted and black [...]. Bubbling brown sugar meets liquid ebony here [...]. Although polished and professional they have not lost any of their streetwise slickness and their performances are still raw and powerful, an explosion of pent-up inner-city energies. (1985: PA)

The terms Ferguson chooses, such as 'bubbling brown sugar' and 'liquid ebony', focus on the dancers' skin colour and evoke associations for her readers. Her choice of the term 'raw' is another example, of which there are many, of an implication that there is a 'natural' element to the performances, as mentioned above, rather than that they are the result of intensive training in daily dance classes and focused rehearsals. While Ferguson seems to be trying to write in an enthusiastic and positive way about this performance, the result is categorisation that limits the dancers to a particular set of stereotypes.

I am now going to consider a review, written by Ismene Brown in *The Daily Telegraph* on 28 April 1998, of the two companies RJC and Phoenix, entitled 'Forget the philosophy – just strut'. As Paul Gilroy points out, 'any discussion of the representation of blackness in British art demands political as well as aesthetic sensitivities' (1996: 1). The title of Brown's article exemplifies precisely an absence of the aesthetic sensitivities to which Paul Gilroy refers.[12] It reinforces a limited view of the African Caribbean performers, implying that their role is to move rather than to think. Such an implication also reinforces the association of people of African heritage with their physicality, which has powerful connections with colonialism and slavery when black peoples' bodies were about economic value for the colonisers (Hall, 1997; Gilroy, 1993). The colonial system established a set of beliefs in which, as Rebecca Schneider argues, 'the imperial white male became culturally and biologically superior to those from whom he *differentiated* himself – the "colored", the colonized, the female' (1997: 137). The binary oppositions of white/coloured, coloniser/colonised and male/female that Schneider discusses are echoed in the opposition of mind/body in the article's title. Such oppositions are problematic because, as Jacques Derrida has argued, one category is usually the dominant one.

Writing such as Brown's is also problematic not only because it offers stereotypical views of people from a specific heritage but also because it invokes dualism: that is, a split between the mind and body as though they were two separate entities. This opposition is one that dance artists

---

[12] Ismene Brown said, however, that she did not write or approve the headline, which she found distasteful (email, 22 December 2004).

and theorists have contested and attempted to replace with a holistic understanding of bodymind, but in her writing Brown is undermining this approach. The review is an example of many of the prejudices that Phoenix have encountered throughout their history and which have been particularly challenging as they have aimed to become fully recognised as one of Britain's leading contemporary dance companies. It appears that in Brown's concern to write hard-hitting copy, she sacrifices accuracy. It is arguable whether the Company was split on such a dilemma as movement styles and repertoire, as she suggests. Nor was it the first 'black company'. There were earlier companies to which that label has been applied, including Les Ballet Nègres and MAAS Movers (see Adair, 1992).

Brown asks, 'How "black" should a black contemporary dance company be? It's a dilemma that split Britain's first black company.' Again Brown's question lacks the sensitivity that Gilroy argues is necessary in relation to issues of blackness in British art, in this case dance. Moreover, the formation of RJC by the founders of Phoenix, Donald Edwards and David Hamilton, and an early member of the Company, Edward Lynch, was a gradual process as people left Phoenix, rather than a dilemma that split the Company. To suggest that there was 'a split' is to reduce the very complex and multileveled nature of the work of each company to one 'dilemma'. The review consists of several comparative oppositions. For example, it is stated that RJC publicised themselves as Britain's 'national' black company and Phoenix were internationally renowned. So what are the reasons for Brown's comparisons? The two companies clearly have a connection between personnel, and the performers are of African Caribbean heritage. The comparisons are inappropriate, however, because the companies have different agendas and, as Brown herself points out, they have significantly different profiles in terms of the range of their audiences and scale of work.

Brown continues her review with the offensive comment that 'Phoenix in the eyes of RJC supporters has become a "coconut" company, black on the outside, white inside; by embracing classic contemporary styles, it is argued Phoenix rebuffs the urban, black, street dance which it sprang from' (PA). This statement raises questions about the reviewer's sources and about the authority with which she writes, which lead her not to question the use of such a derogatory term. Again, accuracy is an issue here. The early videos and photographs illustrate the fact that Phoenix was engaged with contemporary dance from the beginning and street dance was only one element of their style. For example, in the video by Bronwyn Williams for Leeds University Television in 1982, there is a recording of a contemporary dance class

led by David Hamilton with three of the Company members. This is followed by a contemporary dance work choreographed by Donald
Edwards, *Running Shadows* (1982). The photographs of the Company
taken in 1987 and 1989 by Terry Cryer (1992) again illustrate recognisable contemporary dance jumps and extensions.

Her description of *Excuse Da Expression* by De Napoli Clarke for RJC
Company says 'the girls were strutting and the boys were shadow-boxing'. This phrase offers a stereotyped description of racial identity, and
the use of the terms 'girls' and 'boys' is an example of infantilisation as
discussed in Chapter 5.[13] Ismene Brown's description of Mark Baldwin's
Templates of Glory was that it 'looked po-faced, like a twin-set and pearls
on Phoenix's earthy, loose-limbed dancers'. The term 'twin-set and
pearls' has an ethnic and class association of white middle class, and the
term 'earthy' invokes a sense of 'natural, essentialised' identity. Brown
also asserts that 'Living clean doesn't suit Phoenix'. This phrase suggests stereotypes, frequently associated with people of African descent,
of licentiousness, dirtiness and criminalisation.[14] The language used in
this review and the subtext revealed through my analysis are extremely
distasteful. There is little attempt to describe the works in a manner in
which the reader might gain insight into the works themselves, as suggested above by Lavender and Siegel. Instead, readers are subjected to
this critic's perspectives and prejudices without being able to gain
insights into the works discussed in the review. This writing is a good
example of a critic imposing her expectations of the repertoire with little insight or understanding of the artistic aspirations of Phoenix as a
repertory company. In an informal response to this review, Thea Barnes
said, '*What Phoenix and RJC need from critics is acknowledgement that
dance practices are diverse, develop and change frequently [...]. Enough damage has been practised by white/high-art mainstream hegemonic systems that
makes invisible and eliminates the work of most African-descent dance
artists*' (1998).

'Post-colonial melancholia':
Cultural pathology and dance criticism

In light of the above we need to ask if critical responses, particularly
from critics writing reviews, misrepresent a company's progress
through the preconceptions of the writer. Clearly, some of the cited

---

[13] See also Brenda Dixon Gottschild's comments about this point in *Digging the Africanist
Presence in American Performance* (1996, 141).

[14] I appreciate discussing this review with Ramsay Burt and Thea Barnes and hearing their
insightful comments.

examples endorse and support the Company's achievements, but some, as evidenced through the use of specific terms and concepts, do not. To extend this discussion further, I should like to focus on a specific review and consider it in relation to what Paul Gilroy calls 'Post-colonial melancholia' (1999). Gilroy developed this concept to describe a cultural pathology evident in some of the ways in which British society operates. A visible link to this pathology is 'race'. He suggests that, whenever this term is used, the 'residues of imperial and colonial culture live on and they promote a nostalgia and sanction a violence which ensure that Britain stays paralysed by the inability to work through the loss of global prestige and the economic and political benefits that once attended it' (1999: 15).

It is this melancholia and nostalgia that I think is apparent in Nicholas Dromgoole's review published in *The Sunday Telegraph* in 1996 entitled, 'Where did the blackness go?' (8). His topic is a performance by Phoenix Dance Company, which offered a programme of three works: *Never Still* (1995), choreographed by Company member Chantal Donaldson; *Haunted Passages* (1989), choreographed by Philip Taylor, who has a close association with the Company; and *Movements in 8* (1995), choreographed by artistic director Maggie Morris and assistant artistic director Gary Lambert.

Dromgoole is not the only critic to ask such questions. As we have seen above, Ismene Brown asked, 'How "black" should a contemporary dance company be?' (1998). A focus on the categorisation of 'blackness' in relation to discussions of the work of artists of African descent is still prevalent despite the theoretical challenges to the concept by, for example, Stuart Hall, bell hooks, Isaac Julien, Paul Gilroy and Kobena Mercer. A number of the issues raised in Dromgoole's review are also apparent in other reviews; however, my focus initially will be the programme to which Dromgoole is referring, particularly *Never Still*.

I saw the programme in the Company's home town of Leeds at the West Yorkshire Playhouse, where dance performances are the exception in a venue that mainly programmes drama. On this occasion the Company performed to an audience many of whom would be familiar with their work, as the Company has a local following and this is the main venue in Leeds.

The introduction for Chantal Donaldson's choreography in the programme quotes her views:

The joy of creating *Never Still* is reflected in its compendium of movement and dynamics. My inspiration for the piece came from observations of people's everyday lives and relationships and the music of

22. *Haunted Passages*, 1995. Choreographer Philip Taylor; dancers Ricky Holgate, Douglas Thorpe, Sharon Donaldson; photographer Terry Cryer

Hugues Le Bars. *Never Still* is a piece free from the confines of a story-line but full of the passion for life.

This was the second work by Donaldson commissioned for Phoenix and continued a tradition in which dancers make work for the Company. Donaldson was one of the women who joined the Company in 1989 and came from the same school background as the founders. I wrote at the time:

> Lighter moments included flirtatious gestures and a sense of play [...] The dancing was technically sharp with clean lines and at times hurtled along at a breath-taking pace. This was a good example of Chantal Donaldson's work and it illustrated the value of nurturing choreographers from within the company. (1995)

The response of the local critics was positive, as is clear when Jane Tadman in the *Sheffield Telegraph* describes the Company as 'Yorkshire's own Phoenix' (1996: 31). She clearly wanted to claim Phoenix as an example of Yorkshire's cultural practices. Another regional critic, this time of the *Bournemouth Evening Echo*, described the work on tour as 'Exciting, enigmatic, exhilarating [...] brimming with passion for life' (Kosanke, 1996: 24). A London critic, Clement Crisp, writing in the *Financial Times* (1995), commented that the work 'is perceptive about social attitudes, cleverly made, and stunningly danced: the style is smooth-muscled, large in scale, full-blooded'.

Undoubtedly, some critics acknowledge the Company's achievements and its status as a world-class contemporary dance Company, as indicated in its being chosen to represent Britain at the Atlanta Cultural Olympiad. The Company is still, however, frequently defined by the limiting terms of 'black' and 'blackness'. So when Dromgoole asks his question, 'Where did the blackness go?'(1996: 8), what is it that he wants and what is his agenda?

Dromgoole's review begins:

> I remember in 1981, when five young black men,[15] enthusiasts for contemporary dance from Harehills Middle School, Leeds, formed themselves into a dance company, Phoenix Dance and created their own choreography and theatrical excitement by their total commitment and fresh-seeming talent. (1996: 8)

---

[15] In 1981 the Company was founded with just three members.

23. *Never Still*, 1995. Choreographer Sharon Donaldson; dancers Stephen Derrick,
   Ricky Holgate; photographer Steve Hanson

He takes the readers on a nostalgic journey back to the formation of the Company in 1981. So what is it exactly that this critic remembers? He recalls his enjoyment of a programme fifteen years previously, and yet development and change is inevitably part of any company's process. It is legitimate to ask, therefore, why he would expect to see work in 1996 similar to that in 1981. One of the key issues raised in this review is the categorisation of the dancers as black men. As Mills articulates, this is problematic because blackness as a marker excludes one from the 'white body politic' (Mills, 1998: 117) and renders the black person invisible. 'He is not seen in his individuality. To see him as black is to see enough. Hence to see him as black is not to see *him* at all' (Gordon, 1995: 99).

I suggest that one of the difficulties revealed in Dromgoole's review is that he views the dancers in terms of what they can offer to him from the position of the Other, which he places them in. He is, therefore, ill at ease with developments in the repertoire that do not match his expectations. His dissatisfaction with the programme he is discussing tempts him to invoke the memories of the earlier performances and ask, 'What has gone wrong?'(1996: 8). There is an assumption in this first paragraph, as there is throughout the review, that the founders had an essence of 'blackness', which they produced through performance, and that this should have continued as the Company developed. Such a view does not take account of the cultural and social changes in the past fifteen years or of the shifts in performance practices. As Hall makes clear, 'we must recognize that "black" is a politically and culturally constructed category, which cannot be grounded in a set of fixed, trans-cultural or transcendental racial categories, and which therefore, has no guarantees in Nature' (in Morley and Chen, 1996: 18). Dromgoole, however, does not take account of that, nor does he pay attention to the diversity of experiences of people of African descent. His review compounds stereotypes and misinformation. This is partly because he does not consider that, as Hall explains, 'The moment the signifier "black" is torn from its historical, cultural and political embedding and lodged in a biologically constituted racial category, we valorize, by inversion, the very ground of the racism we are trying to deconstruct' (in Morley and Chen, 1996: 472).

In searching for an answer to his question, Dromgoole seeks to blame Arts Council policies. 'I am tempted to say, the Arts Council, mediocrity and layers of bureaucrats have taken over, but that would be unfair simplification' (1996: 8). This comment appears to refer to the funding the Company received, initially in response to a strategic review report, *The Glory of the Garden*. As we have seen, this report recommended that support be strengthened for black and Asian dance, and Phoenix was noted

as a 'good example of talent' (1984: 15). There have been several conferences and numerous articles using or questioning the label 'black
dance'.[16] There has also been debate about the implications for Phoenix
of receiving funding (Briginshaw, 1984: 17).

Dromgoole's next point is the colour of the dancers. 'Why did I not
just say five young men? What has their colour to do with it? In fact a
great deal' (1996: 8). He questions his own description and argues that
the fact that he describes the Company as 'five young black men' (1996:
8) is significant. The term 'black' when used in this way is problematic,
as discussed above. In relation to Phoenix this is because attention is
then paid to the colour/politics of the company rather than to its artistic process and products. What is important at this point is to acknowledge, as bell hooks points out, that 'postmodern critiques of essentialism
which challenge notions of universality and static over-determined
identity within mass culture and mass consciousness can open up new
possibilities for the construction of self and the assertion of agency'
(1990: 28).

In order to justify his description, Dromgoole reflects on the trans-
portation of slaves from Africa and the survival of music and dance culture that has influenced popular music and dance in the west. Is he, in
these comments, searching for an authentic past rather than acknowledging the processes of hybridisation in which people draw on resources
from a number of cultures? Perhaps Dromgoole is making connections
where there are none. The varied and complex culture of the Caribbean
together with British culture may have informed the work of Phoenix.
These influences, however, were not direct but rather came through the
memories and experiences of the dancers' families. The dancers in 1995
were British. So when Dromgoole refers to 'our own popular music and
dance', who is the 'our' to whom he is referring? Such use of language
evokes colonial structures in which the 'our' excludes as well as
includes. So although the colonies may have been dismantled, much of
the thinking and language that evolved from such structures remain
firmly in place. As Homi Bhabha states, 'colonial discourse produces the
colonized as a fixed reality which is at once an "other" and yet entirely
knowable and visible' (1983: 23).

Having set a context of Africa, Dromgoole then turns his attention to
physique and argues that myths about African physique lending itself to
dance are erroneous. Instead he states that the key to such apparent

---

[16] For example, 'Black to the Future', a report of a conference held at the South Bank Centre,
London, as part of the Ballroom Blitz Festival, August 1993.

The Australian *Sunday Times*, 28 December 1986, commented, 'This all-black company
from an inner Leeds suburb has been described as one of the most exciting in the world. Its
work has been called "dance with soul" '(PA).

ease is musicality and an understanding of rhythm, which is learnt. His point here, about cultural acquisition of skills, supports the arguments I am making, but he offers a conceptually muddled context, which locates Phoenix with roots in 'mythical black Africa'. Dromgoole then discusses Phoenix Dance Company and the programme that they performed. In searching for another reason for his dissatisfaction with it, he suggests it is also because the artistic direction and most of the choreography in this programme come from white people. He suggests, therefore, that Phoenix has become an 'ordinary dance company' (1996: 8).

The key to the writer's assumptions and assertions appears to be in the comment that Phoenix 'took advantage of the cultural gifts that black people can so munificently offer us, and enrich our often drab culture in the process' (1996: 8). This statement illustrates Hall's point that:

> The play of identity and difference which constructs racism is powered not only by the positioning of blacks as the inferior species but also, and at the same time, by an inexpressible envy and desire; and this is something the recognition of which fundamentally *displaces* many of our hitherto stable political categories, since it implies a process of identification and otherness which is more complex than we had hitherto imagined. (1999: 444–5)

This positioning is evident in a number of the critics' writings above. So for example, the title to Brown's review discussed earlier is associating the Company with the body rather than the mind. In this binary opposition it is the latter category that is powerful; in such comparisons the body is viewed as inferior, and by association those who engage with physical activities such as dance are also viewed as inferior. The envy and desire that Hall identifies leak through the writings in the descriptions of the dancing as 'exciting', 'energetic' and 'enthusiastic'.

This archive of critical responses is also part of the historical archive of the Company. Phoenix is a highly successful repertory company, and yet its cultural specificity has resulted in it being placed in a position in which it has had to reflect constantly upon its 'identity'. It is as if Phoenix must have an identity, whereas the purpose of a dance company is to produce a practice and it would, therefore, follow that the artistic practice should be the focus of the critical response. This has not necessarily been the case with Phoenix. As we have seen, the critical response often focused on the Company's identity at the expense of writing informatively about the artistic work that it produced. Moreover, the response to Phoenix raises a wider question. If this is the response to a well-respected, successful company, then it would be pertinent to ask how other companies from the African Diaspora have fared. The lack of reflection within dance criticism has resulted in some intolerable prejudices being exposed in the guise of critical judgement. This has meant that critical writing on Phoenix has been limited, and audiences, funders and the Board have seldom had access to informed insights with which to extend their understanding of the Company. Some of these reviews are comparatively recent, and as long as the institution of dance criticism does not address its own prejudices, injustices in relation to evaluations of dance work will continue.

Conclusion

In this book I have located Phoenix Dance Company within the framework of British contemporary dance. This complex narrative of a repertory company and its development from a small-scale regional company to an internationally acclaimed one has many interwoven strands and does not lend itself to a definitive conclusion. Rather, it raises questions with implications for contemporary dance and funding procedures in Britain – questions that highlight the lack of reflection and insight of the funding bodies and the critics, and that have serious implications for the evolving Company in particular, and for the development of contemporary dance in general.

Paradoxically, this cultural history of Phoenix Dance Company is a story of loss at the same time as the Company achieved status in the international dance community. The readings from the archives, together with my interviews, provide a basis for reflecting upon the particularity of this account and the wider issues that emerge from such reflection. A key topic in this respect is institutional racism. The archives, and my interpretation of them, allow a narrative to be uncovered in which the Company has arguably been confronted and contained by institutional racism from the funding bodies and from the critics. Although 'institutional racism' is a term that was used in the context of the Civil Rights Movement in America, it was not until the MacPherson Report (1999) following the death of Stephen Lawrence that the term was widely used in Britain.

The fact that the Arts Council funded the Company as a means of adhering to its own agenda, as articulated in *The Glory of the Garden* (1984) had long-term repercussions for Phoenix. In addition, the funding came with particular obligations, which required the Company to change their organisational procedures and to some extent their artistic practices. In the process of making these changes, the founders were not sufficiently mentored as young artists to help them develop their unique creative approaches, and so a series of losses haunted the Company as it developed. It was expected to adopt a range of inappropriate structures, which inhibited rather than encouraged its artistic growth. The specificity of the Company in relation to the dancers' educational background, their lack of conventional dance training, their youth and the fusion of a range of movement styles was appreciated by their audiences, the dance critics and the funding bodies. Paradoxically however, these were the factors that also contributed to the difficult negotiations which followed their status as a funded Company and which shifted the expectations of stakeholders in relation to their day-to-day organisation and the development of the repertoire.

At first the Company members defined their artistic practice themselves; and although they drew on their experience of contemporary dance, their creative enterprise was not confined by the techniques and choreographic structures that those with formal dance training encountered. The strength of the founders came from their connection to their local community and their perception of dance as being integral to their lives. The first moment of loss was the receipt of funding from the Arts Council. The money obviously enabled them to gain a living wage and acquire resources and offered potential for development, but at the cost of meeting the requirement from the funding body for Phoenix Dance Company to adhere to the criteria and policies that the Council laid down for its clients. The process of reorganisation of the Company to meet the Arts Council's criteria was one of disenfranchisement, and profoundly disempowering for the artists. The experience of Phoenix in relation to resources raises questions about the politically driven funding of contemporary dance in Britain and the implications for artistic development of funded companies. The stated reasons for funding also raise questions. In some ways, providing finance for a regional company was a positive decision and allowed an infrastructure to become established for dance outside the cultural capital of London. It is pertinent to ask, however, whether the artists would have been better served if their work structures, which did not fit the Arts Council's model, had been acknowledged and facilitated.

When I began this study, I anticipated discovering a story of young artists who had benefited from their early success. I was concerned to find that the Eurocentricism of the dance canon and the expectations of the funding bodies and critics meant that, although the artists' achievements were partially acknowledged on the one hand, they were confined by inappropriate criteria and categorisation on the other. I also expected to consider to a greater extent the role that the entry of the four women from the Phoenix Plus project played in the development of the Company. During my research process, however, I considered that this point was another loss for the founding members of the Company. The narrative of the women artists of Phoenix is an equally important account, which in turn highlights important issues in British contemporary dance; but although it has its place, it has not been a central feature of this study. As with the funding, there were some gains to an extended Company, allowing a more diverse repertoire that was received enthusiastically by the press. The question arising from this moment of crisis for the Company, however, is the role of monolithic dance training.

The women had gained professionalism and status from their formal three-year training and their experience as dancers in other companies, which allowed them to some extent to transcend the specificity of their backgrounds. It is arguable, however, that their training affected the experimental edge of their creative work. Moreover, it was a desire for experimentation that led some dancers to rebel against the training and structures of London Contemporary Dance School in the mid-1970s and early 1980s. It was in this era of experimentation, although not directly influenced by it, that Phoenix was founded.

This is a complex narrative played out through gender, ethnicity and class, evident in the body, representation, politics and cultural discourses, economics and critical rhetoric. One of the paradoxes that the Company faced was that of the 'burden of representation' (Mercer, 1994). The dancers were expected by the funding bodies, critics and audiences to represent 'the black community'. Such expectations contained and constrained those artists such as Phoenix who were considered to be representative. Another difficulty with which Phoenix was confronted was how to structure itself as a repertory company. The assumption that accompanied such a structure was that artistic excellence was rewarded and validated by the artistic community, which entailed commissioning well-known choreographers. A repertoire of work from internationally renowned choreographers was considered to be an indication of success, as was a presence on the international touring circuit. Such criteria were the antithesis of the basis on which Phoenix Dance Company was founded, and raise issues about how artistic excellence is judged.

Phoenix encountered certain recurring issues, which were played out with specific nuances under the leadership of each successive artistic director. This study has considered some of these topics. One theme was whether the Company was identified and organised as a dancers' company. Clearly, this concern relates to the early beginnings of the Company when, despite Hamilton's eventual leadership and the co-operation between the dancers, this was its primary organisation. It is arguable that an initial sense of ownership fuelled an ongoing drive from the dancers for the Company to be a dancers' Company. In addition, the perception of both the early dancers and many of those who joined the Company in 1989 was that dance was an important means to express their particularity. They, therefore, wanted a structure in which their expression could be facilitated. Such organisation did not, however, fit with Arts Council policies.

Another emergent theme is that of under-funding which, although not an issue for Phoenix alone, had particular implications for the development of the Company and the acquisition of a diverse repertoire. A third ongoing theme for the Company was its gender and ethnic composition. Phoenix initially emerged in the early 1980s when the paradigm of political separatism was considered valid. In such a context, a Company comprised of men of African descent in an art form in which white European females predominated was read as progressive. In addition, the fusion style of contemporary dance, martial arts and reggae music in some of the choreographies offered an innovative artistic practice, which received early acknowledgement by the national media. This narrative, however, highlights the gradual erosion of the very specificity that ensured the success of the early Phoenix.

This account is one of both success and loss of a specific group at a particular time in contemporary dance history. During the twenty-year period of this study, there have been changes and developments in Arts Council policies and procedures and concern to address cultural diversity. In addition, many institutions have put frameworks in place to challenge institutional racism. It is not clear, however, that such changes are sufficient to provide a structure in which artists such as Phoenix can achieve cultural equity. Unfortunately, it is still questionable whether the funding bodies and critics are sufficiently reflective of their procedures and practices. The issues raised in this book highlight the limitations of the politically driven funding of the art form and have serious implications for the artistic development of evolving companies and for the development of contemporary dance in Britain.

Bibliography

Aalten, A., 1995. 'Femininity as performance/performing femininity: Constructing the body of the ballerina', in *Border Tensions: Dance and discourse* (Guildford: University of Surrey), pp. 11–17

Abel, E., 1990. 'Race, class and psychoanalysis', in M. Hirsch and E.F. Keller, eds., *Conflicts in Feminism* (London and New York: Routledge)

Accolla, J., 1995. 'Part of the problem: language and truth in dance-world politics', in D. Gere, ed., *Looking Out: Perspectives on Dance and Criticism in a Multicultural World* (New York: Schirmer Books)

Adair, C., 1992. *Women and Dance: sylphs and sirens* (Basingstoke: Macmillan)

Adair, C., 1995. 'Black looks: The representation of black dancers', in Butterworth, J., ed., *Dance '95 Moving into the Future* Conference Proceedings (Leeds, Bretton Hall)

Adair, C., 2000. 'Reviewing the reviews: Issues of criticism in relation to Phoenix Dance', in J. Crone-Willis and J. LaPointe-Crump, compilers, *Dancing in the Millennium* Conference Proceedings (conference organised by Congress on Research in Dance, Dance Critics Association, National Dance Association, Society of Dance History Scholars 19–23 July), pp. 1–5 (Washington DC)

Adair, C., 2001. 'Phoenix perspectives: African American influences on a British dance company', in D. Fischer-Hornung and A.D. Goeller, eds., *EmBODYing Liberation: The Black Body in American Dance*, FORE-CAAST series, vol. 4: Munster, Hamburg, London, Litverlag, pp. 127–133

Adair, C., 2001. 'Readings of identities and physicality in the work of Jonzi D', in R. Duerden, compiler, *Dance Theatre: An International Investigation* Conference Proceedings (conference organised by Manchester Metropolitan University 9–12 September 1999), pp. 61–68, www.jonzi_d.co.uk

Adewole, F., 1997. 'On the edge: Jonzi D and Bode Lawal', *Association of Dance of the African Diaspora* (ADAD) *Newsletter*, no. 10, p. 3

Adewole, F., 2003, 'Funmi Adewole interviews Namron', *Dance UK News*, no. 51, Winter, p. 24

Adshead-Lansdale, J., and Layson, J., eds, 1983. *Dance History: A Methodology for Study* (London: Dance Books)

Adshead-Lansdale, J., ed., 1999. *Dancing Texts: Intertextuality and Interpretation* (London: Dance Books)

Alibhai-Brown, Y., 2000. *Who Do We Think We Are: Imagining the New Britain* (London: Penguin Books)

Allen, Z. D., 1976. 'Blacks and ballet', *Dance Magazine*, July, pp. 65–70

Ananya, C., 2003. 'Reading difference: The interventionary perform-ance of Jawole Willa Jo Zollar's *Batty Mores*', *Discourses and Dance*, vol. 2, no. 1, pp. 25–49

Anglesey, N., 2000. '*19: Rewind and Come Again*', *The Stage*, 12 October, p. 17

Araeen, R., 1988. *The Essential Black Art* (London: Chisenhale Gallery in conjunction with Black Umbrella)

Arts Council of Great Britain, 1984. *The Glory of the Garden* (London: ACGB)

Arts Council of Great Britain, 1989. *Towards Cultural Diversity* (London: ACGB)

Arts Council of Great Britain, 1991. *National Arts Strategy and Cultural Equity* (London: ACGB)

Arts Council of England, 1996. *The Policy for Dance of the English Arts Funding System* (London: ACE)

Arts Council of England, 1998. *Cultural Diversity Action Plan* (London: ACE)

Aschenbrenner, J., 1980. 'Black dance and dancers', *CORD Research Annual*, vol. XII, pp. 41–47

Ashcroft, B., Griffiths, G. and Tiffin, H., 1998. *Key Concepts in Post-Colonial Studies* (London and New York: Routledge)

Au, S., 1988. *Ballet and Modern Dance* (London: Thames and Hudson)

Auty, J. and Harrison, K., 1991. *Dance Ideas* (London: Hodder & Stoughton)

Axarlis, N., 1984. 'MAAS National Conference' *Artrage*, vol. 6, Spring, pp. 26–31

Badejo, P., 1993. 'What is black dance in Britain?' *Dance Theatre Journal*, vol. 10, no. 4, pp. 10–13 & continued p. 47

Baddoo, D., 2003. 'Reflections of a dance manager' *Animated*, Spring, pp. 31–33

Bakht, N., 1997. 'Shobana Jeyasingh' *Rewriting the Culture Dance Theatre Journal*, vol. 13, no. 4, pp. 8–9

Baldry, H., 1981. *The Case for the Arts* (London: Secker)

Banes, S., 1994. *Writing Dancing: in the Age of Postmodernism* (Hanover and London: Wesleyan University Press)

Banes, S., ed., 2003. *Reinventing Dance in the 1960s: Everything Was Possible* (Madison: The University of Wisconsin Press)

Barnes, T., 1998. 'Black dance?' *Dance Link*, vol. 4, p. 69

Barnes, T., 1989–99. 'A voyage with parallels' *Animated*, Winter, pp. 28–30

Barnes, T., 1999. 'Be prepared and always be flexible' *Dance Theatre Journal*, vol. 15, no. 1, pp. 32–35

Barnes, T., 2000. 'Individual aesthetic in the African Diaspora' *Dance Theatre Journal*, vol. 15, pp. 24–28

Barthes, R., 1987. 'The discourse of history' in E. Attridge et al, eds, *Post-Structuralism and the Question of History* (Cambridge: Cambridge University Press)

Barzilai, S. and Bloomfield, M.W., 1986. 'New Criticism and deconstructive criticism: or what's new?', *New Literary History*, vol. 18, pp. 151–169

Beckford, R., 1979. *Katherine Dunham* (New York: Marcel Dekker)

Benston, K., 2000. *Performing Blackness* (London and New York: Routledge)

Bernal, M., 1987. *Black Athena: the Afrosiatic Roots of Classical Civilization. Volume 1: The Fabrication of Ancient Greece 1785–1985* (London: Free Association Books)

Berry, K., 2006. 'Phoenix Dance Theatre', *Dancing Times*, vol. 97, no. 1154, October, pp. 27–29

Bhabha, H., 1983. 'The other question: The stereotype and colonial discourse', *Screen*, vol. 24, no. 6, pp. 18–36

Bhabha, H., ed., 1990. *Nation and Narration* (London and New York: Routledge)

Bhabha, H., 1997. *Re-inventing Britain, Identity, Transnationalism and the Arts* (London: British Council)

Blacking, J., 1986. 'Culture and the arts' *National Association for Education in the Arts Take Up Series*, no. 4, pp. 3–22

Bobo, J., 1995. *Black Women as Cultural Readers* (New York: Columbia University Press)

Braden, S., 1978. *Artists and People* (London and New York: Routledge)

Brah, A., 1993. 'Re-framing Europe: En-gendered racisms, ethnicities and nationalisms in contemporary Western Europe', *Feminist Review*, no. 45, Autumn, pp. 9–30

Braham, P., Rattansi, A. and Skellington, R., eds, 1992. *Racism and Antiracism: Inequalities, Opportunities and Politics* (London: Sage Publications)

Bramley, I., 1993–4. 'Letter response', *Dance Theatre Journal*, vol. 11, no. 4, Winter, p. 48

Bremser, M., 1999. *Fifty Contemporary Choreographers* (London and New York: Routledge)

Brennan, M., 1997. 'Knowing the elephant', *Dance Theatre Journal*, vol. 13, no. 4, Winter, pp. 14–17

Brian, B., Dadzie, S. and Scafe, S., 1985. *The Heart of the Race: Black Women's Lives in Britain* (London: Virago)

Briginshaw, V., 1984. 'The rise of Phoenix', *New Dance*, no. 30, Autumn, p. 17

Brooks, A., 1997. *Postfeminisms: Feminism, cultural theory and cultural forms* (London: Routledge)

Brown, C., 1992. '"Same difference": the persistence of racial disadvantage in the British employment market', in P. Braham, A. Rattansi and R. Skellington, eds, *Racism and Antiracism: Inequalities, opportunities and policies* (London: Sage & The Open University)

Brown, C., 1994. 'The possibilities for feminist dance histories', in J. Adshead-Lansdale and J. Layson, eds, *Dance History: An Introduction* (London and New York: Routledge)

Brown, H., Gilkes, M. and Kaloski-Naylor, A., eds, 1999. *White?Women* (York: Raw Nerve Books)

Brown, I., 2000. 'Entranced by a sequined swan and a serpent of ballet shoes', *Daily Telegraph*, London, 26 September, p. 22

Brown, S., Hawson, I., Graves, T. and Barot, M., 2001. *Eclipse Report: Developing strategies to combat racism in theatre* (Nottingham: ACE, Theatrical Management Association and Nottingham Playhouse Initiative)

Bruce, V., 1965. *Dance and drama in education* (Oxford: Pergamon Press)

Bryan, D., 1993. *Advancing Black Dancing* (London: ACE)

Bryson, N., 1997. 'Cultural studies and dance history', in Desmond, J., ed., *Meaning in Motion* (Duke University Press)

Buckland, T. J., 1999. *Dance in the Field: Theory, methods and issues in dance ethnography* (Basingstoke: MacMillan)

Buckland, T. J., 1999. 'All dances are ethnic but some are more ethnic than others: Some observations on dance studies and anthropology', *Dance Research*, vol. 17, no. 1, pp. 3–21

Burt, R., 1983. 'The Phoenix susses Dartington', *New Dance*, no. 25, Summer, p. 21

Burt, R., 1993–4. 'Letter: Women and dance', *Dance Theatre Journal*, vol. 11, no. 1, pp. 3 and 48

Burt, R., 1995. *The Male Dancer* (London and New York: Routledge)

Burt, R., 1998. *Alien Bodies* (London and New York: Routledge)

Burt, R., 1998. 'Re-presentations of re-presentations: reconstruction, restaging and originality', *Dance Theatre Journal*, vol. 14, no. 2, pp. 30–33

Burt, R., 2001. 'Katherine Dunham's *Rite de Passage* censorship and sexuality' in D. Fischer-Hornung and A.D. Goeller, eds., *EmBODYing*

Liberation: The black body in American dance, FORECAAST series, vol. 4, Munster, Hamburg, London, Litverlag, pp. 79–89

Burt, R., 2004. 'Katherine Dunham's floating island of negritude: The Katherine Dunham Dance Company in London and Paris in the late 1940s and early 1950s' in A. Carter, ed., *Rethinking Dance History* (London and New York: Routledge)

Butler, J., 1990. *Gender Trouble* (London and New York: Routledge)

Butler, J., 1990. 'Performative acts and gender constitution: An essay in phenomenology and feminist theory' in S.E. Case, ed., *Performing Feminism: Feminist critical theory and theatre* (Baltimore and London: John Hopkins University Press)

Butler, J., 1993. *Bodies that Matter: on the discursive limits of sex* (London and New York: Routledge)

Carby, H., 1982. 'White women listen! Black feminism and the boundaries of sisterhood', *The Empire Strikes Back: Race and racism in 70s Britain*, University of Birmingham, Centre for Contemporary Cultural Studies (London: Hutchinson)

Carter, A., 1992–93. Book review: '*Women and Dance: sylphs and sirens*', *Dance Now*, Winter, pp. 48–49

Carter, A., 1998. *Dance Studies Reader* (London and New York: Routledge)

Carter, A., 2004. *Rethinking Dance History* (London and New York: Routledge)

Carter Harrison, P., Walker, V. L. II and Edwards, G., 2002. *Black Theatre: Ritual performance in the African diaspora* (Philadelphia: Temple University Press)

Carty, H., 1996. 'Demi-plié bubble shuffle', *Dance Theatre Journal*, vol. 13, no.2, pp. 26–27

Carty, H., 2003. 'Black Dance in England: the pathway here', *Dance UK News*, no. 51, Winter, pp. 6–8

Cass, J., 1993. *Dancing Through History* (New Jersey: Prentice-Hall)

Charlemagne, S., 1984. 'New dance focus', *Artrage*, Spring, pp. 24–25

Charnock, N., 1994. 'Panel discussion, *Ways of working: The difference between female and male ways of working*, with Peter Badejo, Emilyn Claid, Sue Maclennan, Chair: Maggie Semple' in R. Burt, ed., *Redressing the Sylph: The First National Symposium of Women in Dance*, 18–20 February, Artistic Directors Christy Adair and Emilyn Claid (Leeds: Yorkshire Dance Centre)

Claid, E., 2006. *Yes? No! Maybe...: Seductive ambiguity in dance* (London and New York: Routledge)

Clarke, M. and C. Crisp, 1981. *The History of Dance* (London: Orbis Pub)

Clarke, M. and Crisp, C., 1989. *London Contemporary Dance Theatre: The first 21 years* (Dance Books: London)

Cohen, S.J., ed., 1974. *Dance as a Theatre Art: Source readings in dance history from 1581 to the present* (New York: Harper and Row)

Cohen, S.J., ed., 1998. *International Encyclopaedia of Dance*, vols 4 & 5 (New York and Oxford: Oxford University Press)

Commission for Racial Equality, 2003. 'Myths, facts and stats', *Connections*, Spring, p. 9

Cope, E., 1976. *Performances: Dynamics of a dance group* (London: Lepus Books)

Cooper Albright, A., 1997. *Choreographing Difference: The body and identity in contemporary dance* (Hanover and London: Wesleyan University Press)

Cooper Albright, A., 2001. 'Embodying history: Epic narrative and cultural identity in African American dance', in A. Cooper Albright and A. Dils, eds., *moving history/dancing cultures: A Dance History Reader* (Hanover: Wesleyan University Press)

Coveney, M., 1990. 'Artful city at the hub of the West Riding', *Observer*, Sunday 4 March, p. 59

Craine, D., 2006. 'Rekindled Phoenix burns brightly', *The Times*, 27 February, Times Online

Cryer, T., 1992. *one in the eye*, Yorkshire Arts Circus.

Cunningham, J., 1997. *Leading Britain into the Future: Create the Future: A strategy for cultural policy, arts and the creative economy* (London: Labour Party)

Daly, A., 1998. '"Woman", women, and subversion: Some nagging questions from a dance historian', *Choreography and Dance*, vol. 5

Daniels, T. and Geram, J., eds, 1989. *Black Images in British Black TV* (London: British Film Institute)

DeFrantz, T., 1996. 'Simmering passivity: The black male body in concert dance', in G. Morris ed., *moving words: re-writing dance* (London and New York: Routledge)

DeFrantz, T., 1999. 'To make black bodies strange: Social critique in concert dance of the Black Arts Movement', in A. Bean, ed., *A Source Book of African-American Performance: Plays, people, movement* (London and New York: Routledge)

DeFrantz, T., 2002. *Dancing Many Drums: Excavations in African American dance* (Wisconsin: University of Wisconsin Press)

De Marigny, C., 1992. 'Germaine Acogny – New African dance', *Dance Theatre Journal*, vol. 9, no. 3, Spring, pp. 4–7

DeMille, A., 1963. *The Book of the Dance* (London: Bookplan)

Derrida, J., 1981. *Positions*, trans. Alan Bass (London: Athlone Press)

Desmond, J., 1991. 'Dancing out the difference: Cultural imperialism and Ruth St Denis's *Radha* of 1906' *Signs*, vol. 17, no. 1, Autumn, pp. 28–49

Desmond, J., 1997. 'Embodying difference: Issues in dance and cultural studies', in J. Desmond, ed., *Meaning in Motion* (Durham and London: Duke University Press)

Desmond, J., ed., 1997. *Meaning in Motion* (Durham and London: Duke University Press)

Devlin, G., 1989. *Stepping Forward: Some suggestions for the development of dance in England during the 1990s* (London: ACGB)

Dixon, B., 1991. 'Born too late?', *Dance Critics' Association Newsletter*, pp. 5 and 15

Dixon Gottschild, B., 1991, 'The Afrocentric paradigm', *Design for Arts in Education*, January–February, pp. 15–22

Dixon Gottschild, B., 1995. 'Stripping the Emperor: The Africanist presence in American concert dance', in D. Gere, ed., *Looking Out: Perspectives on dance and criticism in a multicultural world* (New York: Schirmer)

Dixon Gottschild, B., 1996. *Digging the Africanist presence in American performance: Dance and other contexts* (London and Westport, Connecticut: Praeger)

Dixon Gottschild, B., 1999. 'Rennie Harris: Pure spirit and sheer joy', *Dancemagazine*, August, pp. 60–63

Dixon Gottschild, B., 2000. *Waltzing in the dark: African American vaudeville and race politics in the Swing Era* (Basingstoke: Palgrave)

Dixon Gottschild, B., 2003. *The Black Dancing Body: A geography from coon to cool* (Basingstoke: Palgrave)

Dixon-Stowell, B., 1984. 'You've taken my blues and gone: A seminar on black dance in white America', *Dance Research Journal*, vol. 16, no. 2, Fall, pp. 37–39

Doolittle, L. and Flynn, A., 2000. *dancing bodies, living histories* (Banff: Banff Centre Press)

Dromgoole, N., 1996. 'Where did the blackness go', *Sunday Telegraph*, p. 8

Dougill, D., 1983. 'The state of play', *Dance and Dancers*, no. 404, August, pp. 12–13

Dunham, K., 1959. *Island Possessed* (Chicago: University of Chicago Press)

Dunham, K., 1969: 1994. *A Touch of Innocence* (Chicago: University of Chicago Press)

Dunlop, R., Moody, D., Muir, A. and Shaw, C., 1995. 'Cultural trends in the 90s, Part 2: The performing arts', *Cultural Trends*, vol. 7, no. 26: 2, pp. 1–25

Dyer, R., ed., 1977. 'Stereotyping', *Gays and Film* (London: BFI)

Dyer, R., 1988. 'White', *Screen*, vol. 29, no. 4, pp. 44–65

Dyer, R., 1992. *Only Entertainment* (London and New York: Routledge)

Dyer, R., 1997. *White* (London and New York: Routledge)

Edgar, D., ed., 1999. 'Plays on playwriting', *State of Play*, vol. 1 (London: Faber and Faber)

Edwards, B., 2004. 'Invisible identity? Invisible voice?', *Animated*, Summer, pp. 14–16

Emery, L. F., 1988. *Black Dance From 1619 to Today* (London: Dance Books)

Engineer, M., 2000. *Between Empire and Equality: Images of race relations in 20th century Britain* (London: Commission for Racial Equality)

Enwezor, O., 1995. 'The body in question: Whose body?: "Black male: Representations of masculinity in contemporary American art"', *Third Text* Summer, pp. 67–70

Evans, K., 2004. *Decibel Overview*: decibel newsletter, p. 1.

Evans, D., 2000. 'Translating traditions', *Dance Theatre Journal*, vol. 15, no. 4, pp. 12–15

Fanon, F., 1952: 1973. *Black Skin, White Masks* (London: Paladin)

Fischer-Hornung, D., 2001. 'The body possessed: Katherine Dunham technique in *Mambo*', in D. Fischer-Hornung and A. D. Goeller, eds., *EmBODYing Liberation: The Black Body in American Dance*, FORE-CAAST series, vol. 4: Munster, Hamburg, London, Litverlag, pp. 91–112

Fisher, J., 1995. Some thoughts on "Contaminations" editorial', *Third Text*, Autumn, no. 32, pp. 3–7

Fleming, B., 1995. 'Looking out: Critical imperatives in writing about world dance' in D. Gere, ed., *Looking Out: Perspectives on dance and criticism in a multicultural world* (New York: Schirmer)

Flockemann, M., 2000. 'South African perspectives on post-coloniality in and through performance practice', in L. Goodman, J. de Gay, eds, *The Routledge Reader in Politics and Performance* (London and New York: Routledge)

Fonteyn, M., 1980. *The Magic of Dance* (London: BBC)

Foster, S.L., 2000. 'Choreographies of gender', in L. Goodman and J. de Gay, eds, *The Routledge Reader in Politics and Performance* (London and New York: Routledge)

Foster, S., 2002. *Dances that Describe Themselves: The improvised choreography of Richard Bull* (Middletown Connecticut: Wesleyan University Press)

Fowler, S.B., 1995. 'Book review: *Women and Dance: sylphs and sirens'*, *Dance Research Journal*, vol. 27, no. 2, Fall, pp. 43–44

Francis, J., 1990. *Attitudes Among Britain's Black Community Towards Arts, Cultural and Entertainment Events* (London: ACGB)

Frankenberg, R., 1993. *The Social Construction of Whiteness* (London and New York: Routledge)

Franko, M., 2002. *The Work of Dance: Labor, movement and identity in the 1930s* (Middletown, Connecticut: Wesleyan University Press)

Fryer, P., 1984. *The History of Black People in Britain* (London: Pluto Press)

Furse, A., 2000. 'Bleeding, sweating, crying and jumping', *Performance Research*, vol. 5, pp. 17–31

Furse, A., 2002. 'Those who can do teach', in M. M. Delgado and C. Svich, eds., *Theatre in Crisis? Performance manifestos for a new century* (Manchester and New York: Manchester University Press)

Gad, T. and Forde, B., 1988. 'Aswad', *Artrage*, Autumn, pp. 12–15

Gatens, M., 1992. 'Power, bodies and difference', in M. Barrett and A. Phillips, eds., *Destabilizing Theory: Contemporary feminist debates* (London: Polity Press)

Geeves, T., 1993. 'The difference between training and taming the dancer', *tomorrow's dancers: The Papers of the 1993 Conference, Training Tomorrow's Professional Dancers*, organised by Dance UK (London: The Laban Centre for Movement and Dance)

Gere, D., ed., 1995. *Looking Out: Perspectives on dance and criticism in a multicultural world* (New York: Schirmer)

Gilbert, H. and Tompkins, J., 2000. 'Post-colonial drama: Theory, practice, politics', in L. Goodman and J. de Gay, eds., *The Routledge Reader in Politics and Performance* (London and New York: Routledge)

Gilroy, P., 1987: 1995. *There Ain't No Black in the Union Jack* (London: Routledge)

Gilroy, P., 1990–91. 'It ain't where you're from, it's where you're at: The dialectics of diasporic identification', *Third Text*, vol. 13, Winter, pp. 3–8

Gilroy, P., 1993. *The Black Atlantic* (London and New York: Verso)

Gilroy, P., 1995–1996. *Picturing Blackness in British Art 1700s–1990s* (London: Tate Gallery)

Gilroy, P., 1999. *Joined-Up Politics and Post-Colonial Melancholia: Diversity lecture* (London: Institute for Contemporary Arts)

Gilroy, P., 2000. *Between Camps: Race, identity and nationalism at the end of the colour line* (London, Allen Lane: Penguin Press)

Goldberg, D.T., 1993. *Racist Culture: Philosophy and politics of meaning* (Oxford: Blackwell)

Golden, T., 1994. *Black Male: Representations of masculinity in contemporary American art* (New York: Whitney Museum of American Art)

Gordon, L., 1995. *Bad Faith and Antiblack Racism* (Atlantic Highlands New Jersey: Humanities Press)

Gore, G., 1995. 'Rhythm, representation and ritual: The rave and religious cult', in J. Adshead-Lansdale, ed., *Border tensions: Dance and Discourse* (Guildford: University of Surrey)

Gowrie, L., 1996. *The Policy for Dance of the English Arts Funding System* (London: ACE)

Graham, H., Kaloski, A., Neilson, A. and Robertson, E., eds, 2003. *The Feminist Seventies* (York: Raw Nerve Books)

Grau, A., 1992. 'Intercultural research in the performing arts', *Dance Research*, vol. 10, no. 2, pp. 3–29

Grau, A., 1993. 'Myths of origin', *Dance Now*, no. 38, Winter, pp. 39–43

Grau, A., 2001. 'Dance and cultural identity', *Animated*, Autumn, pp. 23–26

Grau, A. and Dodson, M., 1993. 'Television series: Dancing', *British Journal of Ethnomusicology*, vol. 2 pp. 166–169

Grau, A. and Jordan, S., eds, 2000. *Europe Dancing: Perspectives on theatre, dance and cultural identity* (London and New York: Routledge)

Gregg, M., 1998. *A Guide to Chapeltown and Harehills: Leeds Urban Initiative and Action Plan*, p. 2 (Leeds)

Griffin, G., 2003. *Contemporary Black and Asian Women Playwrights in Britain* (Cambridge University Press)

Griffin, J.H., 1984. *Black Like Me* (London: Grafton)

Haley, A., 1976: 1977. *Roots* (London: Hutchinson)

Hall, S., ed., 1997. *Representation: Cultural representations and signifying practices* (London: Sage)

Hall, S., 1997. 'The centrality of culture: Notes on the cultural revolutions of our time', in K. Thompson, ed., *Media and Cultural Regulation* (London: Sage)

Hall, S., 1999–2000. 'Whose heritage? Un-settling "The Heritage", Re-imagining the post-nation', keynote speech to the conference *Whose Heritage? The Impact of Cultural Diversity on Britain's Living Heritage*, Manchester, UK, November 1999, published in *Third Text*, vol. 49, Winter, pp 3–13

Hall, S. and du Gay, P., eds, 1996. *Questions of Cultural Identity* (London: Sage)

Hanna, J.L., 1979. *To Dance Is Human* (Austin and London: University of Texas Press)

Harpe, B., Kuyateh, T. and Schumann, Y., 1993. 'What is black dance in Britain?', (Manchester: North West Arts Board, The Blackie, The Nia Centre)

Harper, P., 1967. 'Dance in a changing society', *African Arts/Arts d'Afrique*, vol.1, no. 1, pp. 10–13, 76–77, 78–80

Haslam, J., 1998. 'Rhythms of black history', *Guardian*, London, p. 13

Hebidge, D., 1979. *Subculture: The meaning of style* (London: Methuen)

Henshaw, D., 1991, 'Adzido-Pan-African-Dance-Ensemble', *Dance Theatre Journal*, vol. 8, no. 4, Spring, pp. 43–44

Herbert, I., 2000. 'On the third hit they finally got Clifton "Junior" Bryan, the fourth to die in the Leeds gang war', *Independent*, London, p. 3

Hewison, R., 1995. *Culture and Consensus: England, art and politics since 1940* (London: Methuen)

Hilden, P.P., 2000. 'Race for sale: Narratives of possession in two "ethnic" museums', *The Drama Review* (*TDR*), vol. 44, pp. 11–36

Holgate, D., 1997. *Phoenix Dance: Resource/study pack* (Leeds: Phoenix Dance Company)

hooks, b., 1990. *Yearning: Race, gender and cultural politics* (Boston: South End Press)

hooks, b. and West, C., 1991, *Breaking Bread: Insurgent black intellectual life* (Boston: South End Press)

hooks, b., 1992, *Black Looks: Race and representation* (London: Turnaround)

hooks, b., 1994. *Teaching to Transgress: Education as the practice of freedom* (London and New York: Routledge)

Hylton, C., 1996. *African and African-Caribbean Arts: A perspective from Leeds 'Race' and Public Policy Research Unit* (Leeds: Leeds University)

Jackson, T., 2006. 'The Latin temperament', *The Metro*, 16 May, p. 25

Jasper, L. and Siddall, J., eds, 1999. *Managing Dance: Current issues and future strategies* (Devon: Northcote House)

Jelloun, T.B., 2002. Interview: Tahar Ben Jelloun interviewed by Griselda Pollock: *Translating class: Altering hospitality*, Congress CATH, Leeds Town Hall 21–23 June (Leeds: University of Leeds) pp. 1–6

Jenkins, K., 1991. *Re-Thinking History* (London and New York: Routledge)

Johnson Jones, E.J., 1999. 'The Choreographic notebook: A dynamic documentation of the choreographic process of Kokuma Dance Theatre, an African-Caribbean dance company', in T.J. Buckland, ed., *Dance in the Field: Theory, methods and issues in dance ethnography* (Basingstoke: MacMillan)

Johnson, K., 2003. 'Rise of the independent dancer', *Dance UK News*, no. 51, pp. 14–15

Johnston, J., 1971. *Marmalade Me* (Toronto and Vancouver: Clarke, Irwin)

Jonas, G., 1992. *Dancing* (London: BBC Books)

Jones, A. and Stephenson, A., eds, 1999. *Performing the Body/Performing the Text* (London and New York: Routledge)

Jordan, S., 1992. *Striding Out* (London: Dance Books)

Jordan, S., 2003. 'Radical discoveries: Pioneering postmodern dance in Britain', in S. Banes, ed., assisted by A. Harris, *Reinventing Dance in the 1960s: Everything was possible* (Madison: University of Wisconsin Press)

Judd, L., 1997–8. 'Living history: The legacy of Harehills', *Animated*, Winter, pp. 32–34

Julien, I. and Mercer, K., 1988. 'Introducing: De margin and de centre', *Screen*, vol. 29, no. 4, pp. 2–10

Kanneh, K., 1998. *African Identities: Race, nation and culture in ethnography, pan-Africanism and black literatures* (London and New York: Routledge)

Kant, M. and Karina, L., trans. J. Steinberg, 2004. *Hitler's Dancers: German modern dance and the Third Reich* (New York, Oxford and Berghahn: Berghahn)

Kant, M., 2004. 'German Dance and Modernity': Don't mention the Nazis', in A. Carter, ed. *Re-Thinking Dance History: A reader* (London and New York: Routledge)

Kealiinohomoku, J., 1983. 'An anthropologist looks at ballet as a form of ethnic dance', in R. Copeland and M. Cohen, eds, *What Is Dance?* (Oxford: Oxford University Press)

Khan, N., 1976. *The Arts Britain Ignores* (London: Commission for Racial Equality)

Kirstein, L., 1942. *The Book of the Dance* (New York: Garden City)

Koritz, A., 1996. 'Re-moving boundaries: From dance history to cultural studies', in G. Morris, ed., *Moving Words: Re-writing dance* (London and New York: Routledge)

Kraus, R., 1969. *History of the Dance in Art and Education* (Princeton, New Jersey: Prentice-Hall)

Laban, R., 1948: 1966. *Modern Educational Dance* (London: Macdonald & Evans)

Labour Party, 1997. *Create the Future: A strategy for cultural policy, arts and the creative economy* (London: Labour Party)

Laing, S., 1994. 'The politics of culture: institutional change in the 1970s', in B. Moore-Gilbert, ed., *The Arts in the 1970s: Cultural closure* (London and New York: Routledge)

Lavender, L., 1997. 'Intentionalism, anti-intentionalism, and aesthetic inquiry: Implications for the teaching of choreography', *Dance Research Journal*, vol. 29, no. 1, Spring, pp. 23–42

Lavender, L., 2000–1. 'Post-historical dance criticism', *Dance Research Journal*, vol. 32, no. 2, Winter, pp. 88–107

Lewis, J., 1990. *Art, Culture and Enterprise: The politics of art and the cultural industries* (London and New York: Routledge)

Long, R., 1989. *The Black Tradition in American Dance* (London: Prion)

Loomba, A., 1998. *Colonialism/Post-colonialism* (London and New York: Routledge)

Luckhurst, M. and Veltman, C., eds, 2001. *On Acting: Interviews with actors* (London: Faber and Faber)

Mackrell, J., 1992. *Out of Line: The story of British dance* (London: Dance Books)

Mackrell, J., 1997. *Reading Dance* (London: Michael Joseph)

Mackrell, J., 1997. 'Enough of the B-word', *Guardian*, 21 April, pp. 12–13

MacPherson, W., 1999. *The Stephen Lawrence Inquiry: report of an inquiry by Sir William McPherson of Cluny* (London: Stationery Office)

Magill, F. N., ed., 1998. 'Chronology of twentieth-century history', *Arts and Culture*, vol. 2 (Chicago and London: Fitzroy Dearborn)

Maley, W., 1994. 'Cultural devolution? Representing Scotland in the 1970s', in B. Gilbert-Moore, ed., *The Arts in the 1970s: Cultural closure* (London: Routledge)

Manning, S.A., 1993. *Ecstasy and the Demon: Feminism and nationalism in the dances of Mary Wigman* (Berkley, Los Angeles and London: University of California Press)

Manning, S.A., 1996. 'American document and American minstrelsy', in G. Morris, ed., *moving words: re-writing dance* (London and New York: Routledge)

Manning, S. A., 1997. 'The female dance and the male gaze: Feminist critique of early modern dance', in J. Desmond, ed., *Meaning in Motion* (Durham and London: Duke University Press)

Manning, S. A., 2004. *Modern Dance, Negro Dance* (Minneapolis and London: University of Minnesota Press)

Marchant, G., 1996. *Getting in Step: Choreographing the relations between dance companies and venues* (Eastern Arts Board, Eastern Touring Agency, South East Arts and Sussex Arts Marketing)

Marques, I.A., 1998. 'Dance education in/and the postmodern', in S.B. Shapiro, ed., *Dance, Power and Difference: Critical and feminist perspectives on dance education* (Human Kinetics)

Martin, J., 1933: 1965. *Introduction to the Dance* (Brooklyn: Dance Horizons)

Martin, J., 1936: 1968. *America Dancing* (Brooklyn: Dance Horizons)

McCaw, D., 2001. 'Lifelong listening: An appreciation of the fifty-year career of teacher and choreographer Geraldine Stephenson', *Dance Theatre Journal*, vol. 17, no. 1, pp. 20–24

McGavin, H., 2003. 'All the right moves', *Times Educational Supplement*, 20 May, pp. 10–12

McKim, R., 2001. 'The essential inheritance of the London Contemporary Dance Theatre', *Choreography and Dance*, vol. 6, no. 4, pp. 1–137

McLeod, J., 2000. 'Beginning postcolonialism' (Manchester and New York: Manchester University Press)

McMillan, M., 1990. *Cultural Grounding: Live art and cultural diversity: Action Research Project* (London: Arts Council of Great Britain)

McRobbie, A., 1999. *In the Culture Society: Art, fashion and popular music* (London and New York: Routledge)

Mercer, K., 1994. *Welcome to the Jungle* (London and New York: Routledge)

Miles, R., 1989. *Racism* (London and New York: Routledge)

Mills, C.W., 1998. *Blackness Visible: Essays on philosophy and race* (London and Ithaca: Cornell University Press)

Mirzroeff, N., 1999. *An Introduction to Visual Culture* (London and New York: Routledge)

Mohanti, P., 1985:1989. *Through Brown Eyes* (London: Penguin Books)

Moore-Gilbert, B., ed., 1994. *The Arts in the 1970s: Cultural closure* (London and New York: Routledge)

Morley, C.W., 1994. 'Book review: *Women and Dance: sylphs and sirens*', *Gender Studies*, vol. 3, no. 1, pp. 123–124

Moore-Gilbert, B., 1997. *Postcolonial Theory: Contexts, practices, politics* (London and New York: Verso)

Morley, D. and Kuan-Hsing, C., eds, 1996. *Stuart Hall: Critical dialogues in cultural studies* (London, New York: Routledge)

Morrison Brown, J., ed., 1979. *The Vision of Modern Dance* (Princeton, New Jersey: Princeton Book Co. Pub.)

Mullard, C., *Black Britain* (London: George Allen & Unwin)

Muraldo, C., 2003. 'Terminological inexactitude', *Dance Theatre Journal*, vol. 19, no. 1, pp. 32–36

Murray, J., 1979, *Dance Now* (Middlesex: Penguin Books)

National Campaign for the Arts, 1997. *Evidence to the National Advisory Committee on Creative and Cultural Education*, London, pp. 1–11

Ngcobo, L., 1987: 1990. *Let It Be Told: Essays by black women in Britain* (London: Pluto)

Nicholas, J., 1984. 'Letter', *Dance and Dancers*, no. 417, September, p. 3

Norton-Taylor, R., 1999. *The Colour of Justice* (London: Oberon Books)

Norton-Taylor, R., 1999. *The Colour of Justice: The Stephen Lawrence Inquiry*, programme, Leeds, West Yorkshire Playhouse

Novack, C., 1990. *Sharing the Dance: Contact improvisation and American culture* (Madison, Wisconsin: The University of Wisconsin Press)

Novack, C., 1992. 'Artifacts (The empire after colonialism)', *Women and Performance: Feminist Ethnography and Performance*, vol. 5, no. 2, pp. 83–89

Novack, C., 1995. 'The body's endeavours as cultural practices', in S.L. Foster, ed., *Choreographing History* (Bloomington and Indianapolis: Indiana University Press)

Parekh, B., 2000. *The Future of Multi-ethnic Britain* (London: Profile Books)

Parry, J., 1992. 'Now for something completely different', *Observer Review*, 8 November, p. 54

Parthasarathi, S., 1993. *What is Black Dance in Britain?: A meeting for practitioners*, Nottingham (London: Arts Council of England)

Pavis, P., ed., 1996. *The Intercultural Performance Reader* (London and New York: Routledge)

Peneff, J., 1990. 'Myths in life stories', in R. Samuel and P. Thompson, eds., *The Myths We Live By* (London and New York: Routledge)

Percival, J., 1969. 'Moving being at Liverpool University', *Dance and Dancers*, May, p. 43

Percival, J., 1971. *Experimental Dance* (London: Studio Vista)

Percival, J., 1981. 'Comprehensive cover?', *Dance and Dancers*, no. 384, December, pp. 27–35

Perinpanayagam, A., 2000–1. 'What really happened?', *Dance UK News*, no. 39, Winter, p. 18

Perpener, J.O. III, 2001. *African-American Concert Dance: The Harlem renaissance and beyond* (Urbana and Chicago: University of Illinois Press)

Petridis, A., 2002. 'Ska for the madding crowd', *Guardian*, 8 March, pp. 2–4

Phelan, P., 1993. *Unmarked* (London: Routledge)

Phillips, C., 2002. 'United we stand', *Guardian Weekend*, 22 June, pp. 36–42

Phillips, M. and Phillips, T., 1999. *Windrush: The irresistible rise of multiracial Britain* (London: Harper Collins)

Phillips, M., 1998. *Windrush: A guide to the season* (London: BBC)

Phillips, M., 2003. 'From slaves to straw men', *The Guardian*, 30 August, p. 10

Phillips, Y., 2001. 'The aesthetics of hip-hop theatre: Jonzi D talks to Yvonne Phillips', *Dance UK News*, pp. 4–5

Phoca, S. and R. Wright, 1999. *Introducing Postfeminism* (Cambridge: Icon Books UK)

Pollock, G., ed., 1996. *Generations and Geographies* (London and New York: Routledge)

Pollock, G., 1999. *Differencing the Canon: Feminist desire and the writing of art's histories* (London and New York: Routledge)

Pollock, G., 2002. 'Introductory remarks', *Translating Class: Altering Hospitality*, Congress CATH, Leeds Town Hall, 21–23 June (Leeds: University of Leeds) pp. 1–13

Powell, R.J., 1997. *Black Art and Culture in the 20th Century* (London: Thames and Hudson)

Prashar, U., 1997. *The Landscape of Fact: Cultural diversity* (London: Arts Council of England)

Prescod, C., 1986. 'Black artists: White institutions', *Artrage*, no. 12, Spring, pp. 32–35

Preston-Dunlop, V., 1988. 'Laban and the Nazis: Towards an understanding of Rudolf Laban and the Third Reich', *Dance Theatre Journal*, vol. 6, no. 2, Summer, pp. 4–7

Prickett, S., 1991. 'Stacey Prickett on the *Spring Loaded* Season '91 at the Place' *Dance Theatre Journal*, vol. 9, no. 1, Summer, pp. 34–37

Ramdin, R., 1987. *The Making of the Black Working Class in Britain* (Aldershot: Gower)

Ramdin, R., 1999. *Reimaging Britain: 500 years of black and Asian history* (London: Pluto Press)

Rassool, N., 1997. 'Fractured or flexible identities', in H.S. Mrza ed., *Black British Feminism: A reader* (London and New York: Routledge)

Read, A., ed., 1996. *The Fact of Blackness* (London and Seattle, ICA: Bay Press)

Rex, P., 2006. *Phoenix Dance: A notebook* (Leeds: Rex)

River, S.B., 1997. *Plays: Moor Masterpieces, To Rahtid, Unbroken* (London: Oberon Books)

Robinson, H., 1992. 'Bodies of knowledge', *Women's Art*, no. 49, November–December, pp. 18–19

Rodrigues, F., 1984. 'Minority Arts Advisory Service', *Artrage*, no. 7, Summer, p. 1

Rose, T., 1997. 'Cultural survivalisms and marketplace subversions: Black popular culture and politics into the twenty-first century', in J.K. Adjaye and A.R. Andrews, eds., *Language, Rhythm and Sound: Black popular cultures into the twenty-first century* (Pittsburgh: University of Pittsburgh Press)

Rowell, B., 2000. *Dance Umbrella: The first twenty-one years* (London: Dance Books)

Roy, S., 1997. 'Shobana Jeyasingh and cultural issues, part 1', *Dance Theatre Journal*, vol. 13, no. 4, pp. 4–7

Sachs, C., 1937: 1963. *World History of the Dance* (New York: W.W. Norton and Company)

Said, E.W., 1978. *Orientalism: Western representations of the Orient* (London: Routledge and Kegan Paul)

Sayers, L.A., 1987. *A Study in the Development of Twentieth Century British Dance Criticism*: Master of Philosophy thesis, Council for National Academic Awards, London

Sayers, L.A., 1995. 'Book review: *Women and Dance: sylphs and sirens' Gender History*, vol. 7, no. 1, April, pp. 135–137

Sayre, H.M., 1989. *The Object of Performance* (Chicago and London: University of Chicago Press)

Schneider, R., 1997. *The Explicit Body in Performance* (London and New York: Routledge)

Schechner, R., 2003. '"Women's work"?', *The Drama Review (TDR)*, vol. 47, no. 4 T180, pp 5–7

Semple, M., 1992. 'african dance and adzido', *Dance Theatre Journal*, vol. 10, no. 5, Autumn, pp. 26–27

Sheikh, A., 1983, '"Ethnic Arts" or white power of definition?', *Artrage*, Autumn, no. 5, p. 2

Sherlock, J., 1988. *The Cultural Production of Dance in Britain, with particular reference to Ballet Rambert and Christopher Bruce's 'Ghost Dances'* (London: Goldsmiths College, University of London)

Shinkansen, 2001. *Choreography as Work (UK)* (London Arts and Yorkshire Arts Board, p. 42

Shohat, E., 1992. 'Notes on the "post-colonial"', *Social Text*, Spring, nos. 31–32, pp. 99–113

Siddall, J., 2001. 'Making art while living in the marketplace', *Dance UK News*, no. 43, Winter, pp. 6–7

Siddall, J., 2001. *21st Century Dance* (London: ACE)

Siegel, M., 1972. *At the Vanishing Point* (New York: Saturday Review Press)

Siegel, M., 1995. 'On multiculturality and authenticity', in D. Gere, ed., *Looking Out: Perspectives on dance and criticism in a multicultural world* (New York: Schirmer)

Siegel, M., 1998. 'Bridging the critical distance', in A. Carter, ed., *Dance Studies Reader* (London and New York: Routledge)

Sillars, S., 1994. '"Is it possible for me to do nothing as my contribution?" visual art in the 1970s', in B. Moore-Gilbert, ed., *The Arts in the 1970s: Cultural closure?* (London and New York: Routledge)

Skoog, M., 2001. 'On being a new artistic director', *Dance UK*, Winter, pp. 4–5

Skellington, R. and Morris, P., 1992: 1996. *'Race' in Britain Today* (London: Sage Publications)

Solanke, A., Hilaire, P. and Woodley, K., 1986. 'Black artists: White institutions', *Artrage*, no. 12, Spring, pp. 2–3

Sontag, S., 1963: 1982. 'Against interpretation', in *A Susan Sontag Reader* (London: Penguin Books)

Sorrell, W., 1967. *The Dance Through The Ages* (New York: Grossett and Dunlap)

Sorrell, W., 1981. *Dance In Its Time: The emergence of an art form* (New York: Anchor Press/Doubleday)

Spivak, G., 1985. 'The Rani of Sirmur: An essay in reading the archives', *History and Theory*, vol. xxiv, no. 3, pp. 247–72

Spivak, G., 1988. 'In Other Worlds: Essays in cultural politics' (New York and London: Routledge)

Sutcliffe, D. and Wong, A., 1986. *The Language of the Black Experience* (Oxford: Basil Blackwell)

Swift, O., 1999. 'Phoenix's identity crisis', *Dance Theatre Journal*, vol. 8, no. 3, pp. 84–85

Taylor, B., 1995. *Avant-Garde and After* (New York: Harry N. Abrams)

Taylor, E., 1997. 'Soaring to success', *Animated*, Spring, pp. 13–14

Theodores, D., 1996. *First We Take Manhattan: Four American women and the New York school of dance criticism* (Amsterdam: Harwood Academic Publishers)

Thiong'o, N.W., 1986. *Decolonising the Mind: The politics of language in African literature* (London: James Currey)

Thiong'o, N.W., 1993. *Moving the Centre: The struggle for cultural freedom* (London and Nairobi: Heinemann)

Thomas, H., 1995. 'New formations in dance studies: A critical appraisal', *Border Tensions: Dance and discourse* (Guildford: University of Surrey)

Thomas, H., 2003. *The Body, Dance and Cultural Theory* (London: Palgrave Macmillan)

Thompson, K., ed., 1997. *Media and Cultural Regulation* (London: Sage)

Thorpe, E., 1989. *Black Dance* (London: Chatto & Windus)

Tonkin, E., 1990. 'History and the myth of realism', in R. Samuel and P. Thompson, eds., *The Myths we Live By* (London and New York: Routledge)

Ugwu, C., 1995. *Let's Get It On: The politics of black performance* (London, Institute of Contemporary Arts)

University of Birmingham: Centre for Contemporary Cultural Studies, ed., 1982. *The Empire Strikes Back: Race and racism in 70s Britain* (London, Hutchinson in association with the Centre for Contemporary Cultural Studies)

Vucko, A., 1995. 'Dance for all the peoples of the world: Angela Vucko in conversation with Germaine Acogny', *Ballet International/Tanz Aktuell*, vol. 5, no. 4. pp. 42–43

Wainwright, M., 1996. 'Random death in the life of a Leeds suburb', *Guardian*, 13 April, p. 27

Wallace, M., 1970. *Black Macho and the Myth of the Superwoman* (New York: Dial Press)

Webster, W., 1998. *Imagining Home: Gender, 'race' and national identity, 1945–64* (London: UCL Press)

West, C., 1990. 'The New cultural politics of difference', in R. Ferguson, M. Gever, T.T. Minh-ha and C. West, eds., *Out There: Marginalization and contemporary culture* (New York: The New Museum of Contemporary Art and Massachusetts Institute of Technology)

White, H., 1987. *The Content of the Form* (Baltimore & London: John Hopkins University Press)

White, J.W., ed., 1985. *Twentieth-Century Dance in Britain: A history of major dance companies in Britain* (London: Dance Books)

Williams, D., 1974. 'Review of Frances Rust, *Dance in Society: An analysis of the relationship between the social dance and society of England from the Middle Ages to the present day*' (London: Routledge and Kegan Paul, 1969) in *CORD News*, vol. 6 no. 2, pp. 29–31

Williams, D., 1991. *Ten Lectures on Theories of Dance* (New Jersey: Scarecrow Press)

Williams, P.J., 1997. *Seeing a Colour-Blind Future: The paradox of race* (London: Virago)

Williams, R., 1976. *Keywords: A vocabulary of culture and society* (London: Fontana)

Wimsatt, W.K. and Beardsley, M.C., 1970. 'The intentional fallacy' in M. Weitz, ed., *Problems in Aesthetics* (London: Collier Macmillan)

Winnearls, J., 1958: 1973. *Modern Dance: The Jooss Leeder Method* (London: Adam & Charles Black)

Wolff, J., 1995. *Resident Alien: Feminist cultural criticism* (Cambridge: Polity Press)

Woodley, K., 1984. 'The Phoenix Dance Company' *Artrage*, no. 7, Summer, p. 12

Yorkshire Arts, 1988. *Extending Frontiers: Black artists at work* (Bradford: Visual Arts and Media Department, Yorkshire Arts)

Young, L., 1996. *Fear of the Dark: 'Race', gender and sexuality in the cinema* (London and New York: Routledge)

Young, R.J.C., 1990. *White Mythologies: Writing history and the West* (London and New York: Routledge)

Young, R.J.C., 1995. *Colonial desire: Hybridity in theory, culture and race* (London and New York: Routledge)

Youngerman, S., 1974. 'Curt Sachs and his heritage: A critical review of world history of the dance with a survey of recent studies that perpetuate his ideas', *CORD News*, vol. 6, no. 2, pp. 6–19

Zimmer, E., 1987. 'Parallels in black', *Dance Theatre Journal*, vol. 5, no. 1, Spring, pp. 5–7

Zollar, J.W.J., 1995. 'Listen, our history is shouting at us', in D. Gere, ed., *Looking Out: Perspectives on dance and criticism in a multicultural world* (New York: Schirmer Books)

Unpublished references

Barnes, T., 1998. 'Phoenix'

Farrar, M., 1997. 'Is racial integration possible in Leeds?', Leeds West Yorkshire Playhouse, School of Cultural Studies, Leeds Metropolitan University, unpublished paper, p. 3

Saimbhi, H., 2000. 'Welcome to Leeds Racial Harassment Project', Leeds Racial Harassment Project, unpublished presentation, p. 22

Trevithick, 1985. *Working Class Women*, unpublished paper

Walkerdine, V., 2002. 'Rethinking classed subjectivity', *Translating Class/Altering Hospitality*, Congress CATH, Leeds, Town Hall (Leeds University), unpublished paper

Phoenix archives

These archives are uncatalogued and incomplete: Leeds Company Offices

Reviews

Anderson, L., 1987. 'Phoenix rise in striking style', untitled newspaper, Perth, Australia

Anglesey, N., 2000. '*19: Rewind and Come Again*', *The Stage*, 12 October

Anon, 1981. 'Dance group takes first step', *Yorkshire Evening Post*

Anon., 1981. 'Leeds Festival of Youth Theatres', *Yorkshire Post*

Anon., 1982. 'Dance in the region', *Sports News*

Anon., 1985. 'Dance', *Spalding Guardian*, 18 October

Anon., 1986. 'Phoenix Dance return to the Civic', *Leeds Other Paper*, 14 February

Anon., 1986. untitled, *Sunday Times*, Perth, Australia, 28 December

Anon., 1987. 'Phenomenal Phoenix in powerful finale', *Evening Express*, Aberdeen, 26 October, p. 3

Anon., 1991. 'Hot to trot', *The Voice*, 8 October

Balford, H., 1991. 'Inside entertainment', *Sunday Gleaner*, Jamaica, 17 March

Berry, K., 1994. 'Phoenix Dance Company', *The Stage and Television Today*, no. 5921, 6 October

Brown, A., 1991. 'Profile: Phoenix Dance Company', *Artscene*, November, p. 11

Brown, A., 1991. 'Phoenix Dance Company', *Artscene*, p. 11

Brown, I., 1995. 'The right moves at the right time', *Daily Telegraph*, 16 September

Brown, I., 1998. 'Forget the philosophy – just strut', *Daily Telegraph*

Burt, R., 1992. 'Phoenix Dance Company: West Yorkshire Playhouse', *Yorkshire Post*, 10 September

Craine, D., 1991. 'After a decade a new bird arises', *The Times*, 9 October

Crisp, C., 1988. 'Phoenix Dance Company/The Place', *Financial Times*, 14 March

Crisp, C., 1991. *Financial Times*, 11 October

Crisp, C., 1995. 'Dance for the people', *Financial Times*, October

Dawson, J., 1991. 'Phoenix Dance Company: West Yorkshire Playhouse' *Yorkshire Evening Post*, 18 September

Dougill, D., 1987. 'The Phoenix flight lacks destination', *Sunday Times*, 13 September

Dougill, D., 1989. untitled, *Sunday Times*, 22 October

Dougill, D., 1989. 'David Dougill assesses a blueprint which sets out to dictate the development of dance in this country for the next decade', *Sunday Times*, 5 February

Dougill, D., 1998. 'At *Spring Loaded*: David Dougill encounters the highs and lows of contemporary dance', *Sunday Times*, 3 May

Dowle, J., 1997, 'Phoenix rising' *Telegraph Magazine*, 13 July, p. 41

Ferguson, S., 1983. 'The angry young man of dance', *Yorkshire Evening Post*, 28 February

Ferguson, S., 1985. untitled, *Yorkshire Post*, undated

Ferguson, S., 1986. 'Leeds Civic Theatre: Phoenix Dance Company', *Yorkshire Post*, 18 February

Ferguson, S., 1989. 'Last dance?', *Yorkshire Post*, Leeds, 13 December, p. 5

Ferguson, S., 1991. 'Phoenix', *Yorkshire Post*, 13 September

Ferguson, S., 2000. 'Phoenix', *Guardian*, London, p. 25

Hutchinson, C., 2000. 'Phoenix rewinds its old hits', *Evening Press*, York

Javin, V., 2001. 'Stylish Phoenix', *Huddersfield Daily Examiner,* 12 February

King, J., 1985. 'Dangerous, fast and funny', *Morning Star*, undated

Kosanke, S., 1996. 'Don't miss this dance', *Bournemouth Evening Echo*, p. 24

Lee, D., 1986. 'Calls for Phoenix to rise again', *Yorkshire Evening Post*

Levene, L., 1990. 'Soft footfalls, as liquid as a dropped silk scarf', *Independent on Sunday*, 14 October

Mackrell, J., 1990. 'The problem with roots', *Independent*, 12 September

Mackrell, J., 1990. 'Dance for the sheer joy of it', *Independent*, 11 October

Mackrell, J., 1997. 'Not a lot of people know that', *Guardian*, p. 6

Manning, E., 1987. 'Phoenix Dance Company: Waterman Arts Centre', *The Stage*, 24 September

Nugent, A., 1990. untitled, *The Stage*, 18 October 1990

Nugent., A., 1991. 'Hot on their heels', *The Stage*, 16 October

Parry, J., 1988. 'Black arts' grey areas', *Observer*, 24 January

Parry, J., 1992. 'Now for something completely different', *Observer Review*, 8 November, p. 54

Percival, J,. 1992. 'Distinctive whatever the disguise', *The Times* 12 November

Patch, A., 1989. 'A big plus for Phoenix', *Yorkshire Evening Post*, Leeds

Powell, N., 1987. 'The soul power in modern dance', *Wall Street Journal*

Robertson, A., 1990. 'Trouping the colour', *Time Out*, 21–19 September

Robertson, A., 1990. 'The fabulous rebirth of this Phoenix', *Daily Mail*, 12 October

Robertson, A., 1991. 'Savouring the spice in variety', *Daily Mail*, 10 October

Robertson, A., 1992. 'Phoenix rises to meet new challenge', *Daily Mail*, 18 November

Sacks, A., 1999. 'There are no black and white answers', *Evening Standard*, 16 April

Scott, H., 1982. untitled, *Yorkshire Evening Post*

Springham, C., 1982. 'Phoenix rising', *Rendezvous*, p. 26–27

Steel, A., 1982. 'Dancers take on world', unsourced, July

Tadman, J., 1996. 'Phoenix Dance, Crucible', *Sheffield Telegraph*, 31 May, p. 31

Thorpe, E., 1991. 'It's just a smooth operation', *Evening Standard*, 9 October

Upton, D., 2000. 'This is one party invite not to miss', *Lancashire Evening Post*, 27 September

Company documents

Adair, C., 2003. *Phoenix in Motion – York, Research and Evaluation Document for Phoenix Dance Company*

Barnes, T., 1997. *Artistic Directors' Report*, 1 February

Barnes, T., 1997. *Artistic Directors' Report*, 5 May

Barnes, T., 1997a. *ERDI (Educational Research and Development Initiative) – What happens next? Summary*, Leeds: Phoenix Dance Company

Barnes, T., 1998. *A Stance for Growth*: unpublished paper, p. 2

Barnes, T., 1999. *Archive Project*, Leeds, Company documents, p. 1

Battersea Arts Centre publicity for Dance Days Festival, July 1987

Campbell, N., 1987. 'Informal discussion with Company dancers Salisbury', September, pp. 1–2

Fitzmaurice, P., 1985. untitled Company document, September

Fitzmaurice, P., 1986. 'Letter to Jane Nicholas, Dance Director ACGB', 31 March

Fitzmaurice, P., 1987. 'Phoenix Dance Company', pp. 1–4

Fitzmaurice, P., 1990. 'Further developments', 26 June 1990, p.1

Harrison, S., 1989. 'Letter: re: Phoenix Dance Company' from Assistant Director (Arts) Yorkshire Arts, 21 June

Hoyle, S., 1987. 'Notes on meeting in Leeds to discuss devolution of Phoenix Dance Company', 30 October pp. 1–2

Huggins, T., 1988. 'Phoenix Dance Company', 18 June, pp. 1–3

Huggins, T., 1992. 'Culture', unpublished paper, pp. 1–2

Maunsell, P.B., 1988. 'Report', 22 October, pp. 1–3

Nicholas, J., 1986. 'Letter to Pauline Fitzmaurice, Company Administrator', 24 March

Petty, R., 1986. 'Letter to Jane Nicholas re: Phoenix Dance Company', from Director Midlands Arts Centre, 19 March

Wood, H., 2000. *Report on the Archives of Phoenix Dance Company, Leeds* (London: Business Archives Council)

Board minutes

22 September 1985, 18 January 1987, 18 March 1987, 29 March 1987, 26 April 1987, 6 September 1987, 1 July 1990, 27 July 1991, 24 September 1992, 12 December 1992, 22 May 1993, 12 February 1994, 24 May 1994, 21 July 1994, 13 July 1996, 5 October 1996

Other meetings
Meeting with YHA advisers, 2 March 1992, 10 September 1992
Meeting with report writers, 21 April 1993
Meeting between dancers and Board member C. Morrison, July 1992

Other Company documents
Audience survey, McCann, Matthews and Millman, 1992
Business plans, 1987, 1989, 1992, 1993
Company programmes, 1982–2006
Funding application, 1992–1993
Letter Liza Stevens, Company Administrator, 28 April 1993
Publicity document, 'Phoenix Dance Company', 1987
Telephone research, McCann, Matthews and Millman, 1992
'The Future of Phoenix', 1993 pp. 1–4

Northern School of Contemporary Dance archives
Leeds NSCD Library
Anon., 1982. untitled, *Yorkshire Post*: Leeds, Phoenix File
Bayliss, S., 1985, 'Queen of the dance', *Times Educational Supplement*,
    London, NSCD Archive File
Hitchens, 1984. untitled, NSCD Archive File
Lightbrown, C., 1981, 'Youth in sport', *Sunday Times*, London, NSCD
    Archive File

Personal communication
Barnes, T., 6 July 1997, 28 September 1998, 12 April 1999,
    6 September 2004 (a selection)
Goddard, 1982. Villmore James's Certificate of Work Experience
Preston Dunlop, V., 2004, 3 June
Simpson, V., 2003, interview, July, Civic Theatre

Videography
Being White, Dir. R. Martin, London, Albany Video Distribution, The
    Albany, 1987
Breaking the Mould, Dir. Tim Leoandro, producer John Wilcox, *Eye to Eye*,
    Channel 4, 1989
Dancing, programmes 1–7, Dir. and producer Rhoda Grauer, BBC, 1993
Expressive Arts Sportsbank Special, Dir. Paul Wang, BBC 2, BBC
    Education, 1998

Phoenix Dance, Dir. Bronwyn Williams, Leeds University Television, 1982

'Phoenix Dance Company', *The South Bank Show*, Dir. and producer Kim Evans, 1984

Phoenix Plus, Dir. Roger Keech, producer Mike Murray, BBC North East Leeds, 1989

The Magic of Dance, Producer Patricia Foy, BBC, 1979

This OBE is Not for Me, Dir. Giovanni Ullieri, BBC2, 19 December 2004

Windrush Gala, Dir. Julia Knowles, producer Sharon Ali, BBC Manchester, 1998

Radio

Dance at Harehills Middle School: Woman's Hour, J. Hitchens, London, Radio 4, 1985

Harehills Middle School: interview with Nadine Senior: Woman's Hour, S. Talbot, London, Radio 4, 1985

Phoenix Dance Company: interviews with Company members and others, Anon., Leeds, BBC Radio Leeds, 1988 (Those interviewed included Neville Campbell, Donald Edwards, Robert Edwards, Pauline Fitzmaurice, Edward Lynch, Nadine Senior and Douglas Thorpe)

Interviews

Founding members

Edwards, Donald	Leeds, my office at NSCD, February 1997; telephone, August 2004, November 2006
Hamilton, David	Leeds, my office at NSCD, November 1997; NSCD foyer, September 2003; telephone, November 2006
James, Villmore	Leeds, my office at NSCD, February 1997, November 2006
Jones, Merville	Reading, my parents' house, December 1997
Lynch, Edward	Leeds, NSCD foyer, May 1997, November 2006

Phoenix Plus

Donaldson, Sharon	Leeds, my office at NSCD, June 1996, July 1998
Holgate, Dawn	Leeds, Company rooms, February 1998
Johnson, Pamela	Leeds, my office, January 1997
Thomas, Seline	Leeds, Company rooms, April 1998
Donaldson, Holgate, Johnson and Thomas	Leeds, Dawn Holgate's flat, December 1998

Dancers from 1989

Adams, Warren	Leeds, foyer at YDC, September 1997
Davis, Hughie	Leeds, my office at NSCD, January 1998
Goodison, Ricardo 'G'	Leeds, Company rooms, April 1998
Holgate, Ricky	Leeds, YDC studio, April 1998
Hylton, Martin	Leeds, foyer at YDC, April 1999
Louis, Booker T. (Tony)	Leeds, Company rooms, April 1998
Moses, Nicola	Leeds, Company rooms, April 1998
Teall, Melanie	Leeds, Company rooms, April 1998

Artistic directors

Campbell, Neville	Darlington, café, January 2000
Morris, Maggie	Leeds, West Yorkshire Playhouse restaurant, June 1996

| Barnes, Thea | Leeds, Company rooms, May 1997, September 1997, November 1998, April 1999; my house, January 2001, December 2003 |
| Bhuller Singh Darshan | Telephone, November 2006 |

Company teachers and rehearsal directors

Douglas, Norman	Leeds, my office at NSCD, June 1998
Hukham, Gurmit	Leeds, my office at NSCD, November 1998
Namron	Leeds, my office at NSCD, March 1997
McMahon, Niall	Leeds, NSCD staff room, July 1998
Walker, Heather	Leeds, Heather Walker's house, September 1998

Others

Auty, John (Director, Theatre Arts course, Intake High School)
    John Auty's house, July 2006

Claid, Emilyn (Choreographer)
    London, Emilyn Claid's house, January 2000

Corner, Lee (External consultant)
    Telephone, January 2001

Drjaca, Milena (YHA Dance Officer)
    NSCD foyer, March 1998

Jonzi D (Choreographer)
    London, South Bank, August 1999

Fitzmaurice, Pauline (Company administrator, Teacher at Harehills Middle School)
    Leeds, my office at NSCD, March 1996; NSCD Foyer, April 2003, November 2003

Huggins, Tyrone (Chair of Board)
    Leeds, bar, March 2000

Senior, Nadine (Teacher at Harehills Middle School, Principal NSCD)
    Leeds, her office at NSCD, December 1998

Thorpe, Douglas (Dancer with the Company) 1987–91 and from 2005
    York St. John University, October 2006

Abbreviations

ACE	Arts Council of England
ACGB	Arts Council of Great Britain
AD	Artistic Director
BDDT	Black Dance Development Trust
BM	Board Minutes
BP	Business Plan
CD	Company Documents
Dir.	Director
LCDS	London Contemporary Dance School
LCDT	London Contemporary Dance Theatre
MAAS	Minority Arts Advisory Service
NSCD	Northern School of Contemporary Dance
NSCD AF	Northern School of Contemporary Dance Archive File
PA	Phoenix Archives
YAA	Yorkshire Arts Association
YAB	Yorkshire Arts Board
YDC	Yorkshire Dance Centre
YHA	Yorkshire and Humberside Arts

Appendix 1. Choreochronicle 1981–2001

Information on works dated 1982–83 is taken from a choreochronicle compiled by Dawn Holgate that gives the title of the work, its choreographer and its costume designer. Villmore James did most of the lighting in collaboration with the Company in the early years. The details of music and lighting were not listed until later programmes, and are often incomplete.

The information for 1984 is taken from programmes, which omit some details of costume, music and lighting. From 1985 onwards, the Company received funding that enabled it to create more in-depth programmes and therefore credit those involved – although, unfortunately, some of the records are missing. In a Company document (1989) entitled General Information, it was stated that 'lighting is provided by the venue along lines suggested by the company.'

Performance	Year	Choreographer	Costume designer	Lighting	Music
Triad within the Tao	1982	David Hamilton	Moira Smith	Company	Vangelis
Hats	1982	David Hamilton	Moira Smith	Company	Duke Ellington
Running Shadows	1982	Donald Edwards	Moira Smith	Company	Chris Benstead
Tribal Vibes	1982	Villmore James	Moira Smith	Company	Chris Benstead
Forming of the Phoenix	1982	David Hamilton	Moira Smith	Company	New Chapter of Dub, Aswad
Reach	1982	Ross McKim	Moira Smith	Company	Ross McKim
Reflections	1982	Donald Edwards	Moira Smith	Company	[Unknown]
Healing of the Lame Man	1982	David Hamilton	Moira Smith	Company	*The Planets*, Gustav Holst
Ritual for Death	1982	Donald Edwards	Moira Smith	Company	*Moses*, Ennio Morricone
Buddha	1982	David Hamilton	Moira Smith	Company	Gamelan
Solitude	1982	David Hamilton	Moira Smith	Company	*Apocalypse*, Vangelis
Mind	1983	David Hamilton	Moira Smith	Company	*Dance Macabre*, Camille Saint-Saëns
If I See You	1983	Donald Edwards	Moira Smith	Company	[Unknown]
Sweet Black Angel// Black Sweet Angel	1983	Neville Campbell	Moira Smith	Company	Old blues songs
Midnight Movers	1983	Villmore James	Moira Smith	Company	*Flight of the Condor, Incantations*
Boo Bam	1983	Neville Campbell	Moira Smith	Company	Howling Wolf
Nightlife at the Flamingo	1983	Edward Lynch	Moira Smith	Company	Europa Jazz

Performance	Year	Choreographer	Costume designer	Lighting	Music
Traffic Variations	1983	Veronica Lewis	Veronica Lewis	Company	Loillet Flute Suite
Speak Like a Child	1983	Darshan Singh Bhuller	Moira Smith	Company	David Heath
Cry of the Ancient Warriors	1984	Donald Edwards	Moira Smith	Company	*My Life in the Bush of Ghosts*, Brian Eno and David Byrne
Blessed Are They That Mourn For They Shall Be Comforted	1984	Donald Edwards	Moira Smith	Steve Curtis	*Requiem*, Berlioz
Frames from the Ocean Dance Album	1984	David Hamilton	Moira Smith	Steve Curtis	Aswad, UB40
Sam	1984	David Hamilton	Moira Smith	Steve Curtis	Aswad, Steel Pulse
Square Won	1985	Edward Lynch	Moira Smith	Steve Curtis	*The Maze*, The Maze
The Story of the Phoenix – A Journey into the Past and Back	1985	David Hamilton	Moira Smith	Steve Curtis	Maca B, Third World, Dub Council
Primal Impulse	1985	David Hamilton	Moira Smith	Steve Curtis	Live music, Edward Lynch
Running	1985	Jane Dudley	Craig Givens	Steve Curtis	*Night Dancing*, Joe Farrell, *Headhunters*, Herbie Hancock, *Quiet Riot*, Metal Health
Blood Wedding	1986	David Glass	[Unknown]	Steve Curtis	Malcolm McLaren
Divine Child Within Us All	1986	David Hamilton	Moira Smith	Steve Curtis	Stevie Wonder and music by Company
Brain Voice	1986	Villmore James	Moira Smith	Steve Curtis	*Zoo Look*, Jean-Michel Jarré
Political Ties	1987	Neville Campbell	Moira Benoit	Steve Curtis	John Coltrane

Performance	Year	Choreographer	Costume designer	Lighting	Music
Where There Has Been Water It Will Begin Again	1987	Neville Campbell	Jean Kerr	Steve Curtis	Mick Marra
X3	1987	Neville Campbell, collaborating with the sculptor Phil Powers and Moira Benoit	Moira Benoit	Jill T. Ellis	John Hoare, *Down to the Moon*, Andreas Vollenweider
Misfits	1987	Neville Campbell	Moira Benoit	Jill T. Ellis	*Lazy River, Dipper Mouth Blues*, Louis Armstrong
Alpha/Omega	1987	Donald Edwards	Moira Benoit	Jill T. Ellis	Chakk
Leave Him Be	1988	Villmore James	Jonah Pattinson	Jill T. Ellis	*Domino Theory*, Weather Report
Revelations	1988	Donald Edwards	Moira Benoit	Bill Deverson	*The World is my Womb*, Nocturnal Emissions, *Let the Dog Out*, Gondwonlam
The Path	1988	Donald Edwards	Isabelle Hargrave	Jill T. Ellis	Terence Trent Darby, Tradition, James Brown, Krush, Smokey Robinson and The Miracles
Spirit of Rebellion	1988	Neville Campbell	Design by Loughborough College of Art and Design	Mark Smith	Tangerine Dream
Harlequins	1988	Villmore James	Moira Benoit, realised by Pat Anderson and Jean Brier	Mark Smith	Terry Oldfield, Klaus Kruger, John Holloway
Breakdown in Dralon	1989	Emilyn Claid	Emilyn Claid / Bill Deverson	Bill Deverson	Sound collage by Bill Deverson with the company. Nat King Cole, Penguin Café Orchestra, June Tabor

Performance	Year	Choreographer	Costume designer	Lighting	Music
Gang of Five	1989	Aletta Collins	Andy Papas	Mark Smith	'B' Word, John Matsuura
Nightlife at the Flamingo	1989	Edward Lynch	Heidi De Raad	Mark Smith	Arranged and recorded by Andrew Keeling
Don't Speak my Name in Whispers	1989	Neville Campbell	Neville Campbell and Pat Anderson	Mark Smith	Peter Gabriel, Jan Garbarek
Haunted Passages	1989	Philip Taylor	Heidi De Raad, realised by Babette Van den Berg	Mark Smith	*Lachrymae*, Benjamin Britten
One Love	1989	Gary Lambert	Gary Lambert	Company technician	*One Love*, poem by Linton Kwesi Johnson, spoken by Clinton Blake
Human Scandals	1990	Neville Campbell, in collaboration with the Company	Heidi Da Raad, realised by Babette Van den Berg	Mark Ridler	Sound tape created by Shaun Campbell and Paul Cantillon
Solo	1990	Neville Campbell	Emma Tregidden, realised by Malooli	Mark Ridler	*Density*, Edgar Varèse
Rights	1990	Michael Clarke	Michael Clark, realised by Pearl	Mark Smith	Big Hard Excellent Fish
Manic	1990	Simon Rice	Simon Rice, Fiona Brockway, Luke Heydon	Mark Smith	*Complete Studies for Player Piano*, Volumes 1–3, Conlan Nancarrow
Tainted Love	1990	Tom Jobe, assisted by Anita Griffin	Paul Dart, realised by Pat Issitt	Mark Ridler	Sound tape compiled and recorded by Stephen Smith
Shock Absorber	1990	Darshan Singh Bhuller	Sonja Kirkham	Mark Ridler	*Johnny Handsome* and *Crossroads*, Ry Cooder, *One World*, John Martyn

Performance	Year	Choreographer	Costume designer	Lighting	Music
Heavy Metal	1991	Neville Campbell	Carole Waller	Jim Simmons	Compiled and recorded by Michael Swann
Subject of the City	1991	Pamela L. Johnson	Pamela L. Johnson, realised by Pat Issitt	Mark Smith	Compiled and recorded by Michael Swann. *Wildlife*, Penguin Café Orchestra
Even Cowgirls Get the Blues	1991	Tom Jobe	Peter Docherty, realised by Pat Issitt	Peter Docherty	k.d. lang
Interlock	1991	Darshan Singh Bhuller	Darshan Singh Bhuller	Darshan Singh Bhuller	Clem Alford
Sacred Space	1991	Philip Taylor	Heidi De Raad, assisted by Babette von den Berg	Philip Taylor, Norman Perryman, Mark Smith	*Pari Intervallo, Fratres, Arbos,* Arvo Part
Family	1992	Shapiro and Smith	Joanie Smith, realised by Malooli	Mark Smith	Kamikaze Ground Crew, Astor Piazzola, compositions by Scott Killian
Spartan Reels	1992	Bebe Miller, assisted by Renée Lemieux	Katherine Maurer, assisted by Malooli	Mark Smith	Jonathan Kane, George Sempepos and Chris Lawrence, Fred Frith
Heart of Chaos	1993	Darshan Singh Bhuller	Malooli	Guy Dickens	*E Lucevan Le Stelle* (*Tosca*, Act III), Giacomo Puccini, *Overture, L'Italiana In Algeri,* Gioachino Rossini, *Sonata for Cello Op.8 – Adagio,* Zoltan Kodaly, *Sex,* Thomas Newman
Fatal Strategy	1993	Donald Byrd assisted by Michael Blake and Leonora Stapleton	Paul Dart, realised by Gillie Hastie and Elspeth Threadgold	Guy Dickens	Mio Morales

Performance	Year	Choreographer	Costume designer	Lighting	Music
Face Our Own Face	1993	Pamela L. Johnson	Christiane Ewing, realised by Gillie Hastie and Elspeth Threadgold	Mark Ridler	Malcolm Swann
Windrush (retitled *Shoot No. 526*)	1994	Emilyn Claid	Gillie Hastie	Guy Dickens	Sylvia Hallett
Shaded Limits	1994	Chantal Donaldson	Emma Tregidden	John Stevens	Bhiah Black
Longevity	1994	Gary Lambert	Alison Amin	Guy Dickens	Text by Martin Luther King
Covering Ground	1994	Shapiro and Smith	Alison Amin, realised by Gill Lightfoot	Guy Dickens	Scott Killian
Never Still	1995	Chantal Donaldson	Malooli, realised by Judy Gray	Spike Mosley and Guy Dickens	*Hugues Le Bars*, soundtrack by Spike Mosley
Haunted Passages (revived)	1995	Philip Taylor	Heidi De Raad, realised by Babette van den Berg	Mark Smith	*Lachrymae*, Benjamin Britten
Movements in 8	1995	Maggie Morris and Gary Lambert	Alison Amin, realised by Jane Hunter	Guy Dickens	*42 Shades in the Black*, Orphy Robinson
Chasing the Moon	1995	Stephen Derrick	Emma Tregidden, realised by Gill Lightfoot	Spike Mosley	Steve Reich
White Picket Fence	1996	Darshan Singh Bhuller	Claire Sheriker, realised by Beverley Vas	Lucy Carter	Oboe Concerti Vol. 1, Vivaldi, Stefan Schilli, Diethelm Jonas Oboes/Failoni Chamber Orchestra

Performance	Year	Choreographer	Costume designer	Lighting	Music
Eve's Reflection	1996	Pamela L. Johnson	Heidi De Raad, assisted by Babette von den Berg	Mark Ridler	*In Her Own Time*, Jason Yarde
Covering Ground (revived)	1996	Shapiro and Smith	Alison Amin, realised by Gill Lightfoot	Guy Dickens	Scott Killan
Unbroken	1997	Thea Nerissa Barnes	Clare Burton,	Spike Mosley	Text by Sol B. River. Voices of Wayne Buchanan, Mica Derrick, Jhardine Farnell, Luciana Lang, Karen Lopez, Joe Williams, Angela Wynter
Templates of Glory	1997	Mark Baldwin	Andrew Flint-Shipman, realised by Gill Lightfoot	Guy Dickens	*Le Temple de la Gloire* Suite 1, Rameau
Diction	1997	Dwight Rhoden	Ricky Lizalde, realised by Gill Lightfoot	Guy Dickens	*Instruments of Darkness from In Visible Silence*, Art of Noise, *We Live Here*, Pat Metheny Group
Cornered	1999	Warren Adams and Andile Sotiya	Emma Tregidden and Gill Lightfoot	Spike Mosley	*A la Vie a la Mort*, Rene Aubrey, *Gangart*, Pichler/Poor
Us Must Trust Us	1999	Jonzi D	Emma Tregidden and Gill Lightfoot	Spike Mosley	*OverYa Head*, KRS One, reworked by DJ Biznizz
Peregrinations	1999	Dwight Rhoden	Julie Watson, realised by Gill Lightfoot	Spike Mosley	Tim Fleming
4	1999	Thea Nerissa Barnes in collaboration with the dancers Andile, Joanna, Maria, Martin, Melanie, Misha, Nicola, Sharon	Emma Tregidden and Gill Lightfoot	Spike Mosley	*4' 33"*, John Cage, performed by Matthew Bourne, Richard Herriot, Eileen Hunter, Chris Wood

Performance	Year	Choreographer	Costume designer	Lighting	Music
The Last Word	1999	Thea Nerissa Barnes	Emma Tregidden and Gill Lightfoot	Gail Hirsch	Derived from *Vous Faites Partie de moi*, Porter-Henneve-Palex, sung by Josephine Baker
19 Rewind & Come Again (included excerpts from *Spartan Reels, Templates of Glory, Subject of the City, Never Still, Tainted Love, Cornered, Longevity, Family and Unbroken*).	2000				
The programme also included new works inspired by Phoenix Dance makers of the1980s, including:					
Brawta	2000	Thea Nerissa Barnes and Andile Sotiya	Design team: Rachel Baynton, Rosella Maria Murphy, Amy Pope	Spike Mosley	*Dongogun* Bawren Tavaziva
Strange Fruit	2000	Thea Nerissa Barnes and Andile Sotiya	Design team: Rachel Baynton, Rosella Maria Murphy, Amy Pope	Spike Mosley	*Strange Fruit*, Nina Simone
Key Club	2000	Thea Nerissa Barnes and Andile Sotiya	Design team: Rachel Baynton, Rosella Maria Murphy, Amy Pope	Spike Mosley	*Frisco Frog*, arranged and performed by Jimmie Lunceford and his Orchestra

Appendix 2: Dancers, 1981–2000/01

Dancer	Dates
Warren Adams	1996–98
Dwayne Barnaby	2000–
Jeanette Brookes	1993–96
Neville Campbell	1987–91
Joanne Cansell	1998–99
Clare Connor	1991–93
Naomi Czuba	2000–
Hugh Davis	1994–2000
Seline Derrick, née Thomas	1989–99
Stephen Derrick	1989–99
Donald Edwards	1981–92
Junior (Robert) Edwards	1987–89
Ricardo 'G' Goodison	1991–2000
Delene Gordon	1999–2000
David Hamilton	1981–87
Dawn Holgate, née Donaldson	1989–2000
Rick Holgate	1989–98
Andiambolanoro Holisoa	2000–
Martin W. Hylton	1992–93, 1998–2000
Vanessa Hoyle	2000
Robert Hylton	1995–96
Villmore James	1981–89
Carl Johnson	1993–94
Pamela Johnson	1989–99
Merville Jones	1982–87
Booker T. Louis	1989–99
Edward Lynch	1982–91
Godiva Marshall	1994–96
Pauline Mayers	1999–2000
Nicola Moses	1996–2000
Misha Movingo	1998–2000
Jake Nwogu	2000–
Tia Ourila	1999–
Colin Poole	1985–87
Dwight Powell	1993–94
Martin Robinson	1991–92
Maria Ryan	1998–2000
Gary Simpson	1987–89

Mikah Smillie	2000
Andile Sotiya	1998–2000
Sharon Sterne	1998–99
Bawren Tavaziva	2000–
Melanie T. Teall	1995–2000
Douglas Thorpe	1987–91
Sharon Watson, née Donaldson	1989–97

This list of dancers is from the Company archive, but I have amended it from information in Company programmes. Phoenix had guest dancers and apprentices, but there is not a complete record. The following were noted in relevant programmes or in Company documents:

- B. Claxton Payne (no date)
- R. Hylton (1995, as an apprentice)
- Sigourney Robinson (1993)

The dancers in the company in 2000 danced *19: Rewind and come again* before the company temporarily closed in 2001.

Appendix 3:
Board of Directors, 1985, 1986, 1992, 2000

1985: The Proposed Management Committee
A meeting took place in Leeds on 22 September 1985.

Chair

Dave Fitzmaurice	Deputy headteacher, Leeds

Assessors

Jane Nicholas	Dance and Mime Director of the Arts Council of Great Britain
Roger Lancaster	Yorkshire Arts Association
Sue Harrison	Yorkshire Arts Association

Present

John Auty	Education specialist, Intake High School
Philip Broadhead	Head of Securities, Barclays Bank
Terry Cryer	Photographer
Jane Dudley	Director, London Contemporary Dance School
Penny Greenland	Director, Jabadao Dance Project
Jeremy Hughes	Ex-director, British Council
Jude Kelly	Battersea Arts Centre
Bill Kilgallon	Director, St Anne's Housing Action
Donald McLennan	Assistant artistic director, London Studio Centre
John Travis	Head of Education Unit, Festival Ballet

Apologies

Jean Davenport	Shaw Theatre, London
Brian Goddard	Civic Theatre, Darlington

1986: The Board of Directors

John Auty	Inspector for dance, ILEA
Terry Cryer	
Jean Davenport	
Jane Dudley	
Dave Fitzmaurice	

Jeremy Hughes
Bill Kilgallon
Donald McLennan
John Travis

1992: The Board of Directors

Graham Devlin (*Chair*)	Writer, librettist, and director in theatre, opera and television
John Auty	Head of the Arts Support Service for Nottinghamshire
Pam Bone	Freelance in arts and media
Chris de Marigny	Editor, advisor at National Dance Agency, London
Dave Fitzmaurice	
Garth Frankland	British Library
Tyrone Huggins	Playwright, actor, producer
Martin Jobbings	Solicitor, Harrison Jobbings
Oliver Jones	Performer and co-founder of Leeds-based Drumming, Dance and Drama Group.
Edward Lynch	Dancer and choreographer for Phoenix until 1991, training as a Dance Education Officer
Elizabeth Minkin	Leeds City Councillor and Chair of Education Committee
Stella Murrell	Lecturer and arts management specialist
Chester Morrison	Community Education specialist
Chris Thomson	Founder of Ludus Dance Company, and Director of Community and Education programmes at London Contemporary Dance Theatre
John Travis	Classical ballet teacher at NSCD
Will Weston	Musician, concert manager and Executive Director of West Yorkshire Playhouse

2000: The Board of Directors

Tyrone Huggins (*Chair*)	Writer, director, performer
Janet Archer	Dance agency director, Dance City, Newcastle upon Tyne
Carol Beckford	Consultant, PricewWaterhouseCoopers
Jeff Dean	Human resources manager
Liza Kellett	Head of Development, West Yorkshire Playhouse
Michael Morgan	Personnel Director, Northern Foods, Hull

Appendix 4: Company Publicity circa 1982

Phoenix Dance Company, was founded in 1981, as an all male contemporary company with a special commitment to bring dance to young people, especially those living in under privileged and inner city areas.

Phoenix have chosen to work as a co-operative using the varied and youthful talents of individual members of the Company in conjunction with some of the leading young professional choreographers working in Britain. They have already earned the reputation of being one of the most exciting and original young Companies to emerge upon the dance scene.

The Company have performed in small and middle-scale theatres, colleges, universities and schools, where their performance has been described as dynamic, powerful and highly original with 'moves not seen before and not even thought possible' (Yorkshire Post).

In Rehearsal

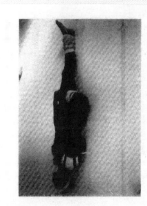

The Dancers
David Hamilton   Merville Jones   Donald Edwards   Vilmore James   Edward Lynch

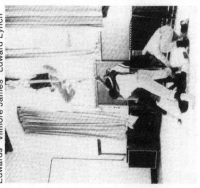

Phoenix are also willing to give master classes, both in technique and choreography and participate in workshop sessions in schools and colleges. This will usually be on the morning of a performance.

Their repertoire can be adapted to either a young or adult audience.

For further information contact:

David Hamilton
Harehills Middle School
Harehills Road
Leeds 8
Tel: 492181 – 783579

PHOENIX DANCE COMPANY

Printed by The Parkgate Press, Borough Road, Darlington
Tel (0325) 63207. 63846

Fees and Availability

Phoenix are now available for performances, residencies and workshops.

Fees:

Technical or choreographic workshops

Classes lasting one hour and a half

£25 + travelling expenses to and from the venue

Classes lasting two hours

£30 + travelling expenses to and from the venue

Performances:

School's matinee: £100 + travelling expenses

Evening performance: £150 + travelling expenses

Appendix 5:
Programme insert (p. 49) for Phoenix Dance
Company performance at the Harrogate
International Festival 1985

8pm Royal Hall

Phoenix Dance Company

Leo Hamilton, Donald Edwards, Vilmore James, Merville Jones, Edward Lynch

Speak Like a Child
Choreographer **Darshan Bhullar**
Music **David Heath**
Dancers **The Company**

In 'Speak Like a Child', Darshan reflects on his memory of a childhood spent on the same streets and in the same environment as the Company. The piece attempts to explain the reality of life in Harehills and Chapeltown.

Solitude
Choreographer **Leo Hamilton**
Music **Apocalypse, Vangelis**
Dancer **Leo Hamilton**

Being alone is not necessarily lonely. In this poignant solo, Leo explores the relationship between the two states of mind.

Nightlife and the Flamingo
Choreographer **Edward Lynch**
Music **Various Jazz Artists**
Dancers **The Company**

Set in an imaginary American night club of the '30s, the piece shows the dreams of the night club owner offset against the incompetence of the cabaret. The dance was featured on 'The South Bank Show' and is one of the most popular pieces in the present rep. It contains a very fast-moving duet reminiscent of the work of the Clarke and Nicholas brothers.

Interval

Blessed are they that mourn, for they shall be comforted
Choreographer **Donald Edwards**
Music **Requiem, Berlioz**
Dancers **The Company**

This is Donald's third choreography for the Company and moves into a new, more lyrical style. Dealing with the themes of anguish and consolation, the piece becomes a personal and moving statement of faith.

Story of the Phoenix — *'a journey to the past and back again'*
Choreographer **Leo Hamilton**
Music **Selections from Maca B, Third World, Dub Council**
Dancers **The Company**

'Down the corridors of the past I travelled
There I found an abundance of movement
Akin to the Ocean Dwelling'. *Leo Hamilton.*

Founded in 1982, the **Phoenix Dance Company** has achieved a remarkable degree of national recognition. They have already earned the reputation of being one of the most exciting and original young companies to emerge upon the dance scene. Phoenix tour extensively throughout the British Isles, performing for and working with a wide variety of people. Because the believe that 'Dance is for everyone' they have performed in many different sorts of venues — from major theatres to school halls, community centres and open prisons.

The five dancers continue to work together in a partnership that began in their school days at Harehills School in Leeds. Although their work takes them all over the country, they remain Yorkshire-based.

Phoenix are noted for their innovative and exciting choreography of the company members as well as guests such as Jane Dudley (founder member of Martha Graham's Company), Darshan Bhuller (Dancer/Choreographer with London Contemporary Dance Theatre), Veronica Lewis and David Glass. Their programmes use a wide range of totally accessible music from reggae and jazz to baroque flute.

Although Phoenix are primarily a performing company they have a great interest in working with community, school and youth groups. They have a special interest in linking performances and workshops — especially as a way of encouraging boys to dance. The have been enormously successful in stimulating and encouraging dance activities during residences in theatres, arts centres and summer schools.

Phoenix do not consider themselves just as dancers — all members are creatively involved in preparing work and each member of the company has choreographed dances.

Appendix 6: Reviews

Judith Mackrell, 'The problem with roots', *Independent*, 12 September 1990

Dance: Judith Mackrell considers the troubled identity
of black dance in the light of a new season at Sadler's Wells

The blithely unselfconscious racism with which reviewers thrilled to Les Ballet Negres (Europe's first non-white ballet company) shows how simple it was in 1940s Britain to regard black culture as a species of primitive exotica. Despite the fact that the company's founder Berto Pasuka was classically trained and that many of his works were fuelled by a militant political consciousness, the company was seen as fascinatingly and unthreateningly Native – 'barbaric exultant', 'an atavistic appeal to the savage in us all'.

It is arguable that the company's demise in the 1950s was hastened by large-scale immigration and hardening racial tension. Certainly black dance all but disappeared from the theatres until the 1970s, when black arts in general began to assert themselves and white dance audiences became more receptive to non-western dance. Attuned to a Graham-based idiom, they could see the beauty of articulate pelvises, weighted steps and curved spines; accustomed to the laid-back repetition of minimalist choreographers, they could relax into the slow, subtle transition of African dance.

At first the black scene was restricted to a smattering of fringe groups presenting modern choreography or a small range of traditional Ghanaian dance. But in 1984 George Dzikumu founded Adzido, a group of African dancers and drummers which not only sought to match the professionalism and scale of the bigger white companies but also to open up the repertoire of African dance.

By dint of Dzikumu's exhaustive travel and research, a typical Adzido programme came to include Zulu war dances, Ghanaian initiation rites and South Ugandan social dances, performed in full costume and with full drumming accompaniment. On one level the company's mission was to preserve and present a major body of world dance, on another it was to give second and third generation British blacks access to their own cultural roots. Yet while the magnitude of Dzikumu's ambition remains unquestioned, companies like Adzido have become the focus of sometimes bitter debates about the identity of black dance and its place within the dance community as a whole.

Dzikumu's critics – black and white – claim that Adzido's style of work reinforces a regressive grass skirts and mud huts stereotype of black dance. Given Brixton, given Broadwater Farm, they argue, black dancers shouldn't be trading in cosy *National Geographic* images but developing dance forms that address issues relating to their own life.

In any case, they say, these dances don't work in a western theatre. Their intrinsic religious or social significance is violated by ripping them out of the rituals within which they evolved.

Adzido's administrator, Hilary Carty, finds arguments about the company's lack of contemporary relevance both ill-informed and patronising. 'We have a huge black following,' she counters, 'who see our work as a celebration of what is truly theirs – it's a glorification of their own art form which they'd normally only get from reading or watching television.' As for the traditional nature of Adzido's repertoire, she argues: 'People accept that classical ballet has developed over centuries, and it's just the same with African dance. We need to establish our own core repertoire, the same as ballet.' What she does accept is that the company has to do a lot of tinkering to make these dances work on a British stage. Although Dzikumu gets teachers from all over Africa to teach the raw material, much of this may consist of a small range of steps, repeated at considerable length with little variation in floor pattern. 'The British eye', says Carty, 'is used to more intricate imagery.' So Dizkumu adjusts the dances – giving variety to the grouping, compressing the dances' length, tactfully developing certain movements.

Their current show, for instance, features a Ghanaian religious dance called Tigari which, *in situ*, is performed by fetish priests and can last for several days. Adzido not only has to generate an equivalent build-up of energy in a mere five minutes but has to reconstruct the ritual from which it came, casting the dancers as priests, onlookers and participants. Over a full programme they then have to find a pretext for linking what may otherwise be an unrelated string of dance rituals, and this in the past has proved the weakest point of their work.

Coming Home, for instance, essayed the somewhat artless scenario of a young British black being given a guided tour of his own dance roots. For their latest show, *Under African Skies*, however, they've rather more inventively commissioned a sequence of poems from the Nigerian poet Odia Ofeimun which dovetail with the dances to give an impressionistic survey of African history.

This device doesn't, however, overcome the fact that the theatre audiences remain divided from the performers in a way that is alien to the dances' original spirit. But Carty says their public have developed a way of participating which restores some sense of community to performances. 'Blacks', she says 'are completely uninhibited about clapping and chanting', while whites tend to release their enthusiasm by dancing in the aisles. To white audiences outside London she suspects 'the company have a kind of 'Out of Africa' appeal, but she claims there is a large public who 'love dance and come to watch us because they're more comfortable with what we do than with some of the more difficult modern choreography.'

Carty's arguments would certainly be echoed by organisations like the Black Dance Development Trust, who fight for the national support and recognition of African dance. Also by Greater London Arts, who will often give preferential funding to African companies at the expense of possibly more accomplished original white work. Both claim that African dance represents an essential aspect of British culture which, having only recently become 'visible', needs all the positive discrimination it can get. Under-funded white dancers in London occasionally mutter that they'll be driven to spears and grass skirts in order to survive. But such policies aren't universally welcomed by black dancers either – some of whom say that to be protected/patronised by positive discrimination is to trap themselves within a set of unwanted expectations.

The Leeds-based company Phoenix, for instance, started out as a model minorities dance group – its membership exclusively male, working-class, black. The work they presented, though far from the traditional repertoire of Adzido, conformed to a very black and very street-cred image, with an up-tempo jazzy style, and heavy use of blues and reggae music. To some they were a flagship modern black company. But Neville Campbell, who became the group's director in 1987, felt that the qualities which made Phoenix dear to sociologically-minded funding bodies militated against it artistically. The dancers' energy and muscle power were impressive, but descriptions like 'exuberant' stuck to them as doggedly as clichés about natural rhythm and the company seemed increasingly imprisoned in its style of urban dance machismo.

Campbell decided on drastic change, and in his second year not only recruited four women dancers but enlarged the repertoire to include unquestionably non-black works by choreographers like Aletta Collins and Michael Clark. Even more courageously, he chose to flout the company's 'unwritten policy' of maintaining an all-black membership and started to look for white or Asian dancers. He hasn't found any of the right style but insists that Phoenix is now 'first and foremost a modern dance company. I'd be appalled to think we were ever funded because of the colour of our skin'.

Having taken this line he is understandably irritated by the fact that Phoenix is to appear at Sadler's Wells in what by implication is a season of black dance, *Dance for the Sheer Joy of It*, which also includes Les Ballets Africains and Adzido. 'If they book a lot of ballet companies, they don't call it a festival of white dance. It should be irrelevant what colour a company is.' Even the Black Dance Development Trust says that ultimately it would like to see its clients 'take their place naturally' in the dance world rather than shelter under a black banner. But while black artists are still so badly represented in dance it's not surprising, given the dreariness of today's funding situation, that those companies who benefit from black/white segregation should exploit their minority status for every penny it's worth.

Nicholas Dromgoole, 'Where did the blackness go?', *Sunday Telegraph*, 16 June 1996

Dance: Phoenix Dance Company, *The Turning World*

I remember in 1981, when five young black men, enthusiasts for contemporary dance from Harehills Middle School, Leeds, formed themselves into a dance company, Phoenix Dance, and created their own choreography by their total commitment and fresh-seeming talent. Last week I went to see Phoenix Dance Company at the Derngate Theatre, Northampton, and found them far less satisfying. What has gone wrong?

I am tempted to say, the Arts Council, mediocrity and layers of bureaucrats have taken over, but that would be an unfair simplification. The reasons are more complex. Why did I not just say five young men? What has their colour to do with it? In fact a great deal.

Oppressed, enslaved, carried by force across to the New World and thrust into a new and different culture, when in a few generations they were stripped not only of self-respect but of their language and history, vestiges of Africans' culture still survived when they were transplanted against their will to the West. Their African languages may have been lost, but the language of African music and dance survived, and is still massively influencing our own popular music and dance.

We tend to think that Africans have a physique that somehow lets them dance more naturally than we do. Not so. They have a music tradition that is different from ours. Where European music has tended to emphasise the melody, African music has emphasised the rhythm.

Africans can keep going in their minds at the same time far more different rhythms than we can. We are not nearly so sophisticated. And with this appreciation of the different rhythms comes what seems a natural ability to dance. It is nothing of the kind. It is culturally acquired, and a spin-off, as it were, of a greater sophistication and understanding of different rhythms.

What I suppose really lowered me as I watched Phoenix Dance was how depressingly unmusical they looked. They were simply not moving to the beat of the different music they played. Could it be, I thought, that within one generation, immersed in the sadly unmusical depths of British society, they have already lost so much of their enviable heritage? I remember watching the auditions for the Royal Ballet School, where youngsters were not asked to dance, but simply to walk around the room in time to the music. Nearly two-thirds of them could not do it. What a condemnation of our musical and physical education!

Imagine asking a group of children in Africa to do the same thing. Would there be a single child unable to do it? But they, of course, are not told to sit still at their desks and stop fidgeting, and generally treated as if they existed only from the neck up.

When I looked more closely at the Phoenix programme, I saw that they now have a white artistic director and assistant director. Two out of the three ballets on offer had been choreographed by whites; even the black Chantal Donaldson's work was a sort of compendium of all that is fashionable in the avant-garde world of contemporary dance.

Now there is nothing wrong with having yet another ordinary contemporary dance company, and that is what Phoenix has become, but originally it was special. It took advantage of the cultural gifts that black people can so munificently offer us, and enrich our often drab culture in the process. The original impetus that set it going has been smothered by the doubtless good intentions of the Arts Council and the boards and bureaucrats that accompany, like locusts, Arts Council grants.

I found this particularly infuriating in the final work. On stage were the jazz musicians of Orphy Robinson's group, playing Orphy's gorgeously rhythmic music. On stage was a largely black group of dancers, moving almost against the grain to this exhilarating danceable music, in choreography that brought together a whole set of clichés from barefoot contemporary dance. The programme pompously claimed the affair 'pushes the boundaries of our perceptions with a new synergy of music, poetry and dance'.

Oops. Are they really unaware that this is what theatre dance has been doing since at least the Renaissance? Unfortunately it is not what was happening on stage at Northampton. No synergy between music and dance was taking place there and poetry was nowhere. We watched dancers whose talents seemed largely wasted in remarkably insensitive choreography.

My sympathies went back to those five happy spirits who set up the company. Let us hope that they are not too bitter about the bureaucrats.

As a straightforward contemporary piece, Phillip Taylor's *Haunted Passages* set to Britten's *Lachrymae* was far and away the most inventive piece of the evening. For three dancers it created a strange atmosphere, attempting to catch the last waking moments before sleep, and in doing so kept its audience vividly awake and all attention.

I wish I had more space to praise *Paulo Riberio* and his Portuguese company at the Place Theatre last week as part of the Turning World festival. Three couples in unusual and striking choreography explored human relationships in effectively dramatic movement in *Solardo 2*. Two days before, we watched a Spanish company, directed by Vicente Saez, who choreographed, a shade too ambitiously, a dance for six dancers to Mozart's *Requiem*. In the nature of things, they could not do Mozart justice.

Ismene Brown, 'Forget the philosophy – just strut', *Daily Telegraph*, 28 April 1998

Dance: RJC Touring, Phoenix Touring

How 'black' should a black contemporary dance company be? It's a dilemma that split Britain's first black company.

From Leeds in 1982 sprang the three teenage boys of the Phoenix Dance Company. Two of them, Donald Edwards and Leo Hamilton, now run RJC, billing itself as Britain's 'national' black dance company, while Phoenix went on to become a group of international renown, a guest of Atlanta Olympics in 1996, and is now run by an American.

Phoenix, in the eyes of RJC supporters, has become a 'coconut' company, black on the outside, white inside: by embracing classic contemporary styles, it is argued, Phoenix rebuffs the urban, black, street dance which it sprang from. RJC stands for 'reggae, jazz, contemporary', so you know where you are with them.

By coincidence, both companies were in London last week – and each looked trapped in a struggle for a suitable philosophy: Phoenix lured by smooth modern American voices, RJC by African 'roots' ones. Predictably, there was preaching to endure in both programmes, and neither was an unmixed blessing choreographically.

The palm went to RJC (whom I saw at the Cochrane Theatre, WC1) because once they'd journeyed through lost tribal innocence, slavery and the healing power of bad dance we got De Napoli Clarke's *Excuse Da Expression*, a joy of a piece. By this stage the symbolic piles of books on stage (signifying oppressive white laws) had tottered over, the sound-track was thumping, the girls were strutting and the boys were shadow-boxing and everyone was having a good time.

Phoenix – stopping off on its tour at the South Bank's Queen Elizabeth Hall until tomorrow – had a loftier tone, with three new commissions and a homegrown creation. The white Mark Baldwin's *Templates of Glory* was much the finest choreography, but its twiddly contemporary moves to some tricky Rameau music looked po-faced, like a twin-set and pearls on Phoenix's earthy, loose-limbed dancers.

They looked much chirpier in Dwight Rhoden's *Diction*, a hip-hop-cum-ballet love-game for four. The new American artist director Thea Nerissa Barnes contributed a starchy solo for the heroic Booker T. Louis. While Mom, Pop and a preacher exhorted him to live clean and virtu-ous, he wandered about looking understandably condemned. Living too clean doesn't suit Phoenix – RJC have a point.

Index